BORDERS AND MIGRATION

BORDERS AND MIGRATION
The Canadian Experience in Comparative Perspective

Edited by
Michael J. Carpenter,
Melissa Kelly,
Oliver Schmidtke

University of Ottawa Press
2022

University of Ottawa **Press**
Les **Presses** de l'Université d'Ottawa

The University of Ottawa Press (UOP) is proud to be the oldest of the francophone university presses in Canada and the oldest bilingual university publisher in North America. Since 1936, UOP has been enriching intellectual and cultural discourse by producing peer-reviewed and award-winning books in the humanities and social sciences, in French and in English.

www.press.uottawa.ca

Library and Archives Canada Cataloguing in Publication

Title: Borders and migration : the Canadian experience in comparative perspective / edited by Michael J. Carpenter, Melissa Kelly, Oliver Schmidtke.
Names: Carpenter, Michael J. (Writer on the Middle East), editor. | Kelly, Melissa, 1981- editor. | Schmidtke, Oliver, editor.
Series: Politics and public policy (University of Ottawa Press)
Description: Series statement: Politics and public policy | Includes bibliographical references.
Identifiers: Canadiana (print) 20220394636 | Canadiana (ebook) 20220394741 | ISBN 9780776638065 (hardcover) | ISBN 9780776638058 (softcover) | ISBN 9780776638072 (PDF) | ISBN 9780776638089 (EPUB)
Subjects: LCSH: Emigration and immigration—Government policy. | LCSH: Immigrants—Government policy. | LCSH: Refugees—Government policy.
Classification: LCC JV6038 .B67 2023 | DDC 325/.1—dc23

Legal Deposit: First Quarter 2023
Library and Archives Canada

Production Team

Copy-editing	Robbie McCaw
Proofreading	Tanina Drvar
Typesetting	Nord Compo
Cover design	Lefrançois, agence marketing B2B

Cover Image	Tony Studio

The University of Ottawa Press gratefully acknowledges the support extended to its publishing list by the Government of Canada, the Canada Council for the Arts, the Ontario Arts Council, the Social Sciences and Humanities Research Council and the Canadian Federation for the Humanities and Social Sciences through the Awards to Scholarly Publications Program, and by the University of Ottawa.

ONTARIO ARTS COUNCIL
CONSEIL DES ARTS DE L'ONTARIO
an Ontario government agency
un organisme du gouvernement de l'Ontario

Canada Council   Conseil des arts
for the Arts   du Canada

Canadä

uOttawa

Table of Contents

PART II – BORDERS ABOVE THE LAW: LEGAL LIMITS AND LOOPHOLES

PART III – NEW PERSPECTIVES, CHALLENGING OLD THINKING

PART IV – DENATURALIZING AND DECONSTRUCTING NATIONAL INTEREST AND BORDER POLICY

List of Figures

Borders and Migration: Integrating Conceptual and Comparative Perspectives

Michael J. Carpenter, Melissa Kelly, and Oliver Schmidtke

Until 2020, the annual number of cross-border migrants had been increasing for many years, with more than a quarter of a billion people residing outside the country of their birth in 2019 (IOM 2019).[1] Of the 272 million international migrants, 29.4 million are refugees, including 3.5 million asylum seekers (UNHCR 2019).[2] The recent numbers of people who fled or were forced across borders are unprecedented, surpassing, in 2016, the record number of people displaced in the aftermath of the Second World War, and they continue to rise. Yet borders are more pervasive and impenetrable than ever. Militarized walls and security fences proliferate along international boundary lines (Andersson 2015; De Genova 2017; Milivojevic 2019; Vallet 2016). Surveillance and biometrics allow states to meticulously screen and police their territorial limits (Ackleson 2017; Muller 2011; Muller et al. 2016; Popescu 2015; Salter 2013; Topak et al. 2015). Contrary to some assumptions of recent decades, borders have not withered away under

---

1   As a proportion of the world's population, the number of cross-border migrants has risen slightly, from 2.2 percent to 3.5 percent, since 1975, meaning the vast majority of people are not migrants (though increasingly more are).

2   The numbers of refugees and asylum seekers has risen dramatically in the last decade, almost doubling since 2009 (and the number of internally displaced people, within their countries of origin, is even higher, about double that of cross-border displacement). There have been spikes over the decades, but this is the highest.

globalization; rather, they have thrived and proliferated. The exclusionary quality of borders is only half the story. Borders connect and bridge, making possible the transfer of people, goods, and services from one jurisdiction to another (Mezzadra and Neilson 2013). Borders are complex and adaptable policy arenas, an assessment that is not captured in the simple open-versus-closed juxtaposition.

In this context, the Canadian experience of borders and migration offers comparative insights and lessons. Canada is one of the largest countries in the world by land mass and relatively small by population, with about 38 million people. With oceans on both the east and west coasts, the Arctic to the north, and a sprawling land border with the United States to the south, the country is not immune to global trends, though in some respects it has been somewhat sheltered from them. In the past few years, Canada's annual immigration numbers increased from about 250,000 to 300,000. Most recently, the government of Prime Minister Justin Trudeau has announced that it intends to bring about 400,000 new permanent residents to Canada annually from 2020 to 2023.[3] In per capita terms, that number is higher than most other countries. In the last five years, responding to global crises, Canada has resettled over 100,000 refugees and accepted the claims of thousands more asylum seekers at the border. These numbers are several times higher than the previous five-year period and unsurpassed in Canadian history. Canada is often regarded as a leader in refugee policy, partly because of the high number of refugees that the country receives, and because it has adopted innovative policy approaches and taken leadership in international humanitarian crises.

For liberal-democratic countries such as Canada, the protection of human rights and civil liberties is considered a priority. Large migration flows, however, pose governance and political challenges. For example, there are widespread concerns that mismanaged or overextended immigration policies threaten the viability of welfare and social services, and the socio-cultural cohesion of the nation. Moreover, security discourses in the post-9/11 and post-Islamic State eras have cast new and prospective arrivals as potential threats. In some cases, politicians have taken advantage of xenophobic and Islamophobic

---

3 See Kathleen Harris, "Federal Government Plans to Bring In More than 1.2M Immigrants in Next 3 Years," *CBC News*, October 30, 2020, https://www.cbc.ca/news/politics/mendicino-immigration-pandemic-refugees-1.5782642.

sentiment among voters, and capitalized on it for political gain. Migrants are frequently scapegoated and seen as responsible for a range of domestic issues, such as unemployment and a weakening social-welfare state (Goodfellow 2019). On these bases, most countries have tried to restrict the flow of migrants, including refugees, while simultaneously (and somewhat contradictorily) claiming to uphold human rights (Joppke 2007; Moreno-Lax 2018; Perkowski 2016). In this former respect, we have witnessed an increasingly polarized contestation of migration. Migration-related issues have taken on a pivotal and controversial role in public debate and party politics. Borders are politicized in a way that is widely detached from the practical consideration of governing borders on the ground (see Krzyżanowski, Triandafyllidou, and Ruth 2018; Vila 2000).

Despite facing similar challenges, national governments have adopted divergent policy responses. While some countries have left their doors relatively open, others have fortified their borders and largely banned asylum seekers from access to their territory (Kallius, Monterescu, and Rajaram 2016; Hansen and Randeria 2016). The Canada-U.S. comparison is striking. Justin Trudeau, who was first elected as Canada's prime minister in 2015 on a platform of increased openness and support for refugees from Syria, stood in stark contrast to the American president at the time, Donald Trump, and his push for hardened borders and fewer migrants. The divergent approaches adopted by governments has led to an interest in comparative migration and border-policy analysis (Brettell and Hollifield 2014). More broadly, they have raised ethical questions concerning who should and should not be allowed to cross borders, and on what terms (Bauder 2016; Bigo 2014; Fine and Ypi 2016).

As we write this, late in the manuscript process, we are in the midst of the coronavirus (COVID-19) pandemic, which has only increased the salience of questions about borders and migration. While the spread of the virus is clearly a global phenomenon, the response to COVID-19 has primarily been a national one, based on the policy decisions of individual nation states. Many federal governments have chosen to close their borders, albeit selectively, to the international movement of people. However, the specific ways in which countries are handling mobility across borders during the pandemic period has differed, with countries allowing the movement of citizens, temporary residents, asylum seekers, and other categories of migrants to varying degrees. Since the majority of the chapters included in this volume were completed before the outbreak of COVID-19, its impacts on borders and migration are not explored in detail, and, in some cases, specific trends and policies discussed here may have been affected or overtaken by unprecedented governmental responses to the virus. These developments will have fundamental consequences for border/migration policy for years to come, and likely in ways that few can presently anticipate. We hope this volume will help readers view the border-migration nexus in a new way, and to better understand the relationships between borders and migration as they evolve in the post-COVID era.

This volume aims to advance the understanding of borders and migration through an exploration of the Canadian experience in comparative perspective. It is a contribution to the wider Social Sciences and Humanities Research Council and Erasmus+ Jean Monnet Network-funded Borders in Globalization program, which studies how the function and meaning of borders are evolving under conditions of globalization.[4] The contributors to this volume come from diverse disciplinary backgrounds in the social sciences, humanities, and law, as well as non-academic backgrounds with professional experience in related civil-society and industry sectors. Most of the authors came together through collaborative work based at the University of Victoria and a series of workshops held between 2017 and 2018 in Europe, Japan, and Canada, focusing on borders and migration in comparative perspective.[5]

We adopt the comparative approach because it allows a clearer understanding of how borders work, and how different modes of governance affect the relationship between migration and borders. This allows us to situate Canada globally, while acknowledging similarities and differences in comparative contexts. Most of our chapters focus on Canada, while several others consider Europe. This volume also touches on other jurisdictions, including Turkey, Mexico, and Japan. We deliberately chose to focus primarily on the Global North, and especially Canada and the European Union, because these regions are often held up as humanitarian models of border and migration policy,

---

4   For more details on Borders in Globalization, also known as BIG, see https://biglobalization.org/.

5   For an overview of the project and its four workshops, see JMN 2020; see esp. BIG, "Canada Workshop–Canada's Border and Migration Policies in Comparative Perspective," November 13, 2018, https://biglobalization.org/content/canada-workshop---canada's-border-and-migration-policies-comparative-perspective.

despite hosting a disproportionately small percentage of the world's refugees and asylum seekers, and despite reinforcing an international status quo that tightly controls and often restricts human movement. We believe a comparative look at these regions reveals critical insights on the role and functioning of borders.

This volume explores several emerging areas of interest to researchers, policy-makers, and concerned members of the public. First and foremost, human mobility is a fixture of contemporary global politics, and borders and migration are more deeply entangled than their respective research literatures often recognize. We are learning that borders are not simply territorial lines or zones of division and exclusion maintained by adjoining national governments. Instead, borders are shaped by multiple actors (not only state authorities but also civil-society and economic sectors) at varying scales (including local, regional, national, international, and global), and through new technologies (especially electronic and biometric). Additionally, bordering processes, which designate people (and things) as included or excluded, increasingly happen far from the boundary line, not only across border regions but also deep inside a state's territory and far beyond. Borders are present in functions and flows as much as space and geography.

In this introduction, we examine the wider global context in which borders are governed and sketch our conceptual approach to investigating these phenomena. We begin with catalyzing events in other parts of the world and some of the varying policy responses from governments in Europe and North America, highlighting the value of a multidisciplinary and comparative method from a Canadian perspective. In a next step, we develop an expanded reflection on the notion of a "borderless world," coupled with an elaboration of the potentially constructive intersections between border studies and migration studies. Then, in an effort to advance our research program, we sketch an analytical model based on the border–migration nexus, noting the many contradictions at play. Finally, the introduction describes the four parts of this volume and outlines the individual contributions.

Canada in a Global Context

Canada is known for its selective and comprehensibly managed migration policies. Most migrants who enter Canada are in fact selected through competitive economic immigration programs, while a smaller number enter as family-reunification migrants or as resettled refugees (IRCC 2020). Moreover, unlike Europe, Mexico, and the United States, Canada's geographical positioning has largely deterred irregular arrivals. However, in recent years, Canada too has felt increasing pressure to welcome an extraordinary number of regular and irregular refugees and asylum seekers. The so-called refugee crisis of 2015–2016 brought into clearer focus the challenges that Canada faces in responding to global migration patterns. During this period, the movement of refugees and migrants reached unprecedented levels and began posing exceptional challenges to many countries and regions around the world. War, persecution, destitution, and desertification impelled millions to flee their homes in central Asia, the Levant, and North Africa. Many migrants set their sights on Europe and embarked on dangerous land and sea journeys. European countries scrambled to accommodate surges of hundreds of thousands of asylum seekers, while millions more languished in camps around the eastern Mediterranean and extending as far as Afghanistan. The EU's common asylum policy largely failed to deliver a pan-European solution to the challenge (Andersson 2015; Crawley 2018).

The governance of borders and migration developed into a fundamental political challenge to the EU, its asylum policy, its border regime, and its commitment to fair burden sharing (Bauböck 2018; Schmidtke 2018; Wolf and Ossewaarde 2018). Partly due to key elements of the European integration project, most notably the single market and cross-border mobility, the EU had to address challenges that exceeded the regulative capacity of individual member states. However, when facing pressure due to an influx of asylum seekers, a coherent and effective response by the EU proved to be difficult. The proposal of an EU distribution scheme for refugees across all member states was vigorously opposed in particular by countries in central and eastern Europe. A series of EU summits on the issue demonstrated how divided heads of state and government were on the refugee issue. It also showed how sensitive the policy domain of borders and migration has been, particularly with a view to domestic electoral politics (Trauner 2016).

In the end, a series of emergency summits led to a compromise that was too limited in scope to provide a sufficient answer to the challenge. Instead, individual member states adopted their own policies that were directed primarily at border control. The principle of a

Europe without borders was compromised, at least temporarily. The crisis was addressed by externalizing the policy response: a controversial 2016 agreement with Turkey provided the EU with a means of protecting the continent from unwanted irregular migration and establishing stricter migration control. Still, the issue of refugees and border protection looms large in public debate and party politics in contemporary Europe (Brubaker 2017; Geddes and Scholten 2016).

In the United States, rising numbers of refugee claimants have been perceived as a threat to the country's economic and national security (Pierce and Selee 2017). Unlike some European countries that made a clear effort to resettle refugees, such as Sweden and Germany, the U.S. approach was to reduce the openness of America's borders toward migrants in general and refugees and asylum seekers in particular (Pierce and Selee 2017). Trump's presidential campaign had a strong anti-immigration focus, which he used to mobilize anti-immigrant and anti-refugee sentiment among voters. He appealed to the xenophobic fears of some voters by promising to build a wall between Mexico and the United States to prevent undocumented migration (Gilmartin, Wood, and O'Callaghan 2018). After coming into office, Trump cited perceived security threats as a legitimate reason to restrict asylum flows, and to cancel the right of Syrians to apply for refugee status. People from certain countries—Iran, Iraq, Libya, Somalia, Syria, Yemen, North Korea, and Venezuela—were also temporarily banned from travelling to the United States regardless of their reasons for visiting. More recently, in 2018, Trump responded to the arrival of large groups of migrants from Central America (who passed through Mexico to arrive at the southern U.S. border, largely to escape poverty and violence) with threats to close the U.S. southern land border. Appalling stories of detention, human-rights abuses, and unauthorized deportations ensued.

Trump's approach to dealing with migratory flows was frequently criticized by international organizations such as the United Nations High Commissioner for Refugees as a breach in international asylum law (UNHCR 2019). Despite this violation of international law, he continued his aggressive pursuit to strengthen U.S. borders in the name of protecting American citizens against perceived external threats. Echoing the rhetoric of other nationalist-populist parties, for Trump the defence of the border was an essential matter of protecting the sovereignty of the nation-state. As he famously stated in 2018, "Every nation has not only the right, but the absolute duty, to protect its borders and its citizens. A nation without borders is a nation not at all."[6] More recently, in spite of promises to the contrary, the administration of U.S. President Joseph Biden has, to date, largely proven unwilling or incapable of addressing the humanitarian crisis at the Mexico-U.S. border. Governing the border and irregular migration has proven to be a thorny policy problem for successive U.S. governments.

The term "refugee crisis" is typically used to describe the unprecedented pressures receiving countries have faced in trying to accommodate large numbers of asylum seekers and refugees, as opposed to the humanitarian crises from which these migratory movements extend (Mountz 2020).[7] The global refugee crisis in 2015, led but not exclusively driven by the war in Syria, led to a different political reaction in Canada than it did in the United States and most of Europe. At first, and in line with the Trump administration's approach, Canada only committed to resettling a small number of refugees under the Conservative government of Stephen Harper. Yet when Trudeau and the Liberals came to power, the Canadian government responded to domestic pressure and mobilized to resettle more than 25,000 Syrian refugees in under two years, establishing partnerships with civil-society organizations to do so (Robinson 2016). In addition to government-sponsored refugees, many individuals organized to bring in high numbers of privately sponsored refugees. In 2018, Canada resettled more refugees than any other country, with 28,000 finding permanent homes across the country, almost a third of the global total resettled (UNHRC 2019, 32) (see figure I).

Amid this influx of mostly Syrian refugees from overseas, Canada experienced a large number of irregular border crossings at its southern border with the United States. While there have been spikes in irregular border crossings in the past, recent numbers have been out of the ordinary. Partly driven by measures put into place by the Trump administration, 2018 and 2019 each saw nearly 28,000

---

6   Remarks by President Trump on Signing the Agriculture Improvement Act of 2018, December 20, 2018, https://www.govinfo.gov/content/pkg/DCPD-201800856/pdf/DCPD-201800856.pdf.

7   Putting "refugee crisis" in quotation marks is meant to draw attention to the constructed and problematic nature of the term, which has now come into widespread use. As scholars such as Mountz (2020) point out, the humanitarian disasters causing refugee movements are the real crisis, not the fact that many countries have experienced pressure to admit growing numbers of refugees.

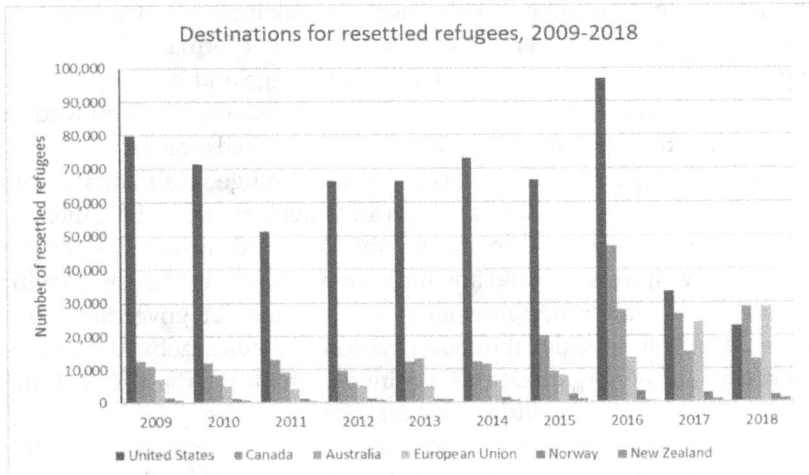

FIGURE I. Destinations for Resettled Refugees, 2009–2018.
Source: Markusoff 2019.

asylum seekers arrive in Canada, from diverse places including Latin America, Africa, and the Middle East (Canada 2020a; Grant 2018). The rise in numbers of asylum seekers by land, mostly crossing the U.S.-Canada border between official ports of entry, heightened political debate and public concern, while the Canadian government showed considerable support, offering a humane and non-militarized, non-criminalized reception.

The divergent policies toward migrants adopted by Trudeau and Trump contributed to persistent calls in Canada to end the Safe Third Country Agreement (STCA) in effect between the two countries since 2004. The agreement stipulates that asylum claims can only be made—with some important exceptions—at the first country of arrival (Canada 2020b). The primary concern voiced by the critics of this agreement is that it threatens to weaken Canada's commitment to refugee protection and to deter legitimate claimants from filing their asylum claim in Canada (Arbel and Brenner 2013). The agreement is based on the assumption that Canada and the United States are both safe countries, but critics argue that the United States does not provide asylum claim-ants with adequate legal protections. Those who are sent back to the U.S. may therefore be at heightened risk of removal, or placed in the U.S. detention system, which has been criticized for failing to meet interna-tional standards (UN News 2019). The agreement also contributed to the increase in the number of unauthorized crossings at the Canada-U.S. border, because the agreement is only enforced at formal border crossings. This has made the border harder to manage and has jeopardized the safety of those who cross it. In July 2020, federal courts moved to strike down the agreement, disputing that the United States was a "safe" country and arguing that the STCA violated refugee claimants' rights that were guaranteed under Canadian and international law. Neither the Liberal government in Canada nor the Biden administration in the United States have expressed any indication of wanting to do away with or substantially alter the agreement, and the Canadian government has so far effectively appealed the court decision (Canada 2020b). At the same time, civil-society organizations continue to challenge the STCA on the grounds of its effects on vulnerable refugee claimants.

These examples—the cases of the Syrian refugees and the Canada-U.S. STCA—are not meant to be comprehensive of the Canadian experience of borders and migration, but they are prominent and illustrative of key themes of this volume. The cases, along with many others, are elaborated in subsequent chapters (as outlined below). The Canadian experience should be of interest to researchers and policymakers in Canada and in other countries, in part because of Canada's particular international reputation. Canada is widely perceived as a policy leader and model with a view to its multiculturalism and its multi-layered system of recruiting migrants (Winter 2015). At the same time, contextualizing and critically assessing this reputation reveals that there is no Canadian exceptionalism (Bloemraad 2012; Trebilcock 2019). Canada is very much an integral part of the global Age of Migration (de Haas, Castles, and Miller et al. 2019), sharing many of the challenges associated with dramatically increased magnitudes of cross-border mobility and displaced people around the world (Cresswell 2006).

Borders *and* (not *or*) Migration

One of this volume's underlying aims is to repudiate the notion that borders are inherently good or bad, and specifically the notion that borders are inherently barriers to migration. In some ways, borders generate harmful social costs, yet in other ways they serve desirable and necessary governance functions. Borders are complex institutions that simultaneously open and close political communities in a multiplicity of ways. We strike this balance in this section, warning against discourses that reduce borders and migration to (often false) dichotomies. Borders and migration are not antithetical, or zero-sum; one does not rise as the other falls. Borders exclude *and* include, separate *and* integrate. They are boundaries *and* ports, walls *and* gateways. Recognizing this, policy responses to twenty-first century migration challenges must include borders, not eliminate them. Relatedly, this section bridges the research literatures on borders and migration, drawing insights from both fields of study, which have so far remained too discrete.

Without question, borders are associated with social costs. Economically, borders have long been associated with restricting markets and trade (Ohmae 1989, 1990). Sociologically, scholars have argued that borders divide people, establish systems of control, and reinforce inequality (Bauböck 2011; Jones 2016; Juss 2016; Oberman 2016). In citizenship studies, some scholars have argued that modern categories of political membership remain too tightly restricted by the borders of territorial nation-states, and that actual meanings and practices of civic life are increasingly cross-border and global (Dauvergne and Marsden 2014; Isin 2012; Marshall 1963; Shachar 2009; Tully 2014). Moreover, borders cast outsiders and foreign countries as "others" and potential security threats, reinforcing tendencies toward xenophobia and war (Booth 2005; Campbell 1992; Walker 1993; Waltz 1959). From a humanitarian perspective, borders exclude unwanted and often vulnerable people who might have good reason for crossing (IOM 2019; UNHCR 2019). Ecologically, borders complicate concerted efforts to tackle climate change; extreme weather events, droughts, and rising sea levels have no regard for international boundaries, and policies confined to territorial units cannot hope to impact global warming (Dalby 2020; Jones 2016).

And without question, borders can be violent toward people (Bissonette and Vallet 2020; Jones 2012, 2016; Mountz 2020). Some borders are maintained in a state of emergency, in which unauthorized approaches are regarded as security threats and likely to be greeted with lethal force. Extreme examples include portions of the borders between North and South Korea, India and Pakistan, and Israel and the Gaza Strip. Borders everywhere are increasingly militarized and seldom welcoming to unwanted or unexpected visitors. As noted above, the U.S. southern border is increasingly walled and guarded, and would-be migrants and asylum seekers are often denied entry or even a hearing. Similarly, European countries, including Italy, Greece, Balkan states, Hungary, Austria, and others, have sealed their borders to varying extents in recent years against the influx of refugees from North Africa, the Middle East, and South Asia. The closed-border policies of states have in turn transformed rugged geographies into deadly border zones. The deserts of the U.S.-Mexico border regions claim the lives of hundreds of northbound migrants every year, and the Mediterranean Sea separating Africa and Europe has become a deadly space where borders are secured and cross-border mobility is often violently restricted. Among those irregular migrants who seek to reach the shores of Europe there are thousands of victims every year, especially in the years since 2011 (IOM 2020; Jones 2016).[8] The willingness of nation states to use borders as a way of controlling migration flows became apparent during the COVID-19 pandemic. Many countries quickly made the decision to close their borders to foreign residents with the objective of stopping the spread of the virus. This led to dire consequences for migrants prevented from seeking asylum or who found themselves stuck in transit, with limited means and precarious legal status. So-called pushbacks forcing migrants back by force and without legal licence have become a recurrent scene at the EU's external borders, with mounting evidence of human-rights abuses and mortalities.[9]

Borders are clearly obstacles to freer and fairer movement of people. In a world that is increasingly globalized, interconnected through trade, communications, and climate change, the movement of people seems to lag behind, one foot still caught firmly in the imaginary world of perfectly compartmentalized Westphalian states. Migration more than other global flows remains subject to a norm of closure. In a globalizing world it has become blatantly manifest that communications, merchandise, tourists, and capital have more rights to cross

---

8   Beginning in 2011, the number of documented migrant deaths in the Mediterranean Sea began to soar, from hundreds annually (where it had been for decades) to thousands, with more than 25,000 fatalities at sea from 2011 through 2019, peaking in 2016 with 5,143 fatalities. Migrant deaths in the Mediterranean account for more than half of all migrant deaths globally (IOM 2020).

9   *The Guardian* reported in May of 2021 that EU member states have been involved in pushing back at least 40,000 asylum seekers at its external borders, leading to the death of over 2,000 people; Lorenzo Tondo, "Revealed: 2,000 Refugee Deaths Linked to Illegal EU Pushbacks," *The Guardian*, May 5, 2021, https://www.theguardian.com/global-development/2021/may/05/revealed-2000-refugee-deaths-linked-to-eu-pushbacks.

borders than people in need or seeking to migrate. However, while states are anxious to reap the benefits of globalization, including those stemming from international trade, they are reluctant to allow admission to migrants who may become a potential strain on the society, economically, socially, and politically.

Across the Global North, there are of course many exceptions to the rule of human immobility if deemed to be in the national interest. Travel and tourism is a multi-trillion dollar industry, experiencing steady growth over the decade preceding 2020 (UNWTO 2020). Border-crossing businesspeople, academics, and tourists, however, are a small minority of the human population, generally coming from affluent and upper-class backgrounds (Bianchi and Stephenson 2019; Breen 2012). While these privileged travellers "cross relatively soft borders regularly without difficulties, migrants and particularly asylum seekers often face the hard side of borders and bordering practices" (Paasi et al. 2019, 2). The other exception many countries welcome is migrant labour, both in terms of a highly skilled and internationally mobile workforce (Kerr et al. 2016) and with a view to low-skilled or even forced international workers (Skeldon 2014). The COVID-19 crisis that unfolded in 2020, for example, brought migration to a near halt, but exceptions were quickly made in several countries, including Canada, to ensure the uninterrupted flow of "essential workers," including health-care professionals and temporary foreign workers engaged in vital sectors such as agriculture.

The extent to which countries are open to foreigners is felt well beyond the borderline itself. Borders are places where forms of belonging and collective identity are negotiated and enacted; for example, through citizenship regimes (Paasi 2009; Scott 2012; Laine 2016). As borders regularly refer to issues that are fundamental to political community (security, sovereignty, identity) the discursive evocation of borders plays a critical role in modes of social inclusion and exclusion. Less privileged migrants may experience deteriorating living conditions in the destination countries primarily due to their precarious legal status as noncitizens. As "unwanted" or "undocumented" migrants, they are exposed to forms of social exclusion, precarious living conditions and, on a regular basis, detention and deportation. Such bordering practices are commonly racially coded and reproduce racial and gendered hierarchies through policing and categorization as unwanted, "illegal," or threatening (Basham and Vaughan-Williams 2012). Borders are places that, as Bosworth, Parmar, and Vázquez put it (2018) "enforce boundaries of belonging" critically shaped by racial categories. In this respect, borders can be conceptualized both as mirrors that reflect broader societal and political exclusionary attitudes and as sites where the "spectacle" of—racialized—modes of exclusion are staged, dramatized, and amplified (De Genova 2013; Parmar 2020).

For instance, temporary labour migrants are often racialized as a group and lack social welfare, political rights, and job security that citizens take for granted (see ch. 1 by Schmidtke). In this latter regard, borders are not only physical, territorially distinct dividing lines but also reference points for reproducing and giving meaning to legal and symbolic boundary markers. Borders, in this way, may inspire and fuel nationalist sentiments and ethnocentrism. While this insistence on protecting community by fortifying borders may benefit those who belong, it is likely to result in the exclusion of others. It is not by accident that borders have taken on such a prominent role in the discursive practices of, in particular, right-wing populism (Wodak 2015).

Given all these factors, some analysts have called for moving toward a borderless world (Bauder 2016; Chen 2005; Heller, Pezzani, and Stierl 2019; Isin 2012; Jones 2016, 2019; Mezzadra and Neilson 2013; Ohmae 1990; Tabarrok 2015). To liberalize migration, reduce structural inequalities, and meet humanitarian needs, border controls should be substantially reduced or eliminated. This is a normative position, a moral and practical critique of the status quo, arguing for reform in favour of increased migrant rights, even universal migration rights. For many in this camp, the notion of a "borderless world" is figurative and signifies a policy of *open* borders rather than *no* borders (more on this distinction below). For others in this camp, however, the notion is not merely metaphoric or reformist; some analysts from radical left, anarchist, and libertarian traditions object to borders per se as part of a fundamental rejection of states themselves (Anderson, Sharma, and Wright 2009; King 2016; Walia 2013). According to these more radical critiques, serious change requires taking the notion of a borderless world literally.

The editors of this volume take the position that borders serve desirable and often indispensable governance functions, while also recognizing the concerns outlined above. This position is supported by other studies as well (Agnew 2008; Espejo 2018; Longo 2018; Mezzadra and Neilson 2013). Most basically, borders delineate and integrate different political jurisdictions. In the modern international system, where two different states meet, there is a seam zone, and people and goods may transfer from one system of governance to another. States intersect at borders, and delineations of sovereignty sometimes blur and overlap within the shared infrastructures of borders, for example, through security cooperation. Borders are functional prerequisites for the spatial organization of political communities whose governance structures and social systems require clearly established modes of assigning membership, legal status, and associated privileges. Political jurisdictions are constituted by a bordered space within which members become entitled, for instance, to participate in elections or access social programs. In the absence of a one-world political jurisdiction, it is impossible to envision what could possibly replace bordered spaces as the socio-structural foundation of an effective polity.

Borders serve a range of important social, political, and economic functions. In addition to facilitating transfer of people and goods between jurisdictions, borders are also access points to government institutions. Locals, tourists, migrants, and asylum seekers routinely seek out borders and bordering processes, including for humanitarian reasons (Meena 2019; Pallister-Wilkins 2018; Sahlins 1989; Walters 2011). Bypassing a border, or crossing illicitly without documentation, makes it difficult to interact with institutions. Legal, financial, and social services often require state recognition of specific individuals, and borders are gateways into these institutions. Public-health objectives are also served by borders, for example, as sites for screening and testing imported food, plants, animals, and merchandise to ensure they meet safety standards. Borders may also help slow the spread of infectious disease—as many countries quickly seemed to discover in early 2020. Borders cannot stop pandemics, but they can be utilized as much-needed mitigation tools or lines of defence. Borders may also serve state-security objectives, screening for violent threats, and, in politically hostile or volatile regions, maintaining a posture of military defence in anticipation of possible foreign aggression.

Migration itself is largely governed and, to a certain degree, defined by borders. International movement of people, like international trade, happens *through* borders, not without them or "behind their backs." Migrants, like goods, require borders to transit from one jurisdiction to another, otherwise the passage becomes smuggling or trafficking, black market, "off the grid" of governance. For example, an international student wants to be registered in a host country and integrated into local governance systems, just as an immigrant worker wants to be contributing to a social-welfare system and earning a pension, or sending money back to their home country through international banking. These and many other forms of governance require *recognition* from the state, and for individuals coming from outside the state, that recognition happens, or begins, at the border, which is not necessarily at the territorial boundary line. The notion that borders inherently restrict movement is based on an oversimplification or misconception that borders are essentially barriers. Scholars have recognized that "borders are equally devices of inclusion" (Mezzadra and Neilson 2013, 7) and "function to allow passage as much as they do to deny it" (Casas-Cortes et al. 2014, 3). Borders typically fill the function of bridge, gateway, filter, and barrier simultaneously (Diener and Hagen 2012, 68). Whether permissive or restrictive of immigration and other forms of mobility, borders play an indispensable role.

Even a policy of unlimited and unrestricted immigration would still require border governance, at least short of conditions of anarchy and the disappearance of states. The literature on open borders (Bauder 2016; Carens 1987, 2013; Espejo 2018; Jones 2019; Nail 2019) argues that all people should be free to cross borders, with some practical exceptions in cases of criminality or specific risks to the public. Free movement of people does not mean *no* borders, or eliminating borders as such. Rather,

> "open borders"…envisions no, or hardly any, restrictions on cross-border migration while at the same time not necessarily striving toward a borderless world. Demands for open borders are not equivalent to those for no borders, since (state) control at border crossings would still occur, for example in order to sift out potential threats and to retain control and knowledge over who and what enters. (Heller, Pezzani, and Stierl 2019, 56)

Borders remain necessary for the governance of any immigration policy, including universal freedom of movement across borders. Arguments for open borders are therefore quite different from the more revolutionary vision of *no* borders. Free movement need not erase boundaries or eliminate border infrastructure, nor recklessly "throw open the gates."[10]

------

10 One way to think about an open-border policy is as a *reversal of the burden of proof* at the border. Under the current international paradigm, all border crossers must prove their specific authorization of passage via nationality status or approved

These distinctions are important. The role of accountable policy-makers is to make migration as orderly and ethical as possible (the 2018 Global Compact for Safe, Orderly and Regular Migration is a good example for such efforts at the international level). Misconceptions about the relationship between borders and migration complicate the politics of immigration reform. Public opinion often associates the idea of increased migration with weakened borders, as if the two were inversely related. But as this volume demonstrates, borders are not inherently anti-migration and migration not inherently anti-borders. For the purposes of progressive immigration reform, the language of *no* borders and a *borderless* world, whether intended figuratively or literally, seems counterproductive. Building public consent around the idea of a world without borders or states, even if a coherent or laudable goal, seems far less realistic than building support for more liberal immigration policies while retaining borders. Conflating the open-borders agenda with the no-borders agenda saddles the reformist agenda with the baggage of fundamental change that has the considerable potential of inviting a populist-nationalist backlash in political terms. Some proponents of open borders nevertheless welcome the work of the more radical no-borders camp, arguing that their ethical commitments and militant activism have influenced discourse and pushed the agenda (Jones 2019; Heller, Pezzani, and Stierl 2019). In order to meet the challenges of the twenty-first century, however, this volume insists on borders as much as migration, borders *and*—not *or*—migration.

---

passport, visa, or other special arrangement; otherwise, the border is closed. Free movement means inverting this paradigm. Free movement means that anyone can pass through official ports of entry unless authorities have specific reason to bar specific individuals, in accordance with the law, such as evidence of criminal or terrorist activity. Presently, the norm is exclusion, and passage is the exception. Under constitutional free movement, passage would become the norm and exclusion the exception. The burden of proof would shift from migrants having to justify their right of entry, to states having to justify refusals of entry.

Another way to think about an open-border policy is as *democratization* or *socialization* of borders.

Currently, the selective benefits that derive from borders and the right to participate in their governance are determined based on historically contingent, identity-based categories of national belonging (Wimmer 2002). Democratizing or socializing borders would mean extending a say in how borders are governed to all individuals impacted by them, as well as a share in the social goods they produce, regardless of nation or clout, on either side of the border, including migrants and asylum seekers.

Our integrative approach naturally bridges the research fields of border studies and migration studies. There is much to gain from their cross-fertilization, though the literatures have remained too discrete, often siloed from each other. In the past decade, especially since the so-called refugee crisis, both literatures have seen a resurgence, partly due to widespread interest in the unprecedented border challenges posed by millions of displaced people, where the two fields intersect. Of course, the respective literatures on borders and migration cannot be precisely delineated or singularly defined, nor are they entirely separate.

It is tempting to assume the research literature on international boundaries is technocratic, neoliberal, conservative, and fixated on structures—in contrast to a migration studies that puts people at its centre and can be portrayed as more liberal, progressive, ethical, and concerned with human agency. The field of migration research is certainly inherently more driven by humanitarian concerns than border studies, and border studies would do well to integrate more explicitly critical humanitarian questions. While border studies has tended to neglect ethical questions in comparison to migration studies (Paasi et al. 2019, 1–3), border scholars have nonetheless challenged conventions of political science and promoted critical and sometimes emancipatory research agendas. For example, border studies often focus on "borderlanders" and their lived experiences (Ellis 2015; Konrad and Kelly 2021; Rogan 1999; Sahlins 1989). Political geographers have popularized the term "borderscapes" to capture the rough, layered, multifaceted, and contested environments that constitute borderlands (Brambilla 2015; Rajaram and Grundy-Warr 2007). The ideas of "borderities" and "mobile borders" can help reframe popular understandings of boundaries into critical methodologies and modes of resistance (Amilhat Szary and Giraut 2015; Konrad 2015; Mezzadra and Neilson 2013; Pinos 2018). Other studies have investigated the dynamics of cross-border flows, revealing functional compatibilities between robust borders and the free passage of things, including goods, capital, finance, and information (Agnew 2017; Blatter 2004; Brunet-Jailly 2005, 2007; Castells 1996; Hale and Bartlett 2018; Khanna 2016; Paasi 1998). Each of these research programs—around borderlands, borderscapes, borderities, and flows—offer critical lexicons that decentre the centralized state, de-stabilize the boundary line, and introduce ways of (re)thinking transgressive politics. They are part of the post 1990s/2000s critical border-studies movement.

The field of border studies offers more fertile ground for adapting to contemporary global migration challenges than predominant political realist or structural realist schools of thought, which presuppose a reified system of territorial nation-states. Insights from border studies should encourage migration researchers to consider that the international system can be reformed, and working with borders is key to improving migration governance. Neither territorial boundary lines nor the academic field of border studies are simplistic, one-dimensional, or unchanging.

The literatures on borders and migration have expanded to meet the increased urgency of the largest number of displaced people since the end of the Second World War. Yet border studies have conventionally paid little attention to flows of people, and migration studies have simultaneously underappreciated the malleability of borders and the innovative work coming out of border studies. This lack of cross-fertilization between these two research traditions may be changing, and we hope to contribute to narrowing the gap with this volume.

We develop the position that the governance of borders has become increasingly multifaceted under globalization. Borders must be understood as complex and often contested policy instruments in particular contexts, not reduced to Manichaean boundaries that are either good and ideally impenetrable (from a conservative or reactionary perspective) or bad and ideally abolished (from a progressive or radical viewpoint). Our consideration requires moving beyond simplistic and either/or notions of borders and migration, integrating findings from both fields of border studies and migration studies. It also requires—as the next section elaborates—more nuanced and adaptive approaches to borders, cognizant of multiple actors, scales, and technologies, and understanding that the bordering of people increasingly happens far from the boundary line.

A Global Approach to the Border-Migration Nexus

Linking the contributions of two seemingly disparate fields, migration studies and border studies, requires a broader understanding of the current border-migration nexus. The nature, role, and purpose of borders has changed significantly in recent years in response to larger structural processes, with profound implications for how migration is managed and understood.

While borders once divided what were relatively distinct territorial units, today these units have become increasingly interconnected through globalizing processes. Broad economic and social processes such as the growth of global capitalism, technological developments, and the flow of goods, people, and information have transformed places at different levels of geographical scale, thereby complicating the concept of borders and challenging the distinctiveness of nation-states (Brunet-Jailly 2005; Diener and Hagen 2012; Konrad and Kelly 2021; Laine 2016; Mezzadra and Neilson 2013; Rumford 2014; Salter 2007). Despite the increasing interconnectivity between countries, however, borders have not disappeared. On the contrary, they have proliferated. In an effort to successfully reap the benefits of globalization (such as international trade) while maintaining sovereignty and avoiding the challenges associated with the unfettered movement of people, national governments have taken new approaches to managing their borders. Borders have changed in form and function as a result; they have become increasingly multi-dimensional institutions, responding to a variety of social and economic processes simultaneously and with new techniques, often in contradictory ways.

One critical point in this regard is that actors responsible for managing migration have increased and diversified. In countries such as Canada, non-state actors such as employers, corporations, and educational institutions play an increasingly important role in immigration policy and, in particular, the selection of immigrants (Flynn and Bauder 2015; Schmidtke 2018). In the same vein, security at and beyond the physical borderline itself is progressively becoming the responsibility of private companies, which sometimes have a greater capacity to manage the border than do existing state institutions. The consequent blurring of the private and the public (Sassen 2015) has changed the way borders work.

In tandem with this shift, a new spatiality of border control has emerged. The territorial governance of the border has changed considerably in response to globalizing forces. The nation state continues to have preeminent power over border governance; however, it has been adapted to accommodate other levels of power. On the one hand, sovereignty has been scaled up. Increasingly, national governments have to negotiate with supranational blocks such as the UN or the EU, or through bilateral or multilateral agreements. On the other hand, power has also been scaled down, with localities and regions playing an increasingly important role in managing cross-border flows. In Canada, for example, provinces and municipalities have both come to take on more competence in designing and implementing immigration and integration policies (Gunn 2020; Schmidtke 2019). Similarly, Europe has witnessed a substantial diffusion of competence across different governance levels in this policy domain (Caponio and Jones-Correa 2017; Schmidtke 2021; Zapata-Barrero, Caponio, and Scholten 2017).

Whether power scales up or down, supranational and subnational policies must still be negotiated through national governments. Recently scholars have therefore begun to promote a multi-scalar approach to understanding borders (see Laine 2016). Such an approach investigates the different but intersecting levels of scale that affect the regulation of people's mobility across borders and challenges the conception of international migration as a strictly state–state phenomenon (Brambilla, Laine, and Bocchi 2016). The ways in which different levels of geographical scale work together are by no means uniform, and may take on different forms. As Cooper and Rumford (2013) point out, this has important implications for the role of borders. As they put it:

> borders may span but also entrench traditional markers or politics of scale, but, at the same time, they also corrupt this logic by operationalising horizontal forms of spatial connectivity that cut across traditional scale politics. In this sense, the border becomes a crucial catalyst for the transformation of, and relationships between, the local, national and global. (114)

While the world has become increasingly bordered (Mezzadra and Neilson 2013), emerging borders are not necessarily territorially fixed. Some scholars have argued that borders are increasingly mobile (Popescu 2015). Far from being simple lines that separate sovereign states, borders are now found in a multiplicity of places away from the actual territorial line itself (Mountz 2020). Many governments, for example, may patrol territory within a certain number of kilometres of the actual borderline, in order to anticipate unauthorized crossings. Surveillance often happens much further away from the borderline, including in airports on the other side of the world (Shachar 2020a). The American government, for example, has made it possible for airline passengers departing from select airports in several countries to complete activities such as immigration, customs, and other types of controls before even departing for the United States.

As Shachar (2020b) has pointed out, measures taken by govern-ments in response to the novel coronavirus have led to the intensification of these trends. Following the World Health Organization's announcement that COVID-19 had become a pan-demic, the Canadian government, for example, did not allow anyone with symptoms of COVID-19 to board a plane to Canada, even if they held Canadian citizenship or permanent residency. This effectively moved control of the Canadian border to foreign airports, where peo-ple were subject to health screenings and other types of controls, remarkably overriding the most basic national right of entry, at least temporarily, on public-health grounds.

While the ability of states to flexibly extend their borders out-ward may be justified as a way of expediting migration flows while simultaneously monitoring the security of state borders, it has also made it possible for some governments to shirk their humanitarian responsibilities. It is much easier to avoid addressing the rights of asy-lum claimants, for example, if they are never permitted to arrive at the country in which they hope to seek asylum. Processing the prospec-tive claims of asylum seekers offshore (as Australia does, for example) reduces the risk that rejected applicants may try to stay in the country anyway. Moreover, the treatment of claimants receives less scrutiny by key stakeholders such as opposition parties, human-rights groups, and the media (Dickson 2015).

The mobility of borders has been facilitated by technology that is increasingly used to monitor and manage migration in new and highly innovative ways (Popescu 2015). This development has, in some cases, changed the physical nature of borders themselves, as they have become zones where one can find the latest technological devices used to identify individuals and detect security threats. Increasingly, bor-der crossings are managed by iris scanning, facial-recognition technologies, and advanced fingerprinting techniques. In order to pre-emptively identify unauthorized border crossers, a range of additional technologies may be used within the vicinity of border crossings. These include ground sensors, X-rays, lasers, surveillance towers, sat-ellites, aerostats, and drones (Muller et al. 2016; Schindel 2016; Topak et al. 2015).

The use of technology to control and monitor migration has been promoted as a way to expedite the movement of people across bor-ders and weed out terrorists, drug dealers, and others who lack authorization to cross. Following the terrorist attacks on New York

City and the Pentagon in September 2001, for example, the United States and Canada implemented the NEXUS program, which allows pre-approved citizens and permanent residents from either country to cross the Canada-U.S. border in an expedited manner. In order to acquire a NEXUS pass, however, one must agree to fingerprinting, the taking of digital photographs, and iris scanning.

The increasing use of technology at and beyond the boundary line has raised a number of new concerns. One is the ability of states to control the use of personal information and the ability to protect individuals' privacy. As data are increasingly shared between governments, it may become increasingly difficult to control how they are used. Also, as Wevers (2018) points out, the collection of biometrical data is far from neutral and objective. Facial recognition technology, for example, cannot recognize all faces with the same degree of accuracy, and may, therefore, unintentionally discriminate against certain categories of people, as they will be subject to more scrutiny than others. Furthermore, while one might assume that technology could be used to reduce profiling and discrimination at the border, this is not necessarily the case. In fact, technologies may be used to intentionally single out certain groups. For example, people from certain countries may be subject to biometric controls while others are not. In other cases, technology may be used to detect people with certain attributes, which may be associated with criminality. In short, the technologies that have been developed to control and monitor border crossings have changed the way people experience borders, in both positive and negative ways.

Viewed collectively, it could be said that the changes associated with borders have resulted in a "restructuring of the relationship between borders, the governing, and the governed" (Diener and Hagen 2012, 73). Borders have become increasingly diverse in the roles that they play, and may be seen as constantly adapting. They are the product of various intersecting types of processes, but they also impact society and economics, particularly concerning the mobility of people.

The chapters in *Borders and Migration* engage with these developments in the border-migration nexus, and reflect on their implications for how migration and cross-border flows are managed in Canada and other countries. This volume argues for an improved understanding of the complex role that borders play in the governance of migration, and the associated challenges and opportunities, especially as they concern the protection of human rights. Our contributors maintain that borders and migration are not necessarily in opposition, and that the problems typically attributed to either are instead problems of governance. Specifically, we can identify six interrelated themes or developments that our contributors illuminate, each in their own ways and to varying extents. First and foremost, states regularly minimize or shirk their legal and humanitarian responsibilities toward migrants in need, particularly irregular migrants and asylum seekers. Sometimes this neglect is inertial; other times it involves sophisticated manoeuvres around international convention. This theme, which recurs in most of our chapters, contains within it a reminder that border policy is never simply pregiven, or fixed across time, but subject to contingent social and political construction.

A second major thematic focus in the following chapters is the importance of scalar perspectives, especially in chapter 1 (Schmidtke), chapter 2 (Watson), chapter 7 (Lehr), and chapter 9 (Simmons). This means paying attention to multiple levels of governance, not just the national level, but also the local level, the municipal, provincial, or mid-regional levels of governance, and the supra-national in the form of international regimes and institutions, and the interactions between these scales. On this topic, see also Brunet-Jailly (2005), Laine (2016), Kurian (2019), and Vivekanandan (2019).

Closely related to scalar analysis, a third research area advanced by our volume is the proliferation of non-governmental actors in the governance of borders and migration, especially in chapter 1 (Schmidtke), chapter 7 (Lehr), chapter 8 (Wong), and chapter 9 (Simmons). This analysis includes civil-society organizations and private industry, and also at various levels, including cross border. For more on non-governmental policy actors, see also Agnew (2017), Brunet-Jailly (2005), Kraler, Hendow, and Pastore (2016), and Kurian (2019).

Fourth, we present new research on the construction of discourse and identity in shaping who belongs and who does not. News and other media play a powerful role in shaping policy and opinion, even though the causal relationships are complex and not always clear. Chapters 11 (Fischer) and 12 (Beaupré) respectively employ media analysis in their studies of identity in first Europe and then Canada (see also Triandafyllidou [2018] and Wallace [2018]).

Fifth, we highlight the increasing importance of technology in shaping the conditions of the international movement of people, including new technologies of digital and biometric identification.

These involve a range of privacy concerns, yet also tease decentralized solutions that could enhance both security and privacy. The theme of border technologies is explored especially in chapter 8 by Wong; see also Amoore (2006), Beauchamp (2016), Kraler, Hendow, and Pastore (2016), Muller (2011), Muller et al. (2016), Norfolk (2019), Popescu (2015), Salter (2007), and Walters (2006).

Sixth, multiple chapters contain evidence of borders operating far from the boundary line. The sorting of people into "included" and "excluded" by national status and special permit is not primarily confined to the territorial frontier. Bordering can happen deep inside the territory of a state, and it can happen far beyond a state's territory. Borders, in this sense, have become "unbounded" or "aterritorial." The theme of bordering detached from boundary lines is evidenced especially in chapter 1 (Schmidtke), chapter 2 (Watson), and chapter 9 (Simmons); for more on the topic, see also Brunet-Jailly (2011), Burridge et al. (2017), Carpenter (2019), Konrad and Brunet-Jailly (2019), Salter (2007), Walters (2006, 2008).

Overview of Chapters

The key idea of the volume is to address the theoretical debates and empirical developments in migration and border studies with a view to what a comparative perspective focused on the Canadian context could offer to this scholarly and policy field. Authors were asked to advance their current work, paying attention to theory, practice, policy, and the links between borders and migration. The themes and connections that emerged are organized into four clusters of three chapters each, bookended by this introduction and a conclusion.

The chapters in Part I introduce the Canadian experience of borders and migration by providing a scholarly overview of contemporary issues and important global context. In the first chapter, political scientist and historian, and co-editor of the volume, Oliver Schmidtke takes up Canada's Temporary Foreign Worker Program (TFWP) to reflect on the country's immigration policy more widely and the implications for borders in the twenty-first century. In particular, the TFWP highlights the differential treatment and precarity of a recently greatly expanded immigrant population, thereby challenging Canada's commitment to promoting the equitable social inclusion of immigrants. Moreover, Schmidtke traces the involvement of multiple levels of government (federal, provincial, municipal) and the expanding role of non-governmental actors, as private business interests and the promise of cheap labour have shaped Canada's policy on temporary foreign workers. The chapter also shows bordering extending far inward from Canada's territorial perimeter, tracking temporary foreign workers as "outsiders on the inside." This chapter depicts the border and bordering practices as critical reference points in reproducing the marginalization of this migrant group and in reflecting significant legal and policy changes in Canada's migration regime.

In chapter 2, political scientist Scott Watson critically places Canada within the global governance of migration. Perhaps exemplary within the parameters of the liberal international order for being a "benevolent" actor on migration and inclusion, Canada is no champion of more democratic global migration. Watson situates Canada's international posture in terms of its vested interest in the current international system. Despite a reputation for humanitarian immigration, the Canadian government has not backed human-rights centred campaigns for migrants, standing instead firmly on the side of nation-state sovereignty, of territorially delineated rights and privileges of movement. Indeed, Canada has primarily based its criteria for permitting newcomers on economic self-interest rather than humanitarian concerns or human rights. Watson reinforces these points through an analysis of the government's divergent responses to two prominent international agreements on immigration: the human-rights oriented International Convention on the Rights of All Migrant Workers and Members of Their Families (1990) and the more state-friendly Global Compact for Safe, Orderly and Regular Migration (2018).

In chapter 3, political scientist Can Mutlu shifts the spotlight to a crucial area of the contemporary global context, an area that sharply contrasts with the relative tranquility of Canadian shores. This chapter revisits the origins of the 2015 refugee and migration movements from the Middle East to Europe, beginning with Syria's political crisis in the wake of the 2011 Arab Spring uprisings. Mutlu portrays the European Union's 2016 bilateral agreement with Turkey as an abrogation of normative liberal values, or an unmasking of its façade, for denying asylum seekers their legal rights and treating them instead as geopolitical bargaining chips. He demonstrates how the European Commission's humanitarian commitments and values have been compromised by the EU's systematic push toward securitizing its external borders. The chapter provides important global context for understanding the Canadian experience of borders and migration; trends around the Mediterranean in 2015 set a precedent for Canada's increased reception of refugees and asylum seekers, and for its increasingly politicized public discourse on the topic.

The chapters of Part II each prominently feature some of the ways that borders have made a resurgence, including legal maneuverings around humanitarian responsibilities. Continuing with the regional focus on Europe, chapter 4, by historian Birte Wassenberg, traces the initial debordering processes within the European Union across the second half of the twentieth century, which culminated in the Schengen Agreement that opened borders to free movement across member states. She then extends the analysis into the contemporary period with the re-bordering that followed divergent European responses to the refugee crisis of 2015. Wassenberg's chapter offers a historian's perspective on Europe's fraught pursuit of a "borderless" ideal.

Chapter 5 returns to North America as legal scholar Asad Kiyani explores Canada's Safe Third Country Agreement (STCA) with the United States, which he portrays as a kind of legal scheme to shirk humanitarian responsibilities. Kiyani argues that the STCA is not really about safety for people but strengthening the hand of states to turn away would-be asylum seekers. Moreover, he raises questions about whether or not the United States warrants the designation "safe" for many migrants in its midst. The focus on the STCA and the challenges posed by the substantially increased number of irregular migrants on Canada's southern border allows Kiyani to address Canada's politically contested role and responsibility in the international governance of refugees.

In chapter 6, legal scholar Donald Galloway highlights the paradox that the "universal" legal principle of non-discrimination ends at the border. The chapter illuminates the role and the limits of courts and judicial oversight in immigration law, importantly detailing how, in some ways, the court's limits are self-imposed and self-enforced; Galloway shows that the courts' reticence to challenge immigration policy is based on questionable legal analysis coupled with an alarming failure to recognize the likelihood of xenophobia skewing legislators' judgement toward the rights of non-citizens and non-permanent residents. Though not explicitly grounded in the research literature on borders and migration, the chapter's legal analysis offers sharp insights into the workings of jurisdiction in the governance of cross-border movement of people and, therefore, clues about where new research and advocacy can be directed.

Part III highlights new approaches to the governance of borders and migration that challenge convention. First, in chapter 7, with a civil-society background in community organizing around refugee resettlement, Sabine Lehr showcases the increased role and importance of the Private Sponsorship of Refugees Program. As soaring numbers of citizens took action to sponsor refugees through the program in 2015 and after, the federal government pledged to raise its own resettlement targets by matching the level of private sponsorships. The program empowered civil-society actors and decentred the state. But Lehr warns of decentring the state too far. By allowing the government to link its responsibilities to civil-society participation, there is a risk of limiting government involvement to popular support, public opinion, and political calculation rather than legal obligations. This policy thus subjects migrants' lives and human rights to the whims of public opinion more than would otherwise be the case. Lehr's chapter also offers insights into multiple levels of governance (federal, provincial, municipal) and new forms of civil-society actors.

Chapter 8, by industry specialist Solomon Wong, explores emerging traveller preclearance technologies in historical and theoretical contexts. With a focus on bilateral arrangements between Canada and the United States, Wong shows how the border has been shifted and displaced into airports and seaports far from the 49th parallel. Moreover, he explores new digital and biometric technologies that could dramatically enhance the capacity to screen and preclear travellers anywhere in the world. For all the privacy concerns these developments raise, Wong also shows that the new technologies have the capacity to strengthen privacy, empower individual users, and break the state's monopoly on security screening through, for example, decentralized blockchain. The chapter is less a scholarly study and more a thematic overview by an industry insider, set within the context of conceptual shifts about borders in the twenty-first century, particularly the recognition that borders increasingly extended beyond boundary lines in both space and time.

Chapter 9, by sociologist Victoria Simmons, turns to Mexico for insights into the ways that borders can be made to serve migration. Supplemented with fieldwork, Simmons details the case of Mexico's state-led agency Grupos Beta de Protección al Migrante. These teams combined police work with social services, official state actors working with civilian volunteers and nongovernmental organizations. Simmons shows that "humanitarian bordering," or the provision of good governance to foreign migrants, even undocumented or irregular migrants, "bulked up" the state, bolstered state sovereignty rather than weakening it, by enhancing its governance capacity and strengthening its presence throughout its territory. This is counterintuitive because facilitating the safe passage of undocumented migrants is often associated in the popular imagination with weakening or eroding borders and sovereignty.

The chapters of Part IV are particularly effective at denaturalizing national interest around borders/migration, reminding that policy and opinion are constructed. In chapter 10, political scientists Edward Boyle and Naomi Chi offer a fresh perspective with a case study of Japanese immigration policy. The authors argue that Japan's reputation as a nation closed to immigration must be understood as historically contingent and partially externally imposed—not culturally essentialist. The chapter offers a striking reminder that the governance of borders and migration is everywhere a work in progress, even in insular Japan.

In chapter 11, Franziska Fischer, political scientist, takes a closer look at how the "refugee crisis" was constructed in Europe through media, discourse, and identity. This chapter addresses the promises and limitations of cross-border solidarity in the European Union as it manifested itself with a view of the extraordinary challenge of assisting and settling hundreds of thousands of refugees over the past couple of years. By assessing whether the EU has developed into a transnational normative power, Fischer conceptualizes borders as shaping the capacity for solidarity and collective action.

Finally, in chapter 12, political scientist Claude Beaupré explores the mediation of Europe's "refugee crisis" through Canadian newspapers. Her research illustrates the influence of the press on domestic Canadian discourse and politics, focusing especially on mediated and sensationalized events (turning points) in 2015 and 2016, including the tragic death of a Syrian child, depicted in a widely disseminated photograph, and impactful coverage of terrorist attacks in Paris. The chapter highlights the extent to which popular attitudes and public policy on issues of borders and migration are fundamentally constructed and contested.

In the conclusion, political scientist and policy specialist Emmanuel Brunet-Jailly reviews the major themes discussed by our co-authors, our collective findings, and some lessons and data in a plea for more comparative research on borders and mobility policies. A first idea is that human mobility is a defining feature of global politics and contemporary history. Another is that since the Second World War, the governments discussed in this book, along with many others, assumed mobility was conjunctural and could be addressed with piecemeal policies only marginally confronting the lacunae of the international agreements that followed the war. Third, what emerges from the chapters of this volume is that border and migration policies are much more intertwined than siloed scholarly knowledge assumes, whereby borders are legal and regulatory policies that participate in controlling mobility, not particularly bounded by international boundaries but reach both inside and beyond the territoriality of states. And, fourth, it is clear that borders and migration policies emerge from legislations that attempt to control territory and mobility across territories. These findings call for much more comparative research by teams of migration and border scholars.

References

Ackleson, Jason. 2017. "Securing through Technology? 'Smart Borders' after September 11th." In *Technology and Terrorism*, edited by Francis Cullen and David Clarke, 55–78, New York: Routledge.

Agnew, John. 2008. "Borders on the Mind: Re-framing Border Thinking." *Ethics & Global Politics* 1(4): 175–191. https://doi.org/10.3402/egp.v1i4.1892.

———. 2017. *Globalization and Sovereignty: Beyond the Territorial Trap*. Lanham, U.K.: Rowman & Littlefield.

Amilhat Szary, Anne-Laure, and Frédéric Giraut, eds. 2015. *Borderities and the Politics of Contemporary Mobile Borders*. New York: Palgrave Macmillan.

Amoore, Louise. 2006. "Biometric Borders: Governing Mobilities in the War on Terror." *Political Geography* 25(3): 336–351. https://doi.org/10.1016/j.polgeo.2006.02.001.

Anderson, Bridget, Nandita Sharma, and Cynthia Wright. 2009. "Editorial: Why No Borders?" *Refuge* 26(2): 5–18. https://doi.org/10.25071/1920-7336.32074.

Andersson, Ruben. 2015. "Hardwiring the Frontier? The Politics of Security Technology in Europe's 'Fight Against Illegal Migration.'" *Security dialogue* 47(1): 22–39. https://doi.org/10.1177/0967010615606044.

Arbel, Efrat, and Alletta Brenner. 2013. "Bordering on Failure: Canada-U.S. Border Policy and the Politics of Refugee Exclusion." Harvard Immigration and Refugee Law Clinical. http://papers.ssrn.com/sol3/papers.cfm?abstract_id=2420854.

Basham, Victoria M., and Nick Vaughan-Williams. 2012. "Gender, Race and Border Security Practices: A Profane Reading of 'Muscular Liberalism.' *The British Journal of Politics and International Relations* 15(4): 509–527.

Bauder, Harald. 2016. *Migration Borders Freedom*. London: Routledge.

Bauböck, Rainer. 2011. "Temporary Migrants, Partial Citizenship and Hypermigration." *Critical Review of International Social and Political Philosophy* 14(5): 665–693. https://doi.org/10.1080/13698230.2011.617127.

———. 2018. "Refugee Protection and Burden-Sharing in the European Union." *JCMS: Journal of Common Market Studies* 56(1): 141–156. https://doi.org/10.1111/jcms.12638.

Beauchamp, Toby Cason. 2016. "When Things Don't Add Up: Transgender Bodies and the Mobile Borders of Biometrics." In *Trans Studies: The Challenge to Hetero/Homo Normativities*, edited by Yolanda Martinez-San Miguel and Sarah Tobias, 103–112. New Brunswick: Rutgers University Press.

Bianchi, Raoul V., and Marcus L. Stephenson. 2019. "Tourism, Border Politics, and the Fault Lines of Mobility." In *Borderless Worlds for Whom? Ethics, Moralities and Mobilities*, edited by Anssi Paasi, Eeva-Kaisa Prokkola, Jarkko Saarinen, and Kaj Zimmerbau, 121–138. New York: Routledge.

Bigo, Didier. 2014. "The (In)Securitization Practices of the Three Universes of EU Border Control: Military/Navy – Border Guards/Police – Database Analysts." *Security Dialogue* 45(3): 209–225. https://doi.org/10.1177/0967010614530459.

Bissonnette, Andréanne, and Élisabeth Vallet, eds. 2020. *Borders and Border Walls: In-Security, Symbolism, Vulnerabilities*. New York: Routledge.

Blatter, Joachim. 2004. "'From Spaces of Place' to 'Spaces of Flow'? Territorial and Functional Governance in Cross Border Regions in Europe and North America" *International Journal of Urban and Regional Research* 28(3): 530–548. https://doi.org/10.1111/j.03091317.2004.00534.x.

Bloemraad, Irene. 2012. "Understanding 'Canadian Exceptionalism' in Immigration and Pluralism Policy." Reports, Migration Policy Institute. https://www.migrationpolicy.org/research/TCM-canadian-exceptionalism.

Booth, Ken. 2005. *Critical Security Studies and World Politics*. Boulder, CO: Lynne Rienner Publishers.

Bosworth, Mary, Alpa Parmar, and Yolanda Vázquez, eds. 2018. *Race, Criminal Justice, and Migration Control: Enforcing the Boundaries of Belonging*. Oxford: Oxford University Press.

Brambilla, Chiara, Jussi Laine, and Gianluca Bocchi. 2016. *Borderscaping: Imaginations and Practices of Border Making*. Abingdon, U.K.: Routledge.

Brambilla, Chiara. 2015. "Exploring the Critical Potential of the Borderscapes Concept." *Geopolitics* 20(1): 14–34. https://doi.org/10.1080/14650045.2014 .884561.

Breen, Marcus. 2012. "Privileged Migration: American Undergraduates, Study Abroad, Academic Tourism." *Critical Arts* 26(1): 82–102. https:// doi.org/10.1080/02560046.2012.663163.

Brettell, Caroline B., and James F. Hollifield, eds. 2014. *Migration Theory: Talking Across Disciplines*. New York: Routledge.

Brubaker, Rogers. 2017. "The New Language of European Populism Why 'Civilization' Is Replacing the Nation." *Foreign Affairs*, December 6, 2017. https://www.foreignaffairs.com/articles/europe/2017-12-06/new -language-european-populism.

Brunet-Jailly, Emmanuel. 2005. "Theorizing Borders: An Interdisciplinary Perspective." *Geopolitics* 10(4): 633–649. https://doi.org/10.1080/1465004 0500318449.

——. ed. 2007. *Borderlands: Comparing Border Security in North America and Europe*. Ottawa: University of Ottawa Press.

——. 2011. "Special Section: Borders, Borderlands and Theory: An Introduction." *Geopolitics* 16(1): 1–6. https://doi.org/10.1080/14650045.2010.493765.

Burridge, Andrew, Nick Gill, Austin Kocher, and Lauren Martin. 2017. "Polymorphic Borders." *Territory, Politics and Governance* 5(3): 239–251. https://doi.org/10.1080/21622671.2017.1297253.

Campbell, David. 1992. *Writing Security: United States Foreign Policy and the Politics of Identity*. Minneapolis: University of Minnesota Press.

Caponio, Tiziana, and Michael Jones-Correa. 2017. "Theorising Migration Policy in Multilevel States: The Multilevel Governance Perspective." *Journal of Ethnic and Migration Studies* 44(12): 1–16. https://doi.org/10.1080 /1369183X.2017.1341705.

Carens, Joseph. 1987. "Aliens and Citizens: The Case for Open Borders." *Review of Politics* 49 (Spring): 251–273. https://doi.org/10.1017/S00346705 00033817.

——. 2013. *The Ethics of Immigration*. Oxford: Oxford University Press.

Carpenter, Michael J. 2019. "Understanding Aterritorial Borders through a BIG Reading of Agnew's Globalization and Sovereignty." *Borders in Globalization Review* 1(1): 123–126. https://doi.org/10.18357/bigr11201919267.

Casas-Cortes, Maribel, Sebastian Cobarrubias, Nicholas De Genova, Glenda Garelli, Giorgio Grappi, Charles Heller, Sabine Hess, et al. 2014. "New Keywords: Migration and Borders, Cultural Studies." *Cultural Studies* 29(1): 55–87. http://dx.doi.org/10.1080/09502386.2014.891630.

Castells, Manuel. 1996. *The Rise of the Network Society*. Malden, U.K.: Blackwell Publishers.

Chen, Xiangming. 2005. *As Borders Bend: Transnational Spaces on the Pacific Rim*. Lanham, U.K.: Rowman & Littlefield.

Cooper, Anthony, and Chris Rumford. 2013. "Monumentalising the Border: Bordering Through Connectivity." *Mobilities* 8(1): 107–124.

Crawley, Heaven. 2018. "Refugees, Migrants, Neither, Both: Categorical Fetishism and the Politics of Bounding in Europe's 'Migration Crisis.'" *Journal of Ethnic and Migration Studies* 44(1): 48–64. https://doi.org/10.108 0/1369183X.2017.1348224.

Cresswell, Timothy. 2006. *On the Move: Mobility in the Modern Western World.* London: Routledge.

Dalby, Simon. 2020. *Anthropocene Geopolitics: Globalization, Security, Sustainability.* Ottawa: University of Ottawa Press.

Dauvergne, Catherine, and Sarah Marsden. 2014. "The Ideology of Temporary Labour Migration in the Post-global Era." *Citizenship Studies* 18(2): 224–242. https://doi.org/10.1080/13621025.2014.886441.

De Genova, Nicholas. 2013. "Spectacles of Migrant 'Illegality': The Scene of Exclusion, the Obscene of Inclusion." *Ethnic and Racial Studies* 36(7): 1180–1198.

———. 2017. *The Borders of "Europe": Autonomy of Migration, Tactics of Bordering.* Durham: Duke University Press.

de Haas, Hein, Stephen Castles, and Mark J. Miller. 2019. *The Age of Migration: International Population Movements in the Modern World.* 6th ed. New York and London: Guilford Press.

Dickson, Andonea. 2015. "Distancing Asylum Seekers from the State: Australia's Evolving Political Geography of Immigration and Border Control." *Australian Geographer* 46(4): 437–454. https://doi.org/10.1080/oo 049182.2015.1066240.

Diener, Alexander C., and Joshua Hagen. 2012. *Borders: A Very Short Introduction.* New York: Oxford University Press.

Ellis, Matthew H. 2015. "Over the Borderline? Rethinking Territoriality at the Margins of Empire and Nation in the Modern Middle East (Part I)." *History Compass* 13(8): 411–422. https://doi.org/10.1111/hic3.12251.

Espejo, Paulina Ochoa. 2018. "Why Borders Do Matter Morally: The Role of Place in Immigrants' Rights." *Constellations* 25(1): 71–86. https://doi. org/10.1111/hic3.12251.

Fine, Sarah, and Lea Ypi. 2016. *Migration in Political Theory: The Ethics of Movement and Membership.* Oxford: Oxford University Press.

Flynn, Emma, and Harald Bauder. 2015. "The Private Sector, Institutions of Higher Education, and Immigrant Settlement in Canada." *Journal of International Migration and Integration* 16(3): 539–556. https://doi.org /10.1007/s12134-014-0369-x.

Geddes, Andrew, and Peter Scholten. 2016. *The Politics of Migration and Immigration in Europe.* Newbury Park, CA: Sage.

Gilmartin, Mary, Patricia Wood, and Cian O'Callaghan. 2018. *Borders, Mobility and Belonging in the Era of Brexit and Trump.* Bristol, U.K.: Policy Press.

Goodfellow, Maya. 2019. *Hostile Environment: How Immigrants Became Scapegoats*. London: Verso.

Government of Canada. 2020a. "Asylum Claims by Year." Immigration, Refugees, and Citizenship Canada. https://www.canada.ca/en/immi gration-refugees-citizenship/services/refugees/asylum-claims /asylum-claims-2020.html.

———. 2020b. "Canada-U.S. Safe Third Country Agreement." Immigration, Refugees, and Citizenship Canada. https://www.canada.ca/en/immi gration-refugees-citizenship/corporate/mandate/policies-operational -instructions-agreements/agreements/safe-third-country-agreement. html.

Grant, Tavia. 2018. "Are Asylum Seekers Crossing into Canada Illegally? A Look at Facts behind the Controversy." *Globe and Mail*, September 11, 2018. https://www.theglobeandmail.com/canada/article-asylum-seekers -in-canada-has-become-a-divisive-and-confusing-issue-a/.

Gunn, Alexander. 2020. "Immigration and Integration Policy and the Complexity of Multi-level Governance: A Case Study of British Columbia." *Journal of Borderlands Studies* 35(4): 603–618.

Hale, Geoffrey, and Cailin Bartlett. 2018. "Managing the Regulatory Tangle: Critical Infrastructure Security and Distributed Governance in Alberta's Major Traded Sectors." *Journal of Borderlands Studies* 34(2): 257–279. https://doi.org/10.1080/08865655.2017.1367710.

Hansen, Randall, and Shalini Randeria. 2016. "Tensions of Refugee Politics in Europe." *Science* 353(6303): 994–995. https://doi.org/10.1126/science .aag1556.

Heller, Charles, Lorenzo Pezzani, and Maurice Stierl. 2019. "Toward a Politics of Freedom of Movement." In *Open Borders: In Defence of Free Movement*, edited by Reece Jones. Athens: University of Georgia Press.

Immigration, Refugees and Citizenship Canada (IRCC). 2020. *2020 Annual Report to Parliament on Immigration: For the Period Ending December 31, 2019*. https://www.canada.ca/en/immigration-refugees-citizenship/corpo rate/publications-manuals/annual-report-parliament-immigration -2020.html.

International Organization for Migration (IOM). 2020. "Missing Migrants Project: Tracking Death Along Migratory Routes." Last modified March, 2020. https://missingmigrants.iom.int/.

———. 2019. *World Migration Report 2020*. International Organization for Migration. https://publications.iom.int/books/world-migration-report -2020.

Isin, Engin. 2012. *Citizens without Frontiers*. London: Bloomsbury.

Jean Monnet Network (JMN). 2020. "Comparing and Contrasting EU Migra- tion and Border Policies." EU Borders & Migration. https://www.uvic.ca /humanities/intd/europe/eu-grants/network/eubamp-16-19/index.php.

Jones, Reece. 2012. *Border Walls: Security and the War on Terror in the United States, India, and Israel*. London and New York: Zed Books.

——. 2016. *Violent Borders: Refugees and the Right to Move*. London: Verso.

——, ed. 2019. *Open Borders: In Defence of Free Movement*. Athens: University of Georgia Press.

Joppke, Christian. 2007. "Beyond National Models: Civic Integration Policies for Immigrants in Western Europe." *West European Politics* 30(1): 1–22.

Juss, Satvinder. 2016. "Exodus after Conflict." In *Towards a Refugee Oriented Right of Asylum*, edited by Laura Westra, Satvinder Juss, and Tullio Scovazzi, 97–128. Abingdon, U.K., and New York: Routledge.

Kallius, Annastiina, Daniel Monterescu, and Prem Kumar Rajaram. 2016. "Immobilizing Mobility: Border Ethnography, Illiberal Democracy, and the Politics of the 'Refugee Crisis' in Hungary." *American Ethnologist* 43(1): 25–37.

Kerr, Sari Pekkala, William Kerr, Çağlar Özden, and Christopher Parsons. 2016. "Global Talent Flows." *Journal of Economic Perspectives* 30(4): 83–106. https://doi.org/10.1257/jep.30.4.83.

Khanna, Parag. 2016. *Connectography: Mapping the Future of Global Civilization*. New York: Random House.

King, Natasha. 2016. *No Borders: The Politics of Immigration Control and Resistance*. London: Zed.

Konrad, Victor. 2015. "Toward a Theory of Borders in Motion." *Journal of Borderland Studies* 30(1): 1–17. https://doi.org/10.1080/08865655.2015.1008387.

Konrad, Victor, and Melissa Kelly, eds. 2021. *Culture, Borders, and Globalization: A Canadian Perspective*. Ottawa: University of Ottawa Press.

Konrad, Victor, and Emmanuel Brunet-Jailly. 2019. "Approaching Borders, Creating Borderland Spaces, and Exploring the Evolving Borders between Canada and the United States" *The Canadian Geographer / Le Géographe canadien* 63(1): 4–10. https://doi.org/10.1111/cag.12515.

Kraler, Albert, Maegan Hendow, and Ferruccio Pastore. 2016. "Introduction: Multiplication and Multiplicity—Transformations of Border Control." *Journal of Borderlands Studies* 31(2): 145–149. http://dx.doi.org/10.1080/08865655.2016.1201431.

Krzyżanowski, Michał, Anna Triandafyllidou, and Ruth Wodak. 2018. "The Mediatization and the Politicization of the 'Refugee Crisis' in Europe." *Journal of Immigrant & Refugee Studies* 16(1–2): 1–14. https://doi.org/10.1080/15562948.2017.1353189.

Kurian, Nimmi. 2019. "Re-engaging the 'International': A Social History of the Trans-Himalayan Borderlands." *Journal of Borderlands Studies* 35(2): 243–254. https://doi.org/10.1080/08865655.2019.1646149.

Laine, Jussi. 2016. "The Multiscalar Production of Borders." *Geopolitics* 21(3): 465–482. https://doi.org/10.1080/14650045.2016.1195132.

Longo, Matthew. 2018. *The Politics of Borders: Sovereignty, Security, and the Citizen after 9/11.* Cambridge: Cambridge University Press.

Markusoff, Jason. 2019. "Canada Now Brings In More Refugees than the U.S." *Maclean's*, January 23, 2019. https://www.macleans.ca/news/canada /refugee-resettlement-canada/.

Marshall, T. H. 1963. *Class, Citizenship, and Social Development.* New York: Anchor Books.

Meena, Krishnendra. 2019. "Borders and Bordering Practices: A Case Study of Jaisalmer District on India–Pakistan Border." *Journal of Borderlands Studies* 35(2): 183–194. https://doi.org/10.1080/08865655.201 9.1646148.

Mezzadra, Sandro, and Brett Neilson. 2013. *Border as Method, or, the Multiplication of Labor.* Durham, NC: Duke University Press.

Milivojevic, Sanja. 2019. *Border Policing and Security Technologies: Mobility and Proliferation of Borders in the Western Balkans.* New York: Routledge.

Moreno-Lax, Violeta. 2018. "The EU Humanitarian Border and the Securitization of Human Rights: The 'Rescue-through-Interdiction/ Rescue-without-Protection' Paradigm." *JCMS: Journal of Common Market Studies* 56(1): 119–140. https://doi.org/10.1111/jcms.12651.

Mountz, Alison. 2020. *The Death of Asylum: Hidden Geographies of the Enforcement Archipelago.* Minneapolis: University of Minnesota.

Muller, Benjamin J. 2011. "Risking it all at the Biometric Border: Mobility, Limits, and the Persistence of Securitisation." *Geopolitics* 16(1): 91–106. https://doi.org/10.1080/14650045.2010.493775.

Muller, Benjamin, Thomas N. Cooke, Miguel de Larrinaga, Philippe M. Frowd, Deljana Iossifova, Daniela Johannes, Can E. Mutlu, and Adam Nowek. 2016. "Collective Discussion Ferocious Architecture: Sovereign Spaces/Places by Design." *International Political Sociology* 10(1): 75–96. https://doi.org/10.1093/ips/olv002.

Nail, Thomas. 2019. "Sanctuary, Solidarity, Status!" in *Open Borders: In Defence of Free Movement,* edited by Reece Jones. Athens: University of Georgia Press.

Norfolk, Alexander. 2019. "Shifting, Securitizing, and Streamlining: An Exploration of Preclearance Policy in the Pacific Northwest." *Journal of Borderlands Studies* 35(4): 527–543. https://doi.org/10.1080/08865655.2019.1 619473.

Ohmae, Kenichi. 1989. "Managing in a Borderless World." *Harvard Business Review*, May–June, 1989. https://hbr.org/1989/05/managing-in-a-border less-world.

———. 1990. *Borderless World: Power and Strategy in the Global Marketplace.* London: HarperCollins.

———. 2016. "Immigration as a Human Right." In *Migration in Political Theory: The Ethics of Movement and Membership,* edited by Sarah Fine and Lea Ypi, 32–57. Oxford: Oxford University Press.

Paasi, Anssi. 1998. "Boundaries as Social Processes: Territoriality in the World of Flows." *Geopolitics* 3(1): 69–88. https://doi.org/10.1080/146500 49808407608.

———. "Bounded Spaces in a 'Borderless World': Border Studies, Power and the Anatomy of Territory." *Journal of Power* 2(2): 213–234. https://doi.org /10.1080/17540290903064275.

Paasi, Anssi, Eeva-Kaisa Prokkola, Jarkko Saarinen, and Kaj Zimmerbauer, eds. 2019. *Borderless Worlds for Whom? Ethics, Moralities and Mobilities.* New York: Routledge.

Pallister-Wilkins, P. 2018. "Médecins Avec Frontières and the Making of a Humanitarian Borderscape." *Environment and Planning D – Society & Space* 36(1): 114–138. https://doi.org/10.1177/0263775817740588.

Parmar, Alpa. 2020. "Borders as Mirrors: Racial Hierarchies and Policing Migration." *Critical Criminology* 28(2): 175–192.

Perkowski, Nina. 2016. "Deaths, Interventions, Humanitarianism and Human Rights in the Mediterranean 'Migration Crisis.'" *Mediterranean Politics* 21(2): 331–335.

Pierce, Sarah, and Andrew Selee. 2017. "Immigration under Trump: A Review of Policy Shifts in the Year since Election." Washington, D.C.: Migration Policy Institute. https://www.migrationpolicy.org/research/immigration -under-trump-review-policy-shifts.

Pinos, James. C. 2018. "Borderities and the Politics of Contemporary Mobile Borders." *Journal of Borderlands Studies* 33(4): 665–666. https://doi.org/10 .1080/08865655.2016.1222882.

Popescu, Gabriel. 2015. "Controlling Mobility: Embodying Borders." In *Borderities and the Politics of Contemporary Mobile Borders*, edited by Anne-Laure Amilhat Szary and Frédéric Giraut, 100–115. New York: Palgrave Macmillan.

Rajaram, Prem Kumar, and Carl Grundy-Warr, eds. 2007. *Borderscapes: Hidden Geographies and Politics at Territory's Edge.* St. Paul: University of Minnesota Press.

Rogan, Eugene. 1999. *Frontiers of the State in the Late Ottoman Empire: Transjordan, 1850-1921.* Cambridge: Cambridge University Press.

Robinson, Vaughan, ed. 2016. *The International Refugee Crisis: British and Canadian Responses.* New York: Springer.

Rumford, Chris. 2014. "'Seeing Like a Border': Towards Multiperspectivalism." In *Cosmopolitan Borders*, edited by Chris Rumford, 39–55. Basingstoke and New York: Palgrave Macmillan.

Sahlins, Peter. 1989. *Boundaries: The Making of France and Spain in the Pyrenees.* Berkeley: University of California Press.

Salter, Mark B. 2007. "Governmentalities of an Airport: Heterotopia and Confession." *International Political Sociology* 1(1) 2007: 49–67. https://doi. org/10.1111/j.1749-5687.2007.00004.x.

———. 2013. "At the Threshold of Security: A Theory of International Borders." In *Global Surveillance and Policing*, edited by Elia Zureik and Mark B. Salter, 48–62. Abingdon, U.K., and New York: Routledge.

Sassen, Saskia 2015. "Bordering Capabilities versus Borders: Implications for National Borders." In *Borderities and the Politics of Contemporary Mobile Borders*, edited by Anne-Laure Amilhat Szary and Frédéric Giraut, 23–52. New York: Palgrave Macmillan.

Schindel, Estela. 2016. "Bare Life at the European Borders: Entanglements of Technology, Society and Nature." *Journal of Borderlands Studies* 31(2): 219–234. https://doi.org/10.1080/08865655.2016.1174604.

Schmidtke, Oliver. 2018. "The Civil Society Dynamic of Including and Empowering Refugees in Canada's Urban Centres." *Social Inclusion* 6(1): 147–156. http://dx.doi.org/10.17645/si.v6i1.1306.

———. 2019. "The Local Governance of Migration: Evidence from the Immigrant Country Canada." *DISP- The Planning Review* 55(3): 31–41. https://doi.org/10.1080/02513625.2019.1670986.

———. 2021. "Policy Formation and Citizenship Practices: Germany's Regions as Laboratories for Immigrant Integration." *Journal of International Migration and Integration.* https://doi.org/10.1007/s12134-021-00804-6.

Scott, James W. 2012. "European Politics of Borders, Border Symbolism and Cross-Border Cooperation." In *A Companion to Border Studies*, edited by T. M. Wilson and H. Donnan, 83–99. Hoboken: Wiley-Blackwell Publishing.

Shachar, Ayelet. 2009. *The Birthright Lottery: Citizenship and Global Inequality.* Cambridge, MA: Harvard University Press.

———. 2020a. *The Shifting Border: Legal Cartographies of Migration and Mobility.* Manchester: Manchester University Press.

———. 2020b. "Borders in the Time of COVID-19." *Ethics and International Affairs*, March 27, 2020. https://www.ethicsandinternationalaffairs.org /2020/borders-in-the-time-of-covid-19/.

Skeldon, Ronald. 2014. *Migration and Development: A Global Perspective.* Abingdon, U.K.: Routledge.

Tabarrok, Alex. 2015. "The Case for Getting Rid of Borders—Completely." *The Atlantic*, October 10, 2015. https://www.theatlantic.com/business /archive/2015/10/get-rid-borders-completely/409501/.

Topak, Özgün E., Ciara Bracken-Roche, Alana Saulnier, and David Lyon. 2015. "From Smart Borders to Perimeter Security: The Expansion of Digital Surveillance at the Canadian Borders." *Geopolitics* 20(4): 880–899. https://doi.org/10.1080/14650045.2015.1085024.

Trauner, Florian. 2016. "Asylum Policy: The EU's 'Crises' and the Looming Policy Regime Failure." *Journal of European Integration* 38(3): 311–325. https://doi.org/10.1080/07036337.2016.1140756.

Trebilcock, Michael. 2019. "The Puzzle of Canadian Exceptionalism in Contemporary Immigration Policy." *Journal of International Migration and Integration* 20(3): 823–849. https://doi.org/10.1007/s12134-018-0633-6.

Triandafyllidou, A. 2018. "A 'Refugee Crisis' Unfolding: 'Real' Events and Their Interpretation in Media and Political Debates." *Journal of*

Immigrant & Refugee Studies 16(1–2): 198–216. https://doi.org/10.1080/1556 2948.2017.1309089.

Tully, James. 2014. *On Global Citizenship: James Tully in Dialogue*. London: Bloomsbury.

United Nations High Commissioner for Refugees (UNHCR). 2019. "Global Trends: Forced Displacement in 2018." https://www.unhcr.org /globaltrends2018/.

United Nations World Tourism Organization (UNWTO). 2020. *Compendium of Tourism Statistics Data 2014 – 2018, 2020 Edition*. Madrid: World Tourism Organization. https://doi.org/10.18111/9789284421459.

UN News. 2019. "UN Rights Chief 'Appalled' by US Border Detention Conditions, Says Holding Migrant Children May Violate International Law." UN News, July 8, 2019. https://news.un.org/en/story/2019/07/1041991.

Vallet, Elisabeth. 2016. *Borders, Fences and Walls: State of Insecurity?* New York: Routledge.

Vila, Pablo. 2000. *Crossing Borders, Reinforcing Borders: Social Categories, Metaphors, and Narrative Identities on the U.S.-Mexico Frontier*. Austin: University of Texas Press.

Vivekanandan, Jayashree. 2019. "No Mountain Too High? Assessing the Trans-territoriality of the Kailash Sacred Landscape Conservation Initiative." *Journal of Borderlands Studies* 35(2): 255–268. https://doi.org/10 .1080/08865655.2019.1646150.

Walia, Harsha. 2013. *Undoing Border Imperialism*. Oakland, CA: AK Press.

Walker, R.B.J. 1993. *Inside/Outside: International Relations as Political Theory*. Cambridge: Cambridge University Press.

Wallace, R. 2018. "Contextualizing the Crisis: The Framing of Syrian Refugees in Canadian Print Media." *Canadian Journal of Political Science* 51(2): 207–231. https://doi.org/10.1017/S0008423917001482.

Walters, William. 2006. "Rethinking Borders Beyond the State." *Comparative European Politics* 4:141–159. https://doi.org/10.1057/palgrave.cep.6110076.

——. 2008. "Bordering the Sea: Shipping Industries and the Policing of Stowaways." *Borderlands* 7(3): 1–25.

——. 2011. "Foucault and Frontiers: Notes on the Birth of the Humanitarian Border." In *Governmentality: Current Issues and Future Challenges*, edited by Ulrich Brocking, Sussanne Krasmann, and Thomas Lemke, 138–164. New York: Routledge.

Waltz, Kenneth. 1959. *Man, the State and War: A Theoretical Analysis*. New York: Columbia University Press.

Wevers, Rosa. 2018. "Unmasking Biometrics' Biases: Facing Gender, Race, Class and Ability in Biometric Data Collection." *Journal for Media History* 21(2): 89–105. http://doi.org/10.18146/2213-7653.2018.368.

Wimmer, Andreas. 2002. *Nationalist Exclusion and Ethnic Conflict: Shadows of Modernity*. Cambridge: Cambridge University Press.

Winter, Elke. 2015. "Rethinking Multiculturalism After its 'Retreat' Lessons from Canada." *American Behavioral Scientist* 59(6): 637–657. https://doi.org/10.1177/0002764214566495.

Wodak, Ruth. 2015. *The Politics of Fear: What Right-wing Populist Discourses Mean.* Los Angeles: Sage.

Wolf, Marie, and Marinus Ossewaarde. 2018. "The Political Vision of Europe during the 'Refugee Crisis': Missing Common Ground for Integration." *Journal of European Integration* 40(1): 33–50. https://doi.org/10.1080/07036337.2017.1404054.

Zapata-Barrero, Richard, Tiziana Caponio, and Peter Scholten. 2017. "Theorizing the 'Local Turn' in a Multi-level Governance Framework of Analysis: A Case Study in Immigrant Policies." *International Review of Administrative Sciences* 83(2): 241–246. https://doi.org/10.1177/0020852316688426.

PART I

CANADA IN CONTEXT

CHAPTER 1

Commodifying Migrants: Borders and Canada's Temporary Foreign Workers

Oliver Schmidtke

Borders are places of categorization and selection. While the assessment of who is entitled to cross a border is determined in political-bureaucratic processes, the border is the place where these decisions are regularly administered. At the border, the status and entitlements of migrants are ultimately determined and enforced. Yet the screening process at the border is fundamentally different for a business executive than it is for asylum claimants who have made it to the country irregularly and without the proper legal entitlement. The reference to a seemingly coherent group of migrants conceals the strict and legally enshrined hierarchies that differentiate the privileged from the less privileged, the group of migrants that states commonly target in their recruitment efforts from those who are often prevented from crossing borders. There is a fundamental difference in what the border means that, based on the legal and socio-economic status of the migrant, is determined prior to the arrival at the actual territorial border. The bordering practice of assigning a status and equipping migrants with a particular licence to move into a country takes place with a view to the interests and obligations of the nation-state. Still, in the end it is the border of the state that is the primary reference in determining the right to enter and stay in a country.

In this context, guest workers or temporary foreign workers (TFWs) are a fascinating group of migrants that are subject to a specific mix of inclusionary and exclusionary practices: They come to a country legally and cross borders with their status established by a clearly defined and time-phased professional task. Different from the traditional guest workers, who as denizens (Hammar 1989) are, under normal circumstances, fully endowed with a full range of social and civil rights, TFWs have a far more precarious status, legally and socially. Arguably, it is exactly this hazardous and temporary status that makes foreign migrant workers so attractive to employers around the globe.[1]

They constitute a relatively cheap and flexible workforce that comes with minimum obligations for the employer or the hosting state. According to the labour-migration branch of the International Labour Organization, globally there were an estimated 164 million migrant workers in 2017. Almost half (46.9 percent) of all migrant workers were located in two broad sub-regions: North America and northern, southern, and western Europe.[22] In this respect, foreign migrant workers are integral to the globalizing world and the borders that facilitate or restrict their mobility (Benson 2011; Lutz 2016; Schierup et al. 2015; Van Reekum 2016; Yeates 2009).

In Canada, the number of TFWs has greatly expanded over the past two decades, at some stage even outnumbering the so-called economic immigrants. This development indicates how a flexible, temporary workforce is highly attractive for certain sectors of the economy in particular (most notably, farming, hospitality, or care services). Yet, at the same time, the rising number of TFWs raises serious issues that are related to how the boundary between the temporary workforce and Canadian citizens is defined and legally regulated. There have been repeated concerns about TFWs filling positions that Canadians should have been considered for first, even if the latter group of workers is more costly (because they are due to earn higher wages and benefits). In addition, TFWs have experienced systematic forms of exploitation or abuse that are directly linked to

---

1   According to the OECD, a foreign migrant worker can be defined as follows: "Foreigners admitted by the receiving State for the specific purpose of exercising an economic activity remunerated from within the receiving country. Their length of stay is usually restricted as is the type of employment they can hold. Their dependents, if admitted, are also included in this category" (see: https://stats.oecd.org/glossary/detail.asp?ID=1047).

2   See "Labour Migration," Global Migration Data Portal, https://migration dataportal.org/themes/labour-migration.

their status of being dependent on a work relationship with one employer and being largely deprived of access to legal protection, which regular local workers take for granted. Furthermore, race and gender play an important role in reproducing the precarious working conditions and status of TFWs. From a larger societal perspective, the massive expansion of the TFW program thus threatens to undermine Canada's achievement as a country of immigration that offers its newcomers swift access to permanent residency or citizenship and, linked to this status, facilitates their full inclusion into the fabric of society.

Investigating the Canadian case, and the extraordinary increase in the number of TFWs, in particular, under recent Conservative governments (2006–2015), I consider two analytical perspectives and the following two sets of questions: (i) What are the bordering practices vis-à-vis TFWs as members of the workforce? What forms of social, legal, and symbolic exclusion do they face? How does their treatment reflect a broader commodification of the labour market and international migration? (ii) Who makes decisions concerning the recruitment of TFWs? What we have witnessed in the Canadian context over the past 15 years is not only a massive expansion of the TFW program but also a shift in the way in which this group of migrants is recruited and brought into the country. In this latter respect, I will address modes of decision making in attracting migrant workers and the gradual retreat of the state in recruiting and settling migrants. I will interpret shifts toward a greater responsibility assigned to private business interests as part of a more general push toward commodifying the governance of Canada's border and migration policies.

After a brief introduction of the theoretical framework within which I interpret TFWs, a first section on this group of migrants will explore the effects of expanding this program dramatically over the past 20 years. The central focus is on the dynamic of inclusion and exclusion that TFWs face in terms of their status in Canada. In a second step, I will analyze how the Temporary Foreign Worker Program (TWFP) has been managed and allude to the decentralization and outsourcing of policy competence in favour of private actors. In the concluding section, I provide both a theoretically driven interpretation of the bordering practices in governing TFWs and a range of policy recommendations designed to address the socially and politically negative effects of the enlarged TFWP.

Selecting and Excluding Immigrants:
Multi-Dimensional Bordering Practices

Borders are the site where international migration is controlled, regulated, and managed. Yet the effects of borders on migration are multi-dimensional and, while constituting a critical component, not exclusively tied to the physical control of cross-border mobility. Arguably, the right to cross borders is the most dramatic manifestation of how migration is restricted or facilitated. The contemporary world provides ample examples of how the least privileged and desirable migrants are prohibited to move from one country to another often by force. The regular images of desperate refugees trying to reach the shores of Europe from northern Africa or cross into the United States from Mexico point to the penalizing and controlling power that is exerted at the border. In this respect, borders have the propensity to be places of violence (van Houtum and Boedeltje 2009), where the mobility of people can be restricted with disciplining tools and sophisticated security regimes (Scheel 2019).

   And yet, there is also a broader performative aspect of border enforcement: it is with reference to the border and the national community it demarcates that the status and legal entitlements of migrants are negotiated. De Genova (2010) speaks about the "contested politics of mobility" that plays out and is staged as a "spectacle" (Andreas 2003; De Genova 2002) at the border. From this perspective, a state's border enforcement and security strategies can be interpreted as political attempts to shape public perception about insiders/outsiders and to contribute to producing notions of illegality. Scheel (2018, 271) speaks about the "productivity of border regimes" and the "rationale of differential inclusion" that are decisive in defining the legality or illegality of migrants. The performative dimension of border enforcement critically relates to the bordering practices of establishing legal and symbolic status for migrants. The hierarchization of legal and illegal statuses is the consequence of a process to categorize migratory movements to render them "governable" (Casas-Cortes et al. 2015, 67).

   In terms of legal status, citizenship is the most privileged status for migrants as it offers comprehensive and legally sanctioned access to rights and entitlements. For De Genova, "'illegality' is a social relation that is fundamentally inseparable from citizenship" (2002, 422). At its core, citizenship is a legal status governing membership of a state community that structures the complex relationship between the state and its citizens. Citizenship, however, regulates affiliation in a twofold sense, in a legal and an identitarian social sense. From the classical position of T. H. Marshall, citizenship becomes a mode of social inclusion that expresses politically sanctioned expectations, in particular, how the nationally minded community treats its members and under which conditions nationals of other states can become fully accepted as new citizens (Bloemraad, Korteweg, and Yurdakul 2008, 34; Joppke 2007; Kershaw 2010). Under theoretical guidelines, Turner (1990) has described citizenship as a constitutive condition for the political community, under which social integration and solidarity can be articulated and become social practice.

In the Canadian context, immigrants have a straightforward, direct, and relatively short path to citizenship. The swift and un-bureaucratic awarding of citizenship is central to this country's immigration and integration policies. According to Canada's multi-cultural ethos, immigrants should be turned into citizens as soon as possible after arrival and given equal access to educational and profes-sional opportunities in Canada (Bloemraad 2002, 2006). Until 2010, permanent residents could apply for citizenship after just three years, but this so-called residence requirement has now been extended to six years and is subject to additional conditions. From a comparative per-spective, Canada has relatively high naturalization rates (Picot and Hou 2014). According to Citizenship and Immigration Canada, in 2011, 85 percent of all immigrants qualified to do so opted for naturalization (at the end of Conservative Prime Minister Stephen Harper's time in office, in 2016, this number fell to 82.7 percent).[3] In comparison, these rates are much lower in Europe. For instance, in Germany or France, naturalization rates are at 40 percent each, and around 60 percent in the United Kingdom and the Netherlands.

The rapid acquisition of citizenship allows for the legal equality of immigrants in the labour market and their inclusion in the political system. In her comparative study, Bloemraad (2006, 2015) shows how the high naturalization rates in Canada are a conscious part of state-sanctioned multiculturalism and its goal of equal inclusion of newcomers. In a nutshell, swift access to permanent residency or citi-zenship is a deliberate strategy employed by the Canadian state as a way of governing migration and their social integration. More

---

3   See "Obtaining Canadian Citizenship," Statistics Canada, https://www12.statcan. gc.ca/nhs-enm/2011/as-sa/99-010-x/99-010-x2011003_1-eng.cfm.

specifically, it acts as a promise to overcome quickly the legal and symbolic boundary that divides the Canadian population from its newcomers. For Bourdieu (1986, 1996; Erel 2010; Nohl et al. 2014) citizenship vitally forms the capital that migrants can rely on. In his theoretical view, citizenship constitutes a key mechanism of distinction between migrant and non-migrant workers manifesting in both formal (legal and institutional) and informal (practised and cultural) aspects (Winter 2014). Still, it is worth pointing out that citizenship establishes only one dimension of societal inclusion or exclusion. As explicated in greater detail later, there are other processes beyond the legal status as citizens that can reproduce patterns of precarity and exclusion for TFWs.

The description of the central pillars of the Canadian citizenship regime should not obscure the fact that citizenship can be interpreted as a far-reaching state and civil-society practice, which is always politically controversial. Over a period of ten years, under Harper-led Conservative governments (2006–2015), the gradual abandonment of the Canadian citizenship model of inclusive and equal rights occurred (Schmidtke 2019a). During this period, there was a distinct push toward portraying migrants as commodities that are considered primarily through the lens of their perceived economic and societal value. The utilitarian logic that drives marketization is characterized by a significant normative tension that advocates, on the one hand, the inclusion of highly skilled immigrants (i.e., active and productive individuals) as beneficial to society if they meet the expectations of the skilled labour market. On the other, refugees or low-skilled temporary workers are not portrayed as socially/economically advantageous. Under the auspices of this strictly market-oriented logic, issues of human rights and the state's obligation to social justice are, at best, secondary.

This development has been accompanied by tightening the standards of eligibility under Canada's economic immigration category, the point system.[4] Recently, the Canadian government introduced

---

4   By 1967, Canada had radically reformed its immigration to reflect the socio-economic imperative of expanding the workforce of the country. A new point system was introduced to evaluate applicants based on their education, linguistic skills (ability to communicate in English or French), work experience, age, existing job offer, and "adaptability" to life in Canada. From this point onwards, race and origin were no longer the determining factors for admittance into Canada. Rather, the education, age, and qualifications of potential migrants became important. Although the point system was modified during the late 1970s, migrants' education and occupation were still seen as being important, in particular for independent

new legislation to make command of one of Canada's two official lan-guages a requirement, and to link the category of the economic migrant more closely to the availability of a job offer. The policy on linguistic capabilities is likely to increase immigration from English-speaking countries at the expense of the non-Western world. Furthermore, recent cohorts of migrants have been denied a variety of social services (including access to health care and employment insur-ance) during their initial years of residence (Reitz and Somerville 2004). What these developments indicate is how recent federal govern-ments, in particular under the Conservatives, have sought to shift the costs of immigration on to migrants themselves while substantially reducing the responsibility of the state in providing newcomers with services and assistance. One could argue that recent initiatives in this policy field simply reflect the ongoing struggles to achieve a better match between labour-market needs and the qualifications of migrants (such as streamlining the recognition of educational degrees or tying residency to a job offer). And yet, there is also the persistent trend to exclude those migrants who are deemed too costly or otherwise bur-densome for Canadian society.

Canada's Growing TFW Force

The TFWP, originally designed to mitigate temporary work shortages, has been in place for decades in Canada. However, over the past 20 years the program has experienced a dramatic expansion. The num-ber of TFWs present in the country rose from 52,000 in 1996 to over 310,000 in 2015. As figure 1.1 shows, the issuing of TFWP permits saw a dramatic expansion in the late 2000s. These numbers remained at an unprecedented level for some years, declined when the Liberals, under Justin Trudeau, came to office in 2015, and then started to rise again over the past two years. While recently the federal government has sought to restrict the number of TFWs, it has become manifest that, to a certain degree, Canada has become dependent on these migrant workers to supply its labour market and to support its agricultural, homecare, and other lower-wage sectors. Kendra Strauss, a director at the Canadian Centre for Policy Alternatives, reports that "the number

migrants, one of the categories under which migrants could apply to enter Canada (Li 2003).

of TFW positive labour market opinions doubled between 2005 and 2012 in sectors like manufacturing and mining, oil and gas, and increased more than sevenfold in construction. Even more striking, though, is the increase from 4,360 to 44,740 during the same period in accommodation and food services positions" (Strauss 2014).

The status of having a temporary permit to stay in the country has become a defining feature of contemporary migration regimes. In 2017, 70 percent of all people coming to Canada on a long-term basis were temporary residents without citizenship rights (see figure 1.2).

Canada has a variety of programs that allow for temporary status in the country, the most frequently used are study permits for educational purposes and the International Mobility Program (IMP).[5] The IMP allows employers to hire foreign workers to fill temporary labour and skill shortages without applying for a labour-market impact assessment (which is the case for TFWs). To recruit a foreign

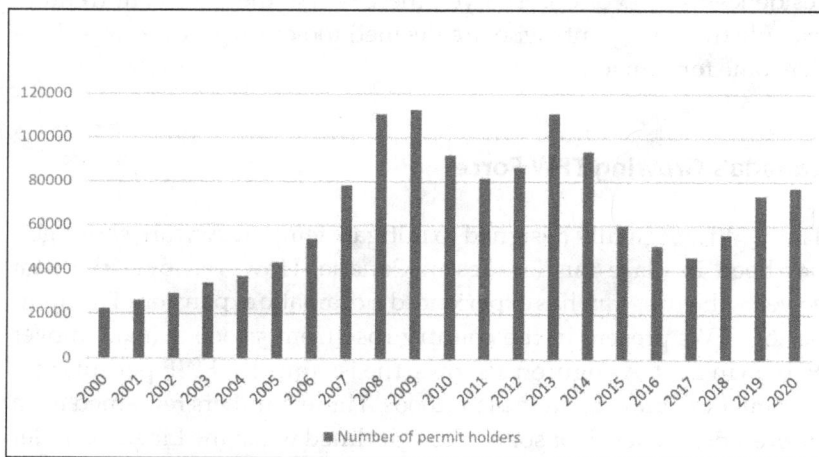

FIGURE 1.1. TFWs Program Work Permit Holders in Canada (2000-2020).

Source: Immigration, Refugees and Citizenship Canada and Statistics Canada (https://open.canada.ca/data/en/dataset/360024f2-17e9-4558-bfc1-3616485d65b9).

---

5   Canada has recently greatly diversified its programs to recruit experienced foreign workers, with a particular view to labour-market needs. For instance, in addition to the programs described, subsequently Canada has also established an "International Experience Canada" scheme designed to attract highly qualified young professionals on a temporary basis.

worker under this program the employer needs to demonstrate that the hire advances broadly defined economic and cultural national interests. The flexibility and relative bureaucratic ease that the IMP offers helps to explain the comparatively high numbers of employer-specific foreign workers brought to Canada under this mobility program (see figure 1.3).

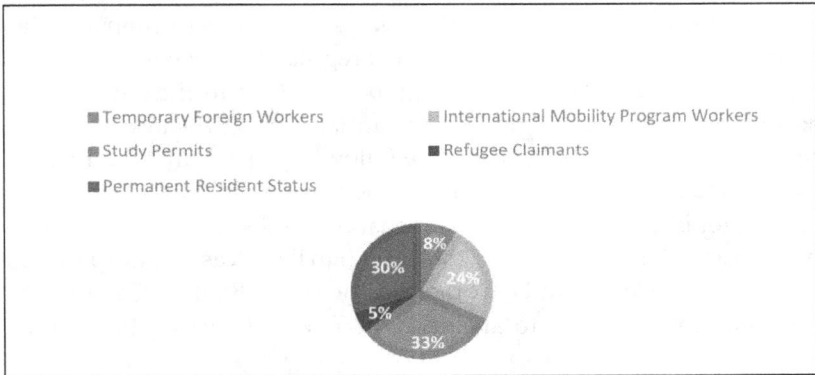

FIGURE 1.2. Immigration Status of People Entering Canada in 2017.

Source: Immigration, Refugees and Citizenship Canada and Statistics Canada (https://open.canada.ca/data/en/dataset/360024f2-17e9-4558-bfc1-3616485d65b9).

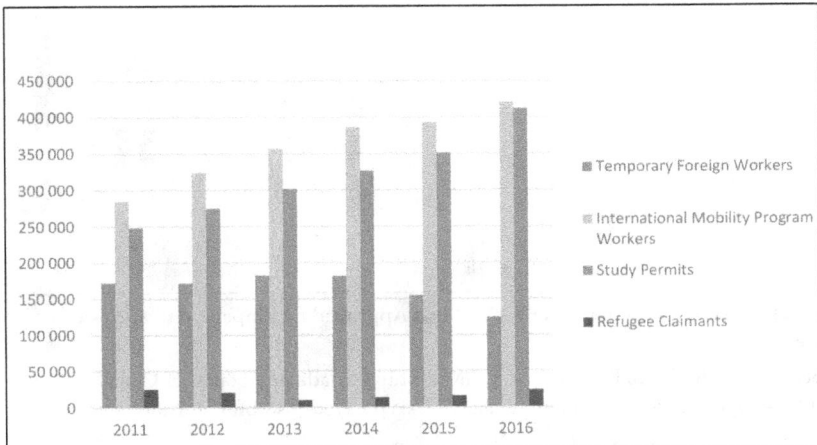

FIGURE 1.3. Temporary Permit Holders with Valid Permits in Each Calendar Year.

Source: Immigration, Refugees and Citizenship Canada and Statistics Canada (https://open.canada.ca/data/en/dataset/360024f2-17e9-4558-bfc1-3616485d65b9).

Entering Canada as a temporary worker is contingent upon a job offer from a Canadian employer. The work permit is tied to this particular position and can be extended for a maximum of four years. It is attractive to employers to hire these temporary workers because they are less expensive and they can easily be fired. For instance, amid the current economic downturn, and more recently during COVID-19, many of these temporary workers lost their employer-specific jobs and had to leave the country. Moreover, Canadian employers are officially entitled to pay temporary workers lower wages than their regular workforce (up to 15 percent less than a regular employee).

Figure 1.4 shows how the number of TFWs in the agricultural sector, in particular, has grown substantially, while the low-wage sector has seen a noteworthy decrease following a peak in 2012. In 2013, there was a series of publicly debated incidents of TFWs being reported to have replaced Canadian workers that compelled the federal government to act. Most prominently, the Canadian Broadcasting Corporation reported that Canadian IT workers at the Royal Bank of Canada lost their employment due to an influx of TFWs.[6] Reacting to a public

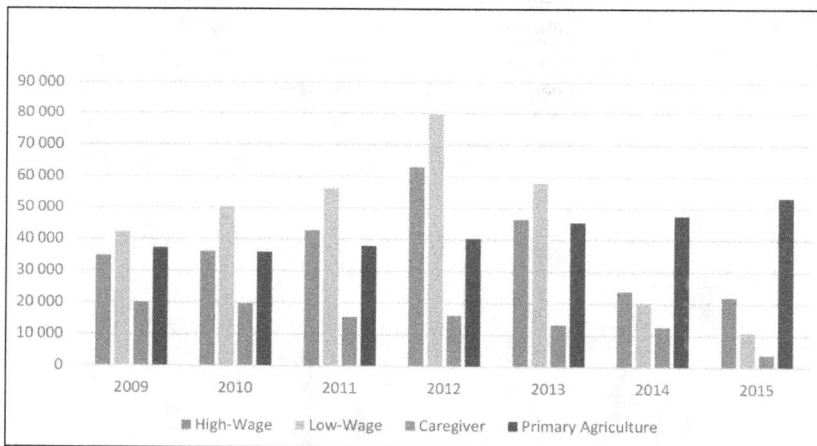

FIGURE 1.4. The Number of TFW Positions Approved by Employment and Social Development from 2009–2015.

Source: Immigration, Refugees and Citizenship Canada and Statistics Canada (https://open.canada.ca/data/en/dataset/360024f2-17e9-4558-bfc1-3616485d65b9).

---

6   See Kathy Tomlinsom, "RBC Replaces Canadian Staff with Foreign Workers," *CBC News*, April 6, 2013, https://www.cbc.ca/news/canada/british-columbia/rbc -replaces-canadian-staff-with-foreign-workers-1.1315008.

outcry, Employment and Social Development Canada rebranded the TFWP and committed it to "Putting Canadians First" in 2014. In agriculture, the concern about replacing parts of the Canadian workforce does not seem to have been a major public concern.

This considerable expansion of Canada's TFWP has brought up concerns at different levels. First, bringing in such a large number of migrant workers raises the question based on what criteria, needs assessments, and recruitment strategies are used for selecting TFWs and placing them in jobs. Does the current practice meet the expectation of this program in terms of filling urgent vacancies in the labour market without replacing Canadian workers?

The second issue relates to the actual working conditions of TFWs in Canada. To what degree does the reliance on one employer and the placement in jobs that are regularly isolated and difficult to monitor lead to forms of abuse critically tied to the precarious legal status of these migrant workers? Finally, is such a high number of TFWs desirable in terms of Canada's legacy of providing an inclusive and equitable environment to newcomers? Is there the danger of replicating some of the pitfalls that have troubled Europe's experience with guest-worker programs (creation of denizens, patterns of social and political exclusion extending over several generations, provoking anti-foreigner sentiments, etc.)? The policy challenge here is the "negotiation of non-citizenship" (Goldring and Landolt 2013) in a country whose approach to immigrant settlement and social cohesion is guided by commitments to turning foreigners into citizens in an accessible and expedient manner. Figure 1.2 shows that over two-thirds of all people entering Canada were temporary residents in 2017. While Canada provides a pathway to citizenship to its permanent residents and, under more restrictive circumstances, to its international student population, TFWs regularly do not have this opportunity even though a large number of this group would be interested in pursuing naturalization. For instance, there has been a long-lasting debate on the structural barriers that live-in caregivers face when applying for permanent-resident status (Canada has a large numbers of Filipina workers recruited through the Live-In Caregiver Program). Legally this group is entitled to apply for permanent status upon completion of 24 months of live-in care work within a four-year period. Yet, in reality, they face multifaceted obstacles related to stigmatization, educational regulations, and immigration requirements in pursuing this goal (Tungohan at al. 2015).

A recent study by Statistics Canada looked into how "temporary" TFWs actually are (Prokopenko and Hou 2018). The results indicate that the majority were temporary in that most TFWs left within two years of their arrival (following the rules stipulated in their contracts). At the same time, the study found a tendency among temporary workers to stay longer, often striving for permanent residence status. The share of TWFs remaining in Canada for various cohorts since 1995 ranged from 11 percent for the earlier and 18 percent for the most recent cohort. The variation can be attributed almost exclusively to changing governmental regulations and extended pathways to a more permanent status in Canada. The analysis confirmed that there is a great desire among TFWs to extend their stay in Canada and, ideally, gain access to permanent residency or citizenship.

The massive expansion of the TFWP is mirrored by other developments that point to a similar structural reconfiguration in Canada's migration regime: the perceived economic utility of newcomers has increasingly become the dominant guiding principle of migrant-selection policy. This policy shift is evident in the priorities guiding the recruitment of new migrants. The proportion of economic migrants has gradually been expanded at the expense of those seeking entry into Canada as family members or on humanitarian grounds. The 1976 Immigration Act defines the three priorities of Canadian immigration policy: (1) family reunification, (2) humanitarian concerns, and (3) the promotion of Canada's economic, social, demographic, and cultural goals. Since then, the emphasis has decisively shifted toward economic goals and recruiting migrants who are deemed as most valuable or desirable, the most obvious example being the introduction of the investor or business class of immigrants.[7] The expansion of the TFWP is the equivalent step primarily for low-skilled workers, who are brought into the country with a view to maximizing the economic benefit of (temporary) migration while reducing the costs associated with it.[8]

---

7   Under this category, access to permanent residence is tied to investing a minimum of $800,000 and creating employment in Canada.

8   The official discourse on migration and integration has shifted accordingly. In tune with the market logic, newcomers are touted as net contributors to the country's economic well-being. This almost exclusive focus on the marketable "value" of migrants is succinctly reflected in a statement by Citizenship and Immigration Canada (2000, 2) from the beginning of the new millennium: "Our

Effects on the Ground: TFWs Subject to Abuse and Marginalization

The largest group of people entering Canada with limited residence permits are workers chosen to fill gaps in the labour market, primarily in the agricultural sector. However, these temporary workers are increasingly filling gaps across many sectors of the service industry and, to a lesser extent, in the manufacturing sector. Still, temporary foreign workers are exposed to a structurally precarious professional environment. Most importantly, as their legal status in Canada is tied to a particular employment, this group of workers tends to be directly affected by economic cycles. For example, many of these temporary workers lost their jobs during the recent economic recession and had to leave the country. Thus, temporary workers are regularly victims of exploitation and marginalization (Worswick 2010).

The challenges that TFWs have faced during the COVID-19 pandemic are a vivid illustration of this propensity for abuse and exploitation. At the beginning of the pandemic there was considerable pressure to prevent a disruption in the food supply chain irrespective of an agricultural labour shortage. As a result, TFWs were regularly exposed to undue workload expectations, long workdays, and unpaid overtime (Han 2020), in addition to exposure to the virus given the working conditions. During the first three months of the COVID-19 crisis, the Migrant Workers Alliance for Change registered over 1,100 complaints from TFWs concerning employers.[9]

The large presence of TFWs has created some considerable unintended consequences and resulting policy challenges that are largely related to the legal status of these groups of migrant workers in Canada. One critical concern is that the recruitment of relatively low-skilled and low-paid workers from abroad will threaten Canadian workers. Canadian media, as noted, have reported the replacement of local by foreign workers. The crux of the matter, though, is that employers are circumventing the rules, illegitimately bringing TFWs into the country.

---

multilingual, multiethnic workforce provides us with a distinct comparative advantage in the global marketplace."

9   For more information, see "Policy," Migrant Workers Alliance for Change, https://migrantworkersalliance.org/policy/.

In addition, fixed-term workers are often exposed to inferior working conditions. Reports of poor accommodation and dangerous working conditions have raised public awareness in Canada of these "second-class immigrants" (Hennebry 2009; Goldring 2010; Goldring and Landolt 2013; Preibisch and Otero 2014). In terms of status, these workers are largely deprived of legal rights and unionized representation, otherwise available to local workers. What emerges is a secondary working class managed by fewer rules and laws. Most importantly, Canada lacks a regulatory or enforcement mechanism to protect TFWs (Horgan and Liinamaa 2017). The lack of legal protection for TFWs in Canada serves to align their social experience more closely to the social reality of immigrants in the United States, although it can be expected that the heavily regulated Canadian labour market has a much lower number of illegal immigrants. The extension of temporary programs has undermined one of the key virtues of the Canadian migration system, as forms of legal exclusion, sometimes officially sanctioned discrimination, are now becoming accepted practice (Ellermann 2014).

The abuse that these workers are exposed to is structurally tied to their status as TFWs, in particular in the low-wage sector. This precarious labour-market position can be illustrated through two examples: caregivers and agricultural workers. First, caregivers, mostly women working in private homes, are frequently vulnerable to abuse, even sexual violence (Robillard et al. 2018). Moreover, they work in isolated workplaces not subject to occupational health and safety inspections. Similarly, TFWs working in the farming industry regularly work under exploitative working conditions and are often deprived of health-care services or legitimately earned income. Reports of poor or dangerous working conditions have raised public awareness in Canada of these "second-class immigrants" (Goldring and Landolt 2013).

With a view to the long-term effects of accepting, in some years, more TFWs than economic immigrants into the country, there is also a significant concern regarding the inclusive and welcoming nature of Canada's immigration and integration regime. Canada's attractiveness as a country that allows immigrants equitable opportunities in the labour market and the educational system is critically dependent on their ability to legitimately become permanent residents or citizens (Bloemraad 2006; Siemiatycki 2012). The broader socio-political question regarding TFWs is whether having a large number of temporary workers in the country could create a class of non-citizens who participate in the workforce under precarious circumstances, excluded from social opportunities and entitlements. Lenard and Straehle (2012) call this phenomenon legislated inequality.

It is worth underlining that the precarious legal status of TFWs is one critical dimension accounting for how they are treated in Canada and what forms of exploitation some are exposed to. One additional factor shaping the professional and social reality that TFWs face is race. As figure 1.5 shows, most TFWs come from the Global South and belong to what is described as "visible minorities" in the Canadian context. There is persistent evidence to suggest that the discrimination and exploitation of TFWs is also related to their racial background (Jubany and Lázaro Castellanos 2021).

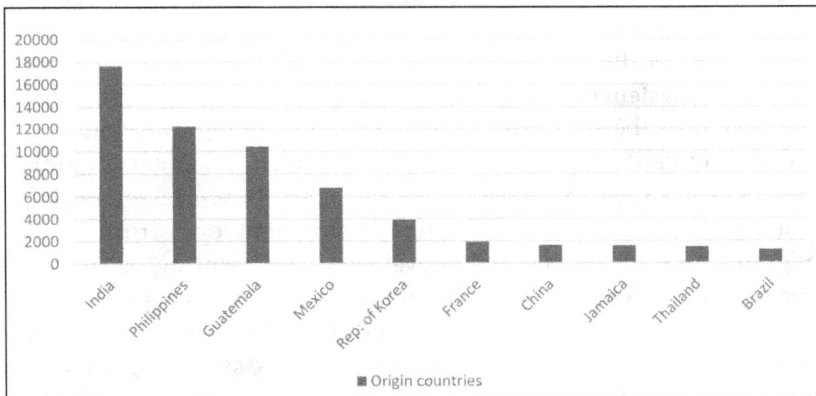

FIGURE 1.5. Top Ten Origin Countries of TFW Program Permit Holders in Canada 2020.

Source: Immigration, Refugees and Citizenship Canada and Statistics Canada (https://open.canada.ca/data/en/dataset/360024f2-17e9-4558-bfc1-3616485d65b9).

Agents of Recruiting Migrants: Privatization under Neoliberal Auspices

It is not by accident that the expansion of the TFWP coincides with another major development in Canada's immigration and integration regime, the decentralization of policy and administrative competences arising from the federal government. A key component in this regard is the provincial nominee program (PNP). First introduced in Manitoba in 1998, it has since expanded to all provinces and territories (except Nunavut and Quebec, which have their own economic-class-selection systems). In 2002, only 1.5 percent of all economic-stream migrants were provincial nominees; however, this figure increased substantially (to 15 percent) in 2008 (Challinor 2011). These programs are designed to allow provincial and territorial governments to operate their own systems of immigrant selection. Under this scheme, migrants are nominated by a province, based on them possessing the skills, language abilities, education, and Canadian work experience to immediately make an economic contribution to the province. In most cases these individuals are temporary migrants or former international students applying from within the country. Compared to the federal economic-immigrant category, with its focus on general skill levels, the PNP instead targets more specific professional groups in the labour market and reacts more directly to short-term shortages in the labour force.

As Li (2012, 106) shows in his detailed study, provinces use the PNP for specific, locally defined socio-economic purposes, thus creating a multitiered system of immigrant selection. Local capacity is an integral dimension of the new streams of recruiting immigrants under the umbrella of PNPs (Schmidtke 2019b). In Manitoba and Ontario, municipalities are formally involved in PNPs primarily through assessing local labour-market needs, identifying employment opportunities for migrants, and, most importantly, developing settlement and recruitment strategies on the ground (Wiginton 2014). Addressing the task of managing migration from below, provinces and cities also rely increasingly on non-state actors to identify labour-market needs, select migrants, and provide them with swift access to professional opportunities. Scholars have framed this development as a marketization of migration, in which private employers and their interests play an increasingly important role in recruiting newcomers (Walton-Roberts 2011).[10]

The empowerment of private business interests in this process has reinforced a more general trend in the Canadian immigration regime.

---

10 Recent census data show that more than three-in-five immigrants (60.3 percent) who arrived between 2011 and 2016 were admitted through an economic program (see Hugo O'Doherty and Eman Katem, "Immigrants Make Up 21.9% of Canada's Population: StatsCan," *CIC News*, October, 25, 2017, https://www.cicnews.com/2017/10/immigrants-make-up-21-9-of-canadas-population-statscan-109735.html#gs.Mzs=_XU). From a critical perspective, Flynn and Bauder (2015) have described how the regulatory process of this policy domain is increasingly driven by a neoliberal, market-based logic—to the detriment of humanitarian considerations (see also Roberts 2020).

While it has long been an integral part of legitimizing Canada's point system, the principle of socio-economic utility has gradually become the dominant guiding principle of the immigrant selection process.[11] In the recruitment of TFWs, employers and private businesses take on a pronounced role in recruiting workers and providing pathways into Canada. This role further weakens the regulatory ability of the state to monitor and shape the stream of TFWs, in particular with a view to their recruitment and the work relationship they enter into with their employer. In this respect, the expansion of schemes to attract TFWs and the outsourcing of the recruitment process speaks to a more general trend in commodifying Canada's immigration and border policies (Bhuyan et al. 2017; Dobrowolsky 2013; Ramos 2012; Walsh 2011, 2014).

Conclusion

Canada has greatly expanded its TFWP, which has highlighted the contradictory nature of border regimes when it comes to governing migration. Temporary international workers are a highly sought-after commodity on the global labour market, particularly in lower-skilled, labour-intensive sectors of the economy. Canada has facilitated the process of recruiting this group of migrant labourers and empowered employers to play a pronounced role (essentially outsourcing key elements of the country's immigration policy to the private sector). However, the relative ease with which TFWs can come into the country contrasts dramatically with the bordering practices this group of migrants is exposed to. Their work environment tends to be precarious and prone to abuse. Although many TFWs would like to become more permanent residents, the pathway to citizenship is difficult. In many ways, the border that divides them from the regular Canadian population remains forcefully intact and defines many aspects of both their professional life and their wider social life. Spatially, TFWs are in the country, yet their status and recognition is widely determined by their prolonged existence as the outside other.

TFWs are the quintessential in-betweens. Subject to multi-layered bordering practices, they are able to cross borders as workers,

---

11 It is worth pointing to massive expansion of Canada's TFWP that, also in its problematic aspects, shows some striking similarities to the German guest-worker programs of the postwar decades.

albeit temporarily. With limited legal status, their entitlements and rights are precarious. In this latter respect, TFWs are subject to a bordering practice that leaves them in a state of legislated inequality.

Yet it is not only legal status that defines the social existence of TFWs. They tend to be perceived and treated by mainstream society as subordinate foreigners. Put into the theoretical categories of Bourdieu, this process of "othering" could be described as follows: TFWs are marginalized as outsiders, they are not recognized as full members of society, and thus, symbolically, are illegitimate. European countries that have experience with guest-worker programs are familiar with this phenomenon. The inferior status attached to those workers led to their social exclusion and to anti-foreigner sentiments (Ehrkamp 2006; Gorodzeisky and Semyonov 2009). In this respect, the recent politicization of the status and vulnerability of TFWs has polarized Canadian public opinion. While the increasingly notable political mobilization of TFWs and their supporters has led to a political backlash, it has also opened the door to policy reforms to redress their marginalization in Canadian society (Isaac and Elrick 2021; Tungohan 2017).

The reliance on TFWs is also a key component of Canada's overall approach to governing migration. The expansion of the TFWP follows a utilitarian reasoning that seeks to maximize the marketable benefits that migrants bring to the country, while also reducing costs. The utilitarian logic driving such a marketization also operates on the basis of an important normative binary: it endorses the inclusion of highly skilled migrants—the active and productive individuals—as being beneficial for society vis-à-vis the labour market. Conversely, it portrays refugees and low-skilled labour as potential threats to or burdens on the well-being of Canadian society. This exclusionary logic applies in particular to those TFWs that work in low-skilled occupations. Thus, under the auspices of a strict utilitarian market-based logic, the inclusive promise of Canadian multiculturalism and the country's citizenship regime are challenged by a growing group of temporary workers with a marginalized status.

Policy Recommendations

Considering the effects of the massive expansion of the TFWP over the past 20 years, three recommendations are put forward: First, while the Canadian government under Conservative leadership introduced amendments to the program that would protect the privileged access of Canadian citizens to job opportunities, replacing Canadian labour is still an endemic problem with the temporary recruitment of foreign workers. In addition, the prevalence of TFWs and their precarity in the labour market has the potential of undermining labour security and privileges more broadly. The fundamental challenge is a creeping process of eroding labour standards irrespective of workers' legal status.

In this respect, a regulatory framework for hiring and employing TFWs is underdeveloped. Thus, a more rigorous system of assessment and adjudication should be established that protects the interests of local workforces and prevents businesses from using TFWs simply as a means of lowering costs. This step would also entail reigning in the increased influence of private interests in recruiting and settling foreign workers on a temporary basis.

Second, the rights of TFWs should be strengthened, as should their ability to address issues of abuse and exploitation. Immigration, Refugee and Citizenship Canada has recently completed its consultation on proposed regulations allowing TFWs to apply for an open work permit if they are facing abuse.[12] After receiving hundreds of complaints about abuse of TFWs via its new established hotline, the federal government has strengthened measures to protect and support them. This is an important first step, but the nature of the threat of abuse that TFWs face is in strong need of additional scrutiny. This group of migrant workers are regularly socially isolated and afraid to speak out against employers on whom they rely for their status in Canada. More transparency and advocacy are required to provide TFWs with realistic avenues to voice their complaints and find proper support.

And third, critics of the current TFWP have claimed that it prevents low-skilled foreign workers from finding access to Canadian citizenship, unlike their high-skilled counterparts. If Canada wants to avoid a considerable class of non-citizens that experience multiple forms of social and political exclusion, it would be desirable to develop additional pathways to Canadian citizenship. At the same time, the acute pressure resulting from the current labour shortage has made

---

12 See the Government of Canada's assessment of the need to update the Immigration and Refugee Protection Act in light of these challenges: "Regulatory Impact Analysis Statement," *Canada Gazette*, Part I, Volume 155, Number 28: Regulations Amending the Immigration and Refugee Protection Regulations (Temporary Foreign Workers), https://gazette.gc.ca/rp-pr/p1/2021/2021-07-10/html/reg2-eng.html.

the TFWP attractive for business and the national economy. The country's immigration and labour-market policies will have to reconcile the pressures coming from the business community, from those demanding a readily available and flexible workforce on the one hand and those voicing concern about the fair and equitable treatment of (temporary) immigrants on the other. Manifestly, the TFWP tests Canada's immigration policy, particularly whether it can effectively combine principles of economic utility with those of fairness and equity when it comes to including newcomers into the labour market and Canadian society more broadly.

References

Andreas, P. 2003. "Redrawing the Line: Borders and Security in the Twenty-First Century." *International Security* 28(2): 78–111.
Benson, P. 2011. *Tobacco Capitalism: Growers, Migrant Workers, and the Changing Face of a Global Industry*. Princeton, NJ: Princeton University Press.
Bhuyan, R., D. Jeyapal, J. Ku, I. Sakamoto, and E. Chou. 2017. "Branding 'Canadian Experience' In Immigration Policy: Nation Building in a Neoliberal Era." *Journal of International Migration and Integration* 18(1): 47–62.
Bloemraad, I. 2002. "The North American Naturalization Gap: An Institutional Approach to Citizenship Acquisition in the United States and Canada." *International Migration Review* 36(1): 193–228.
———. 2006. *Becoming a Citizen: Incorporating Immigrants and Refugees in the United States and Canada*. Berkeley: University of California Press.
———. 2015. "Theorizing and Analyzing Citizenship in Multicultural Societies." *The Sociological Quarterly* 56(4): 591–606.
Bloemraad, I., A. Korteweg, and G. Yurdakul. 2008. "Citizenship and Immigration: Multiculturalism, Assimilation, and Challenges to the Nation-State." *Annual Review of Sociology* 34: 153–179.
Bourdieu, P. 1986. "The Forms of Capital." In *Handbook of Theory and Research for the Sociology of Education*, edited by John Richardson, 241–259. New York: Greenwood Press.
———. 1996. *Distinction: A Social Critique of the Judgement of Taste*. London: Routledge.
Casas-Cortes, M., S. Cobarrubias, N. De Genova, G. Garelli, G. Grappi, C. Heller, S. Hess, B. Kasparek, S. Mezzadra, B. Neilson, and I. Peano. 2015. "New Keywords: Migration and Borders." *Cultural Studies* 29(1): 55–87.
Challinor, A. E., 2011. "Canada's Immigration Policy: A Focus on Human Capital." *Migration Information Source* 1(8).

De Genova, N. 2002. "Migrant 'Illegality' and Deportability in Everyday Life." *Annual Review of Anthropology* 31(3): 419–447.

——. 2010. "Alien Powers: Deportable Labour and the Spectacle of Security." In *The Contested Politics of Mobility*, edited by Vicki Squire, 111–136. London: Routledge.

Dobrowolsky, A. 2013. "Nuancing Neoliberalism: Lessons Learned from a Failed Immigration Experiment." *Journal of International Migration and Integration* 14(2): 197–218.

Ehrkamp, P. 2006. "'We Turks Are no Germans': Assimilation Discourses and the Dialectical Construction of Identities in Germany." *Environment and Planning A: Economy and Space* 38(9): 1673–1692.

Ellermann, A. 2014. "The Rule of Law and the Right to Stay: The Moral Claims of Undocumented Migrants." *Politics & Society* 42(3): 293–308

Erel, U. 2010. "Migrating Cultural Capital: Bourdieu in Migration Studies." *Sociology* 44(4): 642–660.

Flynn, E., and Bauder, H. 2015. "The Private Sector, Institutions of Higher Education, and Immigrant Settlement in Canada." *Journal of International Migration and Integration* 16(3): 539–556.

Goldring, L. 2010. "Temporary Worker Programs as Precarious Status." *Canadian Issues* (Metropolis) 50: 50–54.

Goldring, L., and P. Landolt, eds. 2013. *Producing and Negotiating Non-Citizenship: Precarious Legal Status in Canada*. Toronto: University of Toronto Press.

Gorodzeisky, A., and M. Semyonov. 2009. "Terms of Exclusion: Public Views towards Admission and Allocation of Rights to Immigrants in European Countries." *Ethnic and Racial Studies* 32(3): 401–423.

Hammar, T. 1989. "State, Nation, and Dual Citizenship." In *Immigration and the Politics of Citizenship in Europe and North America*, edited by W. R. Brubaker, 81–96. Lanham, Md.: German Marshall Fund of the United States and University Press of America.

Han, J. Y. 2020. "Temporary Foreign Workers and COVID-19: Investigating Canada's Treatment of Migrant Workers During the COVID-19 Pandemic." Samuel Centre for Social Connectedness. https://www.socialconnectedness.org/wp-content/uploads/2020/10/PDF-Temporary-Foreign-Workers-andCOVID-19.pdf.

Hennebry, J. 2009. "Mobile Vulnerabilities, Transnational Risks: Temporary Agricultural Migrants in Ontario." *International Settlement Canada* 22:10–15.

Horgan, M., and S. Liinamaa. 2017. "The Social Quarantining of Migrant Labour: Everyday Effects of Temporary Foreign Worker Regulation in Canada." *Journal of Ethnic and Migration Studies* 43(5): 713–730.

Isaac, M., and Elrick, J. 2021. "How COVID-19 may Alleviate the Multiple Marginalization of Racialized Migrant Workers." *Ethnic and Racial Studies* 44(5): 851–863.

Joppke, C. 2007. "Beyond National Models: Civic Integration Policies for Immigrants in Western Europe." *West European Politics* 30(1): 1–22.

Jubany, O., and R. Lázaro Castellanos. 2021. "The Gender and Racial Construction of the Working Class: Temporary Mobility of Mexican Women Workers to the US and Canada." *Gender Issues* 38:47–64.

Kershaw, P. 2010. "Caregiving for Identity is Political: Implications for Citizenship Theory." *Citizenship Studies* 14(4): 395–410.

Lenard, P. T., and C. Straehle, eds. 2012. *Legislated Inequality: Temporary Labour Migration in Canada*. Montréal and Kingston: McGill-Queen's University Press.

Li, P. 2012. "Federal and Provincial Immigration Arrangements in Canada: Policy Changes and Implications." In *Managing Immigration and Diversity in Canada: A Transatlantic Dialogue in the New Age of Migration*, edited by Rodriguez-Garcia, 87–111, Montréal and Kingston: McGill-Queen's University Press.

Lutz, H., ed. 2016. *Migration and Domestic Work: A European Perspective on a Global Theme*. London: Routledge.

Nohl, A., K. Schittenhelm, O. Schmidtke, and A. Weiss. 2014. *Work in Transition. Cultural Capital and Highly Skilled Migrants' Passages into the Labour Market*. Toronto: University of Toronto Press.

Picot, G., and F. Hou. 2014. "Immigration, Low Income and Income Inequality in Canada: What's New in the 2000s?" Analysis Branch Research Paper Series, no. 364. Statistics Canada Catalogue no. 11F0019M. Ottawa. Statistics Canada.

Preibisch, K., and G. Otero. 2014. "Does Citizenship Status Matter in Canadian Agriculture? Workplace Health and Safety for Migrant and Immigrant Laborers." *Rural Sociology* 79(2): 174–199.

Prokopenko, E. and Hou, F. 2018. "How Temporary Were Canada's Temporary Foreign Workers?" *Population and Development Review* 44(2): 257–280.

Ramos, H. 2012. "Do Canadians Know How Increasing Numbers of Temporary Foreign Workers Is Changing Immigration?" Focus: Canadian Centrefor Policy. https://www.policyalternatives.ca/sites /default/files/uploads/publications/Nova%20Scotia%20Office/2012/02 /tempforeignworkersinfocus.pdf.

Reitz, J. G., and K. Somerville. 2004. "Institutional Change and Emerging Cohorts of the 'New' Immigrant Second Generation: Implications for the Integration of Racial Minorities in Canada." *Journal of International Migration and Integration / Revue de l'intégration et de la migration international* 5(4): 385–415.

Roberts, S. E. 2020. "The Bureaucratic and Political Work of Immigration Classifications: An Analysis of the Temporary Foreign Workers Program and Access to Settlement Services in Canada." *Journal of International Migration and Integration* 21(3): 973–992.

Robillard, C., J. McLaughlin, D. C. Cole, B. Vasilevska, and R. Gendron. 2018. "'Caught in the Same Webs'—Service Providers' Insights on Gender-Based and Structural Violence Among Female Temporary Foreign Workers in Canada." *Journal of International Migration and Integration* 19(3): 583–606.

Scheel, S. 2018. "Recuperation through Crisis-Talk: Apprehending the European Border Regime as a Parasitic Apparatus of Capture." *South Atlantic Quarterly* 117(2): 267–289.

——. 2019. "Autonomy of Migration within Biometric Border Regimes?" In *Autonomy of Migration? Appropriating Mobility within Biometric Border Regimes*, edited by S. Scheel, 42–74. London: Routledge.

Schierup, C. U., R. Munck, B. Likic-Brboric, and A. Neergaard, eds. 2015. *Migration, Precarity, and Global Governance: Challenges and Opportunities for Labour*. Oxford: Oxford University Press.

Schmidtke, O. 2019a. "Legitimation durch wirtschaftliches Nutzenkalkül und dezentrale Verfahren der Entscheidungsfindung: Das kanadische Migrationsregime." In *Innovation und Legitimation in der Migrationspolitik – Politikwissenschaft, politische Praxis und Soziale Arbeit im Dialog*, edited by R. Pioch and K. Toens, 19–41. New York: Springer.

Schmidtke, O. 2019b. "The Local Governance of Migration: Evidence from the Immigrant Country Canada." *DISP-The Planning Review* 55(3): 31–41.

Siemiatycki, M. 2012. "The Place of Immigrants: Citizenship, Settlement, and Socio-Cultural Integration in Canada." In *Managing Immigration and Diversity in Canada: A Transatlantic Dialogue in the New Age of Migration*, edited by D. Rodriguez-Garcia, 223–247. Montréal and Kingston: McGill-Queen's University Press.

Strauss, Kendar. 2014. "Temporary Foreign Worker Program Changes – Who Do They Help?" *Policy Note* (blog), July 10. https://www.policynote.ca /temporary-foreign-worker-program-changes-who-do-they-help/.

Turner, B. 1990. "Outline of a Theory of Citizenship." *Sociology* 24(2): 189–217.

Tungohan, E., 2017. "From Encountering Confederate Flags to Finding Refuge in Spaces of Solidarity: Filipino Temporary Foreign Workers' Experiences of the Public in Alberta." *Space and Polity* 21(1): 11–26.

Tungohan, E., R. Banerjee, W. Chu, P. Cleto, C. de Leon, M. Garcia, P. Kelly, M. Luciano, C. Palmaria, and C. Sorio. 2015. "After the Live-in Caregiver Program: Filipina Caregivers' Experiences of Graduated and Uneven Citizenship." *Canadian Ethnic Studies* 47(1): 87–105.

van Houtum, H., and F. Boedeltje. 2009. "Europe's Shame: Death at the Borders of the EU." *Antipode* 41(2): 226–230.

Van Reekum, R. 2016. "The Mediterranean: Migration Corridor, Border Spectacle, Ethical Landscape." *Mediterranean Politics* 21(2): 336–341.

Walsh, J. P. 2011. "Quantifying Citizens: Neoliberal Restructuring and Immigrant Selection in Canada and Australia." *Citizenship Studies* 15(6-7): 861–879.

——. 2014. "The Marketization of Multiculturalism: Neoliberal Restructuring and Cultural Difference in Australia." *Ethnic and Racial Studies* 37(2): 280–301.

Walton-Roberts, M. 2011. "Immigration, the University and the Welcoming Second Tier City." *Journal of International Migration and Integration* 12(4): 453–473.

Wiginton, L. 2014. *Canada's Decentralised Immigration Policy Through a Local Lens: How Small Communities Are Attracting and Welcoming Immigrants.* Brandon, MB: Rural Development Institute, Brandon University.

Winter, E. 2014. "(Im)Possible Citizens: Canada's 'Citizenship Bonanza' and its Boundaries." *Citizenship Studies* 18(1): 46–62.

Worswick, C. 2010. "Canadian Issues" (Thematic focus: Temporary Workers). Metropolis. http://boards.amssa.org/research/members/downloadFile /file:1439502517_cdn_issues_CITC_mar10_e_2_.pdf.

Yeates, N. 2009. *Globalizing Care Economies and Migrant Workers: Explorations in Global Care Chains.* London: Palgrave Macmillan.

CHAPTER 2

The "Benevolent" Status Quo State: Understanding Canada's Participation in Global Migration Governance

Scott D. Watson

Canada is frequently portrayed as a global leader in migration management and refugee protection. The UN hailed Canada for resettling the largest number of refugees in 2018, and for its successful policies encouraging integration (Canadian Press 2019). In 1986, the UN bestowed the Nansen Refugee Award to the Canadian people for their "major and sustained contribution" to refugee protection, and Canada is one of only three states that has maintained a large-scale annual refugee-resettlement program. In addition, Canada has among the highest rates of recognition for asylum seekers among Western states, averaging a recognition rate in excess of 47 percent over the past 35 years.[1]

As a country of immigration, Canada has a long-standing history of encouraging and successfully integrating large numbers of immigrants, producing one of the most open and culturally diverse populations in the world. Canada has the seventh-largest foreign-born population in real numbers; and as a percent of total population, Canada ranks in the upper 15 percent of states. Canada's annual immigration target of 0.7 percent to 1 percent of its population is among the highest in the world. Consequently, Canada has emerged in the public and academic discourse as a standard for migrant integration and

---

1   This is based on UNHCR annual reports of asylum-seeker acceptance rates.

refugee protection against which other states, particularly Western democratic states, can and should be compared.

Of course, Canada's historical experience with immigration is not simply a story of openness. Canadian governments used quotas and restrictions to prevent the arrival of certain racial groups, while large-scale immigration was a key mechanism to colonize and settle on Indigenous territory, and to expand the Canadian state's territory (see Abele and Stasiulis 1989; Hawkins 1988). There are many examples of restrictive and discriminatory Canadian immigration policies, including the Chinese head tax (Mawani 2004), the *Komagata Maru* incident (Johnston 2014), the rejection of Jewish refugees during the Second World War (Abella and Troper 1983), recurring incidents calling for more restrictions on asylum seekers, and, more recently, a safe-third-country agreement that limits access to protection in Canada (Macklin 2005). The contrast between Canada's openness and restrictiveness reveals that migration in the Canadian context is complex, and it cannot be understood exclusively through reference to particular immigration policies or episodes.

Rather, it is necessary to examine the international environment in which Canadian immigration policy is formulated. Canada's immigration policies are not simply determined by national, domestic considerations; they are both a response to larger international events in which Canada is necessarily embroiled and represent an attempt to shape various international processes, including the management of global mobility and the management of Canada's position and reputation in the world.

In this chapter, I focus on Canada's engagement with global governance of migration to reveal the international factors that shape Canada's "benevolent" status quo approach to immigration, and its carefully cultivated image of a leader on questions of migration. I argue that Canada acts as a benevolent status quo state to preserve a system from which it benefits by supporting measures that provide marginal benefits to migrants and migrant-hosting states in the developing world. Canada's unique geographical, historical, and political context has meant that it benefits by preserving the existing global migration system, and from acting (or the perception of acting) benevolently within this system. This chapter explores how Canadian governments have responded to global efforts to craft global migration governance, and the factors that influenced Canada's approach to the International Convention on the Protection of the Rights of All Migrant

Workers and Members of Their Families (ICRMW) and the UN Global Compact on Migration.

The Current Global Context

It is a pertinent time to be assessing Canada's engagement with global migration governance. While the response to the COVID pandemic has significantly altered the global migration landscape, the current system was already under severe strain due to high levels of displacement and insufficient resources for migrants and migrant-hosting states. Levels of cross-border migration and displacement are among the highest in the postwar era. The International Organization for Migration (IOM) estimates that the total migrant population now exceeds 257.7 million people globally, which is around 3.6 percent of the global population. International migrants, particularly temporary and low-skilled workers, are vulnerable to exploitation, with many migrants subject to poor working conditions and with limited access to health care and basic workplace protections.

The situation for the forcibly displaced is even more dire. Of those who have migrated across international borders, 11 percent (28.5 million) are forcibly displaced (refugees and asylum seekers).[2] The primary international organization charged with assisting this population—the UNHCR—operates in austerity mode, and in recent years has faced chronic underfunding. The UNHCR's 2018 global appeals report noted that it faced a funding gap of $3.775 billion, which is 47 percent of its proposed budget (UNHCR 2018, 42). According to the UNHCR, increases in funding have not been keeping pace with rates of displacement. Current trends in global migration and displacement, taking into account the prospects of climate change, population growth, and increasing economic inequality, suggest that the number of people moving across international borders will increase in the coming years and decades (Black, Arnell, and Dercon 2011; Hugo 2011). The existing international institutions are insufficient to offer adequate protection for many migrants, and the interests of sending and

---

2   This is the count of refugees and asylum seekers provided by UNHCR, and excludes the 40 million internally displaced and the large number of migrants who have migrated for complex reasons, which may include factors that qualify as forced displacement.

receiving states. With the United States reducing its resettlement places, the global rate of resettlement has declined even as need has increased. In the midst of this protection crisis, Canada has played a prominent role. The Canadian government is being lauded for its approach to refugees and migrants, and is actively taking a leadership role in matters of migration governance. Canada contributed to the creation of two global compacts on migration and refugees; and is working with other states interested in adopting Canada's private resettlement program and its points-based immigration system. During the current protection crisis, Canada is increasingly influential and portrayed as an exemplar of protection.

Calls to enhance international governance of migration often note that the failings of the current governance of global migration stem from its highly complex, fragmented, and de-centralized nature (see Newland 2010; Betts 2011). To date, there is no single overarching global governance framework or regime for migration, meaning that states have significant latitude in how they manage migration, migrants have multiple avenues through which to enact their mobility, civil society has various locations of engagement, and corporations have diverse targets of influence.[3] One problematic aspect of this system is that states and other actors may blur the line between types of mobility, and apply governance mechanisms designed to restrict mobility to migrants whose mobility should be protected (see Mourad and Norman 2019). A fragmented system, however, should not be equated with an accidental or unintentional system. Numerous actors, including many of the most powerful states, support the current system and resist stronger or more coherent forms of global governance.[4] In short, the current fragmented system benefits certain actors in the system, and there is little political will to alter it to enhance migrant protection and to facilitate a more equitable distribution of the costs and benefits of global migration.

---

3   These options are highly constrained, but it is important to recognize the agency of migrants, and the way that the global migration system simultaneously constrains and enables migrant agency.

4   For instance, only 51 states have signed the ICRMW. While 164 states have signed the non-binding Global Compact for Migration, countries such as the United States, Australia, Austria, the Czech Republic, Italy, Hungary, Israel, and Poland have spoken out against the compact; others issued reservations around the compact—including Russia, which articulated a need for differentiation based on responsibility for creating migration flows.

Given this context, it is important to understand how and why Canada behaves as a benevolent status quo state. The concept of a "status quo" state has a long and important history in the field of international relations (IR) and is often used to explain and predict major developments, such as great-power conflict (Schweller 1993; Gilpin 1983). In its most basic sense, status quo states are "those who seek primarily to keep, not increase, their resources" (Schweller 1993, 76). Revisionist states, in contrast, seek to "overturn the status quo order, the prestige, resources and principles of the system" (76). While offering a cursory understanding of a state's orientation toward the current system, the concepts of status quo and revisionist states are "vague and under-theorized," leading to limited theoretical utility (Johnson 2003, 8). These concepts ignore the complexity of international politics and the multiple axes along which states could position themselves as more or less revisionist. Moreover, most actors aspire to improve or diminish global governance and to enhance their position within the system. Consequently, one would be hard pressed to identify any state that does not favor some revision of the current order or their place in that order. Despite the complications surrounding the term "status quo," it does usefully capture a general orientation toward the dominant international institutions and norms. There is a meaningful distinction between preserving the basic foundations of an order and advocating for a new order. For instance, the ICRMW is clearly more revisionist than the Global Compact on Migration.

Consequently, I proceed with the usage of status quo and revisionist states, with three caveats. The first is that "status quo/revisionist" is a spectrum, not a binary—states may be more or less revisionist. The second is that there is an important distinction between minor incremental change, significant alteration, and replacement of the foundational beliefs and norms of an order; status quo/revision is a spectrum that contains meaningful points of delineation. Finally, I emphasize that rather than categorize states as wholly status quo or revisionist, a state's position can only be discerned with reference to a specific object of governance, a specific set of practices/institutions, or a specific set of foundational belief systems. A state could be largely status quo on migration issues or humanitarian intervention, and more revisionist on trade or weapons proliferation—depending on their position in the system and the domestic forces mobilized on these particular issues.[5] Focusing on specific

---

5   It should be noted that I am not advocating status quo/revisionist categories can only be understood issue by issue, because many key issues and regimes hang together as

objects of governance helps explain the various contexts in which China and the United States, for instance, take similar positions during international negotiations, despite claims that one of the states is (or should be) status quo, while the other is (or should be) revisionist by virtue of a changing distribution of power.

At present, global migration governance is so fragmented that it is difficult to fix a state's orientation as more status quo or revisionist. International agreements have constructed various objects of governance in the realm of migration: refugees, asylum seekers, permanent residents, temporary workers, smuggled persons, trafficked persons, tourists, students, business migrants, etc. There are at least seven significant international treaties related to different aspects of international migration (in addition to several smaller agreements) all of which vary in the relative weight placed on migrant or state's rights and situate the management of migration within a larger context.[6] This is because international migration, as an issue area, is nested within larger regimes, such as those that govern international trade, protect human rights, and/or reinforce basic norms of state sovereignty. Because there is no general overarching migration-governance regime, we can understand status quo and revisionist states in reference to individual migration treaties and objects of governance, and efforts to create an overarching global governance regime. Examining two of the more prominent recent efforts to construct a new framework for global migration governance, I conclude that Canada is a status quo state with respect to global migration governance.

The second modifier attached to the Canadian position—benevolent—refers to a state's place within the larger system of migration governance, and to the impact of potential change on the objects of global governance. In this case, various categories of migrants are the primary object of global migration governance, although there are also a number of secondary objects: sending, transit, and receiving states;

---

part of the social order, and most states that support the status quo in some areas are likely to support them in others. However, understanding why states support the status quo in particular areas requires deeper engagement with the issues.

6   This includes the 1951 Refugee Convention and 1967 Protocol; the 1949 ILO Migration for Employment Convention; the 1975 ILO Convention concerning Migrants in Abusive Conditions; the 1990 ICRMW; the 2011 ILO Convention concerning Decent Work for Domestic Workers; the 2000 UN Protocol to Prevent, Suppress, and Punish Trafficking in Persons; the 2000 UN Protocol against the Smuggling of Migrants; to these we could add the 2017 Global Compact on Migration and the 2017 Global Compact on Refugees.

corporations; NGOs; etc. Benevolence is used in this case in reference to a positive potential impact on migrants or developing states that host the vast majority of the world's migrants. There are, of course, differential benefits distributed by the current system of migration governance. As I explore, below, Canada benefits from the existing, fragmented global governance system for migration; while it may support certain policy changes that provide an immediate benefit to some developing states, and to migrants, one would be hard pressed to suggest that the long term, macro-level impact of this policy benefits these actors more than Canada. Analytically, however, policies that benefit others while preserving a system in which the self holds a privileged positioned should be distinguished from policies that harm others while preserving the same system. In more concrete terms, resettling more refugees is better for refugees and refugee-hosting states than reducing refugee resettlement (absent any other structural change), even if refugee resettlement preserves a system from which some states benefit more than others. Similarly, policies may benefit one less-privileged other at the expense of another. For instance, the concept and practice of burden- or responsibility-sharing may be employed to improve the position of developing states hosting large numbers of refugees, while simultaneously making refugees worse off by reducing prospects for protection (see Mourad and Norman 2019). Analytically, this is still a benevolent position because it improves the position of another (developing states) by imposing a cost on the self (to preserve a system from which it benefits).

Consequently, a benevolent status quo state is a state that seeks to distribute short-term benefits to a less-privileged other, while maintaining, in large part, the existing rules, norms, and institutions that preserve the self's privileged position, and from which it accrues long-term benefits. While there are many factors that contribute to the level of benevolence exhibited by a particular state at a particular time, I argue that Canada's benevolent status quo stance toward migration is rooted in Canada's unique geopolitical situation, its history as an immigrant/settler society, and the various advantages Canada enjoys from the current system of global migration governance.

The Canadian Context

Canada's engagement with international governance reflects two orientations: an internationalist orientation strongly committed to

working through multilateral institutions, and a continental orientation committed to cooperation with the United States on continental
security and economic matters. With regard to the former, Canada
behaves as a standard middle power committed to a multilateral,
internationalist foreign policy (Nossal, Rousell, and Paquin 2015, 39).
Defined as a philosophy or policy that "supports active engagement
in international conflict and a commitment to global organizations
charged with maintaining peace," (150) internationalism has been the
dominant Canadian doctrine, with modest fluctuations, since the end
of the Second World War. During that time, Canadian governments
have promoted their interests and influenced international politics
through strong support for multilateral institutions, investment in
effective diplomacy and mediation, coalition building, and institutional innovation (see Cooper, Higgott, and Nossal et al. 1993). Canada's
multilateralist ideology/strategy has entailed a leadership role on a
number of benevolent normative changes: on peacekeeping, environmental issues (acid rain, chlorofluorocarbons), and human-rights
issues (human security, landmines, the "Responsibility to Protect"
doctrine). Canada's benevolent internationalism has led Brysk (2009)
to include Canada as a "global Good Samaritan" that has managed to
make multilateralism and "global humanitarianism into a long-term
national interest" (Cooper, Higgott, and Nossal 1993, 67). Canada's
position on migration matters is largely in keeping with this
orientation.

Nonetheless, Canada's commitment to multilateral internationalism has varied, depending on domestic political factors and its
continental security concerns. Keating (2010) suggests that Canada's
commitment to multilateralism reflects a genuine concern that the
alternative is a "continentalist foreign policy" in which U.S. foreign-
policy interests would dominate. Indeed, the second pillar of Canada's
engagement with the world is a "defence against help" strategy in
which Canada cooperates and participates with continental security
initiatives to ensure the United States does not do so unilaterally—at
the expense of Canada's formal sovereignty (see Orvik 1984; Lagassé
2010). Lagassé suggests that with the expansion of security interests
after 9/11, this strategy is as applicable to refugee policy as it is to
defence spending (2010, 474), as indicated by the passage in Canada of
the Immigration and Refugee Protection Act (IRPA) immediately after
9/11, the creation of the Safe Third Country Agreement (STCA) with the
US in 2002, and the 2011 "beyond the border" security arrangement.

The Canada-U.S. STCA requires asylum seekers to seek protection in the country of arrival.[7] This arrangement had been pursued by previous Canadian governments, as far more asylum seekers traverse through the United States to seek asylum in Canada than the reverse; and upon implementation the STCA has reduced (at least initially) the number of asylum seekers in Canada. In one sense, the agreement represents a rare case where the Canadian government was able to achieve a long-endorsed policy change by drawing on the continental approach to security. The Canadian government first pursued the use of safe-third-country agreements in the late 1980s. Although interest in such an agreement with the United States waxed and waned during the intervening years, the events of 9/11 led both countries to conclude that the STCA would enhance their collective security.

In the case of IRPA, the Canadian government added restrictive measures after 9/11 to assuage American concerns about Canada's immigration policies relative to continental security (Watson 2009). The beyond-the-border arrangement also addressed continental security concerns, and was designed to both enhance border-security cooperation and facilitate greater cross-border economic activity (von Hlatkey 2012). In all these cases, Canada altered its immigration policies to address U.S. perception that Canada's immigration policies were a weak point in America's border security, and to prevent an American response that would reduce cross-border travel and trade. In combination, collaboration with the United States on migration policy in the aftermath of 9/11 reflected a continental orientation that acts as a second pillar (and counter pressure) to Canada's deep-rooted multilateralist strategy.

Canadian governments have to balance these two approaches, and as a result there is some variation in the relative influence of these two pressures in Canadian foreign policy. As Nossal, Rousell, and Paquin (2015, 166–167) demonstrate, there have been periods in Canadian history when political elites have hedged their commitment to multilateral institutions and periods where bilateral cooperation with the United States is prioritized. Under the Harper government,

---

7   The actual parameters of the STCA are more complicated than this, applying to those who arrive at designated points of entry (see Macklin 2005), but the general intent of the agreement is to prevent asylum seekers from arriving in one state then pursuing their asylum claim in the other.

post 9/11, Canadian foreign policy notably shifted away from its inter-nationalist stance that was dominant in the postwar period. More recently, under Prime Minister Justin Trudeau, Canada reaffirmed a strong internationalist position but has, nonetheless, restrained this positioning in response to a number of geopolitical challenges, not least of which is rising Chinese influence, and an American adminis-tration that, under Trump, was strongly opposed to Canada's multilateral internationalism.

These two strains help explain key aspects of Canada's approach to global migration governance; namely, its support for multilateral institutions that maximize Canada's influence and soft power, and cooperation with the United States in ensuring continental security by controlling entry and maintaining a degree of autonomy in setting immigration policy. Canada maintains significant autonomy over its immigration policies and uses this to enhance its international reputation; however, in instances where security concerns become predominant and the possibility of restricting cross-border movement arises, Canadian governments tend to prioritize continental security concerns. One of Canada's primary contributions to continental secu-rity is to ensure the security of its borders, which, due to Canada's privileged global position, essentially entails supporting and strength-ening controlled global migration governance.

Canada's Privileged Global Position

In terms of restricting access to Canadian territory, Canada enjoys a privileged geographic location—an advantage ensured through a highly regulated global mobility regime that prioritizes the interests of destination states in the Global North over sending and transit states, and over migrants themselves. Most migrant-sending states would benefit from a completely reformed migration system in which they could more directly control and benefit from emigration of high-skilled labour, while still facilitating emigration of un- and under-employed citizens (see Stahl 1982; Adams and Page 2005). These states would also benefit from a migration system that ensured greater protection of their citizens abroad, to keep them working, sending remittances, and from returning with work-related injuries that the home state/society would have to address (see Mobed, Gold, and Schenker 1992). In short, most migrant-sending states would benefit from significant revision of the system from which Canada currently benefits and which it actively defends.

Canada enjoys unique advantages even in comparison with other migrant-receiving states. As with other advanced, wealthy countries, Canada is a desirable destination country; however, its geographic location has "insulated Canada from the more difficult challenges" that other destination countries face in restricting unwanted migration (Garcia 1994, 120). The global migration regime severely limits global mobility through the use of passports and visa requirements enforced by transportation companies and states. With a border consisting of three oceans, and a land border with the United States—until recently the most desired country for resettlement and immigration—transcontinental access to Canada is largely restricted to air travel, which is among the most heavily regulated forms of international travel. Accessing Canadian territory requires either complying with Canada's regulated migration system (possession of a valid passport and/or visa) or irregular migration that requires traversing massive bodies of water or crossing the land border with the United States. Until recently, relatively few migrants sought to move to Canada when given the option of staying in the United States; the flow of migrants from Canada to the United States is nearly twice the flow in the opposite direction (Dion and Vezina 2010). Combined with the attractiveness of the United States as a destination country, the SCTA further reduces Canada's exposure to irregular migrants, and initially produced a drastic reduction in the number of asylum seekers in Canada. This geographic advantage has meant that Canada has been able to uphold its commitment to continental security by strengthening international migration governance and participating in international institutions that regulate global mobility.

In a globalized world with readily available transportation technology, a well-managed restrictive system is essential to ensure such geographic advantages. At the height of intense migration in 2016, when Germany received close to 750,000 asylum seekers, Canada received fewer than 25,000 (UNHCR 2018). Even with the recent spike of asylum seekers that saw claims in Canada rise to 55,000, the number is not particularly high relative to other Western countries, to say nothing of the developing states in the Global South that house close to 85 percent of the world's refugees. Just as importantly, of the 55,000 asylum claims in 2018, fewer than 20,000 were irregular arrivals (Canadian Press 2019). In short, the vast majority of asylum seekers to Canada arrive through the regular (highly regulated) channels. This combination (geographic advantage and highly regulated global mobility) means that Canada, when its leaders are determined to do so, can reduce irregular arrivals from specific source countries by use of "remote-control" restrictions. One of the most effective of these is visa requirements. Berthiaume (2007) reports that Canada uses a variety of thresholds to determine whether a country's nationals require visas for travel to Canada, including if that country makes up more than 2 percent of Canada's total annual asylum claims. In 2009, Canada withdrew the visa waiver for the Czech Republic when asylum claims from that country spiked, curbing Czech claimants and travellers (see Salter and Mutlu 2010). As a result of its geographic advantage, Canada has simply not faced large numbers of asylum seekers in comparison with many other Western states—and when it has, it has policy options available to reduce these numbers.

Canada's openness to regular immigration and its prioritization of economic prosperity in its immigration policies have further enhanced Canada's advantages in the existing system. The current global migration system is oriented toward facilitating economic globalization in combination with a high degree of regulation of human mobility. This combination is advantageous for states willing to prioritize their own economic interests in setting national migration policies. As a country of immigration, successive Canadian governments have prioritized economic growth as the primary value informing immigration policy (see Abu-Laban and Gabriel 2002). Early in its history, the Canadian government encouraged large-scale migration in order to gain access to more territory and exploitable resources, dispossess the Indigenous population, and prevent American expansion. These strategies have been a foundational component of Canada's economic growth and membership in the G8 (Abu-Laban and Gabriel 2002). Canada continues to bring in a substantial number of immigrants each year to sustain economic (and demographic) growth, to build a highly educated workforce, and to create a temporary labour pool for low-skilled forms of labour. While such considerations are most evident in the economic stream of migration, Dirks (1977, 255) shows that economic factors have been a significant consideration even in constructing Canada's refugee-resettlement policy.

The economic advantage of immigration is amply evident in Canada's temporary-worker programs and its permanent migration plan, which privileges skills-based immigration over family reunification and humanitarian immigration. Since the 1960s, Canada has employed a points-based system that has facilitated the recruitment of the most highly skilled and educated migrants from around the globe, without having to expend resources on their training (Buzdugan and Halli 2009). For the past decade, this economic class of migrants have comprised 52 percent to 63 percent of permanent admissions to Canada (Government of Canada 2015). Under the current government's immigration targets from 2018–2021, the target for economic immigrants comprises over 57 percent of Canada's total immigration intake, with the other two streams, family and humanitarian/protection, ranging between 25 percent and 28 percent, and 13 percent and 15 percent, respectively. As a consequence of this policy, Canada has the highest proportion of highly educated immigrants in the world, with over 58 percent of immigrants qualifying as highly educated; in comparison, two-thirds of Organisation for Economic Co-operation and Development countries have ratios under 30 percent (Belot and Hatton 2012).[8] The success of this program, as measured by the educational skills of its immigrant population, stems from a global mobility regime in which states set their own admission priorities, while other states are expected to uphold a right of exit and while transport companies, non-governmental, and intergovernmental authorities help enforce these priorities.

Canada has further entrenched the prioritization of economic advantage through the expansion of temporary-worker arrangements for lower-skilled workers rather than offering a path to permanent settlement. In essence, permanent migration to Canada is class-based—those with education, language skills, or financial assets have opportunity for permanent settlement, while those who lack these characteristics are largely relegated to temporary admission with limited rights, or face a more difficult path to permanent residence. Canada has long maintained temporary-worker programs although it was historically far lower than permanent economic immigration. In 2003, the Canadian government began to increase the number of temporary-worker programs and temporary migrants, and by 2006 Canada admitted more temporary workers than permanent migrants

---

8   To limit the impact of this approach on skilled domestic workers and industries (and thus maintain support for large-scale migration), formal and informal foreign-credential-recognition requirements restrict the economic opportunities for those with foreign education credentials or work experience (Buzdugan and Halli 2009, 383). The long-term impact of this has been a decline in employment and income for skilled immigrants in Canada (Reitz 2007).

in the economic class (Dauvergne and Marsden 2014, 228). Schmitdke demonstrates in the previous chapter that Canada's growing temporary foreign-worker programs limit access to full membership associated with permanent programs, while developing a flexible workforce that is responsive to economic shifts. Temporary migrants are a highly disposable and cheap labour force that are subject to exploitation and precarious working conditions, and have limited access to legal and residency rights (Horgan and Liinamaa 2017, 714). As Dauvergne and Marsden (2014, 231) note, these jobs are not temporary; immigrant's access to territory, jobs, and wages are temporary, guaranteed through a well-managed global migration system and restriction of rights domestically.

In short, Canada's multi-tiered immigration system relies on, and benefits from, a well-managed global migration system that ensures migrants a right of exit, while permitting individual states to restrict entry and to design and implement national migration policies based on national priorities. The Canadian system is designed first and foremost for Canada's economic benefit, with sending states exerting very little influence over Canada's migration programs. Consequently, maintaining a well-regulated migration system in which the Canadian government determines who has access to its territory and labour market is a cardinal Canadian objective.

Lastly, Canada has been able to use its openness to immigration and its successful integration efforts to enhance its reputation and soft power. While Canadian immigration policy has largely been driven by economic and domestic political considerations (see Dirks 1995; Knowles 2007), Canadian governments have also used their openness to controlled immigration to exert leadership and influence internationally. As noted in the previous section, Canada's multilateral orientation on a wide range of issues has led to a level of influence beyond what its demographic, economic, and military might would suggest. Migration governance has been one of Canada's notable fields of international leadership, particularly its policies on refugee resettlement and the integration of immigrants. Early architects of Canada's resettlement policy justified the program based on its contribution to meeting Canada's "international objectives," and to "provide leadership" in addressing "major refugee crises facing the international community" (Dirks 1995, 65). Canada has been able to use its migration and refugee-resettlement programs to contribute to international solutions in response to migrant crises, to play a leading role in the ongoing work of the UNHCR, and to take a leadership role in promoting private resettlement initiatives globally.

As part of its leadership initiatives, Canada has facilitated large-scale immigration as a key measure to alleviate international crises. In the aftermath of the Second World War, Canada resettled large numbers of displaced persons in Europe. This response was viewed positively among European states as it helped alleviate the refugee burden and provided an outlet for surplus population for countries whose economies were devastated after the war and unable to integrate large numbers of displaced persons. This program also contributed to early Cold War strategic objectives—by resettling refugees rather than repatriating them to Soviet-controlled territories, as was the USSR's preference (Dirks 1977, 255).

Canada's resettlement of Indo-Chinese refugees in the late 1970s further demonstrates that Canada has used resettlement as a means of demonstrating leadership and alleviating international crises. The large outflow of refugees from Vietnam, Cambodia, and Laos triggered an international crisis, as recipient states in the regions, such as Malaysia, Indonesia, and the Philippines, refused further entry on the grounds that they were unable to accommodate the growing number of boat arrivals, and that the crisis stemmed from the colonial policies of France and the United States in the region. The international community, under UNHCR leadership, hosted several emergency meetings over the exodus of people by boat, with resettlement emerging as a key pillar of the 1979 Geneva Conference and the 1989 Comprehensive Plan of Action. Under the 1979 agreement, Canada agreed to resettle 50,000 refugees, a massive amount at the time, which was geared to resolve the international crisis, encourage resettlement in other Western states, and to end the "push-back" policies of countries of first asylum (Adelman 1982, 38).

In addition to these two major incidents of mass displacement, Canada has used its resettlement program to help alleviate international migration/refugee crises in response to major displacements in Hungary, Czechoslovakia, Uganda, Chile, Kosovo, and more recently Syria. In the Syrian case, Canada's decision to resettle 25,000 Syrian refugees elicited worldwide news, with Trudeau's decision to greet the first arrivals at Toronto Pearson International Airport a key event. Canada eventually resettled close to 45,000 Syrian refugees, and in the aftermath of this effort, several countries approached Canada to help develop private resettlement initiatives. Canada also took a leading role in the 2016 New York Declaration for Refugees and Migrants, the Agenda for the Protection of Cross-Border Displaced Persons in the Context of Disasters and Climate Change, and the resulting UN Global Compacts. Canada chaired the UNHCR Executive Committee in 2017 that pushed forward many of the central features of the Global Compact on Refugees, particularly the concept of refugees as economic and cultural assets to the resettling state (Ugland 2018). Ugland (2018) notes that Canada has been highly influential in spreading ideas and policies to integrate migrants and refugees that have inspired change in a number of countries, and that Canada's leadership on immigration and integration has helped it increase Canada's international influence and reputation.

Milner (2016) argues that Canada's decision to resettle 25,000 Syrian refugees in 2015 had a notable impact on Canada's soft power, increasing its international profile and thrusting Canada into various leadership opportunities. Global media coverage was generally positive and key international leaders specifically identified Canada as an instrumental actor in the ongoing efforts to address the global migration crisis. Milner even suggests that Canada's decision to resettle large numbers of Syrian refugees was connected to its renewed commitment to multilateralism and to its plan to bid for a UN Security Council seat in 2021. While Canada's Security Council bid was unsuccessful, the immediate aftermath of the Syrian resettlement program demonstrated the soft-power impact of taking a leadership role in the area of refugee protection—at the various international conferences on the migration crisis and on the UNHCR Executive Committee.

Canada clearly enjoys numerous advantages from the current global migration-governance system. As noted, Canada exhibits relatively strong multilateral commitments on many issues, including on migration, but also balances this with a continentalist approach favouring Canadian autonomy and border security. Canadian governments have opposed international migration agreements that are perceived to undermine Canadian autonomy in managing its immigration. In the next section, I explore Canada's response to the ICRMW and the more recent Global Compact on Migration. The former represents the most significant revisionist piece of global migration governance ratified by the United Nations, while the latter is the most recent attempt to address the shortcomings of the current system. In both instances, Canada exhibits a strong commitment to the status quo.

Canada and the ICRMW

The ICRMW is among the most ambitious human-rights agreements adopted by the UN. It contains 93 articles that would vastly expand the rights of migrant workers and their families, and requires states to submit to external verification of compliance. Perhaps not surprisingly, then, this convention is among the lowest ratified human-rights conventions. Originally adopted in 1990, the convention currently has fewer than 55 ratifications—and none among major migrant-receiving countries, including Canada. Moreover, the UN largely ignores the convention in its discussion of human-rights law (Grange and D'Auchamp 2009). The initial push for an international convention to protect the rights of migrant workers emerged from the concerns of migrant-sending states with the existing mechanisms of protection (or lack thereof), and the failure of the 1975 International Labour Organization (ILO) Migrant Workers Convention to address these concerns (Gest et al. 2013). Initiated in 1979 by Mexico and Morocco, the ICRMW sought to incorporate and build on rights articulated by the ILO and other human-rights documents, resulting in a comprehensive document that articulates a wide range of general rights, and rights specific to certain types of migrant workers, including undocumented migrants (Pécoud and de Guchteneire 2006, 246–248). Lonnroth (1991, 718) reports that from the outset, negotiations between migrant-receiving and migrant-sending states were tense, as the latter sought to develop differential standards for sending and receiving states, and to draw attention to the "discriminatory policies of industrialized states." In contrast, migrant-receiving states sought to create a single, universal migration regime that applied to all states, one that would ensure state control over migration processes.

During the negotiations, Canada worked with other migrant-receiving states, such as the United States, Australia, and Germany, to promote three core principles: (i) the right of individual states to establish admissibility, (ii) migrant workers' obligation to abide by domestic laws of the hosting state, and (iii) creation of a universal set of obligations rather than one that differentiated responsibility (Lonnroth 1991, 733). These states opposed firm obligations on states or unconditional protection for workers, preferring less-stringent language and "escape clauses" (Gest et al. 2013, 168). In contrast with Canada's general orientation toward multilateral internationalism, its position on the ICRMW exhibited a far greater concern with protecting autonomy in setting migration policy associated with ensuring continental security.

The Canadian government opposed the convention on several grounds: one of which was the claim that it simply was not relevant to the Canadian context, in which permanent settlement was the primary objective of its migration programs, rather than the guest-worker programs dominant in Europe (Piché, Depatie-Pelletier, and Epale 2009, 203). Canada had a number of temporary-worker programs at the time, and has drastically expanded the scale of its temporary-worker arrangements since the convention came into force (Piché, Depatie-Pelletier, and Epale 2009, 196). The increase in the number of migrant workers in Canada with limited or no prospects for full citizenship indicate that the rights outlined in the ICRMW are increasingly relevant in the Canadian context. In addition, as Schmidtke (present volume) amply demonstrates in the previous chapter, the Canadian government has encouraged privatization of the temporary-worker program, by which businesses and corporations have greater control over who enters, and leaves, Canada as a migrant worker. Intense privatization requires greater attention to the protection of migrant workers' rights (Piché, Depatie-Pelletier, and Epale 2009, 210).

Another objection articulated by the Canadian government was that the convention undermined state sovereignty and the right of individual states to determine their own migration priorities and policies. Piché, Depatie-Pelletier, and Epale document repeated assertions by the Canadian government that migration management must be state-led, outside the UN treaty system (204). Moreover, the Canadian government claimed that it already protected the rights of all migrant workers in its territory, that the convention was largely redundant (205). In other contexts, the Canadian government has argued that Canada already provides protection for migrant workers under the Canadian Charter of Rights and Freedom, and that the treaty includes "extraterritorial obligations" that the Canadian government could not uphold (LaViolette 2006, 305).

The Canadian government also worried that the convention undermined its existing bilateral temporary-worker and deportation agreements (Piché, Depatie-Pelletier, and Epale 2009, 203). These agreements, according to Ottawa, were essential for the government to use migration policy to address labour shortages (Ruhs 2012, 1284). These concerns have not lessened over time. In subsequent years, the Canadian government continues to resist calls to ratify the convention.

LaViolette (2006, 303) reports that Canadian officials view the ICRMW as one of the "treaties of the Group of 77" that induce disagreement between "industrialized and non-industrialized countries." In addition, he notes that the Department of Foreign Affairs opposed several provisions of the treaty, such as a right to family reunion, and an obligation to provide "health care, education, and social assistance" to the family of a migrant worker (304).

Of course, Canada is not alone in ignoring the ICRMW. Pécoud and de Guchteneire (2006) argue that the ICRMW suffered from numerous obstacles. The political impetus for it arose in the context of the 1970s, while concerns over migration changed substantially over the two-decade process of ratification, and continued to change over the two-decade post-ratification period (253). Furthermore, there are a host of political, security, and economic reasons why most states, including migrant-sending states, have decided against ratification. Industrialized, primarily migrant-receiving states such as Canada benefit immensely from a migration system in which receiving states maintain a fair degree of autonomy over their migration decisions and can decide, unilaterally or bilaterally, how to manage migrant workers. In addition, many states are part of regional agreements that govern the treatment of migrant workers. The bilateral and regional agreements are far less comprehensive than the ICRMW, especially on the rights of undocumented workers, which limits the appeal of signing on to the ICRMW (262). Patrick Taran (2009, 151) concludes that the convention ultimately failed because many states gain from the availability of a pool of "cheap, docile, temporary and easily removable" workers—a description that aptly describes Canada.

Canada's stance toward the ICRMW is important because it clearly demonstrates that, overall, Canada does not differ significantly from most other migrant-receiving states in its approach to migration governance at the global level, and does not endorse revising the current system to one that is founded on migrant rights. For a country that promotes a human-rights-oriented foreign policy, this approach to migration management may have concrete repercussions. LaViolette (2006) concludes that Canada's failure to ratify the ICRMW is based on the false claim that migrant populations in Canada do not suffer from human-rights violations, or that any additional protections are necessary. There are a number of studies demonstrating that a number of Canada's migrant-worker programs fall well short of ensuring the human rights of migrant workers (see Dauvergne and Marsden 2014; Khan 2009). LaViolette also suggests that it undermines Canada's human-rights-driven foreign-policy objectives. Most importantly for the purposes of this chapter, Canada's treatment of the ICRMW illustrates the problem of identifying Canada as a global leader on issues of migration; in this case, Canada defends the status quo.

In contrast, Canada has endorsed the Global Compact for Safe, Orderly and Regular Migration and the Global Compact on Refugees. Whereas Canada played an obstructionist or indifferent role in the negotiations on the ICRMW, Canada was an active contributor to the Global Compacts. Comparing these agreements, and Canada's orientation toward the two, reveals the general approach that the Canadian state takes toward managing migration.

Canada and the Global Compact for Safe, Orderly and Regular Migration

The Global Compact for Safe, Orderly and Regular Migration was adopted by the UN General Assembly in 2018, following two years of negotiation after the New York Declaration for Refugees and Migrants that recognized the need for greater cooperation on governing migration. The choice to create a compact rather than a treaty or convention, as in the case of the UN's Convention Relating to the Status of Refugees (the Refugee Convention) or the ICRMW, is itself revealing, as it is essentially a choice to create non-binding recommendations rather than legal obligations (Roele 2017; Panizzon 2017; Gemmeltoft-Hansen 2017). Gemmeltoft-Hansen (2017, 9) notes that the choice of a compact reflects a larger international trend toward using soft law to govern highly contested issues. He notes that while this approach has potential to generate new norms, provide normative guidance in areas where hard law does not exist, and to connect existing laws and norms under a coherent framework, it also has the potential to undermine existing hard law and reduce normative coherence and compliance (10). In the case of the Global Compact for Safe, Orderly and Regular Migration, he notes that it calls mostly for "political and practical cooperation" at the expense of legal obligations (7).

Roele (2017) also notes that the choice of compact rather than convention signals political rather than legal commitments. Consequently, the mechanism of fostering change is through "offers of support and assistance" rather than "coercive enforcement" (11). Tying migration-policy choices to conditional development assistance can "build trust" and "create incentives to compromise"; however, it may also reduce commitments or encourage compromise on the protection of migrant rights (Panizzon 2017, 18). Given the failure of states to sign on to the ICRMW, which entrenched a divide between sending and receiving states and contained an implicit threat of monitoring and enforcement, the Global Compact offers an alternative mechanism for spreading norms of migrant protection. This feature of the compact offers an opportunity for states, such as Canada, who have an extensive history in managing migration and that have developed robust and various migration policies and pathways, to exert political leadership by collaborating with other states to help implement similar policies but without any legal obligation to amend their migration policies in line with a new legal standard.

The lack of concrete legal obligations was a key factor in garnering support for the compact. While a small number of states refused to approve the agreement due to fears that it eroded state sovereignty, there was near-unanimous agreement among supporters of the agreements that, in fact, they "reinforced the sovereign rights of states" and imposed "no new obligations for states" (UNGA 2018). The representative for Norway, in announcing support for the compact, suggested that the Norwegian government would not even need to revise existing "laws or practices" to be in compliance with it (UNGA 2018). The Canadian delegation asserted that the agreement did not merit the status of "international law"; that it was, rather, a framework that enables states such as Canada to "share lessons learned" from their extensive experience managing migration (UNGA 2018).

The choice of a compact is ideally suited for a country like Canada. Of the potential options the international community had to restructure global migration governance, the compact adopts an approach that focuses on "policy development, confidence-building, and consensus seeking" (Newland 2010, 340). The advantage that Newland identifies for this approach is that it would protect national migration policies at the outset, with the eventual aim of encouraging cooperation toward policy and normative convergence (340). And it does so without imposing an obligation on states to foreground human-rights commitments, establishing the new standard for migrant protection at the "lowest common denominator" and, in the process, essentially legitimizing the status quo (Roele 2017, 16).

The compact sets out 10 guiding principles and 23 objectives (and 187 sub-objectives) that would underpin international cooperation on migration governance. The Global Compact is a "non-legally binding framework" (Government of Canada 2018, 15b) that offers "a comprehensive menu of options for States from which they can select policy options" that "give states the space and flexibility to pursue implementation based on their own migration realities and capacities" (IOM 2019). Although the compact does encourage the recognition of human rights in the management of migration, the ICRMW itself does not figure prominently at all, which is surprising given that it is the primary human-rights agreement focusing on migration. The peripheral place of the ICRMW in the Global Compact amply demonstrates a shift away from a strong human-rights approach. The preamble to the compact asserts that it rests on two foundations, the primary one being the UN Charter, which asserts the centrality and sovereignty of the state. The preamble then states that it "also rests on" 17 explicitly identified international conventions, treaties, and frameworks, and "other core human rights treaties." The list of 17 treaties starts with the Universal Declaration of Human Rights but does not include the ICRMW, which is named only in a footnote under "other core human rights treaties," and, even then, as the fifth of seven additional "core" human-rights treaties. The compact avoids direct mention of the ICRMW, even when it is most obviously applicable. The sixth objective, to "Facilitate fair and ethical recruitment and safeguard conditions that ensure decent work", calls on states to "promote signature and ratification of, accession to and implementation of relevant international instruments related to international labour migration, labour rights, decent work, and forced labour," without directly mentioning the ICRMW.[9]

It is revealing that a global compact that purports to deal with migration and asserts a foundation in human rights does not foreground the one human-rights convention explicitly devoted to the rights of documented and undocumented workers and their families, which make up the vast majority of migrants globally. In contrast, the ILO (and its standards, guidelines, and principles) does feature in the Global Compact. While there are reasonable and practical reasons for

9   Migrant workers are also mentioned in objectives 7, 14, 16, 18, 20, and 22, but the sixth objective is most directly pertinent to migrant workers, and contains seven of the document's 18 clauses related to migrant workers. None of the other objectives call for recognition or implementation of the ICRMW.

doing so, it is noteworthy to keep in mind that the Group of 77 initiated the ICRMW due to two concerns with the ILO: that it was controlled by developed, migrant-receiving states, and that its principles and guidelines did not offer sufficient protection to migrant workers (Lonnroth 1991). Understood in this context, the foregrounding of the ILO and peripheral placement of the ICRMW in the Global Compact suggests a reassertion of industrialized states' control over the narrative and mechanism of governing global migration.

In their assessment, Atak et al. (2018) argue that the Global Compact privileges states, especially receiving states, over migrants in several ways. First, the document focuses on vulnerable migrants rather than their precarious social environment. This orientation, they argue, directs attention to the characteristics of the refugees themselves rather than the policies of home, transit, and host states. It presents vulnerable migrants as helpless victims due to some inherent characteristic, rather than as agents in precarious situations (19). Furthermore, the document fails to identify border-control policies and practices and other forms of state control of mobility as key contributors to either vulnerability or precarious situations (7). Consequently, the Global Compact offers protection only to a limited range of migrants, and not those in precarious circumstances due to the enforcement of "safe and orderly migration"—the raison d'être of the Global Compact. Indeed, they argue that the key objectives of the Global Compact will be realizable only by adopting a human-rights-based approach in which migrants themselves are empowered and encouraged to defend their human rights, which was a key aspect of the ICRMW (20). The failure of the Global Compact to strongly endorse ratification and implementation of the ICRMW suggests a limited commitment to reducing the vulnerability and precarity of migrants, and of protecting their human rights.

Given its commitment to differential migration policies based on national contexts, to safe, orderly, and regular migration, and to multilateralism centred around sharing policy ideas, the Global Compact is essentially a defence of the status quo, with a commitment to slow and voluntary reform. In short, it is an agreement tailor made for a benevolent status quo state such as Canada. Not surprisingly, Canada's approach to the Global Compact is fundamentally different from its position on the ICRMW. Canada has repeatedly championed the Global Compacts, and has adopted a "whole of government" and "whole of society" approach to its implementation; requiring all levels of government and civil-society actors involved in migration matters to assess policy consistency with the compact (Migration Network 2020). Canada was named as one of the 22 "Champion Countries" of the compact by the UN, recognized for its leadership on implementing the compact and preparing for the first International Migration Review Forum to take place in 2022 (UN Network on Migration 2021). Canada's engagement with the Global Compact is a revealing and stark contrast to its opposition to the ICRMW.

Conclusion

This chapter has shown the use of assessing a state's position on global migration governance through the lens of the status quo/revisionist spectrum. Canada's position with respect to global migration governance has consistently been in favour of the status quo, in which migrant-receiving states have great latitude in setting migration policy based on their perceived national interests. Successive Canadian governments have constructed the Canadian national interest as it pertains to migration predominantly in terms of domestic economic gain, which has been intrinsically tied to territorial control (and Indigenous dispossession), natural-resource extraction, and a highly educated workforce. In addition to these economic concerns, Canada has also sought to ensure national autonomy by contributing to continental security, which has necessitated the prioritization of regulating and restricting access and securing borders against irregular arrivals. The existing global migration system, including the recently negotiated Global Compacts, is exceptionally well-designed for a state in Canada's position to use migration policy to achieve its national priorities.

A further benefit to securing the status quo is that it has enabled Canada to adopt a benevolent position within the existing system, through (relatively speaking) effective integration of migrants and generous levels of refugee resettlement and asylum-seeker recognition. This position is tenable because the existing system enables the Canadian government to make it difficult for irregular arrivals to arrive at Canada's borders; and because Canada has been able, historically, to leverage its benevolent position on migration, and other issue areas, to increase its soft power and reputation. However, as Canada's unsuccessful bid for a UN Security Council seat in 2020 aptly demonstrates, taking a leadership position in endorsing a benevolent position on migration governance is insufficient in itself to achieve major foreign-policy objectives.

Using the analytical lens of status quo/revisionist can be useful when properly understood, not as a binary but as a spectrum, and when supplemented with additional concepts that help explain variations along that spectrum, such as benevolence. Furthermore, these concepts are most useful when used in reference to a state's position on a specific object of global governance, such as migration, rather than a generalized descriptor of the state and its orientation to the full set of international regimes. In doing so, this facilitates examination of the specific identities and interests that shape and sustain international regimes.

References

Adams, R. Jr., and J. Page. 2005. "Do International Migration and Remittances Reduce Poverty in Developing Countries?" *World Development* 33(10): 1645–1669.

Abele, Frances, and Daiva Stasiulis. 1989. "Canada as a 'White Settler Colony': What about Natives and Immigrants?" In *New Canadian Political Economy*, edited by Wallace Clement and Glen Williams, 240–277. Montréal and Kingston: McGill-Queen's University Press.

Abella, Irving, and Harold Troper. 1983. *None is Too Many: Canada and the Jews of Europe: 1933–1948*. Toronto: University of Toronto Press.

Abu-Laban, Yasmeen, and Christina Gabriel. 2002. *Selling Diversity: Immigration, Multiculturalism, Employment Equity and Globalization*. Peterborough: Broadview Press.

Adelman, Howard. 1982. *Canada and the Indo-Chinese Refugees*. Regina: LA Weigl Educational.

Atak, Idil, Delphine Nakache, Elspeth Guild, and François Crépeau. 2018. "Migrants in Vulnerable Situations and the Global Compact for Safe, Orderly and Regular Migration." Queen Mary University of London, School of Law Legal Studies Research Paper, no. 273/2018.

Belot, M., and T. Hatton. 2012. "Immigrant Selection in the OECD." *The Scandinavian Journal of Economics* 114(4): 1105–1128.

Berthiaume, L. 2007. "Visa-Free Travel Still a Dream for Some New EU Members." *Hill Times/Embassy* [Ottawa]. September 19, 2007.

Betts, Alexander. 2011. *Introduction: Global Migration Governance*. Oxford: Oxford University Press.

Black, Richard, Nigel Arnell, and Stefan Dercon, eds. 2011. "The Effect of Environmental Change on Human Migration." *Global Environmental Change* 21(1): S3-S11.

Brysk, A. 2009. *Global Good Samaritans: Human Rights as Foreign Policy*. Oxford: Oxford University Press.

Buzdugan, Raluca, and Shiva S. Halli. 2009. "Labor Market Experiences of Canadian Immigrants with Focus on Foreign Education and Experience." *International Migration Review* 43(2): 366–386.

Canadian Press. 2019. "Canada Resettled More Refugees than Any Other Country in 2018, UN Says." Canadian Press, June 20, 2019.

Cooper, Andrew, Richard Higgott, and Kim Richard Nossal. 1993. *Relocating Middle Powers: Australia and Canada in a Changing World Order*. Vancouver: University of British Columbia Press.

Dauvergne, C., and S. Marsden. 2014. "The Ideology of Temporary Labour Migration in the Post-global Era." *Citizenship Studies* 18(2): 224–242.

Dion, Patrice, and Mireille Vezina. 2010. "Emigration from Canada to the United States from 2000 to 2006." Canadian Social Trends, 11-008-X, no. 90.

Dirks, Gerald. 1977. *Canada's Refugee Policy: Indifference or Opportunism?* Montréal and Kingston: McGill-Queen's University Press.

———. 1995. "Controversy and Complexity: Canadian Immigration Policy during the 1980s." Montréal and Kingston: McGill-Queen's University Press.

Gemmeltoft-Hansen, Thomas. 2017. "The Normative Impact of the Global Compact on Safe, Orderly and Regular Migration" In *What is a Compact? Migrants' Rights and State Responsibilities Regarding the Design of the UN Global Compact for Safe, Orderly, and Regular Migration*, 1–10. Lund, Sweden: Raoul Wallenberg Institute of Human Rights and Humanitarian Law.

Gest, Justin, Carolyn Armstrong, Elizabeth Carolan, Elliott Fox, Vanessa Holzer, Tim McLellan, Audrey Cherryl Mogan, and Meher Talib. 2013. "Tracking the Process of International Norm Emergence: A Comparative Analysis of Six Agendas and Emerging Migrants' Rights." *Global Governance* 19(2): 153–186.

Gilpin, Robert. 1983. *War and Change in World Politics*. Cambridge: Cambridge University Press.

Government of Canada. 2015. *Facts & Figures 2015: Immigration Overview—Permanent Residents*. Ottawa: Immigration, Refugees and Citizenship Canada.

Grange, Mariette, and Marie D'Auchamp. 2009. "Role of Civil Society in Campaigning for and Using the ICRMW." In *Migration and Human Rights: The United Nations Convention on Migrant Workers*, edited by R. Cholewinski, P. de Guchteneire, and A. Pécoud, 70–99. Cambridge: Cambridge University Press.

Garcia y Griego, M. 1994. "Canada: Flexibility and Control in Immigration and Refugee Policy." In *Controlling Immigration: A Global Perspective*, edited by Wayne Cornelius, P. Martin, and James Hollifield, 119–140. Stanford: Stanford University Press.

Hawkins, Freda. 1988. *Canada and Immigration: Public Policy and Public Concern.* Montréal and Kingston: McGill-Queen's University Press.

Horgan, M., and S. Liinamaa. 2017. "The Social Quarantining of Migrant Labour: Everyday Effects of Temporary Worker Regulation in Canada." *Journal of Ethnic and Migration Studies* 43(5): 713–730.

Hugo, Graeme. 2011. "Future Demographic Change and its Interaction with Migration and Climate Change." *Global Environmental Change* 21(1): S21–S33.

International Organization for Migration (IOM). 2019. *The Global Compact for Safe, Orderly and Regular Migration.* https://www.iom.int/global-compact -migration.

———. 2020. *World Migration Report 2020.* Geneva.

Johnson, Alistair I. 2003. "Is China a Status Quo Power?" *International Security* 27(4): 5–56

Johnston, Hugh J. M. 2014. *The Voyage of the Komagata Maru: The Sikh Challenge to Canada's Colour Bar.* Vancouver: University of British Columbia Press.

Keating, Tom. 2010. "Multilateralism: Past Imperfect, Future Conditional." *Canadian Foreign Policy Journal* 16(2): 9-25.

Khan, Sabaa. 2009. "From Labor of Love to Decent Work: Protecting the Human Rights of Migrant Caregivers in Canada." *Canadian Journal of Law and Society* 24(1): 23–45.

Knowles, Valerie. 2007. *Strangers at Our Gates: Canadian Immigration and Immigration Policy, 1540-2006.* Toronto: Dundurn Press.

LaViolette, Nicole. 2006. "The Principal International Human Rights Instruments to Which Canada Has Not Yet Adhered." *Windsor Yearbook of Access to Justice* 67(2): 267–325.

Lagassé, P. 2010. "Nils Orvik's 'Defence against Help': The Descriptive Appeal of a Prescriptive Strategy." *International Journal* 65(1): 463–474.

Lonnroth, Juhani. 1991. "The International Convention on the Rights of All Migrant Workers and Members of Their Families in the Context of International Migration Policies: An Analysis of Ten Years of Negotiation." *The International Migration Review* 25(4): 710–736.

Macklin, Audrey. 2005. "Disappearing Refugees: Reflections on the Canada-US Safe Third Country Agreement." *Columbia Human Rights Law Review* 36: 365–426.

Mawani, Renisa. 2004. "'Cleansing the Conscience of the People': Reading Head Tax Redress in Multicultural Canada." *Canadian Journal of Law and Society* 19(2): 127–151.

Milner, J. 2016. "Canada's Global Refugee Policy: Opportunities for Leadership." Policy Paper for Canadian Global Affairs Institute.

Migration Network. 2020. "GCM Regional Review—Canada's Submission of Voluntary Inputs." https://migrationnetwork.un.org/sites/default/files

/docs/goc_response-voluntary_inputs_to_gcm_regional_review-final.
pdf.

Mobed, K., E. Gold, and M. Schenker. 1992. "Occupational Health Problems
among Migrant and Seasonal Farm Workers." *Western Journal of
Medicine* 157(3): 367–373.

Mourad, Lama, and Kelsey P. Norman. 2019. "Transforming Refugees into
Migrants: Institutional Change and the Politics of International
Protection." *European Journal of International Relations.* https://doi.org
/10.1177/1354066119883688.

Newland, Kathleen. 2010. "The Governance of International Migration:
Mechanisms, Processes and Institutions." *Global Governance* 16(3):
331–343.

Nossal, Kim Richard, Stéphane Rousell, and Stéphane Paquin, eds. 2015. *The
Politics of Canadian Foreign Policy.* Montréal and Kingston: McGill-
Queen's University Press.

Orvik, N. 1984. "Canadian Security and 'Defence Against Help.'" *Survival*
26(1): 26–31.

Panizzon, Marion. 2017. "The Global Migration Compact and the Limits of
'Package Deals' for Migration Law and Policy." In *What is a Compact?
Migrants' Rights and State Responsibilities Regarding the Design of the UN
Global Compact for Safe, Orderly, and Regular Migration,* 17–26. Lund,
Sweden: Raoul Wallenberg Institute of Human Rights and
Humanitarian Law.

Pécoud, Antoine, and Paul de Guchteneire. 2006. "Migration, Human Rights
and the United Nations: An Investigation into the Obstacles to the UN
Convention on Migrant Workers Rights." *Windsor Yearbook of Access to
Justice* 67(2): 241–266.

Piché, Victor, Eugénie Depatie-Pelletier, and Dina Epale. 2009. "Obstacles to
Ratification of the ICRMW in Canada." In *Migration and Human Rights:
The United Nations Convention on Migrant Workers' Rights,* edited by
Ryszard Cholewinski, Paul de Guchteneire, and Antoine Pécoud, 193–
218. Cambridge: Cambridge University Press.

Reitz, J. 2007. "Immigrant Employment Success in Canada, Part II:
Understanding the Decline." *Journal of International Migration and
Integration* 8(1): 37–62.

Roele, Isobel. 2017. "What Are the Forms of UN International Agreements/
Understandings and What is Their Legal Effect?" In *What is a Compact?
Migrants' Rights and State Responsibilities Regarding the Design of the UN
Global Compact for Safe, Orderly, and Regular Migration,* 11–16. Lund,
Sweden: Raoul Wallenberg Institute of Human Rights and
Humanitarian Law.

Ruhs, Martin. 2012. "The Human Rights of Migrant Workers: Why Do So Few
Countries Care?" *American Behavioral Scientist* 56(9): 1277–1293.

Salter, M., and C. Mutlu. 2010. "Asymmetric Borders: The Canada-Czech Republic 'Visa War' and the Question of Rights." Center for European Policy Studies, November.

Schweller, Randall. 1993. "Tripolarity and the Second World War." *International Studies Quarterly* 37(1): 73–103.

Stahl, Charles. 1982. "Labor Emigration and Economic Development." *International Migration Review* 16:869–899.

Taran, Patrick. 2009. "The Need for a Rights-Based Approach to Migration in the Age of Globalization." In *Migration and Human Rights: The United Nations Convention on Migrant Workers' Rights*, edited by Ryszard Cholewinski, Paul de Guchteneire, and Antoine Pécoud, 150–170. Cambridge: Cambridge University Press.

Ugland, T. 2018. *Policy Learning from Canada: Reforming Scandinavian Immigration and Integration Policies*. Toronto: University of Toronto Press.

United Nations Network on Migration. 2021. Champion Countries Initiative. https://migrationnetwork.un.org/champion-countries-initiative.

United Nations High Commissioner for Refugees (UNHCR). n.d. Statistical Yearbooks. https://www.unhcr.org/statistical-yearbooks.html.

———. 2018. *2016 Statistical Yearbook*. Geneva: UHNCR. https://www.unhcr.org/statistics/country/5a8ee0387/unhcr-statistical-yearbook-2016-16th-edition.html.

UNHCR. 2019. *Global Appeals 2018-2019*. Geneva: UNHCR.

United Nations General Assembly (UNGA). 2018. "General Assembly Endorses First-Ever Global Compact on Migration, Urging Cooperation among Member States in Protecting Migrants." https://www.un.org/press/en/2018/ga12113.doc.htm.

von Hlatky, Stéfanie. 2012. "The Rhetoric and Reality of Border Policy Coordination between Canada and the US." *International Journal* 67(2): 437–443.

Watson, Scott. 2009. *The Securitization of Humanitarian Migration: Digging Moats and Sinking Boats*. London: Routledge.

CHAPTER 3

European Union and the Governance of Its External Borders: The EU-Turkey Migration Agreement

Can E. Mutlu

The Romans referred to the Mediterranean as "Mare Nostrum" (Our Sea), implying the centrality of the Mediterranean as a bridge between the empire's Asian, European, and North African territories. In contemporary European political imaginary, however, the Mediterranean is no longer a maritime connector, or a unifying space-in-between. It is a vast space of surveillance, deterrence, policing, and death that separates Europe from its surrounding countries.

The irregular-migration phenomenon has become a central concern of EU officials and European politicians alike. The impetus to externalize the European Union's border-control policies highlights the tension embedded in European integration; a desire to find a balance between free mobility and security. The "European" migration crisis that reached its highpoint in the summer of 2015 underscored this tension, which seems to fuel populist politics in Europe today; how does a union of liberal-democratic states govern migration in the age of political unrest and social, political, and economic inequality surrounding its borders? Whether to admit asylum seekers or force them to stay in neighbouring countries? The answers provided by European leaders ranged from welcoming refugees to xenophobic statements and practices. The diversity of these approaches and proposed policy solutions have highlighted the inconsistency and lack of solidarity across Europe. EU members

seem divided when it comes to finding common ground on governing migration in Europe.

What we witnessed in 2015 is a result of Europe's two-track
mobility structure. One layer focuses on opening space internally
while another is closing it externally. The crisis within this system is
not an exception; it is the norm. One set of rules, structures, and procedures for European citizens and "preferred" travellers are about
openness of borders and deregulation of flows across borders to maintain the EU's "four freedoms" of movement of people, goods, services,
and capital. The other is a system of walls and detention centres that
rely on the vastness of the high seas and deserts that create the conditions of possibility for an "ontology of exclusion" (Mountz 2011) facing
asylum seekers.

EU enlargement has commonly been celebrated for its internal
de-bordering activities leading up to the inclusion of central and eastern European countries. The expansion of the Schengen area in 2004
and the simultaneous re-bordering that happened at the external borders of the EU and beyond were regarded as a necessity to ensure free
and secure circulation within Europe. Discussions of the EU's mobility
governance and border-management policies in the early part of the
2000s often happened in relation to (de)regulation of technical policy
issues and economic prosperity. These discussions were often self-
congratulatory in tone, referring to a borderless continent from Poland
to Portugal. Yet the geopolitical developments of the 2010s demonstrated a lack of solidarity among EU member states, not only in
economic terms but also in terms of governing migration in Europe.

The increasing number of arrivals to the EU via external borders
meant that EU member states such as Greece, Italy, Malta, and Spain
were left to their own devices to absorb the costs of processing irregular migrants.[1] Whereas principles of solidarity and burden-sharing
were embedded in the foundational documents of the Schengen
Agreement, political developments and the rise of populist movements in various member states, including the "illiberal" government
of Prime Minister Viktor Orbán in Hungary and increasingly national-
ists blocks like those in the Netherlands, France, and Austria, meant
that EU officials had to look for alternative arrangements for

---

1   I use the term "irregular migrants" to describe migrants who cross at undesignated
border crossings. My preference is based on the idea that we cannot ethically or
morally consider people seeking a better life to be illegal.

addressing the emerging "migration crisis." Suspending parts of the Schengen treaty; re-instating "temporary" border controls; creating "hot spots" for processing asylum seekers; building a series of walls, fences, and camps to stall the movement of individuals; and committing resources to legally questionable international agreements were put in place to force asylum seekers to stay put in countries outside of the EU.

This chapter looks at the 2016 EU-Turkey migration agreement (officially designated the "statement of cooperation") as a problematic document. I argue that in endorsing the agreement, the European Commission, the executive branch of the European Union, traded short-term migration relief for long-term credibility as a so-called normative power in world politics. The first section of the chapter provides a background on the state of Syrian migrants in Turkey. The second section looks at the EU-Turkey deal and the history of the EU's governance of its external border security and migration policies. The final section discusses the implications of these external governance practices for the EU's global reputation as a normative power.

Syrian Refugee Crisis and the Turkish Government's Response

In March 2011, as the world was reflecting on how to make sense of the Arab Spring protests in Tunisia, Egypt, and Libya over the preceding several weeks, the Syrian people started their own anti-government protests. What began as civil unrest against Bashar al-Assad's authoritarian regime quickly turned into a bloody civil war following the regimes' brutal suppression of demonstrations. By 2013, the Syrian civil war had become a regional and international proxy war with serious implications for the broader Middle East, and indeed the rest of the world. The war included a Western coalition, along with Kurdish fighters affiliated with People's Protection Units/Kurdistan Workers' Party (YPG/PKK) that took on and largely defeated Islamic State forces; allied Syrian government, Russian, Iranian, and Lebanese Hezbollah forces fighting various opposition groups in the country, including Islamic State militants and other extremist organizations, such as the Qatar/Turkey-backed Free Syrian Army and the al-Nusra Front, among other factions; there are also various Sunni and Shia groups fighting against and among each other, backed by regional powers such as Iran, Qatar, Saudi Arabia, and Turkey. The war in Syria became a regional conflict shaped also by the geopolitical interests and interventions of countries such as Russia and the United States (Gelvin 2015; Hinnebusch, Imady, and Zintl 2016).

These parties have used chemical weapons and have directly targeted civilians and civilian infrastructures, including hospitals, schools, and residential buildings. In some of the most gruesome cases of violence, members of the Islamic State committed acts of genocide against various minority groups, including the Yazidis, and established slavery markets. Due to the war, major urban centres such as Aleppo, al-Qusayr, Darrayya, Homs, and Jobar have been destroyed either partially or in full. The subsequent "urbicide" and the destruction of Syrian cities and infrastructure was so vast that the damage to the civil infrastructure in urban centres, and the social and economic damage, would take decades of recovery for the country to reach its pre-war socio-economic and human-development levels. These are important facts for understanding the long-term implications of the war for the Syrian population, especially within the context of the region and elsewhere.

Beyond the material damage to the country, the human cost of the war has been both tragic and tragically underappreciated in the West. According to some conservative estimates, close to half a million people have died in Syria as a direct result of the conflict since 2011. The widely covered cases of chemical weapons use, the vicious cycle of everyday violence, and the horror stories coming out of both rebel-held and government-controlled territories paint a dark picture of life inside Syria. Those who survive in the conflict areas live under some of the harshest conditions in the world, at times without access to the most basic of necessities. It should thus be no surprise that Syrians are seeking stable lives both inside and outside the country, as refugees or internally displaced persons fleeing conflict.

According to the UNHCR (2021), approximately 6.3 million people have been displaced internally within Syria, while another five million have sought refuge in neighbouring countries and beyond, in Europe and elsewhere (UNHCR 2017). According to the UNHCR, of the five million Syrians seeking refuge in neighbouring countries, Turkey has the highest number of Syrians, with approximately 3.7 million living in the country. Lebanon, in turn, has the highest in proportion to its population, with approximately 850,000 Syrians residing there, about a fifth of the country's total inhabitants. These countries are followed by Jordan, with 670,000 Syrians. When we consider the number of Syrian refugees, we get a better sense of the scale of this crisis; it is of historically significant proportions.

Scholarship exploring the nexus between migration and development has demonstrated that people tend to move to seek better lives in developed countries (Geiger and Pécoud 2011). When it comes to forced migration, such as in the case of Syria, people have no choice but to move. Currently, however, Syrians are stuck in neighbouring countries, with developed countries doing very little, if anything, to help them relocate. Irregular migrants do not choose to migrate irregularly, through smuggling networks; by risking their lives in open seas; by being at the whim of authorities and smugglers. They do so because they are often without a legal option to seek asylum and safety.

Once regular passage options are eliminated as part of border-security practices (Jones 2016), asylum seekers are forced to seek dangerous irregular routes charted by human smugglers. Given the discursive differentiation between "good refugees" that wait in UNHCR camps to be relocated upon screening and "bad migrants" who jump ahead on the proverbial queue and pay to be smuggled across borders, the legal status of Syrians living outside of Syria matters a great deal to their prospects of relocation. Whether Syrians have a refugee-status determination in Lebanon or Jordan or a temporary-protection status (TPS) in Turkey makes a difference in terms of being relocated elsewhere. Syrians who receive UNHCR status fall under the protection of the Geneva Convention Relating to the Status of Refugees. These individuals receive support from the UNHCR, including the possibility of relocation to a refugee-receiving state. Whereas those that reside in Turkey and fall under the TPS regime only receive guarantees from the Turkish state.

In the short term, the Turkish government provides basic services to Syrian nationals with valid permits that register them under the TPS framework, including shelter, food, health care, and education (Rygiel, Baban, and Ilcan 2016). While the TPS framework originally provided (1) an open-door policy for Syrians, (2) ensured that there will be no forced returns to Syria in line with the principle of *non-refoulement* established under international law, and (3) gave them the right to have an unlimited duration of stay in Turkey, the TPS policy was a short-term stopgap.

Since 2018, with a declining economy and a Turkish-occupied buffer zone in Syria with the so-called Free Syrian Army, the "welcoming" attitude of the Turkish government started to shift. A closed-border policy was introduced, a wall was built along the Syria-Turkish border and, in some cases, there were forced returns to the Turkish-occupied buffer zone. TPS was never intended by Turkish authorities to be a long-term solution such as the one offered by the UNHCR under the Geneva Convention. TPS does not have a framework for relocation or integration. In many ways, it was a policy that tied the fortunes of Syrians living in Turkey to the hospitality of the Turkish president, Recep Tayyip Erdogan.

In Turkey, the Foreigners and International Protection Law, which came into effect in April 2014, is the legal document that governs the conduct and rights of non-nationals residing in Turkey, including refugees from Syria. The law regulates the procedures and laws that oversee the entry, exit, and stay of non-nationals, and identifies the rights, guarantees, and services provided to those seeking protection in Turkey, and the creation and functioning of the Turkish Directorate General of Migration Management, under the Interior Ministry, responsible for overseeing the implementation of the law.

Currently, most Syrians living in Turkey fall under the TPS regime, which exists as a framework under the Foreigners and International Protection Law. Under the TPS regime, Syrians are not officially considered to be refugees or asylum seekers by the Turkish authorities due to Turkey's "geographical limitation" to the Geneva Convention. Turkey's geographical-limitation clause dictates that Turkey's international obligation to refugees extends only to refugees from European states. As such, Syrians cannot apply for asylum or refugee status in Turkey, nor stay in Turkey in order to gain a path towards citizenship. The legal maze created by Foreigners and International Protection Law, however, had unforeseen consequences for Syrians. Those who arrived before the introduction of the law had been able to apply for residency permits under the old regulations, and, if successful, received residency permits, the so-called blue notebooks, that allowed them to live, work, and be eligible for Turkish citizenship after a residency requirement of three years. Those that entered Turkey after 2014, however, fell under the purview of the TPS regime, forcing them into a precarious legal status vis-à-vis international law.

That there are two separate streams make it complicated to discuss a singular Syrian experience in Turkey. Those who came after the introduction of the law have been granted TPS and have been subjected to the rights and limitations of that governance regime, including limited legal work opportunities that have only been introduced as late as 2016 and remain unattractive due to the bureaucratic hurdles associated with the application process. While all Syrian nationals who enter Turkey legally receive "temporary protection" on humanitarian grounds, their status is not protected under the Geneva Convention. This means that individuals staying in Turkey are not being assisted by the UNHCR in its camps; instead, the Turkish Disaster and Emergency Management Presidency provides assistance in camps established and run by the Turkish government.

While Syrians can apply for and receive UNHCR status in Turkey, that status is only relevant for relocation purposes. UNHCR status does not grant Syrians living in Turkey a path to permanent residency or citizenship. It also does not add any additional benefits or guarantees. Further, many Syrians that live in Turkey are still waiting to be registered with the UNHCR. The lengthy process in Turkey to receive UNHCR status adds anxiety and uncertainty to the lives of an already marginalized, traumatized population supported by minimum aid. With the Turkish economy in a clear decline compared to a decade ago, the integration of Syrians into the Turkish social welfare, health, and education systems presents a massive financial challenge for the Turkish government. Against this bleak background, Erdogan was able to exploit differences within the EU and provide a way to relieve the growing pressures by negotiating a financially lucrative deal with the EU. In return, the EU gained an opportunity to keep a large number of would-be asylum seekers outside its borders.

External Governance of Migration Management and Border Security in the EU: The EU-Turkey Migration Agreement

Especially since 2015, criticisms of the increasingly securitized European responses to irregular migration have become commonplace in academic circles and public debates. As a prosperous region with stable governments, western European countries are a destination for those seeking better lives, and have been for a long time. Whether East Germans crossing into the West in November 1989 or sub-Saharan Africans enduring treacherous journeys across the Sahara and the Mediterranean, the goal is the same: to seek a better life in Europe.

European colonial histories and the related core/periphery dependencies make European countries attractive places to live for many in the Global South. European states, however, have some of the harshest border-security and migration-management policies in the world (Moreno-Lax 2018). Here we need to look at two aspects. The first is the "Europeanization" of migration management under the Schengen Agreement and the subsequent securitization of irregular migration in Europe as part of the re-bordering of the Schengen area at the outer edges of the passport-free travel zone. The second issue is the externalization of border security through partnerships with regional countries such as Morocco and Turkey through so-called mobility partnerships.

Lavenex and Schimmelfennig (2009) coined the term "external governance" as an analytical lens for understanding instances "when parts of the *acquis communautaire* are extended to non-member states" (Lavenex 2004, 683). External governance is an umbrella concept consisting of three kinds of institutional forms that enable its practice, "hierarchy, networks, markets" (Lavenex and Schimmelfennig 2009, 796). This perspective is "both an attempt at conceptualizing important aspects of the EU's international role and a step towards analyzing forms of integration into the European system of rules that remain below the threshold of membership" (792). As such, Lavenex and Schimmelfennig use "governance" to account for "institutionalized forms of coordinated action that aim at the production of collectively binding agreements" (795).

The field of European human mobility is legally defined within the context of the Schengen Agreement, signed in 1985, establishing the Schengen area of free mobility for European citizens. Schengen enables free, or unrestricted, movement of people within the EU territories by eliminating internal borders while standardizing the union's external border-control practices as defined by the Schengen Borders Code (European Council 2006). Whereas internally the Schengen zone requires the elimination of internal borders between EU member states in order to supplement the smooth functioning of the four-freedoms principle, externally it involves a process of re-bordering that includes the harmonization of border-security practices and the implementation of a unified visa code for granting short-term travel visas (Dimitrovova 2008; Grabbe 2000; Guild, Carrera, and Balzacq 2008; Leonard 2009; Neal 2009; Rees 2008; Vaughan-Williams 2007; Zaiotti 2011).

The Schengen Agreement forms the internal dimensions of the union's institutions and technologies of border control and mobility governance. The broader "field" of EU human mobility, however, involves a multi-layered structure that includes several agencies spread across three different levels of governance, private stakeholders, and specialized plans such as the Stockholm Programme, standardized practices such as Schengen short-stay travel visa, and networked databases such as the Schengen Information System (SIS), Visa Information System, and European Dactyloscopy, among others, all of which enable the EU's human-mobility and border-security policies. It is important to note that the current institutional arrangement of the EU's mobility regime is the result of continuous negotiations between various parties—with varying degrees of power over different decision-making processes—interested in the everyday practices of control at the border. As such, the Schengen area is a fragile system that goes through continuous transformations, resulting in institutional and material reconfigurations. The so-called migration crisis represented one such transformation.

The Arab Spring and the subsequent conflicts in Libya (Prashad 2012; Pashakhanlou 2017) and Syria (Aboud 2015) created a migration crisis at the external borders of the EU. Whereas the Libyan conflict had a primary impact on the central Mediterranean route, the Syrian conflict had a more direct impact on the Aegean route. The EU and its member states were unable to cope with the historically high number of migrants arriving every day on the Italian island of Lampedusa (Campesi 2011, 2014), Greek islands (Gkionakis 2016), and the Spanish enclaves in Ceuta and Melilla (Mutlu and Leite 2012; Johnson 2013). This development created a sense of urgency at the EU level, and an asymmetry in the way in which the responsibilities were distributed among different member states, forcing countries at the external borders of the EU to deal with rescuing, processing, and providing care for the asylum seekers entering the EU through their territory. Countries like Germany, France, and the United Kingdom were forced to address the refugees once they started moving freely inside the Schengen area. The effects of this asymmetry were twofold. First, it meant that the solidarity principle behind the Schengen area was undermined, and this, in turn, resulted in the semi-permanent reinstatement of border controls between a number of Schengen-area countries. Second, it meant that the EU started to approach external border controls more aggressively, forcing countries at the external borders to cooperate heavily with Frontex, the EU's border agency, ensuring that security became the central lens to approach this unraveling humanitarian crisis.

While the securitization of irregular migration as a result of the recent migration crisis may seem like a contemporary phenomenon, it is part of an ongoing process that pre-dates the current crisis by at least two decades. The criminalization of irregular human mobility through the adoption of preventative legal measures at the EU level has been a process that started with the creation of the Schengen zone and the pooling of migration-management and border-security responsibilities. In practical terms, this securitization move has resulted in increased cooperation among EU member states to establish a network for active cooperation among judicial and police agencies. Furthermore, it has led to the creation of several EU agencies tasked with overseeing coordination among EU member states in areas pertaining to what eventually became Justice and Home Affairs (JHA), a policy-making domain under the authority of the European Council, covering, among others, asylum and immigration policy, and external border management.

The earliest example of this type of cooperation at the EU-level was the TREVI forum, which was established following the 1990 European Council meeting in Rome as a result of the increasing number of transnational terrorist attacks affecting the European continent, the Black September attacks on Israeli athletes during the 1972 Olympics in Munich being the most influential. Following the Treaty of Maastricht on European Union, the institutional arrangements of the forum were absorbed into the EU's "three pillar" structure, under the JHA pillar. Whereas the TREVI forum originally centred on counter-terrorism measures, the JHA pillar focuses on a wide-range of policies that deal with citizenship, immigration, and judicial and police cooperation, and the external dimensions of these policy areas. The relatively limited cooperation that started with the TREVI forum has turned into a flourishing EU-level policy sector under the Lisbon Treaty, which amended existing EU treaties; the JHA domain now manages the EU's involvement in everyday security practices affecting millions of EU citizens.

Under the EU-level initiatives overseen by the Stockholm Programme, EU institutions are involved in practices controlling two types of human mobility, regular and irregular. The Schengen short-stay visa regime, supplemented by national visa regimes governing long-term residency permits, governs the status of "regular" migrants. A second group of irregular migrants consists of asylum seekers, refugees, and others that enter the EU legally with proper Schengen visas but overstay.

Under the EU's "Global Approach to Migration and Mobility" (European Commission 2011), the European Commission established a framework that encouraged bilateral mobility partnerships and visa dialogues with neighbouring countries that propose possibilities for visa facilitation in return for the successful signing of readmission agreements, among other requirements. These readmission agreements are designed to provide a framework for the legal conditions of return for irregular migrants to their country of entry into the EU rather than their country of origin—in instances when the latter cannot be identified due to missing identification documents.

The requirements of mobility partnerships result in the relocation of the EU's external border practices further away from the actual boundaries of the union, well into third countries' external borders. This extraterritorialization of border-security practices eliminates the possibility of due process for irregular migrants trying to make their way into the EU to apply for asylum at regular border crossings (Mutlu and Leite 2012; Levy 2010; Chou 2009). The legal basis of these extraterritorial practices is embedded in a number of regional frameworks. These practices are often supplemented by bilateral agreements between the EU member states and third countries, and other memorandum-of-understanding agreements between EU agencies such as Frontex and the border agencies of countries flanking the EU.

These existing agreements and frameworks were put to a stress test in 2015; even with all these partnerships, collaborations, and security infrastructures in place between the EU and its neighbouring countries to the south and east, the volume of refugees from North Africa and Turkey crossing irregularly into the EU caught the union's border-security and migration-management authorities unprepared. In 2015, at the height of the migration crisis, approximately 885,000 thousand asylum seekers crossed the maritime border between Turkey and the Greek islands into the EU (Frontex 2021).

The EU authorities, and their trusted risk-management rubrics, failed to predict the multitude of asylum seekers trying to make their way to the EU to seek shelter. They failed to predict this because they did not take seriously the internal dynamics and struggles of bordering countries hosting millions of refugees. In understanding the

Syrian refugee crisis, then, it is important to remember that this crisis does not end and begin at the European borders. This is not simply a European crisis. It is a crisis that includes Europe, but the crisis is far greater than its impact on Europe. Within the context of the Syrian refugee crisis, volatile dynamics in Syria, Lebanon, Jordan, Turkey, and other regional countries, require our attention. To that end, we must pay attention to recent agreements that came into force since the European migration crisis.

The most prominent agreement is the EU-Turkey migration deal, which has come to represent the limits of the EU's technocratic imagination in dealing with a particularly challenging crisis that has tested the union's core principles and credentials. The agreement represents a shift in the way in which EU authorities approach migration stemming from neighbouring countries. It is perhaps the most politically significant agreement the European Commission negotiated with an external partner since the introduction of "Global Approach to Migration."

The EU-Turkey migration agreement is a political document. Its wording and contents represent a shift from the overly technical nature of the existing template for readmission agreements. This may be a direct result of the Turkish government's negotiation strategy that focused on using European insecurities over irregular migration as leverage. Or perhaps it was an outcome of the urgency of the crisis or a by-product of its design and drafting process in general. The agreement demonstrates that EU authorities are no longer simply offering to share "everything but [their] institutions" (Lavenex 2008, 953) when it comes to their relations with their immediate neighbours. The circumstances of the migration crisis are forcing EU authorities to pay hard cash for the cooperation with third countries in migration management and border security, in return for de facto detention of prospective asylum seekers in countries outside of the EU.

The details of the EU-Turkey deal are indicative of the pressure the European Commission and the European Council were under to address the influx of migrants arriving to the EU from Turkey in 2015–2016 (Rygiel, Baban, Ilcan 2016). To close or slow the eastern Mediterranean migration route, EU authorities negotiated and signed the EU-Turkey migration agreement. The agreement asks that Turkish authorities clamp down on human smuggling, and it creates a framework that oversees deportation of irregular migrants from Greece back to Turkey upon the processing of their asylum claim, if deemed unsuitable for asylum. In return, the EU authorities agreed to pay approximately 6 billion euros to cover programs for refugees in Turkey, propose a now defunct roadmap for visa liberalization for Turkish citizens travelling to the Schengen area, and made a promise to re-settle a refugee from Turkey to Europe on a one-for-one basis, meaning that for every person returned to Turkey under the pretext of the agreement, a new refugee waiting in Turkey would be resettled in Europe. With the exception of financial assistance in the form of sup-porting social programs for refugees, the EU did not deliver on its promises set out in the agreement. This was partially due to the aspi-rational nature of some of these promises—like the short-term-visit visa-waiver agreement for Turkish citizens travelling to the Schengen zone, and the clause for the resettlement of Syrians living in Turkey to the EU over a long-term period—and partially due to the lack of co-operation and changing political landscape in Turkey following 2016's failed coup attempt.

The agreement was also criticized by both the UNHCR and Médecins Sans Frontières, which refused to take part in its implemen-tation and pulled its operations out of Greece for the questionable ethics and legality of the proposed practices under the deal. Of par-ticular concern for these organizations was the shirking of international legal obligations on the part of the EU, and reducing asylum seekers to objects of barter by the Turkish government that in turn undermine the international right to political asylum. While the agreement was partially successful, in that the volume of irregular migration from Turkey to Greece dropped to pre-crisis levels, it has also turned migrants in Turkey into a bargaining chip for the Turkish government in its future negotiations with the EU. The agreement has also allowed the EU to pressure Greek authorities to enforce the processing and detention of irregular migrants in Greece, disrupting the Balkan route to Europe. In the meantime, the agreement allowed for authorities along the Balkan route to develop a securitized border infrastructure, consisting of walls, fences, and detention centres in Macedonia, Serbia, Hungary, Croatia, and Bosnia. In that sense, the EU-Turkey migration agreement has allowed the EU to reconfigure its border-security prac-tices both internally and externally to prospectively address similar crises in the future, but that ability came at a price.

Further complicating this picture is the changing socio-political and economic situation in Turkey. The failed coup attempt in Turkey in July 2016, the subsequent crackdown on civil society, the broader breaches of rights and liberties under the ongoing state of emergency, the rekindling of the Kurdish conflict in the southeast, and the desta-bilization of the Turkish economy after a decade of boom have created a renewed impetus for migrants living in Turkey to seek ways into Europe.

The EU-Turkey migration agreement was a response to a par-ticular moment in European history. A traditionally technocratic entity responded to a moment in which widespread xenophobia in EU member states, combined with political insecurities, seemed to force its hand. It was an unusual agreement for the EU to negotiate, and Erdogan's government took advantage of the political moment. The agreement was both a success and a failure. It was a success in that it allowed the border to remain closed for the time being, and allowed the EU to fortify its borders and develop its capacity to deter and detain migrants from crossing the Aegean in such large numbers. It was, however, a failure in terms of its ability to establish Turkey as a reliable partner. In the long run, the agreement also undermined the EU's credentials as a normative power in world politics.

Undermining Europe's Normative Power?

Since the fall of the Iron Curtain in 1989 and subsequent improvement of relations between east and west European states, the external bor-ders of the EU have been a source of vibrant scholarly and public debate (Anderson and Bort 199; Balibar 2002, 2003; Barbe and Johansson-Nogues 2008; Bigo and Guild 2005; DeBardeleben 2005; Delanty 2006; Diez 2006; Grabbe 2000; Rumford 2006; Scott 2005, 2006; van Houtum 2010; van Houtum and Pijpers 2007; Walters 2002, 2004; Zielonka 2001, 2006). Whether using analogies of containers, fences, gates, regulators, or choke points, any discussion of European borders must be grounded in, and specific about, which Europe is being referred to.

The EU, manifested through its numerous metamorphoses, can be both Jekyll and Hyde. The issue of human mobility is an example commonly used in this regard (Boswell 2003; Ceyhan and Tsoukala 2002; Huysmans 2000, 2006). The extent of one's subjection to the EU's mobility-management practices depends on one's citizenship, point of departure, destination, and how that identity and location are per-ceived by the EU authorities and EU member states through a rubric

of risk analysis and related geopolitical calculations. Different interpretations of these factors greatly affect mobility experiences in and
out of the EU. The subjective mobility experience thus provides a tan-
gible data marker for understanding the topologies of the European
project.

Mobility has been an important signifier for normative evalua-
tions of European integration (Maas 2007). The unrestricted mobility
of persons, goods, services, and capital (the four freedoms), and the
policies, practices, and standards are often presented as both the outcome and raison d'être of the European project. In this argument,
mobility and circulation establish a community of networks across
multiple levels and sectors that contribute to a liberal or cosmopolitan
understanding of community as envisioned by Jean Monnet and
Robert Schuman, the architects of the European integration project.
The EU is often referred to as a liberal intergovernmental project (Haas
1958; Hoffmann 1966; Moravcsik 1998) built upon the belief that
increased interdependence and cooperation results in peace and stability. The limits of this community, in terms of participation, however,
depend on one's location, and specifically whether one is inside or
outside the territorial footprint of the project.

In many ways, resurgent populist right-wing politics across
Europe threaten to undermine the normative credentials of the EU as
a kind of polity that adheres to global norms. This is clear in the anti-
migrant, anti-Muslim sentiments of populist politicians. The end of
the Cold War, and the "big bang" of enlargements in 2004, allowed EU
officials to make the case for reunifying Europe and eliminating borders. At the time, the EU was regarded as a "liberal" actor in world
politics. It was painted as an exception to the norm of self-interested
states. The contemporary moment, however, comes to show that the
EU was not an exception to the norm. The exceptions to the global
norms that exist within the founding documents of the EU that prioritize human rights and democracy did not end up defining the norms
of the EU member states, making the union fundamentally not that
different from a traditional state when it comes to border-security discourses and practices.

The EU-Turkey migration agreement is a good example of the
kind of exception that seems to define the European norms these days.
It is an example of realpolitik that focuses on outcomes rather than
ideals and global norms embodied in international law. Paying an
increasingly authoritarian regime to at best delay, at worst detain, a

group of people escaping war is not something a "normative power" in world politics would do. Moreover, the EU's actions violate its own legal commitments. Instead, in many ways, the EU project is business as usual when it comes to international politics.

Conclusion

The EU is currently far from the inspiring liberal organization it once was claimed to be. Today, it makes deals with authoritarian governments on its periphery to slow or stop irregular migration flows. Whether it is Libya, Niger, or Turkey, the EU's efforts to extraterritorialize through readmission agreements, migration deals, and pushbacks at its borders often go against both the word and the spirit of international laws governing international migration.

Today, with shifting geopolitics, the return of Russia as an active power, and continuing destabilization of the Middle East following decades of Western interventions and authoritarian rule, the EU looks a lot different than it did at the end of the turn of the century. To quote the Japanese lifestyle consultant Marie Kondo, the EU "no longer gives joy" to those observing its politics. Far from it. Instead, the so-called European migration crisis illustrates the endurance of old-fashioned nationalism and the impact of populist politics on technocratic governance, undermining the union's claims to being a normative power.

The seemingly "pragmatic" tack that the EU leaders took negotiating the EU-Turkey migration agreement highlighted cracks and divisions among EU member states and their technocratic elite. Developmental and humanitarian discourses that dominate the European Commission's policy documents gave way to discourses and practices of securitization at the external borders. The Turkish government, with its own agendas and internal economic woes took advantage of these cracks. Erdogan, after all, made a name for himself for his ability to shine during such interactional politics, both domestically and internationally.

While in the short term both the EU and Turkish authorities seem to have gotten what they want from their migration agreement, making it appear to be a win-win situation, the long-term outlook is bleak. In many ways, the EU has lost its remaining credibility for its claim to represent a different kind of global polity, a normative power. Readmission agreements, push-back deals, and comprehensive migration agreements made with neighbouring illiberal if not authoritarian regimes allowed the EU to curb the number of migrants entering its borders. That reduction in numbers, however, came at the cost of the rights of migrants seeking a better, safer life in Europe. Turkey, on the other hand, expected financial remedies for the costs it was incurring from providing care for Syrian nationals, a pathway for resettlement in Europe for Syrians, alongside visa-free travel to the EU for Turkish nationals. In Turkey, changing domestic dynamics, the 2016 coup attempt, the increasingly apparent democratic decline, and the downturn in the economic outlook made the introduction of non-financial aspects of the migration agreement even more unlikely.

In the short term, the agreement provided a stopgap in the flow of migration, which allowed the EU agencies to regroup and pursue alternative ways to reduce the number of migrants entering the EU. In the long term, it transformed migration into a leverage issue in Erdogan's approach to the EU, turning the Syrian nationals into proverbial pawns on a chessboard. Whereas we can speak of short-term gains for both the EU and Turkish governments, for Syrians living in Turkey the agreement provided virtually no extra relief. In many ways, it turned Turkey into a long-term "home" for Syrians there, making them the losing party of the agreement, stuck in a country with a declining economic and democratic outlook, with no apparent path to citizenship or return back to their homes in Syria, or onwards to Europe.

References

Aboud, M. 2015. "Can Oman Become a Key Player in The Syrian Crisis?" *Middle East Eye.* http://www.middleeasteye.net/news/can-oman-become -key-player-syrian-crisis-145819127.

Anderson, M., and E. Bort. 1996. *Boundaries and Identities: The Eastern Frontier of the EU.* Edinburgh: University of Edinburgh.

Balibar, E. 2002. *Politics and the Other Scene.* London: Verso.

———. 2003. "Europe: Vanishing Mediator." *Constellations* 10(3): 312–338.

Barbe, E., and E. Johansson-Nogues. 2008. "The EU as a Modest 'Force for Good': The European Neighbourhood Policy." *International Affairs* 84(1): 81–96.

Bigo, D., and E. Guild. 2005. *Controlling Frontiers: Free Movement into and within Europe.* Aldershot, U.K.: Ashgate.

Boswell, C. 2003. "The 'external dimension' of EU Immigration and Asylum Policy." *International Affairs* 79(3): 619–638.

Campesi, G. 2011. "The Arab Spring and the Crisis of the European Border Regime: Manufacturing Emergency in the Lampedusa Crisis." European University Institute Working Paper.

Ceyhan, A., and A. Tsoukala. 2002. "The Securitisation of Migration in Western Societies." *Alternatives* 27: 21–39.

Chou, Meng-Hsuan. 2009. "The European Security Agenda and the 'External Dimension' of EU Asylum and Migration Cooperation." *Perspectives on European Politics and Society* 10(4): 541–559.

DeBardeleben, J. 2005. "Introduction: What Borders for Which Europe?" In *Soft or Hard Borders? Managing the Divide in an enlarged Europe*, edited by J. DeBardeleben, 1–22. Aldershot, U.K.: Ashgate Press.

Delanty, G. 2006. "Borders in a Changing Europe: Dynamics of Openness and Closure." *Comparative European Politics* 4(2): 183–202.

Diez, T. 2006. "The Paradoxes of Europe's Borders." *Comparative European Politics* 4: 235–252.

Dimitrovova, B. 2008. "Re-making of Europe's Borders through the European Neighbourhood Policy." *Journal of Borderlands Studies* 23(1): 53–68.

European Commission. 2011. "Global Approach to Migration and Mobility (GAMM)." https://ec.europa.eu/home-affairs/pages/glossary/global-approach-migration-and-mobility-gamm_en.

European Council. 2006. Regulation (EC) No 562/2006 of the European Parliament and of the Council of 15 March 2006 Establishing a Community Code on the Rules Governing the Movement of Persons across Borders (Schengen Borders Code). https://eur-lex.europa.eu/legal-content/EN/ALL/?uri=CELEX%3A32006R0562.

Frontex. 2021. "Migratory Routes." https://frontex.europa.eu/we-know/migratory-routes/eastern-mediterranean-route/.

Geiger, M., and A. Pécoud. 2013. "Migration, Development and the 'Migration and Development Nexus.'" *Population, Space and Place* 19(4): 369–374.

Gelvin, J. 2015. *The Arab Uprisings: What Everyone Needs to Know*. Oxford: Oxford University Press.

Gkionakis, N. 2016. "The Refugee Crisis in Greece: Training Border Security, Police, Volunteers and Aid Workers in Psychological First Aid." *Intervention* 14(1): 73–79.

Grabbe, H. 2000. "The Sharp Edges of Europe: Security Implications of Extending EU Border policies Eastwards." Occasional papers, Institute for Security Studies Western European Union.

Guild, E., S. Carrera, and T. Balzacq. 2008. "The Changing Dynamics of Security in an Enlarged Union." CHALLENGE Research Paper 12, Centre for European Policy Studies. https://www.ceps.eu/download/publication/?id=6095&pdf=1746.pdf.

Haas, E. B. 1958. *The Uniting of Europe*. Stanford: Stanford University Press.

Hinnebusch, R., O. Imady, and T. Zintl. 2016. "Civil Resistance in the Syrian Uprising: From Peaceful Protest to Sectarian Civil War." In *Civil Resistance in the Arab Spring: Triumphs and Disasters*, edited by A. Roberts, M. J. Willis, R. McCarthy, and T. G. Ash. Oxford: Oxford University Press.

Hoffmann, S. 1966. "Obstinate or Obsolete: The Fate of the Nation-State and the Case of Western Europe." *Daedalus* 95(3): 862–915.

Huysmans, J. 2000. "The European Union and the Securitization of Migration." *Journal of Common Market Studies* 38(5): 751–777. https://doi.org/10.1111/1468-5965.00263.

———. 2006. *The Politics of Insecurity Fear, Migration and Asylum in the EU*. London: Routledge.

Johnson, H. 2013. "The Other Side of the Fence: Reconceptualizing the 'Camp' and Migration Zones at the Borders of Spain." *International Political Sociology* 7(1): 75–91.

Jones, Reece. 2016. *Violent Borders: Refugees and the Right to Move*. London: Verso.

Lavenex, S. and F. Schimmelfennig. 2009. "EU Rules beyond EU Borders: Theorizing External Governance in European Politics." *Journal of European Public Policy* 16(6): 791–812. https://doi.org/10.1080/13501760903087696.

Lavenex, S. 2004. "EU External Governance in 'Wider Europe.'" *Journal of European Public Policy* 11(4): 680–700. https://doi.org/10.1080/1350176042000248098.

———. 2008. "A Governance Perspective on the European Neighbourhood Policy: Integration Beyond Conditionality?" *Journal of European Public Policy* 15(6): 938–955.

Levy, Carl. 2010. "Refugees, Europe, Camps/State of Exception: 'Into The Zone,' the European Union and Extraterritorial Processing of Migrants, Refugees, and Asylum-Seekers (Theories and Practice)." *Refugee Survey Quarterly* 29 (1): 92–119.

Maas, W. 2007 "The Evolution of EU Citizenship." In *Making History: European Integration and Institutional Change at Fifty: The State of the European Union*, edited by Sophie Meunier and Kathleen R. McNamara, 231–246. New York: Oxford University Press.

Moravcsik, A. 1998. *The Choice for Europe: Social Purpose and State Power from Messina to Maastricht*. Ithaca, N.Y.: Cornell University Press.

Moreno-Lax, V. 2018. "The EU Humanitarian Border and the Securitization of Human Rights: The 'Rescue-through-Interdiction/Rescue-without-Protection' Paradigm." *Journal of Common Market Studies* 56(1): 119–140.

Mountz, A. 2011. "Specters at the Port of Entry: Understanding State Mobilities through an Ontology of Exclusion." *Mobilities* 6(3): 317–334.

Mutlu, C., and C. Leite. 2012. "Dark Side of the Rock: Borders, Exceptionalism, and the Precarious Case of Ceuta and Melilla." *Eurasia Border Review* 3(2): 21–39.

Neal, A. W. 2009. "Securitization and Risk at the EU Border: The Origins of FRONTEX." *Journal of Common Market Studies* 47(2): 333–356.

Pashakhanlou, A. H. 2017. "Decapitation in Libya: Winning the Conflict and Losing the Peace." *The Washington Quarterly* 40(4): 135–149. https://doi.org/10.1080/0163660X.2017.1406712.

Prashad, V. 2012. *Arab Spring, Libyan Winter*. Oakland, CA: AK Press.

Rees, W. 2008. "Inside Out: The External Face of EU Internal Security Policy." *Journal of European Integration* 30(1): 97–111.

Rumford, C. 2006. "Theorizing Borders." *European Journal of Social Theory* 9(2): 155–169. https://doi.org/10.1177/1368431006063330.

Rygiel, K., F. Baban, and S. Ilcan. 2016. "The Syrian Refugee Crisis: The EU-Turkey 'Deal' and Temporary Protection." *Global Social Policy* 16(3): 315–320 https://doi.org/10.1177/1468018116666153.

Scott, J. W. 2005. "The EU and 'Wider Europe': Toward an Alternative Geopolitics of Regional Cooperation?" *Geopolitics* 10(3): 429–454. https://doi.org/10.1080/14650040591003471.

———. 2006. *EU Enlargement, Region-Building and Shifting Borders of Inclusion and Exclusion*. Aldershot, U.K.: Ashgate.

United Nations High Commissioner for Refugees (UNHCR). 2017. "Global Trends: Forced Displacement in 2017." https://www.unhcr.org/statistics/unhcrstats/5b27be547/unhcr-global-trends-2017.html.

———. 2021. Syrian Regional Refugee Response. https://data.unhcr.org/en/situations/syria#_ga=2.11294260.1838920278.1635799571-361023765.1635799571.

van Houtum, H. 2010. "Human Blacklisting: The Global Apartheid of the EU's External Border Regime." *Environment and Planning D: Society and Space* 28(6): 957–976. https://doi.org/10.1068/d1909.

van Houtum, H., and R. Pijpers. 2007. "The European Union as a Gated Community: The Two-Faced Border and Immigration Regime of the EU." *Antipode* 39(2): 291–309.

Vaughan-Williams, N. 2007. "The Shooting of Jean Charles de Menezes: New Border Politics?" *Alternatives* 32(2): 177–195. https://doi.org/10.1177/030437540703200202.

Walters, W. 2002. "Mapping Schengenland: Denaturalising the Border." *Environment and Planning D: Society and Space* 20(5): 564–580. https://doi.org/10.1068/d274t.

Walters, W. 2004. "The Frontiers of the European Union: A Geostrategic Perspective." *Geopolitics* 9(3): 674–698. https://doi.org/10.1080/14650040490478738.

Zaiotti, R. 2011. *Culture of Border Control: Schengen & Evolution of European Frontiers.* Chicago: Chicago University Press.

Zielonka, J. 2001. "How New Enlarged Borders Will Reshape the European Union." *Journal of Common Market Studies* 39(3): 507–536. https://doi.org/10.1111/1468-5965.00301.

———. 2006. *Europe as Empire: The Nature of the Enlarged European Union.* Oxford University Press.

PART II

BORDERS ABOVE THE LAW
LEGAL LIMITS AND LOOPHOLES

De-bordering and (Re-)Bordering in the EU during the 2015 Migration Crisis: The End of "Europe without Borders"?

Birte Wassenberg

"Wir haben so vieles geschafft—wir schaffen das" (We have managed so many things—we will also manage this situation) was the spontaneous reaction by German Chancellor Angela Merkel to the migration crisis, which she expressed in an August 31, 2015, press conference after having visited a refugee camp near Dresden (Wittrock and Elmer 2016). Her message was taken up by the media and spread throughout Europe. It immediately stirred the hopes of tens of thousands of refugees who had travelled through Serbia and were waiting for admission at the Hungarian border. The Hungarian authorities built a fence to stop a massive inflow of refugees, but on September 1 they decided to open the border, thus spurring an immense refugee movement into the European Union (Rothenburg 2016).

But the initial welcoming by Merkel paradoxically led to a process of re-bordering in a growing number of EU member states. This was a challenge to the understanding of European integration as a "borderless Europe." Indeed, the EU is a regional organization whose aim was to lift borders between its member states. As Robert Schuman announced in his declaration on May 9, 1950, leading to the European Coal and Steel Community: "The pooling of coal and steel production should immediately provide for the setting up of common foundations for economic development as a first step in the federation of Europe" (Schuman 1950). The objective of economic integration, which progressively led to the European Community's project of a common market in 1957 and then to a single European market in 1987, was closely linked to the idea of a suppression of trade barriers; that is, of a "Europe without borders." However, borders were here largely considered as economic obstacles—customs duties and tariffs—whereas the reality of EU borders is much more complex (Wassenberg 2020, 39). Indeed, even economic borders are diverse: there is a European monetary zone, a "Europe without currency borders," a European customs union, a "Europe without customs duties," a European free-circulation zone, and a "Europe without work visas." Besides, there are many other borders—political borders, administrative, and cultural borders— which are not considered within the realm of this economic borderless Europe. For example, the Schengen zone, which designates a Europe of free circulation of people, without border controls, reveals an ambiguous relationship between the EU and borders: "While the functioning of the internal market is essentially based on freedom of movement and implies the elimination of borders as barriers to trade, the freedom of movement of the European citizen remains defined largely within the conceptual framework of borders, since nationality is a prime requirement for European citizenship" (Bouveresse 2020, 64). And for these types of borders, the competencies lie outside the realm of EU jurisdiction for it is the member states who control, open, and close national border points. This complexity of borders was little recognized until the migration crisis led to a significant reintroduction of border controls in the EU.

The EU was therefore forced to re-question the different functions of "borders" in European integration. Internally, the ideal of a Europe without borders was crumbling, an ideal which had been propagated by the European Community ever since the ambitious project of the single European market in 1987 and the creation of a "Schengenland" of free circulation in 1997 (Guild et al. 2015, 3). It was the heart of the Schengen Agreement, abolishing internal border checks of EU citizens, which was now at stake. The reintroduction of border controls by member states of the Schengen area not only represented an obstacle to internal mobility within the EU but was also associated with growing protectionism and a new fear of "the other," which diminished the potential of a welcoming policy toward migrants (Saurugger 2017, 23). Concerning external borders, the functioning of the so-called Dublin system of regulation on asylum seekers was disrupted, as it stipulates that asylum seekers have to be dealt with at the external point of entry into the EU, but during the migration crisis, member states at the external borders were no longer fulfilling this requirement and proceeded instead with extreme re-bordering policies; that is, the construction of fences and walls. This left the EU with a vacuum on how to deal with the migrant issue (Berrod 2020, 54).

This chapter assesses the historical ideal of a Europe without borders and its impact on the border regimes of the EU, then retraces the effect of the 2015 migration crisis in terms of de-bordering and (re-)bordering responses by the EU member states in order to, finally, evaluate the long-term consequence of this crisis of European integration. The methodological approach is historical; that is, it is based on an analysis of primary sources (mainly newspaper articles) collected during the examined period (2015–2016). Theoretical models, including European integration theory (functionalism, neo-functionalism, etc.), are therefore not considered, and the engagement with concepts like "Europe without borders" is primarily embedded into a historical assessment that takes into account the origin and development of the concept without any claim of theoretical modelling. In the context of this volume and debates about the role of borders in an era of globalization and unprecedented movements of people, this chapter illuminates how nation-state territorial boundaries persist as fixtures of the modern world, even when and where they appear most dormant and recessed.

The Ideal of a Europe without Borders

The model of a borderless Europe was a founding element of the process of European integration, as initiated at the beginning of the 1950s by the six founding member states of the European Coal and Steel Community.[1] Indeed, one of the listed objectives then was to create "a Europe without borders" (Bitsch 2006, 3–10). This objective primarily (but not exclusively) meant the elimination of economic borders,

---

1   France, Germany, the Benelux states (Belgium, the Netherlands, Luxembourg), and Italy.

and was first realized when the European Economic Community (EEC) was established, in 1957, which provided for the creation of a common market without customs barriers. From the start, therefore, the concept of a borderless Europe was linked to an economic interpretation of borders as obstacles to the free circulation of goods (Wassenberg 2019a, 44).

It took until the mid-1980s for this concept to progressively include the free circulation of people. Though focused on the elimination of economic obstacles, the idea of a single European market therefore foresaw not only the free movement of goods but also those of services, capital, and people—the latter with regard to their free circulation as workers; that is, factors of production in the EEC (Leboutte 2008). This meant the elimination of "all internal borders in Europe," as the then president of the European Commission, Jacques Delors, announced in January 1985, when he presented his white paper on the accomplishment of the internal market (Reitel, Wassenberg, and Peyrony 2018, 7). The Single European Act, signed by the 12 EEC member states on February 17, 1986, provided for the implementation of this single European market "without borders" by 1992. Conceptually, this model of a Europe without borders was based on a study Delors had asked the commission to conduct on the "costs of non-Europe"; that is, the economic costs that would occur if the single European market was not accomplished. The study was published in March 1988 and came to be known as the Cecchini report, named after its author, Paolo Cecchini, a high-ranking civil servant in the European Commission. It contained 6,000 pages of cost assessments, which were collectively estimated as being a minimum of 4.25 percent and a maximum of 6.5 percent of the gross domestic product of the EEC. According to the report, barriers to trade would not disappear if borders were maintained physically (by means of border controls of people and goods within the EEC), technically (by means of national administrative regulations), or fiscally (by means of indirect taxes resulting in lengthy and costly border formalities) (European Commission 1988).

It was the first of these three restrictions highlighted by the Cecchini report—maintaining border controls for people within the EEC—that was tackled by a small number of member states; namely, France, Germany, and the Benelux countries. Three years before the publication of the report, they had already decided to facilitate the implementation of free movement within the EEC by means of an initiative taken outside the European treaty framework. Their approach to a Europe without borders was a reaction to the successive strikes of Italian and French custom officers in 1984, who cited their increased workload at the border following a French truck-driver strike (Cunha, Silva, and Frederico 2015). On June 14, 1985, on a boat on the Moselle River near the town of Schengen, the five states therefore signed an intergovernmental agreement, the Schengen Agreement, which proposed measures intended to gradually abolish border checks at the signatories' common borders (Infantino 2019). The Schengen Agreement had two consequences: First, it expanded on the economic free movement of people (goods and labour) to include a "political" free movement because it abolished not only economic obstacles at borders but also politico-administrative ones; that is, personal identity checks (via passports, identity cards). It was "moving the borders of sovereignty and the borders for persons" (Guild 2001, 13) rather than "removing" them, because they shifted to Europe's perimeter. Second, it created a differentiated approach to the ideal of Europe without borders within the EEC, for only five out of nine EEC member states adopted the Schengen Agreement in 1985.

Not surprisingly, it was difficult to implement this political Europe without borders: it took until June 19, 1990, for the five EEC member states concerned to finally adopt the Schengen Implementing Convention, which entered into force March 26, 1995. The difficulties of applying the Schengen convention were due to the fact that the removal of internal borders had to be compensated by common controls at external borders in order to guarantee checks of arrivals from outside the EU and the security of the Schengen area. For the internal borders, it also implied an increased need for cross-border law-enforcement cooperation in order to avoid international trafficking and abuses within an opened space of free movement among the Schengen member states. A Schengen Information System was put in place to ensure the exchange of data, the sharing of information on criminal matters, and to coordinate investigation of cross-border crimes (Bevers 1993, 83–84). Whereas the Schengen convention had been first developed outside the legal framework of the EEC, it was then integrated into the EU's Amsterdam treaty in 1997 and applied in all EU member states.

However, from the start, the Schengen area did not correspond to the scope of the EU, for the United Kingdom and Ireland negotiated an opting out, and two external states, Norway and Iceland, had already signed an association agreement with the Schengen members in 1996. At present, out of the 26 states which have gradually acceded to Schengen, four (Iceland, Liechtenstein, Norway, and Switzerland) are not members of the EU, and EU member states Cyprus, Romania, and Croatia have yet to prepare their accession. Borderless Europe has therefore become a complex issue, for in economic terms it corresponds to the 28 (27 after Brexit) EU member states, whereas in political terms it comprises 26 states, not all of which are EU member states.

Borderless Europe becomes even trickier when taking into account the implication of the Schengen convention for the EU's external border policies. With a system of internal mobility and the suspension of internal border controls, the management of the external border had to be commonly assured (Poptcheva 2015, 3). Contrary to the Schengen Agreement, the Dublin regulation was elaborated in the framework of the EEC and signed on June 15, 1990, by 12 member states—including Ireland and the UK—and entered into force in September 1998. By January 1999, it applied to all 15 EU member states (thus including Austria, Sweden, and Finland), and was then extended to new EU member states during each enlargement round (Kasparek 2016, 61). The Dublin regulation was mainly established to define not a common but a "concerted" asylum procedure for the EU member states.

Dublin was not established as a refugee-friendly system, but rather to prevent irregular mobility of asylum seekers, irregular migrants, and undocumented refugees in the Schengen area (Lovec 2017, 127). Indeed, the Dublin regulation was not meant to become common EU policy, but was conceived as an intergovernmental tool, where the EU Council maintained jurisdiction and unanimity decision-making was the rule. Its main purpose was to rapidly determine the member state responsible for an asylum claim; that is, the external state that the asylum seeker seeks to enter (Mouzourakis 2014, 4). This then allowed for the transfer of all asylum seekers back to the point of entry. But the Dublin regulation suffered from significant flaws from the start: it did not determine how the asylum seekers, once their claims were admitted, would then be dispatched throughout the EU. Despite successive revisions, neither the Dublin II regulation of 2003 nor the Dublin III regulation of 2013, which introduced some improvements for refugees in terms of a right of appeal or the facilitation of family reunification, introduced the (necessary) principle of distribution of asylum seekers among EU member states according to a quota system (Thielemann and Armstrong 2012, 148–150).

Even before the migration crisis of 2015, the problem with Schengen and Dublin was that they were not sufficiently integrated EU policies and placed the burden of management of refugee/migrant movement to the EU member states at the external borders. This did not change despite that the external border management of the EU was slightly improved in 2004, with the creation of the European Border and Coast Guard Agency, or Frontex. Frontex was designed to monitor migration and detect criminals and terrorists at the EU external land and maritime borders, but its financial and human resources were limited, insufficient to deal with the growing pressure of migrants and refugees trying to enter the EU. Also, Frontex was only a monitoring organization; it was not responsible for controlling EU external borders, as the individual EU member states maintained jurisdiction in this field. After the Arab Spring in 2010 and the beginning of the Syrian war in 2011, this pressure led to the migration crisis, the peak of which arrived in summer 2015, when Merkel made her "Wir schaffen das" declaration.

De-Bordering and (Re-)Bordering Responses of EU Member States to the 2015 Migration Crisis

Migration challenges for the EU did not begin with the 2015 crisis (Blanchard and Rodier 2016). Problems had existed for some EU member states, especially at the external land and sea borders (Besier and Stoklosa 2018). The two major routes to enter the EU, the Mediterranean Sea route from the African shores and the Balkan land route via Turkey, put immense pressure on Italy, Spain, and Greece on the one hand, and on Hungary and Bulgaria on the other (Düvell 2010, 78–79). But even far across the European continent, at the borders of the Schengen area between France and the United Kingdom, French authorities had to deal with the "jungle of Calais," a non-authorized camp of migrants near the Channel Tunnel waiting for a chance to enter the United Kingdom (Agier et al. 2018, 218–230). Apart from the legal tools of Dublin and Schengen, which regulated at minimum the question of how to deal with the procedure of legal asylum seekers at external borders, the EU had no response to this problem: it lacked a common asylum and migration policy, "since member states have not been willing to transfer their authority to the supranational level" (Lovec 2017, 129). Therefore, EU member states at the external borders were often left on their own to tackle the resulting consequences of migration, be it to manage the asylum demands at the Hungarian or Bulgarian borders, or the control of the maritime borders at the shores of Lampedusa in Italy or on the Greek islands. Frontex sea missions were largely insufficient for coping with the growing number of boats packed with refugees, so that they had in fact to be complemented by national coastal-surveillance operations (e.g., the Italian Mare Nostrum operation of 2013–2014).

If the situation came to a peak in the summer of 2015, this was mainly because migration movements were constantly being amplified by a number of push-and-pull factors, or triggers, starting in the 1990s with the consequences of the war in Yugoslavia (in Bosnia and Kosovo), then followed in the 2000s by wars in Afghanistan (2001), Iraq (2003), and then, from 2011 onwards, in Syria and Libya (Becker and Becker 2018, 4–6). The years 2015 and 2016 were indeed record-breaking in terms of human displacement: in 2015, there were 59.5 million people forced out of their homes, and more than 2.5 million applied for asylum in the EU, a far bigger number than what previous years had yielded (European Parliament 2016). The trigger factors caused a sudden and massive increase in migrant numbers in the summer of 2015, both along the eastern Mediterranean and the western Balkan route (Turkey-Greece-North Macedonia-Serbia-Hungary), putting an ever-growing burden on external-border EU member states. According to Eurostat, the union's statistics agency, EU member states received over 1.2 million first-time asylum applications in 2015, more than double that of the previous year. More than one million migrants crossed the Mediterranean in 2015, and in July of that year, several thousand people passed every day through North Macedonia and Serbia (Eurostat 2016).

The situation also had a disastrous humanitarian dimension: after the sinking of a ship laden with refugees in the Mediterranean in April 2015, which resulted in over 800 deaths, EU member states felt an urgency to react. The European Commission published an action plan for the emergency relocation of 40,000 refugees (24,000 from Italy and 16,000 from Greece) within the EU and a resettlement program to take refugees directly from third countries (European Commission 2015a). At that time, Merkel had already expressed the need for fixing "objective relocation criteria" for EU member states, but U.K. Prime Minister David Cameron immediately refused, as migration was one of the main issues during the 2015 U.K. general election (Huggler and Marszal 2015). Cameron was supported by

Hungarian Prime Minister Viktor Orbán, who also opposed the plan, as his country was facing a surge of applications and he feared that a relocation principle would result in even more migration pressure at Hungarian borders (Euractiv 2015).

By spring 2015, then, the Schengen and Dublin regulations had shown their limits: in the intergovernmental relocation system, quotas had to be decided upon by unanimity, and non-Schengen states such as the United Kingdom and Ireland had already announced they would not take part in the relocation plan (Marhold 2016, 14). For the EU member states under pressure, this was regarded as a clear failure of European solidarity, as Italian Prime Minister Matteo Renzi underlined: "If this is Europe, you can keep it" (Graham-Harrison et al. 2015). In the end, the EU Council did reach an agreement, on July 20, 2015, on an emergency relocation of 160,000 refugees, by qualified majority, but the decision had nothing to do with the establishment of "objective criteria" for distribution of refugees among EU member states, and three EU member states, Hungary, Poland, and the Czech Republic, refused to apply the decision (Lovec 2017, 134). It also came too late, for by this time the process of bordering, de-bordering, and re-bordering within the EU had already started.

Indeed, with the increasing number of migrants taking the west Balkan route who first entered the Schengen area in Greece, then continued via Macedonia and Serbia to re-enter the EU in Hungary, the Hungarian government announced, in May 2015, that it would fight illegal immigration by building a border fence. This measure was immediately criticized by Merkel, who argued that "there was no legal limit to refugee numbers" (Graham-Harrison et al. 2015). From a legal point of view, her statement was correct, for the right to asylum is internationally regulated by the Convention Relating to the Status of Refugees, commonly known as the Refugee Convention, which was adopted by the United Nations on July 28, 1951, and it does not limit "authorized" numbers of refugees. However, in August 2015, when Merkel pronounced "Wir schaffen das" in order to underline this, it had serious consequences for the bordering policies in the EU. On August 24, 2015, Germany decided to make use of the "sovereignty clause" to voluntarily assume responsibility for processing Syrian asylum applications, for which it was not otherwise responsible under the criteria of applicable EU law (Schmelter 2018, 163). It, therefore, unilaterally suspended the Dublin regulation, willing and expecting to receive asylum seekers; by the end of July, 302,415 asylum seekers were registered in Germany, and by the end of the year, there were 441,899 refugees in total seeking asylum on German territory (Knortz 2018, 176).

The first effect of this was a de-bordering response by Hungary. The Hungarian authorities opened their borders, letting the migrants travel, via Austria, toward Germany, thus suspending the Dublin regulations that assign responsibility for asylum claims to the first country of arrival, the "first point of entry" into the EU (Martin and Macdonald 2015). After the death of a three-year-old migrant on a Greek beach in early September 2015, which was highly mediatized in Europe, Germany then decided to suspend the Dublin regulation in general. The de-bordering policy was also followed by the Czech Republic, which, on September 2, 2015, decided to offer Syrian refugees who had already applied for asylum in other EU countries and who reached the Czech Republic to either have their application processed there (i.e., be granted asylum there) or to continue their journey elsewhere. However, with the suspension of the Dublin regulation, there was now a massive inflow of refugees who, once in the Schengen area, could move freely in order to reach the country of their preferred destination. At first, one could observe three different blocs of responses to this inflow of migration into the EU: the welcoming countries (Austria, Germany, Sweden), which accepted a massive arrival of refugees; the status-quo countries (France, the Netherlands, Belgium, Denmark), which did not take on increasing numbers of refugees but did not argue against the principle of migration into the EU; and, finally, the refusal countries (Hungary, Bulgaria, Poland), which announced that they would not welcome (any) migrants into their states (Lovec 2017, 139).

At the EU level, the European Commission was incapable of convincing the member states to adopt a European solution for the migration crisis. In September 2015, it proposed a new relocation plan for 120,000 migrants (15,600 from Italy, 50,400 from Greece, and 54,000 from Hungary), but this plan was based on the "objective criteria" for distribution among member states—already rejected in the spring—so it was not surprising that there was significant opposition to the proposal (European Commission 2015b). Within the EU Council, an anti-migration front of central and eastern European states was being formed (Czech Republic, Hungary, Poland, Slovakia, Romania, Slovenia), which rejected the idea of relocation altogether and focused, rather, on security issues and on combatting irregular migration

(Kalius 2017). This revealed the extent of "uncommunication" between the EU and its member states, and a crisis of confidence exacerbated by a lack of solidarity between countries in western and eastern Europe (Withol de Wenden 2017, 191). By the end of 2015, these "nationalist" responses and the departure from the Dublin system of regulation had emphasized the need for reform of EU asylum policy, but there was no consensus on how to proceed as there was no consensus on the most crucial element: the question of a quota system of fair distribution of migrants among EU member states (European Council 2015).

In terms of the ideal of a Europe without borders, the initial de-bordering effect after the suspension of the Dublin system paradoxically led to more bordering within the EU. Hungary started this process, which then led to a ripple effect at the EU's external borders (Cantat 2016). By October 2015, Hungary had finished the construction of new border fortifications to the south: it built a 175-kilometre fence along its border with Serbia and a 40-kilometre fence along its border with Croatia (Almukhtar, Keller, and Watkins 2015, 5). Greece had already built fences along its short land border with Turkey. And when Turkey decided, in September 2015, to expel 1,700 migrants from the border zone, they were diverted to Bulgaria, which consequently also started to build its own fence to block migrants crossing from Turkey (3).

But the ripple effect was also working at internal EU borders. This was due to the fact that, increasingly, EU member states were suspending the Schengen Agreement in order to avoid a massive inflow of refugees once the Dublin regulations had been suspended. The status-quo countries who were affected by the welcoming policies of their neighbours therefore started to argue, by the end of 2015, in favour of re-establishing internal border controls as a reaction to the collapse of the Dublin system. Progressively, therefore, France, Denmark, Belgium, and the Netherlands reintroduced border controls—a measure which the Schengen Agreement allows for, as long as a "temporary measure" (which should normally not exceed a period of six months). In France, these measures were taken when President François Hollande proclaimed a state of emergency on November 13, 2015, after the terrorist attacks at the Bataclan in Paris, thus suspending the Schengen Agreement for an unlimited time. In practice, these border controls were implemented mainly at vehicle crossings by border police, who stopped travellers and checked IDs/passports. This caused considerable disruption of cross-border commutes in the Danish-Swedish border area (Oresund Bridge), the Franco-German cross-border regions, and the Dutch-German Euroregion (Wassenberg 2020, 20). For those in these integrated cross-border regions, this dispelled the notion of Europe without borders in the sense of a free circulation space. It should also be emphasized that under Schengen, border controls were not abolished; they were rather moved from physical border-crossing points to other areas (inside the Schengen space) and were supplemented by new digital tools at external borders (smart borders) (Hermann 2020).

By spring 2016, ironically, the initial "welcoming countries" were also revising their open-border policies. Austria, which had departed from Dublin for the humanitarian objective of maximizing the absorption of migrants, was the first country to impose a daily quota on asylum claims in order to limit the flux of migrants travelling through the country. Even Germany and Sweden, who became overwhelmed by the entry of thousands of refugees, reintroduced internal border controls, and eventually also revised their generous national policies and rescinded the subsidies given to migrants (Kahmann 2016).

In the end, the effects of the refugee crisis emphasised the failings of the EU to find an adequate European response to the crisis, because the EU member states did not agree on a quota solution for an equal distribution of refugees. In fact, the de-bordering process launched by the welcome policy of Merkel ended up with ever-harsher bordering and re-bordering measures in all EU member states, including those favourable to refugees. In the absence of an internal agreement, the EU finally depended on external help to deal with the migration crisis. Thus, it was especially the German government that pushed toward an EU deal with Turkey, signed on March 20, 2016, in order to prevent irregular migrants from entering the union.[2] In exchange for Turkey's willingness to fasten its borders and host irregular migrants, the EU agreed to resettle, on a one-to-one basis, Syrian migrants living in Turkey who had qualified for asylum and resettlement within the EU (Preiss 2016). It was an "externalization" solution for the migration crisis by keeping the refugees outside the external

2   This deal consisted of an agreement between the European Council and to stop the flow of irregular migration via Turkey to Europe. In essence, it meant that migrants and asylum seekers arriving from Turkey to the Greek islands, for example, whose applications for asylum had been declared inadmissible could be returned to Turkey. See chapter 3 of this volume.

borders of the EU. The externalization of the borders was in itself not a new EU strategy. Indeed, it started in 2000 when the EU concluded the so-called Cotonou agreement with the African, Caribbean, and Pacific Group of States, where a readmission clause for migrants was introduced, and then continued with the adoption of the European Neighbourhood Policy and Frontex in 2004. Even before the migration crisis, the willingness to combat clandestine immigration by means of bi- and multilateral treaties with external states was fostered by a treaty between Italy and Libya in 2008, followed by an EU-Libya agreement in 2010 (Buratti 2020, 9). What was new regarding the EU-Turkey deal was its urgency, which led to considerable advantageous conditions for Turkey (the EU agreed to pay Turkey six billion euros). But in the midst of the crisis, this appeared the only viable option for the EU, and this has not changed, because efforts since 2017 to reform the Dublin regulations toward fair distribution of refugees among all EU member states have failed (Walter-Franke 2018, 40). The EU-Turkey deal did, in fact, have an almost immediate effect, reducing the sea arrivals of refugees and migrants in Italy and Greece, as figure 4.1 illustrates.

But the migration crisis of 2015 not only had disastrous consequences for the EU asylum and border policies, but also a deeper impact on the process of European integration, threating basic principles of a Europe without borders.

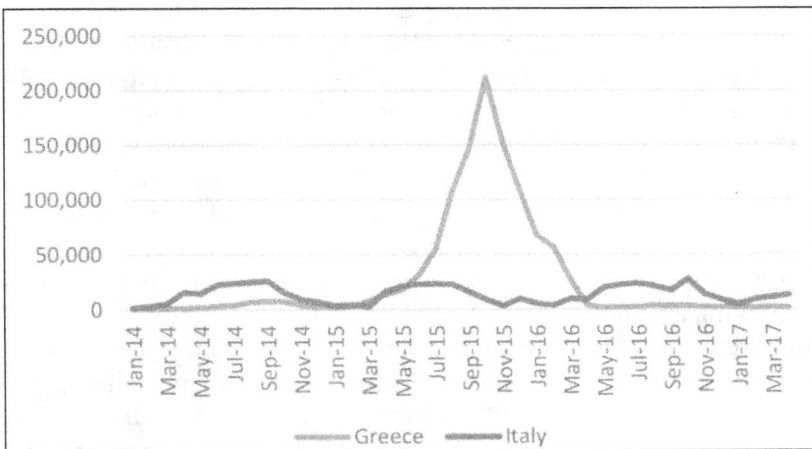

FIGURE 4.1. Sea Arrivals in Greece and Italy, 2015–2017.

Source: Blitz et al. (2017, 4).

The Effects of the Migration Crisis on European Integration

A more profound consequence of the 2015 migration crisis and the re-bordering of the EU was to reveal the end of the ideal of a borderless Europe that, for many observers, meant the end of the project of European integration itself. One consequence was to increase the tendency of Euroscepticism, which, by and large, seeks the breakup of the EU. Indeed, in the context of European crises since 2008 (economic, terrorist, migration), Eurosceptics have increased their presence in the European Parliament (EP). The results of European elections in 2014 and 2019 demonstrate the increase of Eurosceptic political forces in nearly all EU member states (Moreau and Wassenberg 2016a, 2016b; Wassenberg 2019b). Of the 751 EP seats, three anti-European factions—the European Conservatives and Reformists, the Europe of Free and Direct Democracy, and the European United Left/Nordic Green Left—held 171 seats after the 2014 elections, and together with the Europe of Nations and Freedom (ENF) group on the far right, they obtained 176 seats in the 2019 elections. More than 20 percent of the seats in the EP are thus occupied by anti-European or Eurosceptic political parties (Wassenberg 2019b, 281). Migration was one of the main targets for these anti-European political forces (Veivodová 2016, 72–73). Even before the Brexit referendum was an issue for the Cameron government in the United Kingdom, the Eurosceptic politician Nigel Farage had already portrayed migrants as the "other" and as one reason for the British to leave the EU; his party, the U.K. Independence Party (UKIP), had the highest turnout in the 2014 European elections, polling 27.5 percent of British votes and winning 24 of 73 seats (Tournier-Sol 2016, 105). During the Brexit campaign leading to the Leave vote in the 2016 referendum, UKIP used migration as a main argument for the United Kingdom to exit the EU. Other right-wing parties in the EU followed suit. In 2015, when Marine Le Pen and Marcel de Graaff launched the ENF group, mainly composed of the French National Front and Geert Wilders's Dutch Party for Freedom, they introduced a third right-wing anti-European faction of 39 MEPs and frequently used the migration crisis in EP debates to point to failures of European integration (Hanley 2016, 119). While Eurosceptic forces remain a minority in the EP (at around 20 percent), the growing anti-European discourse in the political arena (EP, national parliaments, national governments) nevertheless threatens not only the future development of the EU but also efforts to find a European solution to the migration crisis.

A second consequence was the tightening of the asylum policies of individual EU member states. Among the migration-skeptic policies widespread in central and eastern Europe, there was the so-called Hungarian solution, which consisted of "elective closure of borders, [a] series of deterrents, and governmental xenophobic discourse" (Kallius 2017, 133). Under the pressure of incoming migration, restrictive policies were also applied in more welcoming states; in Italy, for example, which adopted a decree in 2017 in line with the Dublin system in order "to enhance public security especially with respect to the nomads and illegal migrants living in Italian cities" (Ambrosetti and Paparusso 2018, 160). But even in the key migrant-destination country, Germany, the fear that migrants and refugees could become a burden to the welfare state induced the government to introduce more restrictive migration policies. In spring 2016, for example, it decided on a new integration law, "stipulating that persons granted asylum will be obliged to participate in integration measures such as German language courses and job training." Refugees were also restricted in their choice of residence, as they had to stay in a designated place of residency for three years in order to prevent concentrations of migrants in certain areas (Karolewski and Benedikter 2018, 111).

Another consequence of the migration crisis was that re-bordering processes created significant problems in EU border regions. The implementation of the project of a Europe of free circulation had primarily taken place in cross-border regions. Looking at the historical development of cross-border cooperation and its link with European integration, it appears that an awareness of the border as an obstacle had always existed in these peripheral areas, and was even the object of cooperation itself: to overcome the border as "a scar of history" was the main incentive for many border regions to start cooperation. However, following the European Regional Policy reform in 1987, the European Commission introduced in 1990 a Community program—Interreg—in order to support cross-border cooperation. This program was meant to facilitate the contribution of border regions to the Single European Market. Cross-border cooperation was increasingly put forward by the commission as a tool to implement the ideal of a Europe without borders (Reitel, Wassenberg, and Peyrony 2018, 15–17). Indeed, border regions were from then onwards identified as "models for European integration," especially those with a long experience of cross-border cooperation, as, for example, the Greater Region of Saar-Lor-Lux or the Franco-German-Swiss Upper Rhine region (Lambertz 2010, 10).

However, the re-bordering in response to the migration crisis fundamentally changed the perception of the function of the border in these regions: the "separation" function of the border was being reinforced and "the pertinence of the border" seemed to rematerialize (Wassenberg 2018, 34). Indeed, the effects of the unprecedented migration flows since 2015 are extremely palpable in these border regions. What used to be models of integration now exhibit the return of borders to Europe, as images of newly imposed border controls in 2016 in well-integrated cross-border spaces such as the Oresund region or the Strasbourg-Ortenau Eurodistrict illustrated. With the re-bordering process, the more cross-border cooperation had been developed, the more the persistence of the border was felt. In the Franco-German border regions, for example, a significant proportion of French employees worked in Germany (e.g., 22,700 Alsatians in Baden-Wurttemberg, 33,200 in Rhineland-Pfalz, and 18,000 in Saarland). With border controls re-established, cross-border flows were disrupted and cross-border workers were often late for work. On weekends in the Strasbourg-Ortenau Eurodistrict, 80 percent of French consumers travel to German Kehl for their weekly shopping. With frequent vehicle controls on the bridge between Strasbourg and Kehl, this became difficult and time-consuming (Evrard, Nienaber, and Sommaribas 2018). At the border between Denmark and Sweden, where systematic border checks were introduced at the Oresund Bridge in spring 2017, the situation became quickly unbearable for cross-border workers. Thus, the Swedish authorities had to stop these controls after three weeks, as the cross-border workers (20,000 commute daily) began demonstrating against the extraordinary measures that prevented them from reaching their workplace (*The Telegraph* 2017). It was a reversal process, one which reinforced and even multiplied the obstacles to crossing the border (Wassenberg 2017). Cross-border regions were thus becoming "models for European dis-integration" or evidence of the failure of the borderless ideal altogether.

Euroscepticism was even being spurred in the border regions. Doubt emerged about European integration amid the migration crisis, for it was precisely in cross-border spaces where the problems of the lack of European management of the migration crisis became all the more visible (Wassenberg 2019c, 135–136). Administrative, legal, psychological, and linguistic barriers—which emerge when borders persist, when the political and administrative structures of neighbouring countries come up against one another—were again being reinforced, leading to misunderstandings and even to intercultural tension between citizens living on borders (Dussap-Köhler 2011, 139–141). For example, when reinforced border controls caused late arrivals of Alsatian cross-border workers in Germany, German employers deployed stereotypes like "the French are not reliable, they are always late." Or, after the reintroduction of border controls between France and Germany after the November 2015 terrorist attacks in Paris, the Alsatian population would believe that the terrorists came from Germany or that they were German, whereas the assailants had been operating from within French territory (Wassenberg 2018, 23). After the migration crisis, the insecurity and fear of "the other" beyond the border was particularly felt in these border regions, since it was the function of the border as a gatekeeper against danger that was now put forward by the national authorities, not as a place of contact and exchange (Wassenberg 2019c, 142). This created mistrust and ressentiment among the border population, rekindling latent conflicts or resistance to cross-border cooperation (Lambertz and Ramakers 2013, 63–65). Thus, after the migration crisis it was easy, even in those regions where the degree of cooperation was well developed, to emphasize administrative, political, and cultural obstacles, and to identify them as a proof of the failure of the ideal of a Europe without borders (Wassenberg 2018, 25). However, when border controls were lifted, the situation in these border regions returned to normal, and there was little need to continue reflection on how to introduce crisis management at borders or to consider border regions differently with regard to other regions in the EU in order to not disrupt cross-border flows and cooperation. This showed particularly when the COVID-19 crisis led to the hermetic closure of almost all EU borders, entirely stopping cross-border mobility during the first wave of the pandemic, in spring 2020 (Berrod and Wassenberg 2020).

Finally, it was the bordering and re-bordering processes following the 2015 migration crisis that led to an overall reassessment of the function of borders in the context of European integration, and this reinterpretation was doubtful of the concept of a Europe without borders. Attention was drawn to the function of borders as "gatekeepers of sovereignty and security," a function which has gained in significance since the migration crisis (Brunet-Jailly 2018a). At the internal and external borders of the EU, security issues have again become of crucial importance, so that stakeholders are increasingly interested not in the integration but rather in the control function of the border in order to prevent cross-border crime or to increase internal security. However, this function of the border is still mainly reserved for the national states, which regard it as part of their exclusive competence in foreign and defence policy, and as a safeguard of their national sovereignty (Brunet-Jailly 2018b, 89). Military experts highlight this function of national borders as an "invaluable" asset for a nation "to exercise sovereign powers within its territory" (Spindler 2018, 202). The Westphalian border has indeed always been highly relevant from a security and geopolitical perspective, even if borders between postmodern states have lost some of their geopolitical relevance due to globalization, worldwide mobility, and transnational interactions (Ullestad 2018, 235–236).

However, this national re-appropriation of the border may lead to a new round of discussions and appreciations as to the nature of borders in the EU. For it questions the functioning of the EU, especially regarding the principle of multi-level governance, which associates European, national, and regional authorities in order to define and implement European policy. The member states of the EU are indeed reluctant to share power with European institutions (such as the Schengen Information System, Frontex, or Europol, the EU's police agency) on the management of the national border for security reasons; that is, they retain their authority over control of the external border, and they do not favour participation by local and regional authorities either. It can indeed be argued that the migration crisis has proven that the Westphalian order of borders has in no way been overcome in Europe, as the EU is not at all "immune to sovereignty conflicts" (Castan Pinos 2018, 251). These conflicts may even lead, as Brexit has shown, to existential crisis. There has always been an awareness by EU member states that borders as gatekeepers of sovereignty still matter, but the migration crisis of 2015 has underlined this point, and has pointed to the necessity of engaging in a new debate on functions and management of EU borders (Wassenberg 2021).

Conclusion

Although the migration crisis in 2015 was not the beginning of refugee problems for the EU, which have been increasing steadily since the Arab Spring and the Syrian civil war, it was still a significant turning point for migration policies and their role in European integration.

Angela Merkel's "Wir schaffen das" announcement in August 2015 had serious consequences, both for the treaty dispositions of the EU concerning border and asylum policies and for the subsequent responses of bordering and re-bordering by EU member states. In terms of EU law, the effect of the migration crisis was that the two EU conventions for internal and external border management were now at stake: Dublin and Schengen, both signed in 1990 and progressively implemented by EU member states. Merkel's welcoming policy indeed initially led to the suspension of the Dublin system, which established the principle of dealing with asylum seekers at the external borders of the EU at their "first entry point." From a humanitarian perspective, this policy led, in a first phase, to a de-bordering process in the EU, allowing for a massive inflow of migrants. From a political and legal perspective, however, this also led to internal (re)bordering in the EU and to a partial—more or less permanent—suspension of the Schengen Agreement, which normally guarantees free movement of people in the EU and therefore symbolizes a Europe without borders. The diverging migration policies of EU member states have led to a dis-equilibrium of the number of refugees accepted in member states, and to a lack of solidarity and management of the refugee crisis.

Due to the attitude of central and eastern European member states, which refused to accept a catalogue of "objective" criteria for the redistribution of refugees, the EU was incapable of defining a common solution or coming up with a new European asylum policy. Instead, a ripple effect of bordering and (re)bordering spread through the EU between August 2015 and spring 2016. The bordering started with the construction of fences and walls at the external EU borders by those EU member states that were not willing to accept migrants, Hungary and Bulgaria. It then continued with the introduction of internal border controls within the Schengen area by those member states that did not want to increase their share of migrants but did not oppose a welcoming policy by other member states (France, the Netherlands, Belgium, Denmark). Ironically, this non-harmonized process of de-bordering and bordering ended up with the most welcoming EU member states (Germany, Sweden, and Austria) also reintroducing internal border controls.

The migration crisis of 2015 thus not only led to a re-bordering at the external and internal borders of the EU, it also juxtaposed the role of borders with European integration. The Schengen Agreement was the expression of the ideal of Europe without borders, which had been implemented since the single European market of 1987 and had led to an EU space where the free movement of people, goods, services, and capital was the key element for success of the European integration process. The migration crisis of 2015 seemed to signal the end of this ideal, which in reality was more of a progressively constructed myth. Taking advantage of the apparent failure of European integration, growing numbers of Eurosceptic political parties within the EP was but one of the immediate consequences. Other effects of the bordering process were increasing difficulties of cross-border cooperation in border regions and an increasing emphasis placed on the border as a place of conflict, rather than a place of cooperation or integration.

Within the EU, this has led many member states to introduce more restrictive migration policies, to hold on to their national borders as gatekeepers of sovereignty, and to move away from the EU principle of the free movement of people. By dissociating themselves from the European unification process, these member states start "drawing up borders in their minds," thus not only denying the objective of a Europe without borders but the very fundamental principle of the EU as an open space, which is not only a challenge for the future European asylum policy but for the future of European integration itself. For Canada, the lesson to be learned from Europe's de- and re-bordering process during the migration crisis could be to resist the lure of idealized or mythical self-images—that of a borderless space—that elide the persistent and exclusionary quality of national borders. However, this lesson for Canada only applies to the external borders of the EU. It must not be forgotten that the EU is more complex where internal borders are concerned. It is a regional organization, which some do qualify as a quasi-state, but it is not a federation like Canada. Therefore, internal borders in the EU are not intra-state borders and, in times of crisis, they reveal themselves as national borders, just as the external borders. The exclusionary character of borders therefore applies to them just as well, and not only questions welcoming policies toward migrants but also the cohesion of the EU as an integrated space itself. This effect of the migration crisis can therefore not be compared to Canada, where a migration crisis might also lead to external bordering and exclusion, but not to a threat of disintegration.

References

Agier, M., Y. Bougga, M. Galisson, C. Hnappe, M. Pette, and P. Wannesson. 2018. *La Jungle de Calais*. Paris: PUF.

Almukhtar, S., J. Keller, and D. Watkins. 2015. "Closing the Back Door to Europe." *New York Times*, October 16, 2015. https://www.nytimes.com /interactive/2015/09/15/world/europe/migrant-borders-europe.html.

Ambrosetti, E., and A. Paparusso. 2018. "Migrants or Refugees? The Evolving Governance of Migration Flows in Italy during the 'Refugee Crisis.'" *Revue européenne des migrations internationales* 34(1): 151–171.

Becker, J. M., and K. Becker. 2018. "Causes and Triggers of Escape and Forced Migration to Europe." In *How to Deal with Refugees? Europe as a Continent of Dreams*, edited by G. Besier and K. Stocklosa, 3–15. Zurich: LIT.

Berrod, F. 2020. "The Schengen Crisis and the EU's Internal and External Borders: A Step Backwards for Security-Oriented Migration Policy?" *Borders in Globalization Review* 1(2): 53–63. https://doi.org/10.18357/bigr 12202019602.

Berrod, F., B. Wassenberg. 2020. "La frontière franco-allemande au temps du COVID-19 : la fin d'un espace commun." *Bordering in Pandemic Times, Insights into the COVID-19 Lockdown*, Special Issue, UniGR-CBS, June 30, 2020, 39–43.

Besier, G., and K. Stoklosa, eds. 2018. *How to Deal with Refugees? Europe as a Continent of Dreams*. Zurich: LIT.

Bevers, H. 1993. "Police Observation and the 1990 Schengen Convention." *European Journal of Crime and Policy Research* 1(4): 83–107.

Bitsch, M.-T. 2006. *Histoire de la construction européenne*. Brussels: Bruylant.

Blanchard, E., and C. Rodier. 2016. "'Crise migratoire' : ce que cachent les mots." GISTI, *Plein droit, Cairn.info*, 11: 3-6.

Blitz, B. K., A. d'Angelo, E. Kofman, and N. Montagna. 2017. "Health Challenges in Refugee Reception: Dateline Europe 2016." *International Journal of Environmental Research and Public Health* 14(1484): 2–22. https:// doi.org/10.3390/ijerph14121484.

Bouveresse, A. 2020. "The Ambiguous Relationship Between the EU and its Internal Borders: The European Citizen's Point of View." *Borders in Globalization Review* 1(2): 64–70. https://doi.org/10.18357/bigr12202019567.

Brunet-Jailly, E. 2018a. "Borders and the EU: The Consequences of the Schengen Crisis." Communication at the 2nd ABS World Conference, Budapest/Vienna, July 10–14, 2018.

——. 2018b. "Borders and Border Disputes in the European Union." In *Castle-Talks on Cross-Border Cooperation: Fear of Integration? The Pertinence of the Border*, edited by B. Wassenberg, 85–103. Stuttgart: Steiner Verlag.

Buratti, T. 2020, "Externalisation des frontières de l'Union européenne. Enjeux et perspectives." Notes d'analyse, *RSE & Diversité*: 3–17. https://

www.pourlasolidarite.eu/sites/default/files/publications/files/na_2020
_div_externalisation_des_frontieres_de_l_union_europeenne.pdf

Cantat, C. 2016. "La Hongrie, chien de garde de l'Europe." GISTI, *Plein droit, Cairn.info*, 11: 19–22.

Castan Pinos, J. 2018. "Conflicts over Sovereignty in Europe in the So-Called Post-sovereignty Era." In *Castle-Talks on Cross-Border Cooperation: Fear of Integration? The Pertinence of the Border*, edited by B. Wassenberg, 239–253. Stuttgart: Steiner Verlag.

Cunha, A., M. Silva, and R. Frederico, eds. 2015. *The Borders of Schengen*. Brussels: Peter Lang.

Dussap-Köhler, A. 2011. "Les sensibilités interculturelles dans les régions transfrontalières." In *Vivre et penser la coopération transfrontalière (Vol.4) : les régions frontalières sensibles*, edited by B. Wassenberg and J. Beck, 129–145. Stuttgart: Franz-Steiner Verlarg.

Düvell, F. 2010. "Irregular Migration." In *Global Migration Governance*, edited by A. Betts, 78–108. Oxford: Oxford University Press.

Euractiv. 2015. "Hungary's PM Orban Calls Refugee Quota Plan 'Mad.'" *Euractiv*, May 8. https://www.euractiv.com/section/all/news/hungary-s -pm-orban-calls-eu-refugee-quota-plan-mad/.

European Commission. 1988. "Cecchini Report on the Cost of non-Europe." March 13.

——. 2015a. "Joint Foreign and Home Affairs Council: Ten-Point Action Plan on Migration." Luxemburg, April 20. https://ec.europa.eu/commission /presscorner/detail/it/IP_15_4813.

——. 2015b. "Proposal for a Council Decision Establishing Provisional Measures in the Area of International Protection for the Benefit of Italy, Greece and Hungary." September 9. https://ec.europa.eu/home-affairs /sites/homeaffairs/files/what-we-do/policies/european-agenda-migration /proposal-implementation-package/docs/proposal_for_council _decision_establishing_provisional_measures_in_the_area_of_inter national_protection_for_it_gr_and_hu_en.pdf.

European Council. 2015. "Action Plan and Political Declaration." Valletta summit on migration, November 11–12. https://www.consilium.europa. eu/en/press/press-releases/2015/11/12/valletta-final-docs/.

European Parliament. 2016. "Internal Border Controls in the Schengen Area: Is Schengen Crisis-Proof?" LIBE Committee, June. https://www.euro parl.europa.eu/RegData/etudes/STUD/2016/571356/IPOL_STU %282016%29571356_EN.pdf.

European Stability Initiative (ESI). 2017. "The Refugee Crisis through Statistics." January 30. https://www.esiweb.org/pdf/ESI%20-%20The%20refugee%20 crisis%20through%20statistics%20-%2030%20Jan%202017.pdf.

Eurostat. 2016. "Asylum in the EU Member States Record Number of Over 1.2 Million First Time Asylum Seekers Registered in 2015", News

release 44, March 4. https://ec.europa.eu/eurostat/documents/2995521
/7203832/3-04032016-AP-EN.pdf/790eba01-381c-4163-bcd2-a54959b
99ed6.

Evrard, Estelle, Birte Nienaber, and Adolfo Sommaribas. 2018. "The
Temporary Reintroduction of Border Controls Inside the Schengen
Area: Towards a Spatial Perspective." *Journal of Borderland Studies* 35(3):
369–383. https://doi.org/10.1080/08865655.2017.1415164.

Graham-Harrison, E., P. Kingsley, R. Waites, and T. McVeigh. 2015. "Cheering
German Crowds Greet Refugees after Long Trek from Budapest to
Munich." *The Guardian* [UK], September 5. https://www.theguardian.
com/world/2015/sep/05/refugee-crisis-warm-welcome-for-people
-bussed-from-budapest.

Guild, E. 2001. *Making the Borders of Europe.* Nijmegen, NE: University of
Nijmegen.

Guild, E., E. Brower, K. Groenedijk, and S. Carrera. 2015. "What Is Happening
to the Schengen Borders?" *Liberty and Security in Europe* 85:1–26.

Hanley, D. 2016. "The UK Independence Party: Gathering up the Periphery?"
In *European Integration and New Anti-Europeanism I, The 2014 European
Election and the Rise of Euroscepticism in Western Europe*, edited by
P. Moreau and B. Wassenberg, 113–131. Stuttgart: Steiner Verlag.

Hermann, G. 2020. "Smart Borders – intelligente Außengrenzen des
Schengenraums?" Bundeszentrale für politische Bildung, January 13.
https://www.bpb.de/gesellschaft/migration/kurzdossiers/302985
/smart-borders.

Huggler, J., and A. Marszal. 2015. "Angela Merkel Calls for New Rules for
Distributing Asylum Seekers in Europe." *The Telegraph*, April 24. https://
www.telegraph.co.uk/news/worldnews/europe/germany/11561430
/Angela-Merkel-calls-for-new-rules-for-distributing-asylum-seekers-in
-Europe.html.

Infantino, F. 2019. *Schengen Visa Implementation and Transnational Policymaking.
Bordering Europe.* Cham, Switzerland: Palgrave.

Kahmann, M. 2016. "L'Allemagne fait marche arrière." GISTI, *Plein droit,
Cairn.info*, 11: 15–18.

Kallius, A. 2017. "The East-South Axis: Legitimizing the 'Hungarian Solution to
Migration.'" *Revue européenne des migrations internationales* 33(2–3): 133–155

Karolewski, I. P., and R. Benedikter. 2018. "Europe's Refugee and Migrant
Crisis: Political Responses to Asymmetrical Pressures." *Politique
européenne* 2(60): 98–132.

Kasparek, B. 2016. "Complementing Schengen: The Dublin System and the
European Border and Migration Regime." In *Migration Policies and Practice*,
edited by H. Bauder and C. Matheis, 59–78. Cham, Switzerland: Springer.

Knortz, H. 2018. "Migration and European Policy of the Federal Republic of
Germany: An Analysis from and Economic-Historical Perspective." In

How to Deal with Refugees? Europe as a Continent of Dreams, edited by G. Besier and K. Stocklosa, 167–183. Zurich: LIT.

Lambertz, K.-H., ed. 2010. *Die Grenzregionen als Labor und Motor kontinentaler Entwicklungen in Europa. Berichte und Dokumente des Europarates sowie Reden zur grenzüberschreitenden Zusammenarbeit in Europa.* Zürich: Baden-Baden; Dike: Nomos.

Lambertz, K.-H., and J. Ramakers. 2013. "Vielfalt und Hürden kennzeichnen die grenzüberschreitende Zusammenarbeit in Europa." In *Grenzüberschreitende Zusammenarbeit leben und erforschen (Bd.5): Integration und (trans-)regionale Identitäten,* edited by J. Beck and B. Wassenberg, 63–73. Stuttgart: Steiner Verlag.

Leboutte, R. 2008. *Histoire économique et sociale de la construction européenne.* Brussels: Peter Lang.

Lovec, M. 2017. "Politics of the Schengen/Dublin System: The Case of the European Migrant and Refugee Crisis." In *Border Politics. Defining Spaces of Governance and Forms of Transgressions,* edited by C. Günay and N. Witjes, 127–143. Cham, Switzerland: Springer.

Marhold, H. 2016. "The European 'Area of Freedom, Security and Justice': Its Evolution and Three Fundamental Dilemmas." *L'Europe en Formation* 189: 9–24.

Martin, M., and A. Macdonald. 2015. "Germany Re-imposes Border Controls to Slow Migrant Arrivals." *Reuters,* September 14. https://www.afr.com/world/germany-reimposes-border-controls-to-slow-migrant-arrivals-20150914-gjlpmx.

Moreau, P., and B. Wassenberg, eds. 2016a. *European Integration and New Anti-Europeanism I, The 2014 European Election and the Rise of Euroscepticism in Western Europe.* Stuttgart: Steiner Verlag.

———. 2016b. *European Integration and New Anti-Europeanism II, The 2014 European Election and New Anti-European Forces in Southern, Northern and Eastern Europe.* Stuttgart: Steiner Verlag.

Mouzourakis, M. 2014. *We Need to Talk about Dublin: Responsibility under the Dublin System as a Blockage to Asylum Burden-Sharing in the European Union.* Oxford: Refugees Studies Centre.

Poptcheva, E. M. 2015. *EU Legal Framework on Asylum and Irregular Immigration, on Arrival: State of Play.* Luxemburg: European Parliament Research Service.

Preiss, N. 2016. "Turquie-Europe, à qui la faute?" GISTI, *Plein droit, Cairn.info,* 11: 35–38.

Reitel, B., B. Wassenberg, and J. Peyrony. 2018. "European Territorial Cooperation." In *European Territorial Cooperation. Theoretical Approaches to the Process and Impacts of Cross-Border and Transnational Cooperation in Europe,* edited by E. Medeiros, 7–25. Heidelberg, Germany: Springer.

Rothenburg, C. 2016, "Ein Abend im September. Als Merkel die Grenze öffenete." *NTV*, August 29. https://www.n-tv.de/politik/Als-Merkel-die-Grenze-oeffnete-article18520011.html.

Saurugger, S. 2017. "Crise de l'Union européenne ou crise de la démocratie." *Politique étrangère* 1: 23–33.

Schmelter, L. P. 2018. "The Refugee Crisis and the German Question." In *How to Deal with Refugees? Europe as a Continent of Dreams*, edited by G. Besier and K. Stocklosa, 157–167. Zurich: LIT.

Schuman R., 1950. "Declaration". May 9. https://www.robert-schuman.eu/en/declaration-of-9-may-1950.

Spindler, W. 2018. "Borders, Security and Geopolitical Aspects." In *Castle-Talks on Cross-Border Cooperation: Fear of Integration? The Pertinence of the Border*, edited by B. Wassenberg, 201–219. Stuttgart: Steiner Verlag.

The Telegraph. 2017. "Sweden Ends ID Checks on Oresund Bridge Imposed as Migration Peaked." May 3.

Thielemann, E., and C. Armstrong. 2012. "Understanding European Asylum Cooperation under the Schengen/Dublin System: A Public Goods Framework." *European Security* 22(2): 148–164.

Tournier-Sol, K. 2016. "The 2014 Elections to the European Parliament in the UK: The United Kingdom Independence Party (UKIP) and the British National Party (BNP)." In *European Integration and new Anti-Europeanism I, The 2014 European Election and the Rise of Euroscepticism in Western Europe*, edited by P. Moreau and B. Wassenberg, 99–113. Stuttgart: Steiner Verlag.

Ullestad, A. 2018. "Protecting the Security of the EU through its External Borders." In *Castle-Talks on Cross-Border Cooperation: Fear of Integration? The Pertinence of the Border*, edited by B. Wassenberg, 219–239. Stuttgart: Steiner Verlag.

Veivodová, P. 2016. "The Anti-EU Groups in the European Parliament." In *European Integration and new Anti-Europeanism I, The 2014 European Election and the Rise of Euroscepticism in Western Europe*, edited by P. Moreau and B. Wassenberg, 71–85. Stuttgart: Steiner Verlag.

Walter-Franke, M. 2018. "Building a European Asylum Regime in Discordance Polarized Representations of Refugees in the Discursive Process of Policy-making." *Politique européenne* 2(60): 34–70.

Wassenberg, B. 2017. "The 'Myth' of a Europe without Borders and its Consequences for European Integration and Cross-Border Cooperation in the EU." Communication at the ABS Annual Conference, Bridges or Walls? The Case for Open Borders in the XXI Century, San Francisco, April 12–15, 2017.

———. 2018. "Introduction." In *Castle-Talks on Cross-Border Cooperation: Fear of Integration? The Pertinence of the Border*, edited by B. Wassenberg, 25–35. Stuttgart: Steiner Verlag.

———. 2019a. "Frontières, coopération transfrontalière et intégration euro-péenne." In *Frontières, géopolitique et relations internationales*, edited by B. Wassenberg and M. Aballéa, *Cahier Fare* (16): 43–65.

———. 2019b. "Euroscepticism at the EP elections in 2014: Reflection of the Different Patterns of Opposition to the EU?" In *The European Parliament in Times of EU Crisis. Dynamics and Transformations*, edited by O. Costa, 275–299. Cham, Switzerland: Palgrave.

———. 2019c. "Conflict and Cooperation at European Borders." In *Borders and Memories. Conflicts and Co-operation in European Border Regions*, edited by K. Stoklosa, 135–149. Zurich: LIT.

———. 2020. "The Schengen Crisis and the End of the 'Myth' of Europe without Borders." *Borders in Globalization Review* 1(2): 30–39. https://doi.org /10.18357/bigr12202019599.

———. 2021. "Médiation et gestion de crises aux frontières de l'UE." *Cahiers Fare*, n. 20, 2020.

Withol de Wenden, C. 2017, "Uncommunication in Europe on the Refugee and Migrant Crisis." *Hèrmes, La Revie* 77(1): 191–197.

Wittrock, P., and C. Elmer. 2016. "Angela Merkel und Flüchtlingspolitik: Die Bilanz nach einem Jahr 'Wir schaffen das.'" *Spiegel Online*, August 31. https://www.spiegel.de/politik/deutschland/angela-merkels-wir -schaffen-das-bilanz-eines-fluechtlingsjahres-a-1110075.html.

CHAPTER 5

Criminalization, Safety, and the Safe Third Country Agreement

Asad G. Kiyani

Current discourse about Canada's relationship to refugees reflects debates around the world, primarily in Europe, in that it centres around the concept of a crisis fuelled by irregular border crossings. That crisis is exemplified by the large number of migrants that have recently moved across the Canada-U.S. border to claim asylum in Canada. Highly restrictive and punitive migration policies in the United States heralded the advent of this movement, which reached unprecedented levels starting in August 2017. By March 2020, when the COVID-19 pandemic began and led to the complete shutdown of all crossings of the border, irregular border crossers had made 58,322 asylum claims in Canada (IRB 2021a). The federal government otherwise did not distinctly track irregular border crossers until April 2017 (Boyd and Ly 2021). This increase has led to debate about the validity of the Canada-U.S. Safe Third Country Agreement (STCA), which had prompted the irregular crossings by largely denying the right to make an asylum claim for those who crossed the land border at an official entry point.

This chapter addresses Canada's response to this movement of migrants and how it uses ideas of safety and criminality to justify the continuing application of the STCA. These controls depend on the United States and Canada formally and informally criminalizing various aspects of migration and movement, and highlight the continuing overlap between criminal and immigration law in both. While the United States has been thoroughly critiqued as "unsafe," centring a criminal-law understanding of migration regulation in both states shows that Canada is vulnerable to many similar critiques. Understanding these parallels helps expose the poverty of the word "safe" in the STCA, and the true use to which safety and criminalization are put: to create the legal and policy space to institute new measures designed to prevent asylum seekers from reaching Canada, to deter them from making claims if they avoid or ignore the prevention mechanisms, and to limit the available entitlements and procedural protections if they do make a claim. This criminal–safety nexus is directed at securing the state's total control over who it admits into the country, notwithstanding its effective international obligations to at least consider granting refugee status to asylum seekers.

While the COVID-19 pandemic has effectively closed off the border to all migrants, and thus limited the corporeal dimension of this crisis, it remains a relevant subject of study for three reasons. First, the decline in movement may only be temporary. The pandemic has provided governments around the world with a justification for closing their borders to all manner of people, including their own citizens in some cases. As well, the movement was spurred by the initiation of even harsher migrant regulation policies in the United States. While the Biden administration has mitigated some of the harshness of the previous administration's policies, there is always the spectre of a more conservative government assuming power in the future, and the reality that the American migration regime has operated punitively with Democratic governments too.

Second, the volume and reception of asylum seekers remains politically significant in Canada. All major parties in the 2021 federal election addressed refugees and migrants, including some that specifically advocated for changes to the STCA. It is the STCA that shaped the pattern of movement by designating the United States a "safe" country in which to make a refugee claim. Refugee claimants who cross the land border into Canada from the United States are generally ineligible to make a claim in Canada, unless they cross over outside an official entry point. Hence the large migration flow to unofficial crossing points on the Canadian border, subsequent declarations of "crisis," and calls for the STCA—which permits and perhaps even encourages such "illegal" crossings—to be revised, either by eliminating that loophole or suspending or withdrawing from the STCA altogether. Relatedly, the STCA remains a model for Canada: when Canada closed its border to effectively all refugee claimants during the pandemic, the only exemptions were for those individuals who were exempted from the STCA (Kaushal, Hastie, and Eeg 2020).

Finally, the STCA and its implementation not only helped to generate the ostensible crisis but also to illuminate how Canadian refugee law racializes and criminalizes migrants. Canadian immigration and refugee law exhibits a long-standing pattern of constructing migrants as threats and treating them as such. This chapter focuses on how these dynamics played out in the context of this crisis, and—given the potentially temporary nature of the pandemic-induced pause in movement and the importance of refugees to political discourse in Canada—it remains instructive to understand these processes of criminalization and racialization for what they say about North American refugee regulation.

The claimed focus of the international refugee system is to ensure that those individuals with a well-founded fear of persecution are able to find safe haven. States that have ratified the 1951 Geneva Convention Relating to the Status of Refugees (and its 1967 Protocol Relating to the Status of Refugees) are prohibited under article 33 of the 1951 convention from *refoulement*—expelling or returning the person to a place where their "life or freedom would be threatened on account of race, religion, nationality, membership of a particular social group or political opinion." What this effectively creates is an obligation to permit individuals to make an asylum claim—an obligation to assess if these individuals meet the refugee definition as laid out in international law.

In this light, any agreement, designation, or process—such as the STCA—that purports to negate the ability of claimants to make their case poses a risk to their safety. Any defence of such policies must therefore account for this safety concern. In the context of the STCA, Canada has done so by referencing safety concerns. To some extent, this is done by pointing to the United States as a "safe" place. But while Canada insists on the United States as safe for refugee claimants—even as the United States itself treats many migrants as criminals—it also defends the STCA on the basis of supporting *Canadian* safety in various dimensions. Key to this safety-based argument is the portrayal and treatment of migrants entering Canada as criminal and security threats.

Understanding the relationship between criminality and safety is important because it exposes the centrality of criminalization to refugee regimes in both the United States and Canada. While establishing if the refugee law systems in both states comply with international law is important, this approach only explains if the STCA *ought* to be in force. Examining the role of criminalization supports the argument that Canada should not participate in the STCA while also explaining why it *is* in force *in spite of* any deviations from international law. Criminalization is a central justificatory feature of refugee law in both places, and the discourse of criminality is indifferent to concerns about the technical nature of refugee law compliance. Perpetuating that indifference is arguably a key purpose of the discourse.

The first section examines the STCA's key elements, including the requirement for continual monitoring of American refugee law, and the potential consequences of finding that the United States is unsafe. The next part highlights specific aspects of the U.S. migration regime that serve to criminalize claimants. The third part addresses the idea of "crimmigration"—the blurring of immigration and criminal law—as a central way of understanding both U.S. and Canadian refugee law. It applies this theorization of migration law to trends of racializing and criminalizing asylum seekers. The chapter concludes by arguing that portraying asylum seeking as a threat to Canadian safety is not only a misguided reprioritization of whose safety matters in refugee determination but a red herring. This safety–crime justification obscures the very straightforward intention of the agreement to limit the number of asylum seekers arriving in Canada. Safety and the concomitant criminalization of migrants is thus employed to shelter the mundanely racist administrative goals of the refugee system.

Understanding the STCA

Canada contemplated the utility of the safe-third-country concept as a means to limit refugee claims for decades (Lam and Richmond 1995). A tentative concept for such an agreement was incorporated into the Immigration Act in 1988, but was not given effect because no country was designated as "safe" at that time (Sarbit 2003). Extensive contemplation came to fruition following the 9/11 terrorist attacks with the implementation of the STCA in 2004. The STCA permits either state to largely refuse to hear refugee claims made by people crossing the land border at an official entry point from the other state. This is legally justified on the basis that both countries are "safe" places to make refugee claims; laws, procedures, and protections are said to be both compliant with international legal norms and equivalent to one another. Claimants should therefore simply make their claim in the first safe place they arrive.

While absolute on their face, the prohibitions of the STCA do not apply in blanket terms. Exceptions do exist. From the Canadian perspective, the targets of the prohibitions are those claimants arriving in the United States from some other place and then entering into Canada at a land port of entry (not an air or marine port) to make a claim.[1] The majority of the exceptions permit individuals to make their claim in Canada if they have family members already in Canada. In addition, the Minister of Immigration, Refugees and Citizenship is able to exempt any person from the provisions of the STCA (article 6). Finally, the STCA permits individuals to make their claim in Canada as long as they do not enter Canada via an official land-border entry point. This has led to tens of thousands of migrants irregularly crossing into Canada.

The other key component of the STCA is that it requires monitoring of the implementation of the STCA and to ensure that the basis for designating parties as "safe" persists. If a country is unsafe for asylum seekers, then it matters not whether the entire border is a point of entry; the agreement should not apply. Under regulation 159.3 of the Immigration and Refugee Protection Regulations (IRPR 2002), Canada's agreement with the United States is contingent upon an assessment of U.S. compliance with article 33 of the Geneva Convention and article 3 of the UN's Convention Against Torture (CAT 1984). Both of those provisions protect against returning claimants to places where they may be persecuted or tortured. Section 102 of the IRPA further clarifies that the factors to be considered by the Canadian government are whether the third country is a party to the Refugee Convention and CAT, its implementation of its obligations under those conventions, and its overall human-rights record.

The STCA adopts these principles through its endorsement of the protective regimes of the Refugee Convention, its Additional Protocol, and the CAT (STCA 2004, preamble). Article 7 of the STCA requires the United States and Canada to share information about the "laws, regulations and practices" relating to their refugee-determination

---

1   Section 101(1)(e) of the Immigration and Refugee Protection Act permits claims to be made in spite of the STCA when the claimant is fleeing the "country of their nationality or their former habitual residence."

systems. Article 8 requires the two countries to review the agreement and its implementation, and invite the United Nations High Commissioner for Refugees (UNHCR) to participate in these reviews. Under IRPA section 102(1), there must be "continuing review" of the American refugee-protection regime. This understanding was recently affirmed by the Canadian Federal Court of Appeal, which noted that the STCA was open to challenge on the basis that Canada *continues* to affirm the United States as a safe third country (Canadian Council for Refugees 2021).

Negligent, disingenuous, or even well-intentioned declarations of a third country as safe risk legitimating a wide range of abuses against vulnerable asylum seekers. These dangers include those physical insecurity risks in the third state itself, the risk that the claimant will not be able to make a claim because of different legal interpretations of the Refugee Convention, and the risk of *chain refoulement*—that the third state will send the claimant on to yet another state. A finding that the United States is unsafe ought to lead to one of two consequences. Under article 10(3) of the STCA, either party may give written notice and unilaterally suspend the application of the agreement for up to three months (on a renewable basis). Under article 10(2), either party may give six months' notice before withdrawing from the agreement entirely.

The Canadian government has pursued neither of these options, leading to two sets of litigation. In both cases, migrants challenging the STCA succeeded at trial, only to be denied on administrative and procedural grounds on appeal. In both trial decisions, separate judges of the Federal Court, deciding 12 years apart, found the United States to be unsafe (Canadian Council for Refugees 2007, 2020). The first decision was overturned because the migrants were said to have lacked the right to make the challenge, and that the criteria for assessing the decisions of the Canadian government were different than alleged by the applicants (Canadian Council for Refugees 2008). The second trial decision was overturned on the basis that the applicants had challenged the initial decision to designate the United States as safe, rather than a contemporary decision (Canadian Council for Refugees 2021). In both cases, ongoing monitoring of the American refugee system was accepted, as were the potential consequences: a declaration that the government had exceeded its jurisdiction and/or violated the constitutional rights to life, liberty, and security of the person that asylum seekers were entitled to.

American Criminalization of Refugees

Compliance with international refugee-law requirements is (or was, at the time of the alleged crisis) absent in the United States, where systematic and structural restrictions are placed on the ordinary ambit of refugee law as defined by the Refugee Convention, international jurisprudence, and the UNHCR. A number of assessments of the American system have been made in the past, identifying deficiencies such as improperly preventing asylum claims, improperly punishing asylum claimants, and improperly eliminating grounds for asylum claims (Carasco 2003; Sarbit 2003; Macklin 2005; A. Moore 2007), including for gender-based claims (Arnett 2005; Hodgens 2006; Asthana 2011). Each of these steps on its own meaningfully undermines the *non-refoulement* principles of the Refugee Convention and CAT; taken together, it suggests the United States is unsafe. That thousands of people cross from the United States to Canada to make asylum claims is itself evidence of the same (Hyndman and Mountz 2020).

While the argument that the United States is unsafe is not a new one, this section pays specific attention to those aspects of the American refugee regime that criminalize asylum claimants. While it is important to understand how the American interpretation of refugee law may differ from Canadian or international understandings, the United States cannot be understood as "unsafe" for claimants without attention to how those claimants are criminalized.

Criminalization happens first through detention practices. Article 31 of the Refugee Convention prohibits receiving states from punishing illegal entry or presence in that state, as long as the asylum seekers "present themselves without delay to the authorities and show good cause for their illegal entry or presence" (Protocol Relating to the Status of the Refugee Convention 1967). Any restrictions on the liberty or movement of claimants must only be placed when necessary (*B010 v. Canada* 2015). Clarification on article 31 has been offered by the UNHCR, which notes that detention of asylum claimants ought to be both individualized and exceptional; should not impair the right to seek asylum; can only be undertaken for legitimate purposes; and requires that the conditions in which asylum seekers are detained must meet certain minimum standards (UNHCR 2012). American detention policies fail on all these grounds. In April 2017, the United States announced a "zero tolerance" policy, requiring detention for migrants who crossed into the country at unofficial entry points

(Nathan 2018a). Blanket detention policies violate article 31 and the prohibition on arbitrary detention contained in article 9 of the International Covenant on Civil and Political Rights. Evidence suggests that the detention of families is the result of a conscious decision to detain and prosecute adults travelling with their children over adults travelling alone (TRAC 2018a; Bump 2018; Kopan 2018; Detention Watch Network 2015). Detention of children is intrinsically harmful to them and violates the Convention on the Rights of the Child. That convention, along with the principle of giving effect to the best interests of the child, is incorporated into article 3 of Canada's immigration and refugee regime (IRPA 2001) and has been ratified by every country in the world except the United States.

Conditions of migrant detention in the United States further violate international and domestic rules. Holding cells used for overnight detention often do not have beds, heating, or private toilets, and most detainees are held far beyond the 12-hour limit prescribed for these cells (Cantor 2016; Americans for Immigrant Justice 2013). Larger detention facilities are either prisons that criminal convicts share with migrant detainees or facilities that are designed to function as prisons (Amnesty International 2009; U.S. Commission on International Religious Freedom 2016). Solitary confinement is widespread, including beyond the 15-day threshold, thus constituting "torture or cruel, inhuman or degrading treatment" (Special Rapporteur of the Human Rights Council 2011). Depression, suicide, and post-traumatic stress disorder are common in migrant detention facilities (U.S. Commission on International Religious Freedom 2016), as are physical and sexual abuse (Community Initiatives for Visiting Immigrants in Confinement 2017). All these problems are compounded by substandard medical care that has led to the deaths of detainees (Human Rights Watch 2016).

Extensive detention is one aspect of the criminalization of migrants in American refugee law. The routine use of racial profiling, denial of procedural rights and protections, and over-prosecution of migrants further reflects the worst tendencies of criminal law in both the United States and Canada. Asylum seekers at official border crossings were often refused the opportunity to claim asylum, thereby violating the fundamental obligation to assess that arises under the Refugee Convention (Korthuis 2016; Drake 2017). Suspected asylum seekers were frequently singled out because of the colour of their skin or quality of their clothing (R. Moore 2018a, 2018b; Nathan 2018b).

U.S. Customs and Border Protection agents also often fail to inform about half of the migrants they screen that U.S. law offers protection to those who face persecution, torture, or violence in their home country, and frequently fail to refer for hearings those who do make such claims and are otherwise eligible (U.S. Commission on International Religious Freedom 2005, 6, 53; UN Committee Against Torture 2014, para. 18; Human Rights Watch 2014, 26; 2017, 2; Brief of Refugee and Human Rights Organizations and Scholars as Amici Curiae in Support of Petitioners 2017).

On top of these procedural failures and the extensive detention regime, asylum seekers in the United States are often directly criminalized. The United States has sought to deter irregular border crossings through the use of criminal sanctions since 2005 (Fisher 2011). This policy was strengthened during the Trump administration, including through a directive to federal prosecutors that they consider charging migrants and others with offences involving "unlawful" entry, document fraud or identity theft, and transporting or harbouring non-citizens (U.S. Department of Justice 2017). All these leave legitimate claimants vulnerable to criminal prosecution in violation of the Refugee Convention (Puhl 2015, 99, 101). Moreover, prosecuting immigration offences has become the primary focus of federal prosecutors. The number of federal immigration charges has annually exceeded the number of federal drug charges for two decades (Hernández 2020). Immigration prosecutions are the majority of federal prosecutions (TRAC 2016, 2018a), and the population of prisoners incarcerated for immigration offences grew seven-fold in 25 years (Hernández 2017).

The rapid growth in migrant incarceration and criminal prosecutions (TRAC 2018b) has been accompanied by a decline in due process. In 2018, there was backlog of over a million cases (equivalent to five years' worth of cases) in immigration courts (TRAC 2018c). Only one in seven immigration detainees has counsel (Eagly and Shafer 2015, 32). The impact is significant, as represented migrants are five times as likely to succeed in their claim for asylum (TRAC 2018c), while detained migrants are 3.5 times more likely to be released if represented (Ryo 2016). For several years now, federal criminal cases that would have taken months have instead been condensed into single-day hearings, often with dozens of defendants being prosecuted simultaneously. While all the defendants are appointed a defence lawyer, they spend minutes with counsel before pleading guilty in a process that one magistrate describes as "a factory putting out a mold"; another says the function of defence counsel is to act as "ushers on the conveyor belt to prison" (Nathan 2018a). The cumulative effects of these decisions exacerbate an increasingly restrictive adjudication regime, and undermine the protective ambits of the Refugee Convention and CAT by either penalizing asylum claimants because of how they entered the United States or risking *refoulement* by failing to consider asylum claims on their merits. Canada's continuing adherence to the STCA endorses this criminalization, a set of practices that align with the discursive and legal approaches to migrants in Canada.

Crimmigration in Canada

Assessing the United States

As it has been for many years, if not from the moment that the STCA was signed, the decision that the United States is safe is contestable on its merits. The reason no country was designated as safe when the rules about safe third countries were introduced in the previous Immigration Act was because of U.S. treatment of refugees from certain countries in Central America, which was so deficient that Canada encouraged asylum seekers from those countries to apply for refuge in Canada instead (Sarbit 2003). Recent analyses, including the preceding one, simply confirm that the status quo was never satisfactory and, if anything, the situation has only worsened over time.

In spite of this, and like governments before it, the current Canadian government has deftly avoided its responsibility to answer to the public on this issue. In a review of the STCA that was undertaken from January to March 2017, the government declared that the United States is still "safe." While this report was released to the press, it only came to light after a freedom-of-information request made by the media; when finally released, the underlying basis for the determination was redacted (Wright 2018). The failure to explain should come as no surprise, as the government would otherwise be compelled to explain what non-doublespeak definition of "safe" includes jailing children in cages, where they can be abused, or encourages mass trials that are barely intelligible to those accused, who are shackled to one another as if in a chain gang. One implication of explaining this explicitly is that the Canadian government would have to admit that the STCA is not particularly concerned with ensuring migrant safety; instead, its overriding priority is reducing asylum-seeking in Canada. Condemning American treatment of refugee claimants would undermine this policy objective. It would also expose the domestic criminalization of migrants, which is itself aimed at the same administrative goal.

Canada and Crimmigration

The well-documented deficiencies of the U.S. refugee system, including many not mentioned here, barely register as political concerns. Arguably, this is because of how irregular border crossers are construed as inherently threatening, thus shifting the political discourse and direction of legal reform from how these individuals can be protected to how Canadians can be protected from them. This is part of an ongoing process of criminalization that has escalated in refugee law, and has resulted in marginalizing the marginalized. It has also operated in a self-fulfilling fashion: justifying more severe restrictions and rules as a response to the purported threat.

Understanding the centrality of criminalization helps explain the consequences of border securitization and the replacement of the figure of the refugee with that of the illegal migrant (Macklin 2005). The 9/11 attacks did not fundamentally change the security priorities of Canadian or American refugee law, but simply created space for newer, more restrictive, and punitive tools to come into force (Okafor 2020), including the STCA. These tools are punitive domestically, but also allow for enhanced border screening, and projecting the border outwards overseas to protect against threats (Crépeau and Nakache 2006). Canada's long-standing adoption, refinement, and use of these legal and policy mechanisms to keep out those migrants it has not pre-approved (Macklin 2005) is evidence that asylum's "obituary begins and ends in Canada" (Mountz 2021).

Yet the numbers of irregular border crossers that entered into Canada starting in 2017 make it clear that the need to move has not been erased. The refugee—or at least, the physical body of the refugee paired with the need to flee—has not disappeared but, in Canada at least, been replaced with a potent, quasi-criminal hybrid. This is a partial explanation of why the United States is still designated as safe, and the logical consequence of the convergence of criminal and immigration law known as "crimmigration."

The recognition of crimmigration in legal scholarship originated around the same time as the STCA, and the STCA's durability can be understood at least in part as a side effect of growing alongside—and arguably reinforcing—what is called the "criminalization of immigration" (Miller 2003). The STCA was negotiated shortly after the 9/11 terrorist attacks, and implemented in 2004. Security was a paramount justification for the agreement. There was particular concern that Canadian migration policy risked the security of North America as a whole (Sarbit 2003), and the STCA was described as part of a collaborative fight against terrorism (Macklin 2005). In contemporary times, right-wing politicians and political parties in Canada have insisted that the STCA can be stronger if applied to the entire border, and not just official entry points (Harris 2019b; Ross and Rauhala 2019).

In crimmigration, criminal law and immigration law are increasingly only nominally separate legal fields, with both regulating the state–individual relationship in ways designed to determine which individuals—if any—can be included as full members of society (Stumpf 2006). Crimmigration theory advises in part that border crossing is or will become increasingly criminalized (Stumpf 2006); that assisting irregular border crossing will become increasingly criminalized (Hernández 2020); and that public discourse will be mobilized to generate support for the criminal–immigration convergence.

Seen in this way, crimmigration has several elements. First is the application of harsher ideologies of punishment to immigration law, so that criminal law is used more frequently to respond to migrants and, particularly, asylum seekers and irregular border crossers (Stumpf 2006). Another element is that while only *some* techniques of criminal law are increasingly employed in immigration law, others are not. Criminalization of migration is notable in part because of the *absence* of procedural protections that would otherwise be available under criminal law prosecutions (Šalamon et al. 2020; Billings 2020; Bourbeau 2019). This may happen formally or informally, but the pattern of procedural erasure is apparent in refugee detentions, appeals, and removals in both Canada and the United States. Finally, crimmigration is marked not just by the application of criminal law tools to immigration and refugee law but the absorption of criminal law's theories, methods, and objectives into immigration law, such that they are seen as integral rather than external to it (Legomsky 2007).

Reflecting on the recent "crisis" of irregular border crossers generated by the combined effect of the STCA and changes to U.S. refugee protection illustrates how criminalization pervades Canada's asylum system. As noted above, the crisis began with the arrival of an increased number of asylum seekers at the border. These arrivals allegedly posed two kinds of threats. First, the sheer number of asylum claims is said to overwhelm the system, and thus threaten the integrity of the system (STCA 2004, preamble). This claim is contestable on several grounds, including that it was *not* unprecedented, and that the refugee system was already overwhelmed, even with the STCA functioning to deter asylum claims from the United States. The statutory wait time for an initial refugee hearing is no more than 60 days (IRPA section 100[4.1]). At the start of the crisis, the wait time was 16 months; one year later, it was 20 months (Pauls 2018). In other words, the arrival of more irregular asylum seekers was far less of a threat to the integrity of the system than was the years-long under-resourcing of the system.

Second, individuals are themselves posited as criminal and security threats (McDougall 1991; Macklin 2005; House of Commons 2012a, 2012b; Wright 2019). They are criminal because they are said—by ministers and Members of Parliament—to arrive *illegally* (Chandler 2018; Rempel Garner 2018a; Connolly 2019; O'Toole 2021). As noted above, this description is incorrect: refugee claimants cannot be penalized for crossing the border in violation of a state's laws *until* their refugee claim has failed. Nor can they be penalized for a variety of possible related offences, including forgery or identity fraud.[2] Crossing the border irregularly is not in itself an illegal act; it is the failure to report to a border official for the purpose of assessing what customs duties (if any) are owed on any goods being imported that constitutes the illegal act (s. 11, Customs Act). In other words, Canadian law does not conceive of irregular border crossings as intrinsically unlawful, yet the search for indicators of migrant criminality is so thorough that illegality is ascribed to *persons* for acts permitted by both the Refugee Convention and the IRPA (and which are domestically unlawful only because of the risk of not paying an importation duty).

Asylum seekers are criminalized in a second way. They are not only characterized as illegal for the violation of border crossing rules but also as *dishonest*. People who are willing to violate the sanctity of a border and the sovereignty of a state—even if only purportedly—are intrinsically untrustworthy "asylum shoppers" looking for the best deal for themselves and harming other refugees who do not break the

2 These provisions include IRPA ss. 122, 124(1)(a) and 127, and ss. 57, 340(c), 354, 366, 368, 374, and 403 of the Criminal Code.

law (Kane 2019; Rempel Garner 2018b). Canada now refuses to hear refugee claims made by any person who has made a refugee claim anywhere in the so-called Five Country Conference of Canada, the United States, United Kingdom, Australia, and New Zealand. No exemptions—not even those that apply to the STCA—are available. Again, safety and threat do important work here: according to the Minister for Border Security and Organized Crime Reduction, "[t]hose are safe countries and their claim in those countries should proceed. But we don't want [refugee claimants] sort of shopping around and making applications in multiple countries" (Harris 2019a). By portraying claimants as frauds, the government strengthens its claim to sovereignty (Hardy and Phillips 1999) through a prohibition that, like the STCA's exclusions, is justified on the basis of "safety." It further stigmatizes asylum seekers as dishonest individuals—either queue jumpers or bogus refugees (Dauvergne 2016)—trying to secure Canadian citizenship or welfare (Rempel Garner 2018c), at the expense of other "legitimate" (Ross and Rauhala 2019) or "patient" refugees (Rempel Garner 2018b).

That this effort is focused on reducing migration numbers is shown not only by the absence of exemptions for claimants but also by the absence of any criteria, other than that Canada has signed an information-sharing agreement with a third country. If anything, the Canadian government has learned its lesson from the constant litigation around the STCA and its visits to Federal Court. All that is required now is a security partnership. Rather than debate whether it properly applied its own criteria and assessed foreign compliance with international norms, the government simply removed international compliance as a criterion. This move is indicative of the intransigence around the STCA, which itself is built on an information-sharing agreement with the United States (A. Moore 2007).

A third dimension of criminalization is the infusion of criminal potency into the form of the irregular migrant. They are either capable of committing other, more serious wrongful acts and/or have crossed the border irregularly *with the intention* of committing such an act. Whether it is the RCMP questioning irregular border crossers specifically on their views of Islamic terrorist groups and face coverings worn by some Muslim women (Shepard 2017; Macklin 2018) or political parties implying or directly declaring the migrants to have criminal motives, the presumption is clear. Having committed one offence, the irregular border crosser is a latent threat to commit more.

The criminalization of asylum seekers is a legal phenomenon that gives teeth to the discursive ascription. While the American detention regime has been extensively criticized, the Canadian scheme has been condemned by the UN Human Rights Committee (2015) for not placing an upper limit on the length of immigration or refugee detention. The Canadian system was also deeply criticized in an external audit for inaccuracies and inconsistencies in factual findings made by adjudicators; for uncritical reliance on the evidence of government officials (who frequently repeated inaccurate assertions at multiple hearings); for the failure to hear evidence from enforcement officers and investigators; for not allowing detainees to hear evidence, question it, or present evidence of their own; and for not giving relevant information—including copies of decisions to detain a person, written reasons for a decision, or even their legal options—to detainees (IRB 2018). After two boats filled with Tamil asylum seekers arrived in 2009 and 2010, Canadian border agents were given written instructions to push for their continued detention even if no evidence justifying the detention existed (Bourbeau 2019). These detention practices reflect the idea that criminal law's protections do not flow with the application of criminal law practices in the immigration context, and suggest that deterring future migrants and the making of claims by those detained is the overriding goal of criminalization.

Laws regulating asylum seekers not only criminalize them but also racialize them. The starkest examples of this criminal–racial exclusion involve turning away Jewish, Sikh, and Chinese refugees arriving to Canada on boats. Two months after the 2010 Tamil migrant boat landing, the government proposed rules on "designated foreign nationals" (DFNs)[3]—which mandate detention for adult asylum seekers who arrive in groups identified by the minister, reduce the opportunities for challenging that detention and lengthen the period of detention, reduce appeal routes, and extend the statutory bars against applying for certain forms of exceptional remedies (IRPA, ss. 55[3.1], 57.1, 20.2 and 110[2][a]; Neylon 2015). Crucially, this can happen regardless of the mode of entry, as long as the arrival is in a group of people (IRPA, s. 20.1). Thus those who irregularly cross the land border with the United States as part of a group are vulnerable to being labelled DFNs, as occurred with a group of Romanian migrants in 2012 (Public Safety Canada 2012). Again, the intention of the DFN

---

3   These rules became law in 2012.

regime was clear: to deter migrants willing to enter the country irregularly (House of Commons 2012a).

The detention provisions and the other punitive dimensions of the DFN scheme simply built upon the racialized logic of criminalization that accompanied previous responses to "boat people" by punishing them for their mode of arrival rather than for any actual wrongdoing. The two boats carrying Tamil claimants were the latest in a series that arrived over the course of a century, carrying asylum seekers who were marked by their race, ethnicity, and religion. A partial list dating back to the 1980s includes 152 Tamil claimants in lifeboats in August 1986, 174 Sikh claimants in 1987, and four ships with 599 mostly Chinese claimants in 1999. Boat arrivals are frequently accompanied by demands for security assessments, procedural shortcuts, or changes to ensure passengers cannot remain or will be criminalized, amid declarations of terrorist infiltration (Mann 2011; House of Commons 2012b).

Boat arrivals also give meaning to the "continuous passage rule," which precluded people from landing in Canada essentially based on their place of origin. By requiring all migrants to arrive directly from their place of origin, and then denying ships leaving Asian ports the right to travel directly to Canada, the continuous-journey rule historically embedded racial discrimination in Canadian migration law (Aulakh 2021). By requiring that the claimant's path to Canada not be routed through the United States, the STCA effectively extends the racial logic of the continuous-journey rule for those asylum seekers too poor to pay for a flight or from those parts of the world that require a visa to enter Canada. This effect bears out in the numbers: during the border crisis, the vast majority of asylum claims by irregular border crossers were made by individuals from the Global South (IRB 2021b).[4]

Racializing refugees is not new or unique to Canada; the figure of the refugee has *always* been racialized (Richmond 1994, 2001; Shah 2000; Methmann 2014; Rajaram 2017; Fiske and Briskman 2009; Ashutosh and Mountz 2012), and that attitude has been reflected in American policy decision-making in pursuit of a "Muslim ban" and the construction of Latino asylum seekers as physical and existential security threats to the United States (Armenta 2016). Those fears and their associated nativism have been operationalized through the myriad of

---

4   The top nine source countries are Nigeria, Haiti, Colombia, Pakistan, Democratic Republic of Congo, Turkey, Sudan, Angola, and Eritrea. They are responsible for two-thirds of all claims.

policy changes in refugee law implemented in recent years, affirmed by Canada, and—importantly—reflected in Canadian refugee law.

Given this state of affairs, it is clear the point of the STCA has never been to ensure that migrants are safe in the United States or elsewhere. At its strongest, the purpose of the STCA has been performative in nature: to show Canadians that the government is keeping them safe from unspecified threats posed by a number of migrants who—at least until their refugee-status hearings fail—are acting in ways condoned by domestic and international law. In this context, the safety argument is incoherent: the idea that Canada is safer because it incentivizes people to cross the border illegally and evade law enforcement defies sense. It denies the reality that the STCA was created in the context of enhanced information-sharing with the United States, on the understanding that states are safer the more they know about who is entering their territory (A. Moore 2007). Congressional testimony is more damning: it shows that the STCA was effectively a trade between the United States and Canada as much as it was a cooperative security venture (Office of the White House Press Secretary 2002). Canada agreed to greater information-sharing in return for the United States agreeing to accept Canada's return of asylum seekers (House of Representatives 2002; U.S. and Canada Safe Third Country Agreement 2002). This points again to the mundane goal of simply keeping out as many people as possible.

In this light, the criminalization attendant in the discourse surrounding the STCA, its implementation, and in the broader Canadian immigration and refugee scheme does not serve an ostensible protective purpose. Rather, it operates to limit scrutiny of the regime, and to enable and normalize the systematic deflection of migrants and asylum seekers that has always been at the core of contemporary refugee law in Canada, by creating the space for misleading safety-based justifications. Criminalization is less about punishing migrants than about expanding the discursive, legal and policy field to create new ways of limiting the arrival of the unwanted.

Conclusion

The "crisis" created by irregular border crossers moving from the United States to Canada has reignited debate about the validity of the STCA. When paired with a renewed legal challenge to the agreement, this material-legal interaction focused attention on the legal regime and practices of refugee law in the United States and its compliance with international norms. Creating this space is a central effect of not only the STCA but also the range of restrictive and punitive approaches employed by Canada to limit claims, and prevent and deter the arrival of asylum seekers in the first place. Criminalization inherently raises safety concerns, which justifies further criminalization in a feedback loop that arrays itself and the sovereign authority of the state against the irregular status of migrants who illegally enter the country. In this interaction, the state is justified in responding to the crisis of irregular border crossings in increasingly stringent ways in order to protect itself and its citizenry. Skewing the balance of this contretemps is the reality that it lies within the ambit of the state to declare the rules of the game; that is, to determine what forms of border crossing and other activities by asylum seekers are legal and acceptable or not.

Yet as unwinnable as this conflict seems from the point of view of the criminalized refugee claimant, the persistence of state efforts to increase exclusion suggests it is equally attritional, if not hollow, from the perspective of the state. That people continue to try to make asylum claims, and consciously cross the border irregularly, either on foot or by boat or some other means, suggests that criminalization is inadequate to the task of limiting unwanted asylum claims in the face of the twinned determination and desperation of asylum seekers. Understanding the centrality of criminalization to refugee law in Canada and the United States may simply be another way of reiterating both the futility of criminalization as a deterrent and the need for more constructive engagements with the underlying motivations for such dangerous migration.

References

American Immigration Lawyers Association. 2018. "Policy Brief—USCIS Guidance on Matter of A-B- Blocks Protections for Vulnerable Asylum Seekers and Refugees." AILA Doc. No. 18072308. https://www.aila.org /infonet/uscis-matter-of-a-b-asylum-refugees.

Americans for Immigrant Justice. 2013. "The 'Hieleras': A Report on Human & Civil Rights Abuses Committed by U.S. Customs and Border Protection Agency." https://aijustice.org/wp-content/uploads/2020/05 /The_Hieleras_A_Report.pdf.

Amnesty International. 2009. "Jailed Without Justice: Immigration Detention in the USA." https://www.amnestyusa.org/pdfs/JailedWithoutJustice.pdf.

Armenta, Amada. 2016. "Racializing Crimmigration: Structural Racism, Colorblindness, and the Institutional Production of Immigrant Criminality." *Sociology of Race and Ethnicity* 3 1:82–95.

Arnett, Amy K. 2005. "One Step Forward, Two Steps Back: Women Asylum-Seekers in the United States and Canada Stand to Lose Human Rights under the Safe Third Country Agreement." *Lewis & Clark Law Review* 9(4): 951–980.

Ashutosh, Ishan, and Alison Mountz. 2012. "The Geopolitics of Migrant Mobility: Tracing State Relations through Refugee Claims, Boats, and Discourses." *Geopolitics* 17: 335–354.

Asthana, Deepti. 2011. "Gender Politics: Refugee Definition & the Safe Third Country Agreement." *Georgetown Journal of Gender and the Law* 12(1): 1–42.

Aulakh, Preet S. 2021 "Law, Identity and Imperial Logics of Exclusion: The Case of the *Komagata Maru* Passengers." *Journal of Imperial and Commonwealth History*. https://doi.org/10.1080/03086534.2020.1848029.

B010 v. Canada (Citizenship and Immigration). 2015. SCC 58. https://scc-csc.lexum.com/scc-csc/scc-csc/en/item/15647/index.do.

Billings, Peter. 2020. "Governing Felonious Foreigners through Crimmigration Controls in Australia: Administering Additional Punishments?" In *Causes and Consequences of Migrant Criminalization*, edited by Neža Kogovšek Šalamon, 43–68. Cham, Switzerland: Springer.

Bourbeau, Philippe. 2019. "Detention and Immigration: Practices, Crimmigration, and Norms." *Migration Studies* 7(1): 83–99.

Boyd, Monica, and Nathan T. B. Ly. 2021. "Unwanted and Uninvited: Canadian Exceptionalism in Migration and the 2017–2020 Irregular Border Crossings." *American Review of Canadian Studies* 51(1): 95–121.

Brief of Refugee and Human Rights Organizations and Scholars as Amici Curiae in Support of Petitioners. 835 F.3d 422 (3d Cir. 2016) (no. 16-812). https://www.scotusblog.com/wp-content/uploads/2017/01/16-812-Refugee-Organization-Cert-Amicus-Brief.pdf.

Bump, Philip. 2018. "Trump's 'Deterrent' of Separating Kids from their Parents Isn't Deterring Many Migrants." *Washington Post*, June 7, 2018. https://www.washingtonpost.com/news/politics/wp/2018/06/07/trumps-deterrent-of-separating-kids-from-their-parents-doesnt-even-seem-to-work/.

Canadian Council for Refugees, Canadian Council of Churches, Amnesty International and John Doe v. Canada, 2007 FC 1262 (Canada). https://www.refworld.org/cases,CAN_FC,474fe8d62.html.

Canadian Council for Refugees, Canadian Council of Churches, Amnesty International and John Doe v. Canada, 2008 FCA 229 (Canada). https://www.refworld.org/cases,CAN_FCA,497f38fa2.html.

Canadian Council for Refugees v. Canada (Immigration, Refugees and Citizenship), 2020 FC770 (Canada).

Canadian Council for Refugees v. Canada (Immigration, Refugees and Citizenship), 2021 FCA72 (Canada).

Cantor, Guillermo. 2016. "Detained Beyond the Limit: Prolonged Confinement by U.S. Customs and Border Protection along the Southwest Border." American Immigration Council. https://www.americanimmigration council.org/sites/default/files/research/detained_beyond_the_limit.pdf.

Carasco, Emily. 2003. "Canada-United States Safe Third Country Agreement: To What Purpose." *Canadian Yearbook of International Law* 41:305–342.

Chandler, Olivia. 2018. "Immigration Department Changed 'Illegal' to 'Irregular' on Webpage about Asylum Seekers as Debate Flared." *CBC News*, October 4, 2018. https://www.cbc.ca/news/politics/asylum -seekers-immigration-illegal-irregular-federal-government-1.4847571.

Community Initiatives for Visiting Immigrants in Confinement. 2017. "Letter to Thomas Horman, Director of U.S. Immigration and Customs Enforcement et. al Re: Sexual Abuse, Assault, and Harassment in U.S. Immigration Detention Facilities."

Connolly, Amanda. 2019. "'Dishonest': Liberals Criticized after Memo Says Safe Third Country Agreement Is Not Working." *Global News*, March 18, 2019. https://globalnews.ca/news/5067181/justin-trudeau-safe-third -country-agreement-no-longer-working/.

Convention against Torture and Other Cruel, Inhuman or Degrading Treatment or Punishment (CAT). 1984. 1465 UNTS 85.

Crépeau, François, and Delphine Nakache. 2006. "Controlling Irregular Migration in Canada: Reconciling Security Concerns with Human Rights Protection." *IRPP Choices* 12(1): 3–39.

Customs Act (Canada). RSC, 1985, c.1 (2nd Supp.).

Dauvergne, Catherine. 2016. *The New Politics of Immigration and the End of Settler Societies*. Cambridge, U.K.: Cambridge University Press.

Detention Watch Network. 2015. "Ending the Use of Immigration Detention to Deter Migration." April 2015. https://www.detentionwatchnetwork. org/sites/default/files/reports/DWN%20Detention%20as%20a%20 Deterrance%20Policy%20Brief.pdf.

Drake, B. Shaw. 2017. "Recording Proves Border Agents Are Illegally Turning Back Asylum Seekers under Trump." *Huffington Post*, July 13. https:// www.huffpost.com/entry/recording-proves-border-agents-are -illegally-turning_b_59678d9fe4b07b5e1d96edbd.

Eagly, Ingrid V., and Steven Shafer. 2015. "A National Study of Access to Counsel in Immigration Court." *University of Pennsylvania Law Review* 164(1): 1–91.

Fisher, M. J. 2011. "Testimony before House Committee on Homeland Security." Department of Homeland Security, October 4, 2011. https:// www.dhs.gov/news/2011/10/04/written-testimony-cbp-house -homeland-securitysubcommittee-border-and-maritime.

Fiske, Lucy, and Linda Briskman. 2009. "The Empire Strikes Back: Refugees, Race and the Reinvention of Empire." In *People, Place and Power: Australia and the Asia Pacific*, edited by Dawn Bennett, Jaya Earnest and Miyume Tanji, 217–238. Perth, Australia: Black Swan Press.

Hardy, Cynthia, and Nelson Phillips. 1999. "No Joking Matter: Discursive Struggle in the Canadian Refugee System." *Organization* 20:1–24.

Harris, Kathleen. 2019a. "Liberals Move to Stem Surge in Asylum Seekers— but New Measure Will Stop just Fraction of Claimants." CBC News Online, April 10. https://www.cbc.ca/news/politics/refugee-asylum-seekers -border-changes-1.5092192.

———. 2019b. "Scheer Vows Crackdown on Those Trying to 'Game' Canada's Refugee System." CBC News Online, May 28. https://www.cbc.ca /news/politics/scheer-immigration-policy-refugees-economy -1.5153043.

Hernández, César Cuauhtémoc García. 2017. "Immigration Prison Populations Since 1990s." *CrImmigration* (blog). September 19. http:// crimmigration.com/2017/09/19/immigration-prison-population-since -1990s/.

———. 2020. "Criminalizing Migration, Ending Rights: The Case of the United States Crimmigration Law." In *Causes and Consequences of Migrant Criminalization*, edited by Neža Kogovšek Šalamon, 27–42. Cham, Switzerland: Springer.

Hodgens, Lynn S. 2006. "Domestic Silence: How the U.S.-Canada- Safe-Third-Country Agreement Brings New Urgency to the Need for Gender-Based-Asylum Regulations." *Vermont Law Review* 30(4): 1045–1078.

House of Commons Debates. 2012a. 41st Parl, 1st Sess, No. 108 (April 23, 2012) at 7048 (Jason Kenney, Minister of Citizenship and Immigration).

———. 2012b. 41st Parl, Bill C-31 2nd Reading (June 8, 2012) (Rick Dykstra, Parliamentary Secretary to the Minister of Citizenship and Immigration).

House of Representatives. 2002. "United States and Canada Safe Third Country Agreement: Hearing before the Subcommittee on Immigration, Border Security, and Claims of the Committee on the Judiciary." 107th Congress, Second Session. Washington, D.C. http://commdocs.house.gov /committees/judiciary/hju82363.000/hju82363_of.htm.

———. 2014. "You Don't Have Rights Here: US Border Screening and Returns of Central Americans to Risk of Serious Harm." https://www.refworld. org/docid/5594f30b4.html.

———. 2016. "US: Deaths in Immigration Detention: Newly Released Records Suggest Dangerous Lapses in Medical Care." https://www.hrw.org /news/2016/07/07/us-deaths-immigration-detention.

———. 2017. "Australia/PNG: Refugees Face Unchecked Violence." https://www.hrw.org/news/2017/10/25/australia/png-refugees-face-unchecked-violence.

———. 2018. "Turkey Stops Registering Syrian Asylum Seekers." https://www.hrw.org/news/2018/07/16/turkey-stops-registering-syrian-asylum-seekers.

Hyndman, Jennifer, and Alison Mountz. 2020. "Seeking Safe Haven in Canada: Geopolitics and Border Crossings after the Safe Third Country Agreement." In *Haven: The Mediterranean Crisis and Human Security*, edited by John Morrissey, 110–128. Cheltenham, U.K.: Edward Elgar Publishing.

Immigration and Refugee Board (Canada) (IRB). 2018. *Report of the 2017/2018 External Audit (Detention Review)*. https://irb-cisr.gc.ca/en/transparency/reviews-audit-evaluations/Pages/ID-external-audit-1718.aspx.

———. 2021a. "Irregular Border Crosser Statistics." https://irb.gc.ca/en/statistics/Pages/Irregular-border-crosser-statistics.aspx.

———. 2021b. "Refuge Protection Claims Made by Irregular Border Crossers." https://irb.gc.ca/en/statistics/Pages/irregular-border-crossers-countries.aspx.

Immigration and Nationality Act, 8 U.S.C. 1231 (1965).

Immigration and Refugee Protection Act (Canada). SC 2001, c. 27.

Immigration and Refugee Protection Regulations (Canada). SOR 2002/227.

International Covenant for the Protection of Civil and Political Rights (1966). 999 UNTS 171.

Kane, Lara. 2019. "Trudeau's 'All Are Welcome' Immigration System Damages Its Integrity: Scheer." Canadian Press, February 1. https://globalnews.ca/news/4917809/andrew-scheer-immigration-justin-trudeau/.

Kaushal, Asha, Bethany Hastie, and Devin Eeg. 2020. "Bordering the Pandemic: COVID-19, Immigration, and Emergency." *National Journal of Constitutional Law* 41(1): 1–29.

Kopan, Tal. 2018. "Trump Admin Thought Family Separations Would Deter Immigrants. They Haven't." CNN, June 8. https://www.cnn.com/2018/06/18/politics/family-separation-deterrence-dhs/index.html.

Korthuis, Aaron. 2016. "Outsourcing Refoulement: The United States and the Central American Refugee Crisis." *Yale Journal of International Law Online*. October 24. http://www.yjil.yale.edu/outsourcing-refoulement-the-united-states-and-the-central-american-refugee-crisis/.

Lam, Lawrence, and Anthony H. Richmond. 1995. "Migration to Canada in the Post-War Period." In *The Cambridge Survey of World Migration*, edited by Robin Cohen, 263–270. Cambridge, U.K.: Cambridge University Press.

Legomsky, Stephen H. 2007. "The New Path of Immigration Law: Asymmetric Incorporation of Criminal Justice Norms." *Washington and Lee Law Review* 64(2): 469–528.

Macklin, Audrey. 2005. "Disappearing Refugees: Reflections on the Canada-U.S. Safe Third Country Agreement." *Columbia Human Rights Law Review* 36(2): 365–426.

———. 2018. "Citizenship, Non-Citizenship and the Rule of Law." *University of New Brunswick Law Journal* 69:19–56.

Mann, Alexandra. 2011. "Refugees Who Arrive by Boat and Canada's Commitment to the Refugee Convention: A Discursive Analysis." *Refuge* 26(2): 191–206.

McDougall, Barb. 1991. "Notes for an Address by the Honourable Barbara McDougall, Minister of Foreign Affairs, to the Conference Commemorating the 60th Anniversary of the Statute of Westminster." December 10. Ottawa: Department of Foreign Affairs.

Methmann, Chris. 2014. "Visualizing Climate-Refugees: Race, Vulnerability, and Resilience in Global Liberal Politics." *International Political Sociology* 8:416–435.

Miller, Teresa A. 2003. "Citizenship & Severity: Recent Immigration Reforms and the New Penology." *Georgetown Immigration Law Journal* 17(4): 611–666.

Moore, Andrew F. 2007. "Unsafe in America: A Review of the U.S.-Canada Safe Third Country Agreement." *Santa Clara Law Review* 47(2): 201–284.

Moore, Robert. 2018a. "Border Agents Are Using a New Weapon Against Asylum Seekers." *Texas Monthly*, June 2. https://www.texasmonthly.com/politics/immigrant-advocates-question-legality-of-latest-federal-tactics/.

———. 2018b. "At the U.S. Border, Asylum Seekers Fleeing Violence Are Told to Come Back Later." *Washington Post*, June 13. https://www.washingtonpost.com/world/national-security/at-the-us-border-asylum-seekers-fleeing-violence-are-told-to-come-back-later/2018/06/12/79a12718-6e4d-11e8-afd5-778aca903bbe_story.html?noredirect=on&utm_term=.74aad24219fa.

Mountz, Alison. 2021. *The Death of Asylum: Hidden Geographies of the Enforcement Archipelago.* Minneapolis: University of Minnesota Press.

Nathan, Debbie. 2018a. "Hidden Horrors of 'Zero Tolerance' — Mass Trials and Children Taken from their Parents." *The Intercept*, May 29. https://theintercept.com/2018/05/29/zero-tolerance-border-policy-immigration-mass-trials-children/.

———. 2018b. "Desperate Asylum-Seekers Are Being Turned Away by U.S. Border Agents Claiming There's 'No Room'." *The Intercept*, June 16. https://theintercept.com/2018/06/16/immigration-border-asylum-central-america/.

Neylon, Anne. 2015. "Ensuring Precariousness: The Status of Designated Foreign National under the Protecting Canada's Immigration System Act 2012." *International Journal of Refugee Law* 27(2): 297–326.

O'Toole, Erin (@erinotoole). 2021. "Un gouvernement conservateur va fermer la frontière au chemin Roxham, une fois pour toute." Twitter, September 13, 2021, 4:32 p.m. https://twitter.com/erinotoole/status/1437559719019696132.

Office of the White House Press Secretary. 2002. "U.S.-Canada Smart Border/30 Point Action Plan Update." Homeland Security Digital Library. https://www.hsdl.org/?abstract&did=478252.

Okafor, Obiora. 2020. *Refugee Law After 9/11: Sanctuary and Security in Canada and the United States.* Vancouver: University of British Columbia Press.

Pauls, Karen. 2018. "'It Means Everything to Me.' Wait Times to Have Refugee Claims Heard Continue to Rise." *CBC News,* July 18. https://www.cbc.ca/news/canada/manitoba/refugee-board-wait-time-1.4751200.

Protocol Relating to the Status of the Refugee Convention. 1967. 606 UNTS 267.

Public Safety Canada. 2012. "Minister of Public Safety Makes First Designation of Irregular Arrival under Protection Canada's Immigration System Act." December 5. https://www.publicsafety.gc.ca/cnt/nws/nws-rlss/2012/20121205-en.aspx.

Puhl, Emily. 2015. "Prosecuting the Persecuted: How Operation Streamline and Expedited Removal Violate Article 31 of the Convention on the Status of Refugees and 1967 Protocol." *Berkeley La Raza Law Journal* 25(1): 87–109.

Rajaram, Prem Kumar. 2017. "Refugees as Surplus Population: Race, Migration and Capitalist Value Regimes." *New Political Economy* 23(5): 627–639.

Refugee Convention. 1951. 189 UNTS 137.

Rempel Garner, Michelle (@MichelleRempel). 2018a. "By allowing nearly 38,000 people to enter Canada illegally from the safety of upstate New York then claim asylum, Trudeau has undermined the integrity of Canada's borders. Canada's borders should not be compromised by abuses of our asylum system, and should not sign this compact." Twitter, November 20, 2018. https://twitter.com/MichelleRempel/status/1064995703103975424.

———. 2018b. "FACT: The wait times for Privately Sponsored Refugees - those patiently waiting overseas, many in UN refugee camps is over seven years in some areas. Under Trudeau, the wait time to enter Canada illegally from the US is zero days." Twitter, July 15, 2018, 8:40 a.m. https://twitter.com/MichelleRempel/status/1018520727203414016.

———. 2018c. "Department of Citizenship and Immigration—Main Estimates, 2018-19: Business of Supply Government Orders." House of Commons—Hansard #300 of the 42nd Parliament, 1st Sess. May 24, 2018. https://openparliament.ca/debates/2018/5/24/michelle-rempel-13/.

Richmond, Anthony. 1994. *Global Apartheid: Refugees, Racism, and the New World Order.* Toronto, ON: Oxford University Press.

———. 2001. "Refugees and Racism in Canada." *Refuge* 19(6): 12–20.

Ross, Selena, and Emily Rauhala. 2019. "In a Twist, Canada Asks U.S. for Help Cracking Down at Its Southern Border." *Washington Post*, April 17, 2019. https://www.washingtonpost.com/world/the_americas/in-a-twist -canada-asks-us-for-help-cracking-down-at-its-southern-border/2019 /04/16/75d9e1b6-5bb8-11e9-b8e3-b03311fbbbfe_story.html.

Ryo, Emily. 2016. "Detained: A Study of Immigration Bond Hearings." *Law & Society Review* 50(1): 117–153. https://doi.org/10.1111/lasr.12177.

Safe-Third Country Agreement (Canada–U.S.) (STCA). 2004. CTS 2004/2.

Šalamon, Neža Kogovšek, Barry Frett, and Elizabeth Stark Ketchum. 2020. "Global Crimmigration Trends." In *Causes and Consequences of Migrant Criminalization*, edited by Neža Kogovšek Šalamon, 3–27. Cham, Switzerland: Springer.

Sarbit, Lara. 2003. "The Reality beneath the Rhetoric: Probing the Discourses Surrounding the Safe Third Country Agreement." *Journal of Law and Social Policy* 18(1): 138–158.

Shah, Prakash. 2000. *Refugees, Race and the Legal Concept of Asylum in Britain*. London: Cavendish Publishing.

Shepard, Michelle. 2017. "RCMP Officers Screened Quebec Border Crossers on Religion and Values, Questionnaire Shows." *Toronto Star*, October 11. https://www.thestar.com/news/canada/2017/10/11/rcmp-officers -screened-quebec-border-crossers-on-religion-and-values-question naire-shows.html.

Special Rapporteur of the Human Rights Council. 2011. "Interim Report on Torture and Other Cruel, Inhuman or Degrading Treatment or Punishment." UN Doc. August 5, 2021. A/66/268. undocs.org/a66/268.

Stumpf, Juliet. "The Crimmigration Crisis: Immigrants, Crime, and Sovereign Power." *American University Law Review* 56(2): 367–420.

Transactional Records Access Clearing House (TRAC). 2016. "Immigration Now 52 Percent of All Federal Criminal Prosecutions." TRAC Reports, Syracuse University. https://trac.syr.edu/tracreports/crim/446/.

———. 2018a. "Zero Tolerance at the Border: Rhetoric vs Reality." TRAC Reports, Syracuse University. https://trac.syr.edu/immigration /reports/520/.

———. 2018b. "Stepped Up Illegal Entry Prosecutions Reduce Those for Other Crimes." TRAC Reports, Syracuse University. https://trac.syr.edu /immigration/reports/524/.

———. 2018c. "Immigration Court Backlog Surpasses 1 Million Cases." TRAC Reports, Syracuse University. https://trac.syr.edu/immigration /reports/574/.

UN Committee Against Torture. 2014. "Concluding Observations on the Third to Fifth Periodic Reports of United States of America." UN Doc, December 19, 2014. CAT/C/USA/CO/3-5. undocs.org/cat/ac/usa/co3-5.

UN High Commissioner for Refugees (UNCHR). 2003. "Summary Conclusions on the Concept of 'Effective Protection' in the Context of Secondary Movements of Refugees and Asylum-Seekers." Lisbon Expert Roundtable, December 9–10, 2002. https://www.refworld.org /docid/3fe9981e4.html.

———. 2012. "Detention Guidelines: Guidelines on the Applicable Criteria and Standards relating to the Detention of Asylum-Seekers and Alternatives to Detention." United Nations High Commissioner for Refugees. https://www.refworld.org/docid/503489533b8.html.

———. 2018. "Global Trends: Forced Displacement in 2018." Geneva: UNHCR.

UN Human Rights Committee. 2015. "Concluding Observations on the Sixth Periodic Report of Canada." Geneva: United Nations Human Rights Committee—International Covenant on Civil and Political Rights.

"Migrating to Mexico for Safety: The Need for Improved Protection and Rights." Policy Report 03/08. Barcelona.

U.S. Department of Justice. 2017. "Attorney General Jeff Sessions Delivers Remarks Announcing the Department of Justice's Renewed Commitment to Criminal Immigration Enforcement." Nogales, Arizona, April 11. https://www.justice.gov/opa/speech/attorney-general-jeff-sessions -delivers-remarks-announcing-department-justice-s-renewed.

United States and Canada Safe Third Country Agreement. 2002. "Hearing Before the Subcommittee on Immigration, Border Security, and Claims of the Committee on the Judiciary." 107th Cong. 1–53. https://www. hsdl.org/?abstract&did=706267.

U.S. Commission on International Religious Freedom. 2005. *Report on Asylum Seekers in Expedited Removal, Volume I: Findings & Recommendation.* https://www.uscirf.gov/publications/report-asylum-seekers-expedited -removal.

———. 2016. "Barriers to Protection: The Treatment of Asylum Seekers in Expedited Removal." https://www.uscirf.gov/sites/default/files/Barriers %20To%20Protection.pdf.

Wright, Teresa. 2018. "Canada Deemed U.S. a Safe Third Country for Asylum Seekers." *Canadian Press*, October 22. https://ipolitics.ca/2018/10/22 /canada-deemed-u-s-a-safe-country-for-asylum-seekers-after-internal -review/.

———. 2019. "Andrew Scheer Vows to End 'Illegal' Border Crossings as Part of Conservative Immigration Plan." *Global News*, May 28. https:// globalnews.ca/news/5327265/scheer-immigration-plan/.

CHAPTER 6

Border Control and Xenophobia: Joining the Dots

Donald Galloway

The well-documented, steady increase in the number of people transiting from one country to another has not bypassed Canada.[1] Although the actual number of those seeking to enter Canada in recent years is minuscule compared to the number of those fleeing or migrating elsewhere, the recent Canadian experience is of interest because of the reactions sparked by the arrival of foreign nationals.[2] Of particular note are the political and legal responses to the arrival of those who have not been selected by the government to enter and remain in Canada, including those seeking Canada's protection and those seeking to join family members already here.[3] Under Conservative governments from 2006 to 2015, severe measures were imposed on such individuals, including mandatory detention of arrivals designated as irregular (including children over 16), denial of timely review of detention, impossibly short timelines for refugee claimants to prepare their claims, and even shorter timelines imposed on individuals

---

1   In a report published by the Legatum Institute Foundation, it is noted that "[t]he number of people globally living outside of their country of birth shows an upward trend, from 13 million in 2000 to 258 million in 2017" (Stroud, Jones, and Brien 2018).

2   The point has been made frequently, particularly by Volker Turk, the assistant high commissioner for protection at the UNHCR (quoted in Kawai 2019).

3   As is noted in the same report: "Refugees and asylum seekers account for approximately 10% of the international migrant stock, or an estimated 25.9 million people at mid-2017" (Stroud, Jones, and Brien 2018).

whose country of origin has been designated as safe, who were also denied appeals (Amnesty International 2012). Health care was also denied to many applicants. The Canadian government, like many others, augmented the number of individuals in transit by facilitating the removal of individuals from Canada through expansion of the grounds of removal and reduction of procedural safeguards. In other words, it "flexed its muscle" over the border both by impeding entry and by expediting and more readily resorting to deportation.

Not only has the current Liberal government failed to dismantle some of the harsh restrictions placed on border crossers by its predecessor, it has also revealed its willingness to impose further constraints and restrictions.[4] Most notable are the measures included within the Budget Implementation Act (2019), that render refugee claimants who have made a claim in a country with whom Canada has an information-sharing agreement ineligible to have a claim determined by the Immigration and Refugee Board (IRB) in Canada (Canadian Association of Refugee Lawyers 2019).

In addition, the reaction of the Canadian courts has been particularly noteworthy. Canadian judges have not been silent on the constitutional issues raised by the government's introduction of barriers to cross-border movement and have relied on the human-rights protections guaranteed in the Canadian Charter of Rights and Freedoms and in other international instruments to curtail implementation of some of the more egregious legislative measures. For example, the denials of health care and access to appeals to individuals from designated countries did not survive judicial review; see, for example, *Canadian Doctors for Refugee Care v. Canada (Attorney General)* (2014); *YZ v. Canada (Citizenship and Immigration)* (2016).

However, the judicial response to the various legislative measures can be critiqued as sporadic and piecemeal. In what follows, I reveal what I consider to be a severe deficiency in the response of the Canadian judiciary to various border controls implemented by the

---

4   It must be conceded that the Liberals have made some changes. Most notably, on May 17, 2019, the government removed all countries from the list of those designated as safe (Government of Canada 2019). However, it should be noted that the former Conservative government also created severe difficulties for those seeking to sponsor spouses, thus perpetuating the hardship of spousal separation. For example, a person who was sponsored as a spouse but whose relationship has broken down must be a permanent resident or citizen for five years before they can themselves sponsor a new partner as their spouse. This measure remains in force.

government.[5] In particular, I suggest that the courts have paid insufficient attention to the question of whether xenophobic impulses have informed legislative measures that have been introduced to regulate cross-border movement, and have, therefore, shied away from a major constitutional question, whether xenophobic laws are constitutional. Ultimately, I aim to show that current levels of cross-border movement test our commitment to basic human-rights principles and require us to go further than the position developed by the courts to date. When developing a response to the increased mobility of needy people, Parliament has drawn distinctions between citizens and foreign nationals and has taken it for granted that, everything being equal, it has constitutional authority to do so. By and large, the judiciary has accepted this development and, in most circumstances, has not demanded justification for drawing such distinctions. I suggest that the judiciary fails in its role as steward of our rights-based legal regime when it declines to investigate more thoroughly legislative measures that impose restrictions on non-citizens that are not imposed on citizens. I trace this failure to the fact that it has overlooked the pernicious impact of xenophobia within our political and legal institutions.

I begin by analyzing, in simple terms, the general underpinnings of the applicable law. Canadian immigration law classifies the population of the world into three groups. The largest is that of foreign nationals. It is a wide-ranging category, membership in which is defined by referring exclusively to the other two categories. According to section 2(1) of the Immigration and Refugee Protection Act, a foreign national "means a person who is not a Canadian citizen or a permanent resident" (Immigration and Refugee Protection Act 2001).

The law relies heavily on this tripartite division, by specifying both the category to which each person belongs and the channels through which a person may move from that category to another. In the case of foreign nationals, it also specifies how they may gain admission to Canadian territory, to the Canadian labour market, and to Canadian educational institutions without changing category.[6] In

---

5 I am equally interested in judicial supervision of regulations that restrict entry to Canada and judicial supervision of regulations facilitating removal of individuals. As noted above, I consider both types of regulation to be a form of border control.

6 This includes the processes that govern those who may arrive in Canada seeking refugee status. They enter as foreign nationals and there is no demand that they become permanent residents or citizens (although it is usually to their benefit that they do so).

the case of permanent residents, it provides an intermediate bridging status, and grants a right to enter and remain in Canada while also defining and imposing mandatory and discretionary conditions that restrict this entitlement. In the case of citizens, it provides an unqualified right to enter and remain.

This tripartite structure is by no means unique to Canada. On the contrary, most jurisdictions have adopted similar regimes. The structure also resembles the three-part division among subjects, denizens, and aliens long recognized in English common law (Blackstone 1765). Historically, schemes that distinguish among subjects (or citizens), aliens, and those holding an intermediate status have been regarded as falling within the broad ambit of sovereign-state authority, unconstrained by international law. An authoritative statement of this view is found in Lord Atkinson's speech in *Attorney General for the Dominion of Canada v. Cain* (1906, 546):

> One of the rights possessed by the supreme power in every State is the right to refuse to permit an alien to enter that State, to annex what conditions it pleases to the permission to enter it and to expel or deport from the State, at pleasure, even a friendly alien, especially if it considers his presence in the State opposed to its peace, order, and good government, or to its social or material interests.

However, in the modern era, this unconditional authority has come to be perceived as bounded by side constraints identified in international human-rights instruments.[7] In Canada, the legislative decision to place legal restrictions on non-citizens is also restricted by domestic constraints, found in constitutional provisions that guarantee basic

---

7   The list of relevant human-rights instruments is lengthy and includes the Universal Declaration of Human Rights; the International Covenant on Civil and Political Rights; the International Covenant on Economic, Social and Cultural Rights; the International Convention on the Elimination of All Forms of Racial Discrimination; the Convention on the Elimination of All Forms of Discrimination against Women; the Convention against Torture and Other Cruel, Inhuman or Degrading Treatment or Punishment; the Convention on the Rights of the Child; the International Convention on the Protection of the Rights of All Migrant Workers and Members of Their Families; the International Convention for the Protection of All Persons from Enforced Disappearance, Convention on the Rights of Persons with Disabilities. Most importantly, it includes Convention on the Status of Refugees.

rights to everyone with whom the Canadian government interacts.[8] Various sections of the Charter recognize that the rights enumerated therein vest in "everyone." In *Singh v. Minister of Employment and Immigration* (1985), the Supreme Court acknowledged that non-citizens who are subject to the jurisdiction of the Canadian government are included within the ambit of this broad term. Thus, it is unconstitutional to deprive a person of the rights to life, liberty, and security of the person, except in accordance with the principles of fundamental justice no matter to which immigration category the person in question belongs. Similarly, *everyone* has the "fundamental freedoms" enumerated in section 2 of the Charter.

However, the Charter also guarantees some rights to citizens.[9] Section 6(1), for example, guarantees the right to enter, remain in and leave Canada to "[e]very citizen of Canada." It also explicitly recognizes that some constitutional rights vest in both citizens and permanent residents, but not in foreign nationals. For example, section 6(2) states that "[e]very citizen of Canada and every person who has the status of a permanent resident of Canada has the right (*a*) to move to and take up residence in any province."

These differentiations among right holders produce some knotty legal difficulties, particularly in relation to the rights identified in section 15 of the Charter, which stipulates that "*Every individual* is equal before and under the law and has the right to the equal protection and equal benefit of the law without discrimination and, in particular, without discrimination based on race, national or ethnic origin, colour, religion, sex, age or mental or physical disability" (emphasis added).

As a consequence of the broad scope of this provision—the entitlement vests in *every* individual—we are faced with the major difficulty of explaining how the differentiations on which immigration law is based, and which are endorsed within the Charter itself, can evade challenge under section 15. Are we going to say that the differential treatment envisaged both by the Charter and by Canadian immigration law does not infringe rights to equal treatment or equal protection? After all, section 15 does not require that all individuals be

---

8 There is important but not entirely convincing jurisprudence that limits the extraterritorial application of the Charter that I do not consider here; see *R v. Hape* (2007)

9 As an aside, it has not yet been settled authoritatively whether the Charter grants these unqualified rights *exclusively* to citizens, thereby preventing the legislature from expanding the relevant group to include non-citizens.

accorded the *same* treatment. It may be that a distinction between sameness and equality can be developed to allow for different but equal treatment. Or are we going to emphasize the element of discrimination and say that any distinction drawn between citizens and non-citizens is not discriminatory in the way that a distinction made on the basis of one of the enumerated factors listed in section 15 is? Another option would be to concede that distinctions between citizens and non-citizens are proscribed under section 15, but to argue that in most circumstances they will be justifiable under section 1 of the Charter (which provides that "The *Canadian Charter of Rights and Freedoms* guarantees the rights and freedoms set out in it subject only to such reasonable limits prescribed by law as can be demonstrably justified in a free and democratic society").

Instead of evaluating these and other options in the abstract, I shall first examine how the Canadian Supreme Court and other subordinate courts have unpacked these issues and then comment on the most obvious shortcomings of the analysis that they have offered.

Immigration and Equality: Judicial Analysis

The Supreme Court has allowed non-citizens to rely on section 15 to challenge laws that permit treatment different from that accorded to citizens, but it has limited severely the fields in which they may do so. In *Andrews v. Law Society of British Columbia* (1989), the court developed its permissive stance when it upheld a challenge by a permanent resident against a provincial law that limited access to the practice of law to Canadian citizens. The court also offered some general, *non-binding* opinion indicating that, in the right circumstances, a foreign national should also be able to win such a challenge.[10] The clearest reasons for the decision are offered by Justice Wilson, who refers generally to "non-citizens" as a group that may legitimately claim discrimination.

> Relative to citizens, non-citizens are a group lacking in political power and as such vulnerable to having their interests overlooked and their rights to equal concern and respect violated.

---

10 This analysis is *obiter* because the litigant in the case was a permanent resident and, therefore, any comment made about foreign nationals should not be regarded as a binding element of the judgement.

They are among "those groups in society to whose needs and wishes elected officials have no apparent interest in attending": see J. H. Ely, *Democracy and Distrust* (1980), at p. 151. Non-citizens, to take only the most obvious example, do not have the right to vote.... I would conclude therefore that non-citizens fall into an analogous category to those specifically enumerated in s. 15. *I emphasize, moreover, that this is a determination which is not to be made only in the context of the law which is subject to challenge but rather in the context of the place of the group in the entire social, political and legal fabric of our society.* While legislatures must inevitably draw distinctions among the governed, such distinctions should not bring about or reinforce the disadvantage of certain groups and individuals by denying them the rights freely accorded to others [...].

I believe also that it is important to note that the range of discrete and insular minorities has changed and will continue to change with changing political and social circumstances [...] It can be anticipated that the discrete and insular minorities of tomorrow will include groups not recognized as such today. (emphasis added) (at para. 5)

In other words, the default generalization is that, because non-citizens are identified as a historically disadvantaged and powerless group, a law that imposes further disadvantages on them will be regarded as discriminatory on a ground analogous to those listed in section 15 and, if it is to survive a challenge, its provisions would have to be justified by the government under section 1 of the Charter.

In *Andrews*, the court's analysis does not hinge on the specifics of the particular harm suffered by the appellant. Instead, it offers a general approach that ostensibly includes all types of harm that reinforce the disadvantageous predicament in which non-citizens find themselves. A similar conclusion is reached in a later case, *Lavoie v. Canada* (2002), that focused on a federal law that offered preferential access to employment in the public service to Canadian citizens. The implication would appear to be that section 15 applies to protect non-citizens from any law that draws a negative distinction between them and citizens, and, by so doing, imposes a disadvantage on them that entrenches or aggravates their precarious status within society.

However, this general analysis has not led the court to conclude that our immigration laws are presumptively discriminatory by virtue of their use of a suspect classification analogous to those listed in section 15. On the contrary, in a number of cases, the court has gone out of its way to stipulate that, *within the realm of immigration*, differentiation between citizens and non-citizens is generally acceptable, and that only in rare circumstances will such differentiation be open to challenge. For the most part, where immigration law imposes a liability on non-citizens that is not imposed on citizens, it will not usually be regarded as discriminatory. The clearest articulation of this view has been offered by former Chief Justice McLachlin in *Charkaoui v. Canada (Citizenship and Immigration)* (2007), where the appellant had challenged his detention while the government attempted to arrange his deportation, as a breach of section 15. She made the following statement:

> The appellant Mr. Charkaoui argues that the *IRPA* [Immigration and Refugee Protection Act] certificate scheme discriminates against noncitizens, contrary to s. 15(1) of the *Charter*. *However, s. 6 of the Charter specifically allows for differential treatment of citizens and noncitizens in deportation matters: only citizens are accorded the right to enter, remain in and leave Canada (s. 6(1)).* A deportation scheme that applies to noncitizens, but not to citizens, does not, for that reason alone, violate s. 15 of the *Charter: Chiarelli.*
>
> It is argued that while this is so, there are two ways in which the *IRPA* could, in some circumstances, result in discrimination. First, detention may become indefinite as deportation is put off or becomes impossible, for example because there is no country to which the person can be deported. Second, the government could conceivably use the *IRPA* not for the purpose of deportation, but to detain the person on security grounds. *In both situations, the source of the problem is that the detention is no longer related, in effect or purpose, to the goal of deportation* [...].
>
> Even though the detention of some of the appellants has been long — indeed, Mr. Almrei's continues — *the record on which we must rely does not establish that the detentions at issue have become unhinged from the state's purpose of deportation.* (emphases added, para. 129)

The general principle articulated in this passage is that, unless there is an independent constitutional reason for striking it down, an immigration law is immune from a section 15 challenge claiming that it violates a non-citizen's equality rights by imposing negative measures that do not apply to citizens. The presence of section 6 within the Charter establishes this immunity and legitimizes the use of the citizen/non-citizen distinction within the limits of the field.

There are a number of caveats that should not be ignored. As mentioned explicitly in the cited passage, where a particular scheme has been introduced for reasons unrelated to immigration or where it is impossible to achieve an immigration purpose by implementing the scheme in question, the immunization no longer holds. It also goes without saying that where an immigration law distinguishes among non-citizens on grounds identified in section 15 or other grounds analogous to those listed, the law will not be insulated from challenge. For example, a racist immigration law or one that distinguishes on the basis of national origin will not pass muster. Indeed, decisions from lower courts, such as *YZ v. Canada (Citizenship and Immigration)* (2016) and *Canadian Doctors for Refugee Care v. Canada (Attorney General)* (2014), have acknowledged this point and have determined that particular immigration laws have discriminated on these bases.

Moreover, a constitutional challenge to an immigration law may succeed when it is based on the claim that the law in question violates rights of non-citizens that are recognized in sections other than section 15.[11] The point being made in *Charkaoui* is not that citizens are the exclusive beneficiaries of the Charter, or that immigration laws are Charter-proof. It is that, because it is legitimate to distinguish between citizens and non-citizens for immigration purposes, this citizen/non-citizen distinction cannot be discriminatory as long as it operates as part of an immigration regime. While in other contexts it may be suspect to draw such a distinction between a vulnerable or historically disadvantaged group, this is not the case within the field of immigration itself. The importance of this point cannot be overemphasized. Effectively, it insulates our immigration laws from an important ground of judicial review. Essentially, the legal concept of equality is shaped by the border, rather than transactions at the border being subject to a transcendental concept of equality.

---

11 The courts frequently examine whether immigration laws and procedures violate s. 7 of the Charter and, in one celebrated decision, certain provisions denying health care to non-citizens were found to constitute cruel and unusual treatment contrary to s. 12; see *Canadian Doctors for Refugee Care v. Canada (Attorney General)* (2014).

The court's approach suffers from two substantial deficiencies. First, it is not at all clear what the court means when it talks about a law that goes beyond "the concerns of immigration law" or is "unhinged" from immigration purposes. Any law that imposes a condition on entry or on continuing residence in Canada may be construed as pursuing or being tied to immigration goals. As noted earlier, measures that limit access to the Canadian labour market or to educational institutions may also be characterized as relating to immigration. It is difficult to identify the criteria that may allow us to distinguish between immigration purposes and non-immigration purposes, and the Supreme Court has not offered any assistance on this issue. I ignore this broad issue, below, since it raises complex problems of general jurisprudence. Instead, I focus on a more pressing and discrete issue that relates to equality rights and discrimination. This second concern can be introduced by focusing on xenophobia.

The critical problem with the Supreme Court's analysis is that it does not recognize the need for a legal remedy to deal with cases where xenophobic antagonism to non-citizens has, or may reasonably be believed to have, tainted or infiltrated our immigration laws. Through its failure to acknowledge that xenophobic sentiments and ideologies may have influenced our immigration laws and policies, it is reasonable to conclude that the court is propounding the view that the penetration of xenophobic views into this field of law is a purely political issue that should be addressed exclusively within our political institutions, rather than as a legal matter to be addressed by the judiciary.

There are three overlapping reasons why this should be considered problematic. First, as noted, the court has recognized that, within other contexts, it is insupportable and objectionable, as a matter of general constitutional principle, to disadvantage individuals on the ground that they are non-citizens. It has acknowledged the need for judicial intervention in these other contexts, and has not demanded that the claimants should base an equality claim on other criteria such as race or national origin or on other grounds. It is sufficient to use lack of citizenship as the relevant fulcrum. The failure to recognize a legal remedy in the immigration context appears to introduce an element of inconsistency in its decision making.

As the quotation from Justice Wilson, cited above, makes clear, the court seems well aware of the vulnerable and precarious predicament in which non-citizens find themselves. By recognizing equality claims, the court is able to ensure that this predicament is not worsened further. To ground an equality claim, litigants have a heavy onus of establishing that they belong to a group that has historically suffered disadvantages. It is this historically entrenched context that allows us to consider any added burden as discriminatory. It is only because the court is willing to concede that non-citizens have met this onus that the court is able to recognize the basis of their claim as analogous to one of the grounds enumerated in section 15.

Yet, according to the Supreme Court's analysis of immigration law, even in a case where one can state categorically, and without any risk of contradiction, that a particular immigration law or a proposed measure was based on unwarranted prejudices against foreign nationals, or was being administered in ways that vilify, demean, or stereotype non-citizens, a court would be unable to provide an adequate correction. This would be the case even though the constitutional kernel on which egalitarian legal principles are based is that our legal institutions should prohibit such beliefs and sentiments from operating within the political realm. The incompatibility between the immigration case law and this basic principle is a major source of concern.

Second, the court's failure to advert to xenophobic antagonism as a relevant threat to non-citizens leaves it open to the critique that it mischaracterizes their experience, and the extent and nature of the harm they have endured and continue to suffer. The court is also open to the reproach that it mischaracterizes and underestimates a number of other factors: the dangers associated with xenophobia, how deeply entrenched it is within social life, the range of ways in which it can manifest itself, and the extent of its penetration of our political processes. While the court does recognize that non-citizens are in a particularly vulnerable position because elected officials have no reason to advert to their interests, there is nothing in Supreme Court jurisprudence to suggest that it recognizes that non-citizens have been and continue to be subject to widespread xenophobic abuse in their social relations, and even in their relations with the government itself. A search of the Quicklaw database reveals that "xenophobia" is not a term that has ever been used in a Supreme Court judgement.

To develop this critique further, it is fruitful to provide some more precision to the idea of xenophobia. Xenophobia is a phobia because it embraces an unfounded or irrational fear. This fear will be irrational where it sees grounds for suspicion of outsiders when none exists; where it magnifies any existing reason for suspicion beyond its actual dimensions or where it expands any reasonably grounded suspicion well beyond its justifiable ambit to include unrelated individuals. The unexamined or uninformed belief that individuals from different cultures are unwilling to respect established cultural practices or to coexist peaceably, and the resulting opinion that laws that facilitate immigration unavoidably increase social turmoil, may also be leading examples of xenophobic beliefs.

Xenophobia also presents itself where social and economic ills are traced to the influence or presence of outsiders without sufficient evidence to justify such a nexus. Where insiders feel seriously threatened by non-citizens—where, for example, they believe that their culture is being replaced by another, originating externally, or that their access to employment has been negatively affected or that non-citizens bear responsibility for the high crime rate within the country—they will demand government action in response and may advocate the imposition of excessive hardships on outsiders because of their general deterrent effect.

While regulation of access into Canada (as is permitted by section 6 of the Charter) may not in itself, and in the abstract, be considered xenophobic, one's suspicions that irrational xenophobic sentiments underlie any specific law or any particular set of provisions may be confirmed by the actual mode of regulation that has been selected.

Generally speaking, one should address five issues when determining whether a particular mode of regulation has xenophobic underpinnings: First, are the measures in question gratuitously harsh? Is their serious impact on various groups necessary to achieve the beneficial or justifiable social purposes for which they are said to be introduced? Do they show an awareness of and adequate concern for the interests of those directly affected?

Second, are the measures over-inclusive? Where the law identifies a legitimate threat, is it tailored sufficiently to target only those individuals whose behaviour is problematic, or does it cast a wider net that imposes a negative impact on others who present no risk?

Third, do they impose serious hardship on some individuals who have merely exercised their rights or who have failed to meet demanding conditions, solely to deter large numbers of others from engaging in similar conduct? In other words, do they impose unreasonably high burdens on some individuals in order to provide a disincentive for others to avoid the conduct in question?

Fourth, are they prompted by antagonism toward outsiders, or by a willingness to pander to groups within the polity who bear such resentment? Does the government's justification for the law include explicit or encoded messages that those who are subject to it are less worthy of respect?

Fifth, can one identify throughout the history of this field of law, or throughout its current iteration, other harsh, over-inclusive, or callously instrumentalist laws that would support the idea that the particular law in question is part of a more general antagonistic response to non-citizens rather than an exceptional or unique measure?

It is also important to note that xenophobic measures need not uniformly oppress all non-citizens in the same way, although they might. The fact that some groups of non-citizens may be able to escape the application of a particular rule does not show that that rule is not an instantiation of xenophobia. As is emphasized in many judicial statements about substantive equality, the discovery of formal differences in treatment among subgroups need not lead to the conclusion that the measure should not be identified as an instantiation of a more general assault on the whole group. In anti-discrimination law, we are familiar with the idea that a group may be targeted as a whole even where that some individuals who belong to a maligned group may be able to escape negative treatment.[12] It is for this reason that it is both misleading and unsatisfactory to require non-citizens alleging discrimination within the immigration regime to show that differential treatment is being imposed on different groups of non-citizens. Xenophobia does not necessarily reveal itself as a consistent pattern of conduct against all outsiders. Excessively harsh rules may be created and implemented haphazardly, with little concern about their effect. It is justifiable to describe a measure as xenophobic even when it has no negative impact on some non-citizens.

---

12 The point is made clearly by Lord Hoffman in *Islam v. Secretary of State for the Home Department* (1999, 648), a refugee case: "Suppose oneself in Germany in 1935. There is discrimination against Jews in general, but not all Jews are persecuted. Those who conform to the discriminatory laws, wear yellow stars out of doors and so forth can go about their ordinary business. But those who contravene the racial laws are persecuted. Are they being persecuted on grounds of race? In my opinion, they plainly are. It is therefore a fallacy to say that because not all members of a class are being persecuted, it follows that persecution of a few cannot be on grounds of membership of that class."

Indeed, a major aspect of xenophobic policies is their arbitrary and inconsistent application, which increases their negative psychological impact. This occurs when the law in question is introduced without adequate consideration being shown for the potential impacts it might have, or when it is part of a series of measures that cumulatively reveal a lack of concern for the well-being of non-citizens. When one group of non-citizens is selected for egregious treatment in one situation, this raises the spectre that other groups will be treated likewise in others. Requiring a non-citizen to show discrimination on another independent ground, when one can discern such a general pattern, is to impose an unjustified burden and misses the point.

In addition, the fact that a law accords the same treatment to all non-citizens does not entail that the law shows adequate levels of respect for non-citizens. As Justice Wilson notes in the passage cited above, the non-citizen is recognized to have rights to be treated with equal concern and respect. The non-citizen has not been recognized to have the right to be accorded the same treatment as other non-citizens.

The claim that xenophobia is an entrenched and systemic aspect of our social relations—that in our social and political life, non-citizens experience antagonism and hardship solely because they are non-citizens—has become familiar and has gained widespread attention (Smith and Levin 2017). Prime Minister Justin Trudeau has noted the continuing presence of xenophobia in society when apologizing publicly for an incident in 1939, when the Canadian government turned away refugee claimants on board the MS *St. Louis*, and has called upon "Canada and all Canadians [to] stand up against xenophobic and anti-Semitic attitudes that still exist in our communities, in our schools and in our places of work" (Trudeau 2018).

Xenophobia has also come to be recognized internationally as a social scourge that, while usually experienced domestically, can also traverse national borders. Hence, collective multilateral solutions are sought. The recently signed Global Compact for Secure, Orderly and Regular Migration (2018) makes multiple references to xenophobia and reveals high levels of concern about its rise. For example, it states:

> By implementing the Global Compact, we ensure effective respect, protection and fulfilment of the human rights of all migrants, regardless of their migration status, across all stages of

the migration cycle. [...] We also reaffirm the commitment to eliminate all forms of discrimination, including racism, xenophobia and intolerance against migrants and their families. (sec. 15[f])

A multilateral response is identified as appropriate: "We commit to eliminate all forms of discrimination, condemn and counter expressions, acts and manifestations of racism, racial discrimination, violence, xenophobia and related intolerance against all migrants in conformity with international human rights law" (Global Compact, sec. 33).

A further source of insight in the Canadian context is the *Report of the Special Rapporteur on Contemporary Forms of Racism, Racial Discrimination, Xenophobia and Related Intolerance,* focusing on Canada, in which Doudou Diène, the rapporteur, makes the following remarks:

Compared with other countries in North America, particularly those bearing a heavy legacy of discrimination and possessing a similar demographic and cultural structure, Canada has undoubtedly achieved remarkable progress in its legal and political strategy for combating racial discrimination. The constitutional, legal and legislative framework established by successive governments provides a solid legal basis and the expression of a clear political will to fight racial discrimination and to offer remedies to its victims. This legal and political strategy, however, does reveal a number of shortcomings. [...]

In the first place, it suffers from a lack of vigilance, flexibility, adaptability and creativeness. Discrimination in fact presents a shifting landscape, whose colours, contours and textures are transformed and evolve, inconspicuously and ineffably, under the pressure of migratory movements or ideological and ethical factors, or as a result of the dilemmas and contradictions of multiculturalism and bilingualism. [...] So the Canadian multicultural landscape is constantly changing under the demographic and cultural influence of successive waves of immigration and the ideological and political impact of the situation and climate in the region and in the world at large. In the Special Rapporteur's view, this environment is particularly exposed to xenophobic and racist political platforms, which emerge like poisonous plants whenever national identity safeguards are disrupted by the thrust of pluralism, arising either from historical events such as slavery, colonization and imperial expansion or from immigration or globalization. [...]

Like most countries, Canada does not appear to have grasped the magnitude of this submerged part of the racist iceberg. And yet it is only by taking account of this intangible dimension of racism, through an appropriate intellectual and ethical strategy, that it will be possible in the longer term, with the help of legal strategy, to ensure the eradication of racism and discrimination. (Diène 2004, 21)

Nevertheless, the Supreme Court has, as yet, declined to mandate that our immigration laws show the levels of "effective respect" that the compact mandates. Moreover, the government generally has failed to heed the special rapporteur's recommendation that it should engage in "an in-depth assessment of the relevance and effectiveness of existing constitutional, legislative, judicial and administrative measures, and on the other hand on the principle of vigilance, flexibility and adaptability to the changing challenges and forms of discrimination, particularly in a country experiencing a major dynamic of migration" (Diène 2004, 24).

Against the established background of resentment and antagonism faced by non-citizens, it should be sufficient to mount a successful section 15 challenge for a non-citizen to point to a law's unnecessary harshness, its over-inclusiveness, its reliance on exemplary mistreatment to achieve instrumental ends, and to a legislative history that reveals xenophobic sentiments. It is particularly unsatisfactory for a court to demand that migrants rely on rights other than those found in the equality section of the Charter: the treatment in question may be insufficient to meet the substantial definitions found in other provisions of the Charter (such as the definition of cruel and unusual treatment, or the definition of the right to life, liberty, and security of the person).

A third problem with the Supreme Court's analysis is that we have come to recognize that it is especially within the field of immigration law that xenophobia is most likely to find fertile ground in which it can establish roots and prosper. It is jarring to find that the court is willing to extend an immunity in a field where the problems are the most severe, and where politicians have failed to offer protection.

For example, in the recent past, we have become familiar with governments, political parties, and demagogues stoking fears and kindling widespread antagonism toward outsiders, and doing so with particular reference to migrants. Electoral successes or increases in public support are sought by promising to address the resulting anxieties by rendering our immigration laws less user-friendly, by criminalizing regulatory breaches. Political power is maintained by pandering to the demands of xenophobic groups, and by adopting their views and constructing policies around them. Without any hint of embarrassment, many governments have notoriously responded to such demands by introducing harsh or callous measures into their immigration laws, justifying them by pointing to exaggerated threats and by vilifying the "barbaric practices" of those seeking citizenship.[13] Frequently, the oppressive measures are not concealed but publicized widely, along with descriptions of the misery that they impose, as a negative incentive for those who might be tempted to circumvent immigration regulations or take positive steps to seek humanitarian relief from the government.

Neither is this solely a modern phenomenon. Historians have recognized the many occasions in which nativist or xenophobic ideologies have gained widespread popular support, influenced immigration policy-making, and led to legal changes. Kelley and Trebilcock (2010, 464) have noted that:

> narrow (nativist) conceptions of community...and ideological hostility to collectivism in the organization of the economy seem largely to explain the exclusion of Asian and black immigrants,... the refusal to admit Jewish refugees before and during the Second World War, the internment of Japanese Canadians during the Second World War, the screening out of alleged Communist sympathizers on national security grounds during the 1950s and 1960s.

Recent immigration restrictions introduced by the United States government have gained worldwide media attention. Measures instituting a travel ban for all individuals from identified countries (Executive Order 13780, 2017) and enforcing separation of children from their

---

13 In Canada, the relevant statute is the Zero Tolerance for Barbaric Cultural Practices Act (2015).

parents, who are subsequently deported, have been accorded particular prominence (Jordan 2019). The full details of the measures taken have been concealed and the reasons behind the need to take such measures have been found to be wanting (Ward and Singhvi 2019). Indeed, recent research has indicated that anti-immigrant rhetoric from the executive branch in the United States has magnified already widespread xenophobic resentment (Flores and Schachter 2018).

With all this in mind, one should return to consider the severe measures introduced within Canada to which reference was made at the beginning of this chapter. Cumulatively, these should give rise to concern that xenophobic sentiments have informed and may continue to inform our immigration policies. The amendments introduced by succeeding governments have been both harsh and over inclusive. The language in which they are expressed has been both general and categorical, with insufficient concern paid to the wide range of extreme hardships that may be suffered by those who fall within their ambit. In many cases, these measures have been introduced unapologetically because of their general deterrent effect. For example, as is noted by the Canadian Association of Refugee Lawyers, the measures found in the Budget Implementation Act (2019) "would bar refugee claimants who have simply 'made a claim' in a country with whom Canada has an information-sharing agreement from having their claim heard by the IRB—without any regard to whether a decision was *ever* made on that claim. As a result, the proposed changes will bar access to the IRB for persons whom no country has ever decided whether they are refugees or not" (Canadian Association of Refugee Lawyers 2019).

Similar overgeneralization, indicating a lack of concern for the predicaments of particular individuals, can be found in measures that are already in force. Various individuals seeking to remain in Canada have been barred from access to an independent tribunal in a number of contexts where the details of their circumstances are regarded as irrelevant; for instance, those seeking to avoid deportation who have committed minor offences may not appear before a tribunal to present their account of what actually occurred.[14] Detention is a more frequent response to irregular entry, and in some cases is a mandatory response applying even to children.[15] The government has also introduced

---

14 See IRPA s.64 (appeals to Immigration Appeal Division unavailable to individuals sentenced to six months' imprisonment).

15 IRPA s. 55(3.1) (mandatory detention for children aged 16 and over).

harsh over-inclusive provisions to deal with fraudulent family sponsorships and has failed to develop workable and nuanced criteria to
distinguish between fraudulent and "genuine" cases.[16] Moreover,
backed by public statements from the immigration minister prejudg-
ing refugee claimants as bogus queue jumpers (Kenney 2012), a variety
of stringent measures have been introduced (Canadian Association of
Refugee Lawyers 2012). In a case in which some of these have been
quashed, the minister has been criticized seriously by the Federal
Court for the use of such rhetoric (Canadian Doctors for Refugee
Care v. Canada [Attorney General] 2014).

It is not unreasonable to suspect that these packages of immigration and citizenship reforms have helped stoke the irrational fears of
those who feel threatened by newcomers, and have appealed to and
increased the confidence and strength of anti-immigrant groups and
organizations. Moreover, it is not unreasonable to suspect that the irrational fears of xenophobes may have reciprocally influenced the
government's decision to develop and implement the relevant measures. It would not be outlandish to conclude that, although each
measure of harsh treatment is directed at a discrete and narrowly
defined category of non-citizen, each measure operates something like
a single pixel that, only in combination with many others, presents the
viewer with a comprehensible image. In this case, the cumulative message from the government could be interpreted as the message that in
our immigration processes the interests of the existing citizenry
always come first and extreme measures may be imposed where these
interests might be in jeopardy. Each prominent example of harsh treatment is intended to assuage the general fears of anxious insiders and
to respond to their demands.

Conclusion

I have argued that the Canadian Supreme Court's decisions that
immunize immigration laws from an important form of judicial
review by denying that they can discriminate on the basis of

---

16 Immigration and Refugee Protection Regulations (2002), s. 130(3), originally
   introduced in 2012, which requires a person who has been sponsored as a spouse
   to be a permanent resident or citizen for five years before they can themselves
   sponsor a person as their spouse.

non-citizenship status fail dismally to respect fundamental principles of equality that underpin the Canadian Constitution and international law. I do not mean to imply that Canada is an outlier within the global community. On the contrary, I suspect that among most, if not all liberal democracies, equality rights have been circumscribed in a similar fashion. It is my lack of familiarity with substantive law in other jurisdictions that prevents me from making this wider claim. However, my arguments have a normative application beyond Canada. While conceding that it may be quite justifiable in the abstract to draw lines that distinguish the rights of foreign nationals, permanent residents, and citizens, it is important to examine each measure within its broad historical and social context before determining that it accords with liberal-democratic norms.

Rather than disallow equality-based challenges to our immigration laws, we should welcome litigation that seeks to prove suspicions that our immigration laws may have been shaped by the influence of xenophobic ideologies which may, in turn, have been fertilized by existing government laws and policies. Even where oppressive immigration laws are applicable to all non-citizens and differentiate them as a class from citizens, we should welcome a forum for review in which we can scrutinize their full impact on non-citizens so that we can appraise accurately the actual harms and benefits they impose on members of the class to which they apply. We should examine each measure within its historical and legislative context to identify whether patterns of antagonism toward non-citizens emerge, and determine whether any particular law conforms to the pattern and further entrenches it. Only then should we consider government reasons for imposing such rules, and if we find evidence of xenophobia within our law, the legal burden on the government to justify the measures should be a heavy one.

References

Cases

Andrews v. Law Society of British Columbia, 1 S.C.R. 143 (1989).

Attorney General for the Dominion of Canada v. Cain, AC 542 (J.C.P.C.) (1906).

Canadian Doctors for Refugee Care v. Canada (Attorney General), F.C.J. No. 679 (2014).

Charkaoui v. Canada (Citizenship and Immigration), 1 S.C.R. 350, 2007 SCC 9 (2007).
Islam v. Secretary of State for the Home Department, and Regina v. Immigration Appeal Tribunal, ex parte Shah, 2 A.C. 629 (1999).
Lavoie v. Canada, 1 S.C.R. 769 (2002).
R. v. Hape, 2 S.C.R. 292 (2007).
Singh v. Minister of Employment and Immigration, [1985] 1 S.C.R. 177.
YZ v. Canada (Citizenship and Immigration), 1 FCR 575, 2015 FC 892 (2016).

International, Constitutional, and Legislative Sources

Canadian Charter of Rights and Freedoms, Part I of the Constitution Act, 1982, being Schedule B to the Canada Act 1982 (UK), 1982, c 11.
Executive Order 13780, Protecting the Nation from Foreign Terrorist Entry into the United States (March 6, 2017) (United States). https://www.federalregister.gov/documents/2017/03/09/2017-04837/protecting-the-nation-from-foreign-terrorist-entry-into-the-united-states.
Global Compact for Safe, Orderly and Regular Migration. Resolution adopted by the General Assembly of the United Nations on December 19, 2018, A/Res/73/195. http://www.un.org/en/ga/search/view_doc.asp?symbol=A/RES/73/195.
Immigration and Refugee Protection Act (IRPA), S.C 2001, c. 27.
Immigration and Refugee Protection Regulations (SOR/2002-227).
Zero Tolerance for Barbaric Cultural Practices Act, S.C. 2015, c. 29.

Books and Articles

Amnesty International. 2012. *Unbalanced Reforms: Recommendations with Respect to Bill C-31*. Brief to the House of Commons Standing Committee on Citizenship and Immigration, April 17, 2012. https://www.amnesty.ca/sites/amnesty/files/ai_brief_bill_c_31_to_parliamentary_committee_0.pdf.
Blackstone, Sir William. 1765. *Commentaries on the Law of England*. Oxford: Printed at the Clarendon Press. https://avalon.law.yale.edu/subject_menus/blackstone.asp.
Canadian Association of Refugee Lawyers. 2012. *List of Bill C-31 Resources*. https://carl-acaadr.ca/bill-c-31-the-new-refugee-system/.
——. 2019. "Clawbacks In Budget Implementation Act." April 26, 2019. https://carl-acaadr.ca/our-work/on-the-issues/clawbacks-in-budget-implementation-act/.
Diène, Doudou. 2004. *Racism, Racial Discrimination, Xenophobia and All Forms of Discrimination*. United Nations Human Rights Office of the High

Commissioner, Economic and Social Council, Commission on Human Rights. Document E/CN.4/2004/18/Add.2, March 1. https://www.refworld.org/docid/3f4a10c34.html.

Flores, Rene D., and Ariela Schachter. 2018. "Who Are the 'Illegals'? The Social Construction of Illegality in the United States." *American Sociological Review* 83(5): 839–868. https://doi.org/10.1177/0003122418794635.

Jordan, Miriam. 2019. "Family Separation May Have Hit Thousands More Children Than Reported." *New York Times*, January 17. https://www.nytimes.com/2019/01/17/us/family-separation-trump-administration-migrants.html.

Kawai, David. 2018. "UN Refugee Agency Official Says Migrant Crises Are 'Far Away from North America.'" *Globe and Mail*, November 8. https://www.theglobeandmail.com/canada/article-un-refugee-agency-official-says-migrant-crises-are-far-away-from/?cmpid=rss.

Kelley, Ninette, and Michael Trebilcock. 2010. *The Making of the Mosaic*. Toronto: University of Toronto Press.

Kenney, Jason. 2012. "Speaking Notes for The Honourable Jason Kenney, P.C., M.P. Minister of Citizenship, Immigration and Multiculturalism." News conference following the tabling of Bill C-31, Ottawa, February 16, 2012. https://www.canada.ca/en/immigration-refugees-citizenship/news/archives/speeches-2012/jason-kenney-minister-2012-02-16.html.

Smith, Craig S., and Dan Levin. 2017. "As Canada Transforms, an Anti-Immigrant Fringe Stirs." *New York Times*, January 21. https://www.nytimes.com/2017/01/31/world/americas/canada-quebec-nationalists.html.

Stroud, Philippa, Rhiannon Jones, and Stephen Brien. 2018. *Global People Movements*. Report published by the Legatum Institute Foundation in partnership with Oxford Analytica. https://lif.blob.core.windows.net/lif/docs/default-source/default-library/legj6267_global-people-movements-180622.pdf?sfvrsn=0.

Trudeau, Justin. 2018. *Statement of Apology on behalf of the Government of Canada to the Passengers of the MS* St. Louis. Prime Minister of Canada, November 7, 2018. https://pm.gc.ca/eng/news/2018/11/07/statement-apology-behalf-government-canada-passengers-ms-st-louis.

Ward, Joe, and AnJali Singhvi. 2019. "Trump Claims There Is a Crisis at the Border. What's the Reality." *New York Times*, January 11. https://www.nytimes.com/interactive/2019/01/11/us/politics/trump-border-crisis-reality.html.

PART III

NEW PERSPECTIVES,
CHALLENGING OLD THINKING

CHAPTER 7

Refugee Sponsorship: Navigating the Borders of Expansion and Restriction of the Protection Regime

Sabine Lehr

Refugee sponsorship by private persons has a long tradition in Canada. It is generally understood that the Private Sponsorship of Refugees Program (PSRP) formally started with the coming into effect of the Immigration Act of 1976, in April 1978, and the subsequent sponsorship of 34,000 refugees fleeing the crisis in Southeast Asia in 1979–1980. However, the origins of the program can be traced back much further. Cameron (2021) has argued that the program evolved along a developmental path from negotiations between religious actors and the Canadian government in the wake of large-scale displacement after the Second World War.[1]

For a long time, there were few other countries in the world that allowed private citizens and permanent residents to become involved in bringing refugees to their respective jurisdictions, and none of these programs matched the Canadian model in size. In 1986, Canada and "the people of Canada" were awarded the Nansen Refugee Award in recognition of their exceptional contribution to the protection of refugees; this was the first and only time a nation was the recipient of this award (Abella and Molnar 2016). In recent years, as a result of the

---

1 There are examples of earlier resettlement following similar patterns, in particular of Mennonite and Jewish displaced persons, in the late nineteenth and early twentieth century. For a detailed discussion, see Kelley and Trebilcock, 2010.

large-scale displacement of Syrians, awareness regarding the scale of the global refugee crisis has risen among the general public internationally. As a consequence, states and citizens on different continents have become interested in exploring private and/or community sponsorship of refugees (PSR/CSR), which has brought the Canadian model into global focus.

To support this interest, the Global Refugee Sponsorship Initiative (GRSI) was announced in New York in conjunction with the UN and U.S. refugee summits of September 2016 and was formally launched in Ottawa in December 2016. GRSI is a joint initiative led by the Government of Canada, the United Nations High Commissioner for Refugees (UNHCR), the Open Society Foundations, the Giustra Foundation, and the University of Ottawa (GRSI 2018b). By July 2018, several countries had committed to developing community-based refugee-sponsorship programs, and other countries were exploring this option. The idea of PSR/CSR was also included in the final text of the Global Compact on Refugees (GCR), adopted December 2018 by the member states of the UN General Assembly (United Nations 2018).

PSR/CSR programs are hailed for a variety of reasons. The GCR identifies PSR/CSR as one of a number of "complementary pathways for admission to third countries" (United Nations 2018, 18–19), signifying that such programs are additional or complementary to regular, state-led resettlement. Due to their complementarity, PSR/CSR programs are supposed to substantially increase the availability of global protection spaces for refugees. The European Resettlement Network (ERN) has identified the following motivating factors regarding complementary pathways to protection, including PSR/CSR schemes:

- Increased opportunities and perspectives for those in need of international protection (added-value approach).
- Quality protection that enhances the possibility of self-development for refugees.
- Greater responsibility-sharing and solidarity with countries of first asylum.
- Involvement of a range of stakeholders, including community engagement and integration leading to a strengthening of public support for refugees (IOM and ICMC 2018b).

PSR/CSR schemes are particularly attractive to states from a cost-benefit perspective: They allow for enhanced engagement in the global refugee regime, which is of increasing importance for states that have signed the GCR, while at the same time limiting the deployment of public resources. The 2016 evaluation of Canada's three resettlement program streams revealed an increase in the cost per decision for government-assisted refugees (GAR) between fiscal years 2011/2012 and 2014/2015, whereas the cost per decision for privately sponsored refugees (PSR) decreased over the same time period (IRCC 2016, 37). The differential between GAR and PSR cost per decision during the last reference year was only $71; however, the real saving for the Canadian government lies in the fact that PSRs do not receive any support from the federal Resettlement Assistance Program (RAP) during their first 12 months in Canada—they are fully supported by their sponsors. Since that evaluation, the gap in the average cost per refugee between GAR and PSR has grown wider. In 2019, Immigration, Refugees and Citizenship Canada (IRCC) indicated that the average cost per PSR refugee was only 26 percent of the cost of a GAR refugee (IRCC 2020a).

In this chapter, I critically examine the idealistic concepts of complementarity and additionality enshrined in PSR/CSR schemes. I view these concepts as "idealistic" because a widely accepted definition of these terms does not exist. The UNHCR (2019, 5) defines complementary pathways for admission as "safe and regulated avenues for refugees that complement resettlement by providing lawful stay in a third country where their international protection needs are met. They are additional to resettlement and do not substitute the protection afforded to refugees under the international protection regime."

The "ideals" enshrined in this definition comprise legality, non-substitution of protection, and separation from resettlement. In this chapter, I problematize this idealistic understanding of complementarity based on the Canadian situation, where refugee sponsorship is part of the country's resettlement regime and therefore does not fit the UNHCR's definition. The definition assumes a clear baseline or quota for traditional, state-led resettlement, with PSR/CSR refugees being "additional" or "complementary" to this baseline. This approach is well aligned with countries that have established resettlement programs but have recently started exploring or implementing PSR/CSR schemes. However, my argument is based on the Canadian experience of a mature refugee sponsorship program with a decades-long tradition, where immigration admissions through refugee sponsorship have become a core component of resettlement immigration planning. I argue that, in this context, the baseline is not the number of refugees admitted through government sponsorship but, rather, the totality of planned admissions in the refugee category, which are divided up among the various subcategories. I assess complementarity and additionality in the context of finite annual refugee-admission numbers, resulting in a situation in which the refugee sponsorship program potentially "competes" with traditional, state-led resettlement and irregular arrivals of refugees. Although it remains unclear what exactly would constitute a breach of additionality, many refugee advocates believe that such a breach occurs when the number of resettled sponsored refugees exceeds the number of refugees resettled through state sponsorship (IRCC 2016, 14). Such number distortion risks "'reverse engineer[ing]' additionality when negotiating the state quota in relation to community sponsorship" (Feith Tan 2020, para. 22). As PSR/CSR programs emerge elsewhere and mature over time, insights gathered from Canada provide reflection points for stakeholders in other jurisdictions. My reflections are further informed by direct experiences and communication with stakeholders I had the opportunity to meet during GRSI visits to Europe.

My contribution is embedded in this volume's broader aspiration to critically interrogate the governance of borders and migration at a time of unprecedented global migration movements. In their introduction, the editors note that state sovereignty is changing, with non-state actors playing an increasingly important role in the management of borders. In spite of this, governments at the national level, frequently in collaboration with lower levels of government, still retain ultimate control over borders. My examination of PSR/CSR offers an illustration of this tension. Private or community refugee sponsorship is an attempt to empower community groups in assisting refugees and settling them in Canada. As such, the PSR program opens an additional avenue for cross-border mobility and immigration for a vulnerable group. However, these refugees are still vetted and approved by the state. Furthermore, adding avenues for protection without a concomitant shift in border governance to a less restrictive paradigm simply increases "congestion at the border": it creates a tension between more protection through civil-society-driven modes of expanding the humanitarian commitment of the state on the one hand and a possible additional vehicle for migration control on the other, as governments may freeze or lower the number of state-sponsored refugees and hope to curb irregular arrivals at their borders by offering "legal pathways" for those with community sponsorship supports.

In light of these tensions, I end my chapter by offering some recommendations on how states can achieve the aspirational nature of complementarity and additionality through PSR/CSR to maximize protection and global responsibility-sharing.

Brief Historical Perspective on the PSRP in Canada

Canada's PSRP has its origins in the European displacement resulting from the Second World War. During the 30 years following the end of the war, civil-society organizations (mostly faith-based) gained increasing influence over refugee resettlement to Canada. Even though this influence was uneven—the postwar burst tapered off and then returned in the lead-up to the Immigration Act of 1976—the trajectory was upward.[2] Civil society lobbied to influence and broaden the parameters for refugee admission, gradually opening resettlement pathways for refugees reflecting more humanitarian selection and less ideologically and labour-market-linked selection (Cameron 2021; Epp 2017, 13–16). These efforts impacted the Immigration Act of 1976 (effected 1978), which formally brought refugee sponsorship into Canada's immigration law for the first time. The new program was immediately tested during the short but intense resettlement of refugees fleeing the crisis in Southeast Asia: over the course of 1979 and 1980, 34,000 privately sponsored refugees arrived in Canada (Labman 2012, 156).

Since the late 1970s, Canada's resettlement programs, and the private refugee sponsorship therein, have evolved in three distinct phases. Figure 7.1 provides a schematic overview of Canada's refugee resettlement from 1979 to 2020 in the three categories of GAR, PSR, and, since 2013, the Blended Visa Office-Referred Program, or BVOR.

Phase one spanned a period of approximately 15 years, from 1978 to 1993, and included two distinct peaks. The first peak signified the resettlement of Southeast Asian refugees following the coming into force of the Immigration Act. The second peak occurred during the last years of the Cold War, with the eastern European designated classes. Designated classes allowed for admission of those who did not fit the Refugee Convention definition but who were in refugee-like situations (Epp 2017, 16)—a normative category that gained increasing importance

---

2   A fuller historic examination of this period is outside the scope of this chapter. For a more in-depth discussion, see Kelley and Trebilcock 2010.

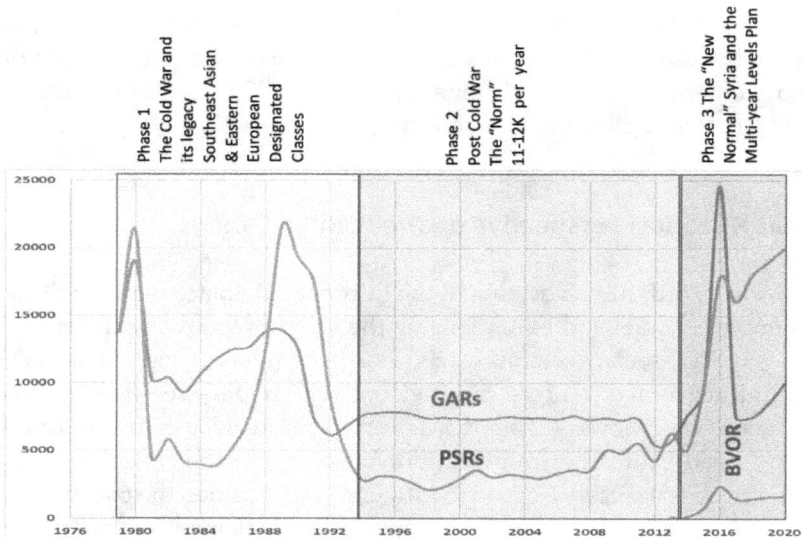

FIGURE 7.1. Canada's Refugee Resettlement, 1979–2020.
Source: Johnson and Smith 2018.

and later morphed into the "Country of Asylum Class" (IRCC 2018d), under which refugees are now regularly resettled to Canada.

During both peak periods, the number of refugees resettled as PSRs exceeded those resettled as GARs. Outside of the peak periods, GARs outnumbered PSRs by a factor of about 2:1. After the end of the Cold War, the Canadian resettlement program moved into a more or less steady phase, during which the country resettled approximately 11,000–12,000 refugees annually. During this 20-year phase, Canada consistently resettled more GARs than PSRs, although the gap between the two programs narrowed toward the end. In 2013, Canada resettled more PSRs than GARs for the first time since the peak at the end of the Cold War. The year 2013 was also the first during which a small number of refugees were resettled under the new BVOR program, introduced by the Canadian government in 2012. The BVOR program drew criticism from refugee advocates because the government's motivation for launching this program was a desire to save money to achieve deficit reduction, while still meeting a commitment to increased resettlement numbers (CCR 2013). Advocates highlighted that the program violated the principle of additionality enshrined in the PSRP. In its departmental performance report for 2011/2012, Citizenship and

Immigration Canada (CIC) stated that "CIC plans increase the number of PSRs to be resettled in a year by 1,000, which *will replace an equivalent number of government-assisted refugees*. Over the coming year, the Department will work with sponsors to identify populations of interest that may be referred by the United Nations High Commissioner for Refugees as PSRs in 2013" (CIC 2013; emphasis added).

The BVOR program was, therefore, initially conceptualized to replace GARs with a refugee category that required less government funding rather than adding to the number of refugees resettled to Canada—a criticism that was clearly articulated at the time by the Canadian Council for Refugees (CCR 2013).

Phase three coincided with the escalation of the Syrian humanitarian crisis, the election of the Liberal government under Justin Trudeau in October 2015, and the mass movement of mostly Middle Eastern refugees from Turkey through Greece and the Balkans toward western and northern Europe. The newly elected government's promise to settle 25,000 government-assisted Syrian refugees, coupled with temporary facilitative measures to allow sponsors to submit high numbers of additional refugees for resettlement to Canada, resulted in the historically largest refugee resettlement effort across all three categories in 2016.[3]

In 2017, the government tabled its first multi-year immigration-levels plan that fixed PSR levels at double the GAR levels for years to come. The levels plan 2018–2020 and 2019–2021 confirm this radical shift in the ratio of GARs versus PSRs (IRCC 2017b, 2018c). For the first time in history, the government quietly positioned the PSRP as the main refugee resettlement program to Canada for the foreseeable future. At the same time, the government promoted the benefits of community refugee sponsorship both through the newly launched GRSI and during the two-year negotiation process on the GCR.

The GRSI and the GCR

As noted, the GRSI was announced in New York and then launched in Ottawa, in December 2016. The GRSI's primary purpose is to assist

---

3   For additional insights on the phases presented in this chapter, the reader may wish to consult the following sources: Carlaw 2017; Hyndman, Payne, and Jimenez 2017; Hynie 2018; Labman 2019; McKinley 2008; Treviranus and Casasola 2003.

states contemplating PSR/CSR schemes to learn from Canada's experience and support interested states in designing and implementing such programs within their specific context. GRSI's main activities encompass:

- Training and public education;
- Community building;
- Advisory services; and,
- Connecting networks (GRSI 2018b).

By July 2018, five countries (UK, Ireland, Argentina, Spain, and New Zealand) had officially committed to developing community-based refugee sponsorship programs in collaboration with GRSI (GRSI 2018a), and other countries (e.g., France, Germany, and Brazil) had also explored this option, in most cases through some level of involvement by Canada (Federal Ministry of the Interior 2018; IOM and ICMC 2018a; Jubilut and Zamur 2018). The GRSI and the idea of PSR/CSR has received a less enthusiastic response in a few other countries, for a number of reasons, including:

- Concern by states regarding admission of additional refugees due to adverse public discourse;
- Reluctance by civil society to take on financial obligations considered to be the state's responsibility; and,
- Opposition by civil society to creating different "tiers" of refugees where sponsored refugees receive more attention and better support than asylum seekers (this based on my personal observations and conversations during participation in GRSI missions).

Canada played a major role in advocating for increased refugee-protection spaces, especially through the inclusion of private/community sponsorship, in the GCR (IRCC 2018a, 10). PSR/CSR was ultimately included in the final text of the GCR, under the heading "Complementary Pathways for Admission to Third Countries," which forms part of the three-year strategy on resettlement called for by the GCR (United Nations 2018, 18–19). GRSI is explicitly mentioned in the text of the GCR, along with a clear indication that such programs ought to be "additional to regular resettlement" (United Nations 2018, 19). The GCR was adopted by UN member states during the UN

General Assembly on December 17, 2018 (UNHCR 2018). Nowhere in the text of the GCR is a clear explanation of the meaning of "additional to regular resettlement" provided; however, the wording assumes that PSR/CSR should be separate from state-led resettlement programs so as not to be confused with resettlement. In the context of Canada's PSRP, the concept of "additionality" goes back to the program's early days, after the coming into force of the Immigration Act in 1978, when private refugee sponsorship was *not* part of Canada's annual refugee-resettlement plan. Employment and Immigration Canada (1979, 2) wrote that "Canadian groups and organizations who are prepared to act as sponsors [...] will have a direct influence on the total number of refugees that can come to Canada. This is because refugees assisted in this way are admitted over and above those planned for in the government's annual refugee resettlement plan."

Although the government's motivations for this policy are not entirely clear, a memo of January 1978 by the deputy minister provides some possible rationale. The memo outlines how sponsors would not only be able to sponsor refugees meeting the Refugee Convention's definition of a refugee, and who the only refugees able to come to Canada under the regular resettlement program are, sponsors would also be able to sponsor "humanitarian cases" under a special program or class—also referred to in the memo as "borderline cases" (Employment and Immigration Canada 1978). The implication is that additionality in private sponsorship was not simply a matter of numbers, but that there was a qualitative component.

This is the basis on which the CCR defined additionality as follows: "Privately sponsored refugees are over and above the refugees resettled by the government (Government Assisted Refugees). Canadians want to know that their government is fulfilling its responsibility, on behalf of all Canadians, to protect refugees through resettlement, and that any refugees they sponsor are additional to those resettled by the government" (CCR, n.d.).

As soon as private sponsorship became incorporated into Canada's annual immigration and refugee resettlement plan, additionality became a contested proposition. By 1990, PSRs were included in annual levels planning (Dolin and Young 2002), and the original meaning of additionality was in jeopardy.

Before I proceed to interrogate complementarity and additionality in the Canadian context, I provide an overview of the conceptualization of sponsorship as a complementary pathway in Europe.

Sponsorship as a Complementary Pathway in Europe

Europe is facing a different geographic reality from Canada. Whereas Canada is surrounded by vast oceans in the north, west, and east, and has up until recently experienced relatively few refugee claimants entering from its southern border (although numbers entering from the United States have risen since 2017 and there have been previous fluctuations), Europe has seen a much larger number of people fleeing their home countries and looking for a new home arrive at its external borders.[4] Contrary to Canada, none of the European countries has a mature refugee sponsorship program, and the concept of community sponsorship has only recently started to be tested in some countries. The realities and discourses in which conversations about complementary pathways in general and PSR/CSR schemes specifically take place differ between Europe and Canada; however, as both jurisdictions find themselves at extreme ends of the sponsorship/asylum-seeker spectrum, they both offer important insights into the discussion about complementarity and additionality.

Much of the exploratory work on expanding and systematizing PSR/CSR in Europe has been carried out by the ERN, a joint initiative coordinated by the International Organization for Migration, the International Catholic Migration Commission, and the UNHCR. In fall 2017, within the EU-funded project ERN+ Developing Innovative European Models for the Protection of Refugees and Providing Support to New Resettlement Countries, the ERN published a scoping paper to take stock of existing sponsorship initiatives in Europe as a basis for exploring the future potential of such programs (IOM and ICMC 2017). The Canadian model was also included in the study for comparison purposes. The scoping paper briefly discussed the concepts of complementarity and additionality. Regarding complementarity, the authors were mostly concerned with the existence of a plethora of refugee statuses across Europe and the possible resulting confusion and differential treatment in regard to social benefits and other entitlements for the same refugee groups (37). Regarding additionality, the authors stressed the centrality of PSR/CSR programs resulting in a net increase to protection places offered under states' resettlement commitments (39). Two

---

4   "Refugee claimant" is the formal term used in Canada for a person arriving at the country's border and making a refugee claim, or making a claim from inside Canada. In many other jurisdictions, such persons are referred to as "asylum seekers."

suggestions were made on how this could be achieved: either by adding distinct PSR/CSR commitments to existing state resettlement commitments (pure numerical addition without criteria distinction) or by offering PSR/CSR programs for refugee nationalities not currently part of a state's resettlement commitment (numerical addition with criteria distinction).

In April 2018, the ERN published a follow-up paper that provided a strategic assessment of three complementary pathways—private or community-based sponsorship, humanitarian-admission programs, and higher-education opportunities—to enhance protection spaces in Europe (IOM and ICMC 2018b). The authors noted that, "in many of their mechanisms and operational procedures, some complementary pathways bear a close resemblance to resettlement" (IOM and ICMC 2018b, 9), thus qualifying the previous call for a clear distinction between resettlement and complementary pathways. In the document, the authors offer a qualitative understanding of additionality that goes beyond the earlier quantitative formulation:

> Complementary pathways can offer additionality beyond numbers and impact, for example by adding methodologies and partnerships other than those used in resettlement to process, receive and integrate refugees. These pathways can also add to existing resettlement programmes by offering opportunities to diversify the refugee populations that can benefit from such third country protection. (10)

In spite of the many references to additionality and complementarity, the ERN's comprehensive strategic assessment of complementary pathways does not offer a detailed discussion of these terms. I will therefore now take a closer look at these concepts, the meanings of which may be clear on the surface but, on closer examination, prove elusive.

Interrogating Complementarity and Additionality

Labman (2012, 141) noted: "Private sponsorship both adds to Canada's resettlement capacity and creates a division in resettlement between refugees entering through the government program and those brought to Canada by citizens." She has thus summarized the fundamental paradox of complementarity and additionality in regard to Canada's PSRP and its function of enhancing protection spaces, while at the same time being part of Canada's overall resettlement regime that operates based on set annual targets. The Canadian government appears to have a conflicted relationship with the principle of additionality. An IRCC (2016) evaluation of the resettlement programs contains two contradictory statements:

> Refugees in the PSR program are intended to be resettled in addition to those arriving under the GAR program, as the PSR program allows Canadians to get involved in refugee resettlement and offer protection space over and above what is provided directly by the government (i.e., principle of additionality). (2)
>
> Although the principle of additionality is not part of the PSR program theory, private sponsors felt that the PSR program was contradicting the principle of additionality, as in 2013, as the number of admitted PSRs was higher than the number of GARs. (14)

As mentioned earlier in this chapter, the fundamental contradiction regarding additionality arises from the fact that Canada's PSRP is formally incorporated into the refugee resettlement program. Canada's Refugee and Humanitarian Resettlement Program relies on the UNHCR and on private sponsors identifying refugees for resettlement (IRCC 2017a). In this way, the PSRP operates on equal footing with the GAR program. The advantage of this system is that private sponsorship is solidly embedded in Canada's policy framework on immigration and refugee protection, making it difficult for the government to challenge the role of private sponsorship. The disadvantage of Canada's system lies in that the lines between state-led resettlement and resettlement through sponsorship as a complementary pathway have become blurred. With finite overall annual immigration landing targets, of which refugee resettlement targets are a subset, resettlement becomes a trade-off between government-sponsored and privately sponsored refugees. As Labman (2016, 68) has noted, "the complementarity of the model risks collapse as it is weighed down by conflicting interests [and] maintenance of private sponsorship's complementary role remains the continual challenge. Additionality can too easily devolve into a relationship of over-reliance and dependence."

The situation becomes even more complicated when targets for accepted refugee claimants are factored into the annual immigration-levels planning process in the refugees-and-protected-persons subcategory. In Canada, sections 94(1) and 94(2)(b) of the Immigration and Refugee Protection Act of 2001 require that the immigration minister table a report in Parliament by November 1 of each year, which includes "the number projected to become permanent residents in the following year" (Government of Canada 2001, 85). Whereas refugee resettlement is a voluntary, humanitarian activity, the right to seek asylum is enshrined in the Refugee Convention, to which Canada is a signatory, and in Canada's Immigration and Refugee Protection Act (Hyndman, Payne, and Jimenez 2016; Labman 2012). The government has limited control over the number of persons that show up at Canada's border to make a refugee claim, and the number of persons subsequently found to be in need of protection—a decision made by the independent Immigration and Refugee Board of Canada. Until recently, Canada's cold ocean geography and the Safe Third Country Agreement with the United States have provided a relatively predictable environment regarding the arrival of refugee claimants (Hyndman, Payne, and Jimenez 2016), enabling Canada's government to include accepted claimants into its annual levels plan with a high degree of numerical confidence. These calculations are further aided by the fact that levels pertain to protected persons receiving permanent-resident status even though they may have received the protected status in previous years—hence, while the number of persons receiving protected status annually is not entirely predictable, immigration levels resulting from this population can be planned. However, with the changing political climate in the United States and a higher number of refugee claimants arriving in Canada, the annually planned targets for this category are no longer adequate to accommodate the number of claimants found to be in need of Canada's protection and, consequently, also being entitled to permanent residency (CCR 2018).

Figure 7.2 indicates the number of permanent residents Canada accepted in all refugee classes between 2006 and the second quarter of 2016.

Immigration Category	2006	2007	2008	2009	2010	2011	2012	2013	2014	2015	Q1-Q2 2016
Government-assisted refugees	7,327	7,572	7,296	7,429	7,266	7,363	5,426	5,728	7,626	9,491	15,647
Privately sponsored refugees	3,338	3,588	3,512	5,037	4,833	5,584	4,227	6,328	5,072	9,743	10,738
Refugees landed in Canada	15,883	11,696	6,995	7,206	9,038	10,743	8,586	8,204	7,944	8,677	6,456
Refugee Dependants	5,953	5,099	6,995	3,183	3,562	4,183	4,853	3,716	3,249	3,389	1,817
Blended Visa Office-Referred refugees	0	0	0	0	0	0	0	153	177	811	2,650
Resettled refugees	10,665	11,160	10,808	12,466	12,099	12,947	9,653	12,209	12,875	20,045	29,035
Accepted refugees claimants + dep	21,836	16,795	11,052	10,389	12,600	14,926	13,439	11,920	11,193	12,066	8,273
Refugees total	32,501	27,955	21,860	22,855	24,699	27,873	23,092	24,129	24,068	32,111	37,308

Source: IRCC, June 30, 2016 Data

FIGURE 7.2. Permanent Residents, All Refugee Classes, 2006–2016 (Second Quarter). *Source:* Adapted from Government of Canada, 2019.

In most years during this 10-year timeframe (with the exception of 2013 and 2015), GAR numbers were slightly higher than PSR numbers. Also noticeable is the reversal in the ratio of resettled refugees versus in-Canada accepted refugee claimants: in 2006 and 2007, accepted claimants were considerably higher than resettled refugees, followed by seven years during which there was a relative balance between these two categories. In the last two years, the number of resettled refugees was considerably higher than the number of accepted claimants. Figure 7.3 shows the same statistics for 2015–2019.

After 2016, the combined PSRs and BVORs (the new "blended" resettlement category introduced in 2013) accounted for more than twice the number of resettled GARs, a trend that is supposed to continue as per the government's multi-year immigration-levels plan (IRCC 2018c).[5] The number of resettled refugees also continued to be much higher than the number of those admitted after receiving protection in Canada.

In a situation where annual refugee admissions in all categories are a finite number determined through a planning process, a "complementarity double jeopardy" exists. Complementarity jeopardy one arises from the interplay between traditional/state-led resettlement and PSR/CSR schemes:

Canada - Admissions of Permanent Residents by Refugee Immigration Category, 2015–2019					
Refugee Category	2015	2016	2017	2018	2019
Blended Sponsorship Refugee	805	4,415	1,285	1,145	990
Privately Sponsored Refugee	9,290	18,315	16,665	18,560	19,140
Government-Assisted Refugee	9,405	23,555	8,630	8,090	9,950
Resettled Refugee - Total	19,500	46,285	26,580	27,795	30,080
Protected Person in Canada	12,060	12,205	14,480	17,680	18,435
Resettled Refugee & Protected Person in Canada - Total	31,560	58,490	41,060	45,475	48,515

FIGURE 7.3. Permanent Residents, All Refugee Classes, 2015–2019.

Source: Adapted from Government of Canada, 2020.

---

5   PSR and BVOR numbers have been combined, even though BVOR refugees receive some level of monetary support from the government. However, sponsors provide the majority of financial support and all non-financial support, and the program can only exist if sponsors are willing to be involved. Also, apart from the significant interest in the program during the government's Operation Syrian Refugees initiative, the program has been unable to meet its targets and is suspended at the time of writing.

Traditional/state-led resettlement and PSR/CSR schemes

Resettlement	Resettlement	Resettlement
° Traditional/state-led ■ Sponsorship	° Traditional/state-led ■ Sponsorship	° Traditional/state-led ■ Sponsorship
Canada 2006–2008 (average)	Canada 2015–2016 (average)	Canada 2017–2018 (average)

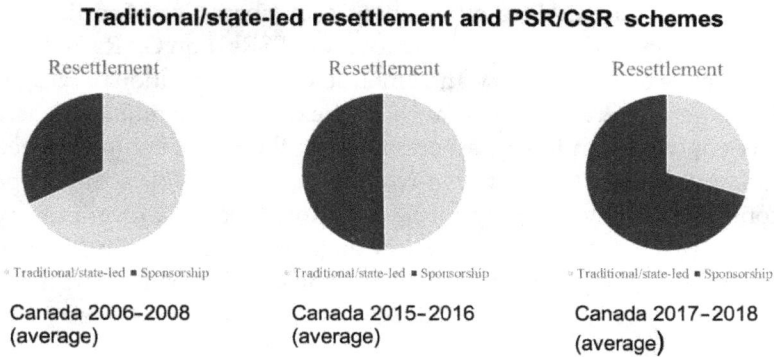

FIGURE 7.4. Complementarity Jeopardy One—Traditional/State-led Resettlement and PSR/CSR schemes.

Source: Adapted from Government of Canada, 2019.

Figure 7.4 shows that in the past 10 to 12 years the ratio between state- and sponsor-led resettlement has been reversed in Canada. A possible consequence highlighted by some refugee advocates is the offloading of state responsibility to private citizens. How does complementarity/additionality fit into this picture? One implied—albeit not explicitly defined in a normative way—understanding of additionality is that the number of sponsored refugees should not exceed the number of refugees resettled by the government: "This complementary protection stream can be put at risk if the government depends on it to fulfill its international obligations. In 2013, for the first year in many decades, the number of PSRs exceeded the number of GARs" (Hyndman, Payne, and Jimenez 2017, 56).

The Canadian Refugee Sponsorship Agreement Holders Association (SAH Association), which represents groups involved in the private sponsorship of refugees, offers a similar perspective on additionality whereby any government commitment to increase Canada's resettlement levels overall should be fulfilled through an increase in GAR levels, with the possibility to also increase the level of PSRs as sponsor capacity exists.

Canadian refugee advocates and academics studying refugee issues seem to be confused, though, in regard to what exactly to ask for when it comes to private sponsorship and additionality. The recommendations formulated by Hyndman, Payne, and Jimenez (2016) and submitted to the Canadian government noted that the 2013 situation of higher PSR than GAR resettlement was an "aberration of additionality" (3). They argued that planning for more PSRs than GARs violated the principle of additionality and amounted to privatization of refugee resettlement in Canada. The authors' next recommendation was a direct contradiction to this assertion about the relationship between GARs and PSRs: "Current *limits* on the number of PSRs should be reconsidered; why are they in place? Prior to 2011 [...] limits were defined by the degree of civil society engagement and willingness to sponsor refugees. Policies should aim to harness and sustain the interest and engagement of Canadians in refugee sponsorship, not undermine them" (3).

In other words, these authors call for unlimited PSR resettlement, to be determined in its entirety by sponsor interest. At the same time, PSR resettlement should never be higher than GAR resettlement. Overall annual resettlement levels planning would be difficult in such a system, where PSR levels would be determined by sponsor activity, and government efforts would be required to keep pace.

Of increasing importance for Canada as higher numbers of refugee claimants arrive is complementarity jeopardy two, which pertains to the interplay between resettlement (state-led and sponsor-led) and the admission of in-Canada protected persons (figure 7.5). This complementarity jeopardy is of particular pertinence for European states where asylum seekers have historically made up a much larger proportion of those who received protection than resettled refugees.

Resettlement (state-led & sponsor-led) and In-Canada Protected Persons

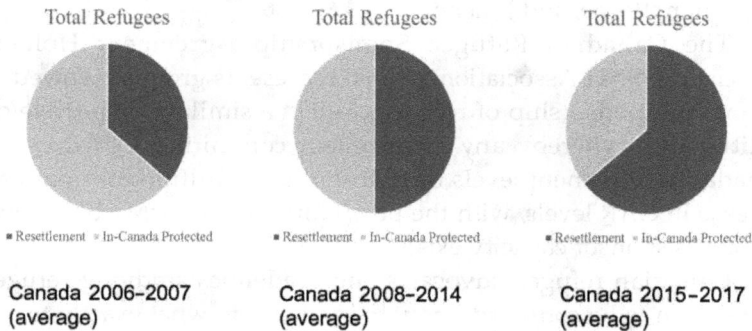

Total Refugees	Total Refugees	Total Refugees
▪ Resettlement ▪ In-Canada Protected	▪ Resettlement ▪ In-Canada Protected	▪ Resettlement ▪ In-Canada Protected
Canada 2006–2007 (average)	**Canada 2008–2014 (average)**	**Canada 2015–2017 (average)**

FIGURE 7.5. Complementarity Jeopardy Two—Resettlement (State- and Sponsor-Led) and In-Canada Protected Persons.

Source: Adapted from Government of Canada, 2019.

Possible consequences arising from complementarity jeopardy two are narrowing of protection space for claimants and/or protracted processes because the annual targeted admission numbers are insufficient to admit the number of claimants found to be in need of protection, and their dependants in Canada or overseas. An analysis of the immigration planning systems of other states is beyond the scope of this chapter; however, states, NGOs, and umbrella organizations working with them on the implementation of PSR/CSR programs are advised to include a country-specific analysis of complementarity/additionality as part of the discussion.

From the perspective of Canada and other states currently operating or contemplating CSR/PSR programs, the argument cannot simply be reduced to numbers, though. I would be amiss if I neglected to acknowledge the benefits of PSR/CSR over and above legal protection. As Hyndman (2011) noted, there exists a gap between the provision of legal protection status and the creation of a substantial state of belonging for resettled refugees. Sponsors undoubtedly play an important role in social-bridging activities, which are conducive to helping resettled refugees gain a sense of belonging at the community/neighbourhood level. The topic of belonging also pervades a recent volume on refugee resettlement, entitled *Refugee Resettlement: Power, Politics, and Humanitarian Governance* (Garnier, Jubilut, and Sandvik 2018). Even though there is no comprehensive quantitative research available yet in Canada that looks at outcomes of refugees' sense of belonging disaggregated by refugee categories, some empirical studies have been carried out that signal how sponsors help resettled refugees with social bonding and social bridging, and thus work toward finding a sense of belonging, in particular because sponsorship often involves kinship ties (e.g., Drolet and Moorthi 2018; Hanley et al. 2018; Hyndman and Hynie 2016). The Canadian government's *Syrian Outcomes Report* (IRCC 2019) also found that "PSRs had stronger connections to community networks" (14) than GARs. Apart from a heightened sense of belonging, other benefits of PSR/CSR that have repeatedly been cited are active citizen engagement in refugee protection—including, in Canada, the selection of refugees—and building meaningful relationships between refugees and their new communities, thus strengthening public support for refugees (e.g., Fratzke 2017; Hiebert 2016). Although there are also possible downsides to PSR sponsorship, such as heightened dependency on the sponsors and being excluded from social benefits such as immediate access to social housing, the balance of advantages over disadvantages is widely seen as positive.

Sponsorship: A Balance between Protection and Additional Vehicle for Migration Control?

In Canada, the finite overall resettlement target as a percentage of total annual immigration means that any increase in private sponsorship comes at the expense of government-sponsored resettlement. This situation has been depicted numerically and graphically earlier in this chapter. The increase in the PSR category between 2015 and 2019 has taken up a disproportionately high share of the overall increase in the resettlement target. In fact, the GAR number for 2019 was almost unchanged from 2015, whereas the PSR number more than doubled during that time. This situation creates a fiscal incentive for government to allow a large number of private sponsorships and filling the remaining spaces with government-assisted refugees, thus turning the principle of complementarity on its head. Even though there are still short- and long-term costs associated with the resettlement of PSRs for governments at federal, provincial, and municipal levels, the per capita cost of a PSR refugee is much lower than that of a GAR refugee, as indicated earlier (IRCC 2020a).

Rising overall immigration numbers have also led to small incremental increases in the GAR target; however, the unequal ratio between GARs and PSRs is now firmly embedded in Canada's immigration levels plan. Relying to such an extent on the goodwill and the capacity of private sponsors is a gamble for the government. Currently, the high number of permanent resident admissions can be serviced out of a significant backlog of applications in process, part of which the current government inherited from its predecessors based on years of relatively low permanent resident admissions without intake management of new applications. The other part of the backlog was created by Trudeau's Liberal government in 2015–2016, when temporary, facilitative policy measures allowed for large numbers of applications to be submitted without any obvious plan on how to clear the resulting ballooning backlog. At the end of 2019, the total backlog (inventory) in the PSR program had grown to 38,820 persons (IRCC 2021, slide 6). Since that time, the IRCC shared with the SAH Association that the backlog had further grown to over 65,000 persons by the end of

April 2021, a result of the pandemic and restrictions on refugee entry to Canada (NGO-Government Committee 2021).

The government had previously committed itself to bringing the PSR processing time down to 12 months by 2019—a goal that sponsorship experts had doubted would be achievable, given the size of the backlog (SAH Association 2018). It is even more unlikely now as the pandemic has taken a heavy toll on the backlog-reduction goal, and the IRCC has acknowledged the difficulties in meeting backlog-reduction targets (IRCC 2018b). Once the backlog is cleared, the Canadian public would need to submit applications in excess of 20,000 persons annually (to account for attrition) and successfully support the settlement process of 22,500 arrivals annually, as per the 2021–2023 immigration-levels plan (IRCC 2020b). Whether such sustained capacity exists in the public remains to be seen. Should the public not be able to meet these expectations, what would happen to Canada's overall resettlement targets? Would the government close the gap and increase GAR resettlement accordingly?

Equally unclear, and potentially more disturbing, are the questions resulting from complementarity jeopardy two. As highlighted by the CCR (2018), the targets for admission of persons with successful in-Canada refugee claims are insufficient in light of permanent-resident admission numbers and the number of claims pending. Given that Canada has a legal obligation to provide protection to persons with valid refugee claims, the government's unwillingness or inability to admit these persons in a timely manner leaves only one option: the creation of backlogs. In the refugee determination system, backlogs can occur either due to unprocessed refugee claims or following a successful claim, as those who have received protection wait for their permanent residence to be processed. At the time of writing, Canada had backlogs in both segments of the process. The increasing backlog of pending refugee claims is readily apparent from figure 7.6. It is more difficult to see the relationship between accepted claimants and protected persons admitted as permanent residents. This is because dependants of protected persons that are part of their application for permanent residence may not show up in the statistics on protected persons if they were not part of the refugee claim. An accepted claimant may result in multiple permanent residence admissions, depending on the number of dependent family members.

Refugee claims and permanent-resident admissions of protected persons in Canada, 2015–2019					
Year	2015	2016	2017	2018	2019
Accepted refugee claims	9,536	10,241	14,411	16,359	25,243
PR admissions of protected persons	12,060	12,205	14,480	17,680	18,435
Pending refugee claims year end	16,256	23,110	47,183	72,260	87,343

FIGURE 7.6. Refugee Claims and Permanent Resident Admissions, 2015–2019.
Source: IRB 2021, and adapted from IRCC 2020.

An analysis in the *Globe and Mail,* from September 2018, revealed that the current wait time for refugee claimants to have a hearing was 20 months (Carbert 2018). The CCR reported that "the processing time for permanent residence for accepted refugees in Canada is two and a half years. Those separated from spouse and children must wait even longer for family reunification: the federal government does not disclose these processing times" (CCR 2018).

European countries are already resorting to other measures in order to limit the number of asylum seekers they have to admit with full protection status. Many European states are limiting protection for those who do not meet the strict Refugee Convention definition by providing them with lower-level subsidiary protection. More extreme measures include the blocking of access routes to their borders through fortifying the EU's external borders and engaging in arrangements with third states under Europe's externalization (containment) strategy (Bloch and Donà 2019).

In this climate, refugee advocates have hopes but also concerns in regard to complementary pathways. The aspirations are clear— "complementary pathways [...] add to the protection and solutions space: they do not infringe on existing policies, programmes or rights for refugees. [...] They should not be used as substitutes for, or have negative impacts on these existing approaches, but rather they should build additional architecture which serves to further strengthen the existing system" (IOM and ICMC 2018b, 16).

However, critics in Europe are sounding the alarm, saying that legal pathways (including resettlement and complementary pathways) are used as a mechanism to justify the narrowing of protection space for migrants: "In the context of the planned EU Resettlement Framework and the Common European Asylum System, the sealing off of Europe, migration control, and development collaboration are being offset against legal pathways (for refugees)" (Refugee Council of Lower Saxony and Caritas Hildesheim, 2008; my translation). The widespread use of the term "legal pathways" in Europe is disturbing in and of itself, as it linguistically seems to suggest that other pathways, including the legal action of seeking asylum, are somehow illegal. Emphasizing the legitimacy of certain pathways meant to enhance the protection space through voluntary actions can—intentionally or unintentionally—drive a public discourse of "legitimate" and "illegal" refugees. In Canada, refugee-rights groups have seen a need to counter this type of misleading discourse as both media and the government have frequently used the term "illegal" when referring to irregular entry by refugee claimants (Citizens for Public Justice 2021).

Conclusion

The purpose of this chapter is not to discourage states and their civil societies from exploring and adopting PSR/CSR programs. In a world of rising refugee numbers and rising populist and xenophobic discourses in many countries, refugee sponsorship offers a powerful mechanism to engage citizens in global solidarity and responsibility-sharing vis-à-vis refugees. Rather, my goal is to point out the dangers of an over-reliance on private citizens regarding what is fundamentally a state's international responsibility. The Canadian government is left with a conundrum: on the one hand, including sponsored refugees in the immigration levels planning process ensures that associated costs can be properly budgeted; on the other hand, the state is unable to plan for citizens' engagement in the same way as it would for state-led resettlement operations. If the good will of citizens wanes, and/or if their capacity to volunteer time, effort, and resources is more limited than the state had anticipated, over-reliance on citizens could result in the state being unable to fulfill its responsibilities. The higher the PSR-to-GAR ratio, the more this conundrum will manifest itself.

Based on the Canadian experience, I offer a few recommendations to states contemplating or newly implementing PSR/CSR schemes:

- Ensure that any new PSR/CSR schemes or expansion of existing schemes are accompanied by at least a proportionate increase in traditional/state-led resettlement, thus ensuring that growth of a country's resettlement program does not rest with community sponsors and volunteers alone.
- Adopt a clear definition of and policy on additionality to avoid a trade-off between state-led and sponsor-led resettlement. Simply declaring that any sponsor-enabled resettlement is in addition to state-led resettlement is insufficient. The state must grapple with complex questions involving, but not limited to: What is the "baseline" for state-led resettlement to which sponsored refugees are complementary or additional? What ratio between the two is acceptable? If privately sponsored or community-sponsored refugees are counted as resettled refugees, do they benefit from the same protection measures and services as state-sponsored refugees?
- Account for admissions under PSR/CSR schemes within a separate category that distinguishes these admissions from state-sponsored resettlement. For states that contemplate blended or mixed models along the lines of the Canadian BVOR program (with state- and sponsor-led components), make sure that these admissions are not subsumed within government-resettlement numbers, but that the complementary sponsorship part is duly acknowledged. Admissions that are only possible because of the existence and support—financial and/or otherwise—of private or community sponsors should be counted as additional/complementary admissions.
- Ensure that any increases in refugees admitted through PSR/CSR schemes and resettlement do not adversely impact the number of protection spaces a country provides to successful refugee/asylum claimants, and that considerations of overall refugee protection (including all three streams) do not result in a zero-sum game.

Ultimately, states contemplating PSR/CSR programs have to grapple with their understanding and the practical implications of additionality. In her remarks at the 2018 Annual Tripartite Consultations on Resettlement, Jennifer Bond, managing director and chair of GRSI, called for the terminology of additionality to be unpacked: does it mean additional spaces for UNHCR referrals? Is it about the overall number of refugees going to particular states? Is it about who is paying? Is it only about a focus on spaces, or is trying to grow support equally important at this time? These are critical questions for all new adopters of sponsorship programs.

References

Abella, Irving, and Petra Molnar. 2016. "Refugees." *Canadian Encyclopedia*. Last modified October 26, 2020. https://www.thecanadianencyclopedia. ca/en/article/refugees.

Bloch, Alice, and Giorgia Donà. 2019. "Forced Migration: Setting the Scene." In *Forced Migration: Current Issues and Debates*, 1–18. New York: Routledge.

Cameron, Geoffrey. 2021. *Send them Here: Religion, Politics, and Refugee Resettlement in North America*. Montréal and Kingston: McGill-Queen's University Press.

Canadian Council for Refugees (CCR). 2013. "Important Changes in Canada's Private Sponsorship of Refugees Program." https://ccrweb.ca/en/changes -private-sponsorship-refugees.

——. 2018. "Low Number for Refugees Accepted in Canada Is a Serious Concern in Immigration Levels." Media release, November 2, 2018. https://ccrweb.ca/en/media/immigration-levels-accepted-refugees -permanent-residence.

——. n.d. "Private Sponsorship of Refugees." https://ccrweb.ca/en/private -sponsorship-refugees.

Canadian Refugee Sponsorship Agreement Holders Association (SAH Association). 2018. "Media Release in Response to the 2019-2021 Immigration Levels Plan." *Canadian Refugee Sponsorship Agreement Holders Association*, November 1. http://www.sahassociation.com/blog /media-release-response-2019-2021-immigration-levels-plan/.

Carbert, Michelle. 2018. "Asylum-Seeker Surge at Quebec Border Choking Canada's Refugee System, Data Show." *Globe and Mail*, Politics, September 11. https://www.theglobeandmail.com/politics/article-asylum -seeker-surge-at-quebec-border-choking-canadas-refugee-system/.

Carlaw, John. 2017. "Authoritarian Populism and Canada's Conservative Decade (2006-2015) in Citizenship and Immigration: The Politics and Practices of *Kenneyism* and *Neo-conservative Multiculturalism*." *Journal of Canadian Studies* 51(3): 782–816.

Citizens for Public Justice. 2021. "Busting myths about refugees in Canada." https://cpj.ca/refugee-myths/.

Citizenship and Immigration Canada (CIC). 2013. "Departmental Performance Report for the Period Ending March 31, 2012." Government of Canada. http://www.cic.gc.ca/english/resources/publications/dpr /2012/dpr.asp#strategic2-5.

Dolin, Benjamin, and Margaret Young. 2002. *Canada's Immigration Policy [BP-190e]*. Government of Canada. http://publications.gc.ca/Collection-R /LoPBdP/BP/bp190-e.htm#app3txt.

Drolet, Julie, and Gayatri Moorthi. 2018. "The Settlement Experiences of Syrian Newcomers in Alberta: Social Connections and Interactions." *Canadian Ethnic Studies* 50(2): 101–121.

Employment and Immigration Canada. 1978. "Memorandum to the Minister: The Sponsorship of Refugees and Humanitarian Cases." Government of Canada.

Employment and Immigration Canada. 1979. "Sponsoring Refugees: Facts for Canadian Groups and Organizations." Government of Canada. http://cihs-shic.ca/wp-content/uploads/2015/03/Sponsoring-Refugees -Facts-for-Canadian-Groups-and-Organizations.pdf.

Epp, Marlene, ed. 2017. *Refugees in Canada: A Brief History*. Ottawa: Canadian Historical Association.

Federal Ministry of the Interior, Building and Community. 2018. "Opening of the Biggest International Conference on Resettlement in Geneva Chaired by Germany." Press release, June 25, 2018. https://www.bmi .bund.de/SharedDocs/pressemitteilungen/EN/2018/atcr-conference -resettlement.html.

Feith Tan, Nikolas. 2020. "Community Sponsorship, the Pact and the Compact: Towards Protection Principles." Centre for European Policy Studies, ASILE Project. https://www.asileproject.eu/community -sponsorship-the-pact-and-the-compact-towards-protection-principles/.

Fratzke, Susan. 2017. *Engaging Communities in Refugee Protection: The Potential of Private Sponsorship in Europe*. Brussels: Migration Policy Institute Europe.

Garnier, Adèle, Liliana Lyra Jubilut, and Kristin Bergtora Sandvik, eds. 2018. *Refugee Resettlement: Power, Politics, and Humanitarian Governance*. New York: Berghahn Books.

Global Refugee Sponsorship Initiative (GRSI). 2018a. *Joint Statement – Ministers from Canada, the United Kingdom, Ireland, Argentina, Spain and New Zealand*. http://refugeesponsorship.org/_uploads/5b4ca01e 5c883.pdf.

——. 2018b. *What we do*. http://refugeesponsorship.org/who-we-are.

Government of Canada. 2001. *Immigration and Refugee Protection Act*. https:// laws.justice.gc.ca/eng/acts/i-2.5/.

———. 2019. *Permanent Residents – Ad Hoc IRCC (Specialized Datasets) - Canada - Admissions of Permanent Residents by Immigration Category, 1980 - Q2 2016.* February 2, 2019. https://open.canada.ca/data/en/dataset/ad975a26-df23 -456a-8ada-756191a23695/resource/a1fca442-1263-4730-a831 -3ad4eeoc2dbo.

———. 2020. *Permanent Residents – Monthly IRCC Updates - Canada - Admissions of permanent resident by province/territory of intended destination and immigration category.* September 30, 2019. https://open.canada.ca/data /en/dataset/f7e5498e-0ad8-4417-85c9-9b8aff9b9eda/resource /5582034d-8f89-49d5-8597-483d628078a1.

Hanley, Jill, Adnan Al Mhamied, Janet Cleveland, Oula Hajjar, Ghayda Hassan, Nicole Ives, Rim Khyar, and Michaela Hynie. 2018. "The Social Networks, Social Support and Social Capital of Syrian Refugees Privately Sponsored to Settle in Montreal: Indications for Employment and Housing during their Early Experiences of Integration." *Canadian Ethnic Studies* 50(2): 123–149.

Hiebert, Daniel. 2016. "What's So Special About Canada? Understanding the Resilience of Immigration and Multiculturalism." Migration Policy Institute, Washington, D.C. https://www.migrationpolicy.org/research /whats-so-special-about-canada-understanding-resilience-immigration -and-multiculturalism.

Hyndman, Jennifer. 2011. *Research Summary on Resettled Refugee Integration in Canada.* Ottawa: UNHCR.

Hyndman, Jennifer, and Michaela Hynie. 2016. "From Newcomer to Canadian: Making Refugee Integration Work." Policy Options, May 17, 2016. http://policyoptions.irpp.org/magazines/may-2016/from-newcomer -to-canadian-making-refugee-integration-work/.

Hyndman, J., W. Payne, and S. Jimenez. 2016. "The State of Private Refugee Sponsorship in Canada: Trends, Issues, and Impacts." Refugee Research Network/Centre for Refugee Studies, policy brief, December 2, 2016. https://refugeeresearch.net/rrn_node/private-refugee-sponsorship -in-canada/.

Hyndman, Jennifer, William Payne, and Shauna Jimenez. 2017. "Private Refugee Sponsorship in Canada." *Forced Migration Review* 54:56–59.

Hynie, Michaela. 2018. "Canada's Syrian Refugee Program, Intergroup Relationships and Identities." *Canadian Ethnic Studies* 50(2): 1–13.

Immigration and Refugee Board of Canada (IRB). 2021. "Refugee Claim Statistics." https://irb.gc.ca/en/statistics/protection/Pages/index .aspx.

Immigration, Refugees and Citizenship Canada (IRCC). 2016. *Evaluation of the Resettlement Programs (GAR, PSR, BVOR and RAP).* Ottawa: Immigration, Refugees and Citizenship Canada. http://publications.gc.ca/site/eng /9.824252/publication.html.

———. 2017a. "How Canada's Refugee System Works." Government of Canada. https://www.canada.ca/en/immigration-refugees-citizenship /services/refugees/canada-role.html.

———. 2017b. "Notice – Supplementary Information 2018-2020 Immigration Levels Plan." Government of Canada, Ottawa, November 1, 2017. https://www.canada.ca/en/immigration-refugees-citizenship/news /notices/supplementary-immigration-levels-2018.html.

———. 2018a. *2018 Annual Report to Parliament on Immigration*. Government of Canada. https://www.canada.ca/en/immigration-refugees-citizenship /corporate/publications-manuals/annual-report-parliament -immigration-2018/report.html.

———. 2018b. "Global Cap for Sponsorship Agreement Holders." Government of Canada. https://www.canada.ca/en/immigration-refugees-citizen ship/corporate/mandate/policies-operational-instructions-agreements /timely-protection-privately-sponsored-refugees.html.

———. 2018c. "Notice – Supplementary Information 2019-2021 Immigration Levels Plan." Government of Canada, Ottawa, October 31, 2018. https:// www.canada.ca/en/immigration-refugees-citizenship/news/notices /supplementary-immigration-levels-2019.html.

———. 2018d. "Resettle in Canada as a Refugee." Government of Canada. https://www.canada.ca/en/immigration-refugees-citizenship/services /refugees/help-outside-canada.html.

———. 2019. *Syrian Outcomes Report*. Government of Canada. https://www .canada.ca/content/dam/ircc/documents/pdf/english/corporate /reports-statistics/evaluations/syria-outcomes-report-may-2019.pdf.

———. 2020a. "IRCC Minister Transition Binder 2019: Refugee Resettlement." Government of Canada. https://www.canada.ca/en/immigration-refu gees-citizenship/corporate/transparency/transition-binders/minister -2019/refugees.html.

———. 2020b. "Notice – Supplementary Information for the 2021-2023 Immigration Levels Plan." https://www.canada.ca/en/immigration -refugees-citizenship/news/notices/supplementary-immigration -levels-2021-2023.html.

———. 2021. *Privately Sponsored Refugees (PSR) Annual Data Summary: Annual Report 2019*. Government of Canada. https://www.rstp.ca/wp-content /uploads/2021/06/PSR-Annual-Dashboard-2019.pdf.

International Organization for Migration and International Catholic Migration Commission Europe (IOM and ICMC). 2017. *Private Sponsorship in Europe: Expanding Complementary Pathways for Refugee Resettlement*. Belgium: European Resettlement Network. http://www .resettlement.eu/sites/icmc/files/ERN%2B%20Private%20Sponsor ship%20in%20Europe%20%20Expanding%20complementary%20 pathways%20for%20refugee%20resettlement.pdf.

——. 2018a. *Feasibility Study: Towards a Private Sponsorship Model in France.* Brussels, Belgium: European Resettlement Network. http://www.reset tlement.eu/sites/icmc/files/ERN%2B%20Private%20Sponsorship%20 Feasibility%20Study%20-%20Towards%20a%20Private%20 Sponsorship%20Model%20in%20France.pdf.

——. 2018b. *Strategic Assessment of Expanding Complementary Pathways of Admission to Europe.* Brussels, Belgium: European Resettlement Network. http://resettlement.eu/sites/icmc/files/ERN%2B%20A%20strategic %20assessment%20of%20expanding%20complementary%20path ways%20of%20admission%20to%20Europe.pdf.

Johnson, Paulette, and Donald Smith. 2018. "The PSRP in a New Era and the Implications: Is this the New Normal?" Presentation at the annual meeting of the Canadian Refugee Sponsorship Agreement Holders Association, Toronto, Ontario.

Jubilut, Liliana Lyra, and Andrea Cristina Godoy Zamur. 2018. "Brazil's Refugee Resettlement: Power, Humanitarianism, and Regional Leadership." In *Refugee Resettlement: Power, Politics, and Humanitarian Governance*, edited by Adèle Garnier, Liliana Lyra Jubilut, and Kristin Bergtora Sandvik, 70–91. New York: Berghahn Books.

Kelley, Ninette, and Michael Trebilcock. 2010. *The Making of the Mosaic: A History of Canadian Immigration Policy.* 2nd ed. Toronto: University of Toronto Press.

Labman, Shauna. 2012. "At Law's Border: Unsettling Refugee Resettlement." PhD dissertation, University of British Columbia. https://open.library .ubc.ca/cIRcle/collections/ubctheses/24/items/1.0071854.

——. 2016. "Private Sponsorship: Complementary or Conflicting Interests?" *Refuge* 32(2): 67–80.

——. 2019. *Crossing Law's Border: Canada's Refugee Resettlement Program.* Vancouver: University of British Columbia Press.

McKinlay, Christine. 2008. "Welcoming the Stranger: The Canadian Church and the Private Sponsorship of Refugees Program." Master's thesis, Ryerson University.

NGO-Government Committee. 2021. "210428 meeting minutes." Communication to Canadian Refugee Sponsorship Agreement Holders Association member organizations, May 13, 2021.

Refugee Council of Lower Saxony and Caritas Hildesheim. 2018. "EU Resettlement Programm: Deutschland beteiligt sich mit 10.200 Plätzen – was verbirgt sich dahinter?" [EU resettlement program: Germany participates with 10,200 spaces – what is behind this?]. https://www .nds-fluerat.org/30949/aktuelles/eu-resettlement-programm-deutsch land-beteiligt-sich-mit-10-200-plaetzen-was-verbirgt-sich-dahinter/.

Treviranus, Barbara, and Michael Casasola. 2003. "Canada's Private Sponsorship of Refugees Program: A Practitioners' Perspective of its

Past and Future." *Journal of International Migration and Integration* 4(2): 177–202.

United Nations. 2018. *Report of the United Nations High Commissioner for Refugees – Part II: Global Compact on Refugees.* https://www.unhcr.org /excom/unhcrannual/5ba3a5d44/report-united-nations-high-commis sioner-refugees-part-ii-global-compact.html.

United Nations High Commissioner for Refugees (UNHCR). 2018. "States Reach Historic Deal for Refugees and Commit to More Effective, Fairer Response." UNHCR, press release, December 17, 2018. https://www. unhcr.org/5c17642a4.

——. 2019. *Complementary Pathways for Admission of Refugees to Third Countries: Key Considerations.* April 2019. https://www.refworld.org /docid/5cebf3fc4.html.

CHAPTER 8

Beyond Preclearance, Future Borders, Digital IDs, and Privacy Management: A Technology and Policy Roadmap for Border Processing

Solomon Wong

Seventy years ago, Canada embarked on transformational changes in border management with the United States. Traditionally, international border clearance takes place *upon arrival* in a country but, starting in 1952 in Toronto, the United States stationed agents to conduct full border clearance *before flight departure*—a standard practice in today's "preclearance" procedures. The Canada-U.S. preclearance model was ahead of its time and expanded to other countries and regions. Subsequently, the U.S. government introduced preclearance operations in the Caribbean, Ireland, and Abu Dhabi, and renewed the Canadian model in 1974, 1999, and 2015. Other countries have adopted similar preclearance procedures. For example, Chinese border authorities are stationed in Hong Kong to process travellers to mainland China on the Guangzhou-Shenzhen-Hong Kong Express Rail Link that opened in 2018. Over the next five years, this operation in Hong Kong will become the largest preclearance site in the world, processing upwards of 100,000 passengers a day.

The ability to conduct pre-departure border checks evolved from a continuum of international travel protocols. Whether a model relies on relocating officers and equipment from one country to another or adopts virtual methods of clearing passengers via remote video calls, there are major consequences for governments, conveyances, ports, airports, and, ultimately, individuals who travel. This chapter focuses on the traveller in the shifting context of privacy and technology. How do travellers exercise their civil rights? Are there enough protections in place? How are the issues of identification changing with the continuous advent of new standards and technologies? Canadian coordination with the United States has attracted global attention to some of these important questions. Furthermore, the movement to examine the future of trade and travel is even more topical relative to the global COVID-19 pandemic.

With an understanding of the contextual history of preclearance, this chapter outlines key considerations to help inform future technology and policy roadmaps, and key implications pertaining to the changing governance of migration and borders. After reviewing theoretical considerations of the physical and temporal location of borders, this chapter outlines the historical context of the U.S. preclearance program with Canada. Subsequently, I explore future possibilities and the incorporation of private actors in the delivery of border clearance. The concept of "privacy by design" is reviewed as a potential key enabler to future border management, before giving a final outline of three key trends that may inform academic literature, stakeholders in border management, and policy-makers.[1]

Conceptual Context

The understanding of borders in recent scholarship includes a burgeoning body of work on the dynamic nature of boundaries and the complexity of the institutions and actors governing movements of people. Bersin (2012) traces the origins of the physical nature of the border as a line to fortify a nation, whether it is the Great Wall of China, the southern border fence of the United States, or the French Maginot Line. Beyond the physical line that typically defines a border, Bersin further argues that borders have existed as flows of capital,

---

1   This chapter is based on work carried out by the author over two decades as a practitioner studying and implementing process and policy changes in borders. Studies drawn upon include white papers delivered for a group of Canada and US border interests in the Future Borders Coalition, and a set of industry and government studies undertaken from 1997 to present regarding the efficiency and effectiveness of borders globally.

goods, people, and ideas for some time: from the Silk Road to the current movement of data across geographies.

Against this backdrop of physical lines and flows, the concept of borders itself is changing. Johnson et al. (2011) trace the idea of a borderless world in the 1990s through to the forces of border securitization, economic protectionism, and anti-immigration sentiments. While a traditional view of borders involves the separation of countries from each other, Johnson et al. outline the evolution of boundaries from a purely "national" to "supranational" view. As a result, there is a duality of countries both reinforcing national boundaries at the same time as finding ways to cooperate with other countries to establish a common set of policies.

The blurring of lines for the concept of borders is further complicated with distance and the notion that a country can exercise authority far beyond its borders. In describing the role of U.S. border officers operating in Canada, for example, Hiller (2010) identifies that "preclearance creates a unique borderland at Canadian airports that goes beyond the type of borderlands found at most international airports or seaports" (28). In other words, the spatial configuration of the border at an airport can, through bilateral agreement, be quite distant from the territorial boundary of a country. Norfolk (2019) extends the analysis further by identifying the "untethering" of border preclearance from official boundaries.[2] In describing preclearance, Norfolk indicates "the application of such bordering functions speaks to the increasingly 'mobile' and a-territorial nature of borders and bordering policy in the twenty-first century" (14). As a result, there is a paradox of borders emerging: while physical boundaries are harder and more prevalent than ever (e.g., border walls), there is also a proliferation of aterritorial borders, particularly with the advent of physical/electronic preclearance of passengers. These analyses lend increasing plausibility to Balibar's claim that "borders are everywhere" (2002, 140). This view is further amplified with the proliferation of smartphone apps that virtually allow people to carry a range of border markers with them anywhere on the planet. The "green pass," for example, serves as a health passport for COVID-19 status in many jurisdictions.

---

2 Researchers involved with the Borders in Globalization research project, which supported this edited volume, developed the idea that borders are increasingly "a-territorial" or "aterritorial"; see also Brunet-Jailly 2011, Carpenter 2019, and Konrad and Brunet-Jailly 2019.

Similarly, the United States has launched CBP One, an app that enables border services in an aterritorial manner.

While space and flows offer one perspective on processing travellers, an emerging area of thought concerns the temporal nature of border management. Tazzioli (2018) argues that "Temporal borders have been mobilised by states as a strategy for regaining control over unruly migrant movements" (21). Examining the prolonged plight of asylum seekers and the use of visas and other authorizations, Tazzioli identifies mechanisms that strengthen border controls by extending them in time. Sontowski (2018) develops this notion by elaborating three temporal elements of biometric border controls within the European Union: first, the use of new controls to require a digital application for third-country nationals long before travel; second, accelerating the speed of border controls through technologies; and third, greater control over the length of stay for third-country nationals to the EU.

However space, flows, and time are constructed and reconstructed for borders, the actors that are working through the concepts described by Sontowski (2018), Norfolk (2019), and Bersin (2012) are not confined to states. Sulmona, Edgington, and Denike (2014) characterize the contribution of nongovernment entities to advanced border controls as a form of technology to accelerate the speed of borders. The "multi-decade symbiotic relationships between the public and private sectors that overcame political, business and technical challenges" (11) they describe outline the critical roles non-government entities—airlines, airports, and other parties—have played in the changing time/place management of border controls.

The following diagram outlines the evolution of physical and temporal borders (see figure 8.1). A traditional border view would have passengers move from an origin point through a national boundary. Border clearance would occur proximate to the boundary. A second evolution relocates the function of border clearance to the moment a passenger boards an airplane—the preclearance model—where the actual border-clearance function is physically far from the national boundary. Finally, an emerging area of analysis for temporal borders includes authorizations far ahead of time, possibly one to two years in advance, with information reviews occurring through biometric/biographical information. This may or may not be accompanied by a form of physical preclearance during the day a flight or other transportation mode is taken. Notably, the passenger journey could occur on multiple modes of transportation, potentially through a

Traditional Borders

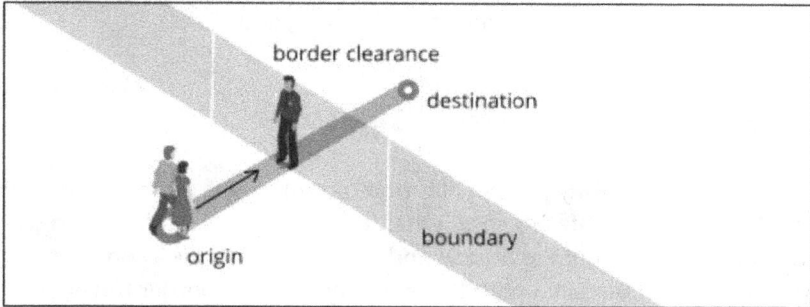

Border Pre-clearance

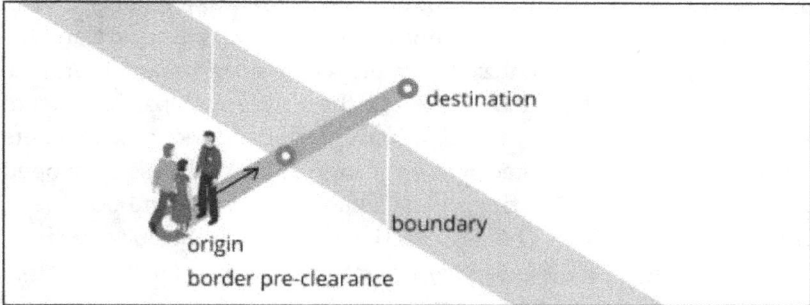

Temporal Borders

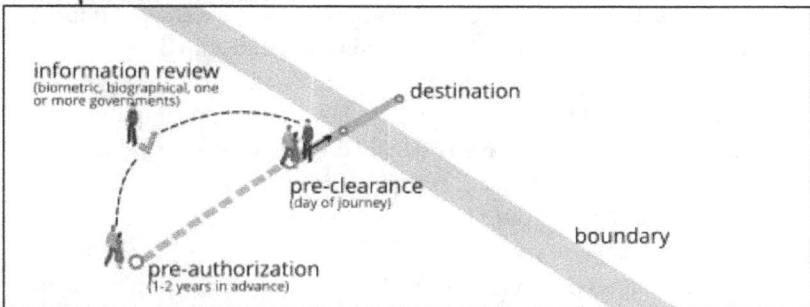

FIGURE 8.1. From Traditional Borders to Preclearance and Temporal Borders.
Source: Solomon Wong.

number of different countries. Today, this includes physical and temporal bordering across air, trains, ships, and the associated connectivity among the different modes. In the future, autonomous vehicles, hyperloops, and yet-to-be-invented modes of transportation will also be built across multiple points of contact and countries.

The History of Preclearance

While the modern-day pre-departure program of U.S. officers stationed on Canadian soil dates to 1952, when they began clearing passengers travelling from Toronto to Boston and New York, there is a considerably longer history associated with the evolution of cross-border travel management. Starting in the 1880s, U.S. immigration authorities started to tighten rules against migration, with different approaches to journeys from across the Pacific and Atlantic Oceans. There was a reliance on racist legislation—namely the U.S. Chinese Exclusion Act, 1882, and Canada's Chinese Immigration Act, 1923. The approach in western Canada and the United States was markedly different than the inbound flows from across the Atlantic. To evade U.S. immigration inspection, travellers chose to travel to the United States through areas with less developed checkpoints, such as entering via a Canadian intermediate point (e.g., Québec City or Halifax). The 1884 reaction from U.S. authorities was twofold—closer work by the U.S. government with transportation operators (rail, marine) and relocation of activities for border clearance to Canada:

> This evasion of immigrant inspection spurred the U.S. government to action. In 1894 the U.S. Immigration Service entered into an agreement with Canadian railroads and steamship lines serving Canadian ports of entry to bring those companies into compliance with U.S. immigration law. The steamship lines agreed to treat all passengers destined to the United States as if they would be landing at a U.S. port of entry. This meant completing a U.S. ship passenger manifest form and selling tickets only to those who appeared admissible under U.S. law. Canadian railroads agreed to carry only those immigrants who were legally admitted to the United States to U.S. destinations.
>
> For its part, the U.S. Immigration Service stationed immigrant inspectors at Canadian seaports of entry to collect the manifests and inspect U.S.-bound immigrants. (Smith 2000)

More than a century later, these powers, which address border risks, are still exercised. For example, maritime and rail pre-inspection operations in Vancouver are rooted in diplomatic notes exchanged in 1894, which permitted immigration checks on Canadian soil by U.S. officers.

While rail and steamships then dominated international travel, the acceleration of commercial aviation prompted a number of changes for the location of border controls. Given the impracticality of stationing a border post mid-air, border controls started to be situated inland—wherever an international airport was located. This could be hundreds or thousands of kilometres away from the actual physical border. Some airports, however, could not cope with the sudden growth of international air travel. American Airlines had a practical problem to address in the growth of commercial aviation—there was limited ability to clear international flights from Toronto in Boston or New York. As a result, American Airlines CEO, C. R. Smith, and the Air Transport Association's president, Stuart Tipton, lobbied successfully to station officers at Toronto's Malton Airport in 1952. Under the old system, passengers inbound from Canada sometimes had to wait as much as half an hour out on the field at LaGuardia before they could even enter the customs gate. Then, depending on their position in the long line, it could take from 10 to 40 minutes for clearance by customs agents (New York Times 1952).

Expansion to Montréal, Winnipeg, Bermuda, and other locales ensued in the 1960s. However, by the early 1970s, significant challenges arose, including matters related to bilateral air-transportation agreements, preclearance processing facilities, and the disruptive Boeing 747 (aka the jumbo jet). With about 150 percent more capacity than the Boeing 707, the Boeing 747 helped meet the growing demand for aviation. However, preclearance facilities faced a considerable processing challenge as a result of higher peak volumes, which some Canadian airports could not accommodate. For some facilities, such as Montréal Airport, preclearance was conducted with U.S. officers standing immediately adjacent to airline check-in agents. Inspections were done in plain sight to the members of the general public, which caused U.S. officials significant concern about the lack of appropriate facilities to conduct inspections.

Complicating preclearance operations further was the set of rules governing route rights: the legal ability for an airline to operate between two cities. While there was unlimited ability for a U.S. airline (United, American Airlines, say) to fly from Calgary or Edmonton to the United States, a Canadian air carrier such as Air Canada was legally barred from flying the same routes. On April 23, 1973, the Canadian transport minister, Jean Marchand, protested the lack of access to U.S. cities for Canadian air carriers by giving 90-days' notice for U.S. preclearance officers to leave Canada (Demarino 1973). After substantial negotiations, two major changes were instituted: the first Preclearance Agreement between the United States and Canada, and a revised bilateral agreement to offer new routes for both U.S. and Canadian air carriers. The 1974 Preclearance Agreement also codified requirements for facilities to be constructed at Canadian airports to meet standards the U.S. government wanted for preclearance. From offices to inspection booths to detention facilities, standards were issued to mandate the size and requirements for the construction of U.S. preclearance facilities in Canada.

Outside of the framework of the Preclearance Agreement, both governments recognized the challenge of modernizing border management to deal with the increasing volumes, new technologies for processing, and the greater complexity of trade and travel. This recognition resulted in four major initiatives, all of which involved the U.S. president, the Canadian prime minister, and senior officials: the Accord on Our Shared Border (1995), the Smart Border Action Plan (2001), the Security and Prosperity Partnership for North America (with Mexico) (2004), and the Beyond the Border Action Plan (2011).

The shared-border accord came just one year after the passage of the North American Free Trade Agreement. The accord recognized "that improving the efficiency of our shared border requires cooperation and coordination. As partners, we share a responsibility to create a border that is flexible enough to accommodate our economic interests and permits us to protect the health and safety of our citizens" (Canada-United States 1995, 3).

Several major changes have been implemented since 1995 to address how identity is managed, further extending preclearance across space and time. For example, in 1997, a pilot project was developed at Vancouver International Airport known as in-transit preclearance. Passengers could use a quicker connection from an international flight from Asia to connect through to the United States. The change instituted was providing passenger-manifest information in advance to allow U.S. border authorities to conduct checks before flight arrival to Vancouver. Similarly, in the 1990s and 2000s, programs such as NEXUS provided voluntary participants access to faster lanes for airports and land borders using biometrics and background checks. In the context of U.S. and Canadian border controls, individuals could submit themselves to more rigorous security checks in exchange for accelerated border crossings.

However, many challenges remained in the exercise of foreign legal powers and handling of data. The response to the terrorist attacks against the United States on 9/11 ushered in a drive to accelerate the handling of data, including the sharing of cargo, manifests, and other information. There are risks associated with government handling of private data, though. In an extreme case, in 2002, as a consequence of information provided by the Canadian government to the United States, Maher Arar, a Canadian citizen, was detained at a U.S. airport and deported to Syria, where he was tortured for alleged ties to terrorist organizations, ties which turned out to be baseless. In Syria, Arar was forced to falsely confess and was held for a year without being charged. Following his release, a commission of inquiry in Canada, led by Justice O'Connor, exonerated Arar and concluded that the actions of the RCMP "provided American authorities with information about Mr. Arar that was inaccurate, [and] portrayed him in an unfairly negative fashion" (CBC News 2006). The case is a powerful example of how government mishandling of private data can result in serious consequences.

While the Arar case occurred outside the preclearance regime, a number of other cases arose about the exercise of rights of individuals associated with information and border processing. To help manage some of the parameters, the 2015 Agreement on Land, Rail, Marine, and Air Transport Preclearance was signed between Canada and the United States to address the rights of individuals more clearly. Instead of restricting preclearance to aviation, a common multi-modal framework was established to allow for more sites to be established, with the conversion of immigration-only rail/marine transportation into the entire scope of border management, including customs and agricultural authorities. Implemented in August 2019, it is expected that efforts will be made to modernize preclearance to the United States and establish a reciprocal arrangement for the movement of people and goods into Canada.

From the inception of pre-inspection regimes, non-government actors have played a growing role in preclearance. The 1894 model of immigration pre-inspection by the United States was largely predicated on cooperation between the U.S. government and rail/steamship lines. Similarly, the 1952 introduction of preclearance for airlines involved operational roles for both air-carrier staff and U.S. government officials. Finally, in 1974, the role of airports in Canada was codified in a formal country-to-country agreement to provide facilities to the United States. As the decades advanced, the role of non-government actors expanded in several ways. The introduction of advanced passenger information in the late 1990s enabled governments to receive passenger manifests before flight departure. In the 2000s, automated kiosks were setup by airports and airlines to help governments accelerate processing and implement biometric recognition. While government retained full legal discretion on the admissibility of individuals into the country, major shifts occurred for non-government entities to provide technologies, staffing, or other aid to facilitate improved processing.

Moving to the Future: Beyond Preclearance and the Future Borders Initiative

While 2011 was a landmark year for the cooperation between Canada and the United States with the release of the Beyond the Border Action Plan, changes in political leadership signalled a shift in priorities for both countries. For the most part, the United States became seized on its southern border with Mexico. Concerns grew among transportation, tourism, and other economic sectors about whether U.S. border management would be stuck in older thinking about how border clearance could work. In particular, the drive to improve both temporal and aterritorial bordering was seen as a way to ensure that border management would not revert back to atavistic policies focused on conducting clearances strictly upon arrival to a country. As a result, a coalition was formed to conduct public–private research into the future of borders.

In 2018, the Beyond Preclearance Coalition, an industry group of bi-national organizations, was formed and commissioned research into the future of the U.S.-Canada border. Border-industry stakeholders across government entities from both countries—alongside futurists, strategists, operations and policy leaders—developed a white paper, *Beyond Preclearance: The Next Generation U.S.–Canada Border*, on the competitiveness of both countries.[3] The coalition held

---

3   See the white paper at https://www.futureborderscoalition.org/publications-1.

an Aviation Border Summit, hosted by Vancouver Airport Authority in October 2018, to launch pilot projects to test new technologies and processes, and to map out supporting policies. They also organized a Transportation Border Summit, hosted by the U.S. Chamber of Commerce in April 2019, to identify potential pilot projects across all modes of transportation.

The *Beyond Preclearance* paper was predicated on projected traffic growth. While severely impacted by the COVID-19 pandemic in the short term, it is expected that international trade and travel will resume growing at a rate of roughly 3–4 percent a year over the next 20 years. As a result, border-clearance activities should anticipate continued long-term growth for international tourism, trade, and travel, and high variability between Canada and the United States (from regional decline to major growth). How will such growth be managed? The paper calls for a dramatic increase in the adoption of more efficient technologies for processing, information management, and early detection of threats in the journey of travellers and goods. Doing so would enhance system resilience against future border threats. Some of the solutions discussed in the white paper point to the ways that borders are increasingly aterritorial and temporally extended.

In 2020, the initiative, renamed the Future Borders Coalition, launched a number of pilot projects related to the COVID-19 pandemic. Given the need to exercise caution in the use of information, pilot projects are designed to give government, industry, travellers, and trade interests time to evaluate the performance of systems to adhere to rules, respect individual rights, and to learn lessons from past mistakes. The concerns outlined in *Beyond Preclearance* are even more pressing due to the lack of usable space from pandemic-related social-distancing requirements. As well, new technologies like health testing, data sharing, and space for temperature screening have been added to border requirements. Practices for sharing personal information that protects individual privacy rights are the core of pilot projects, especially with sensitive information such as vaccination or immigration status across borders.

Preclearance for travellers remains significantly more advanced than on goods movement. While the 2015 Agreement on Land, Rail, Marine, and Air Transport Preclearance allows for legal capabilities for goods preclearance, the development of models for supply-chain clearance is less advanced. Clearance all the way to a U.S. manufacturing plant from third countries, for arrival to Canada (and vice versa), are concepts that are being formulated to also address issues associated with pests and commodity-specific requirements such as food products.

Multi-Country Cooperation on Traveller Identity and Authorization

One of the instruments used to preclear passengers is a visa. Visas can last from several months to as long as 10 years to pre-authorize a visitor to travel to a foreign country. Generally speaking, visa systems are highly antiquated. For some countries, they consist of an application, interview, and subsequent incorporation of a sticker or stamp in a passport. If a country rejects an individual from receiving a visa, then they will be prevented from boarding an aircraft or vessel to travel to that country.

The systems can get quite complicated and risky for travellers to manage. For example, if you are a Chinese national rejected for a visa by the United Kingdom, but accepted by Ireland, then the resulting trip can very much be impacted by the potential airline routings through a different airport hub. As a result, multi-country recognition and cooperation on visas has accelerated in the past decade. For instance, a Chinese national that has a valid visa to go to Japan can, as of 2017, visit Mexico without having to specifically acquire a visa for Mexico; Mexican authorities simply recognize a Japanese visa as equivalent to a Mexican one.

For Canada and the United States, these concepts have been partially implemented. The CAN+ visa, for example, was launched in 2014 by the Government of Canada to expedite visa issuances for individuals who have visited Canada or the United States within the past 10 years. In the same spirit, the vision supported by *Beyond Preclearance* is a greatly simplified methodology of managing authorizations—potentially through a mechanism known as "single window" for multiple countries. This could enable information from an airline booking to be sent seamlessly to different governments. If a foreign national is visiting Canada, the United States, or both countries, then the information needed for travel authorization could be delivered as part of the purchase of the airline ticket.

Although governments have attempted to move to a model of travel authorizations, including the Canadian Electronic Travel Authorization and the American Electronic System for Travel

Authorization, these efforts are separate and cumbersome for travellers who require both documents. Many challenges remain, such as the protection of privacy and potential misuse of information. For instance, if a common travel-authorization framework evolves among Canada, the United States, Australia, New Zealand, the United Kingdom, and South Korea, will there be sufficient protections for individuals who may encounter an issue with one of the six countries?

Similarly, the proliferation of health-information passports related to the COVID-19 pandemic are creating new identity and authorization requirements. Demonstrating vaccination for communicable diseases or the status of a recent test are increasingly being required by governments for travel, and could become the norm, not only for COVID-19 but for a wide range of communicable diseases. Whether one country will fully recognize the health-status indicators of another requires careful coordination on travel identity and authorizations. The Canadian and U.S. case studies are important from an information preclearance standpoint. As of November 2021, the United States recognizes more vaccines approved by the World Health Organization (WHO) than does Canada. Both countries have methodologies to assess information before a flight departs from a foreign country: Canada has a smartphone ArriveCAN application to upload information, and the United States has mandated airlines to review proof of vaccination. However, without Canadian recognition of WHO-approved vaccines, a foreign traveller fully vaccinated for COVID-19 can be cleared to enter the United States without quarantine but cannot do so for a trip to Canada. While the months ahead could potentially create more inclusive global recognition of vaccination status, the different approaches highlight some of the difficulties of achieving a common health-preclearance framework between countries.

New Models of Biometrics

Since the 1990s, biometrics in air travel primarily rested with voluntary programs such as NEXUS and Global Entry. Passengers opt in to submit biometrics to governments in exchange for faster processes at border checkpoints and security screenings. In January 2018, Canada and the Netherlands announced their intent to pilot a Known Traveller

Digital Identity (KTDI) project (Transport Canada 2018), part of a series of initiatives taking place to create the next-generation digital ID for travellers. Launched in July 2019, the Canadian and Dutch governments partnered with their respective national carriers, Air Canada and KLM Royal Dutch Airlines, and Montréal's Trudeau International, Toronto's Pearson International, and Amsterdam's Schiphol airports to test 10,000 passenger journeys using a blockchain to store information. Though the trial was stalled due to COVID-19, additional laboratory tests were conducted to demonstrate the potential of a voluntary system to improve identity management. With future recovery of air-transportation volumes, KTDI is seen as one way of encouraging governments to unify the model for trusted/registered travellers and reduce the number of queues at airports. Furthermore, a trust relationship is developed with individual travellers based on a running log of trips taken by the individual, including hotel visits and other contact points with governments and private-sector entities. Assistant Deputy Minister for Transport Canada Lori MacDonald (2018) described the process as follows:

> KTDI will be for the passenger to share specific pieces of information and stakeholders with their travel continuum to facilitate their process for their departure. It is a voluntary project where I upload my information on a token—what I am doing, where I am going, where I am staying, my traveller info in terms of flights, allowing me to go through the system in a seamless way so I can proceed through the traveller continuum.

The "token" indicates the blockchain solution. The data typically contained in paper documents, or stored on government databases, is instead stored on a form of technology that is designed around information security and privacy. A blockchain is an immutable ledger that is shared across peer-to-peer information systems. Access is limited and controlled by the passenger, while the entire chain is universally available and protected through encryption. The basis of blockchain has enabled the emergence of cryptocurrencies like Bitcoin.

When used in a border context, MacDonald (2018) further added that the benefits would include reducing queues and removing the task of assessing/re-assessing from governments, ultimately allowing a known traveller to move in a more efficient manner. In addition to easing the governmental burden, there are also commercial benefits to the proposed system. Accenture's Rajeev Kaul (2018), one of the developers of the KTDI, said: "The key here really is travel stamps. Every time I cross the border, every time I check into a hotel, we have a stamp that is added…like digital stamps. It allows an individual over time to have this identity that is associated with them…it has already been verified by governments and other trusted entities."

Further, Kaul described a collection of stamps that could include an individual's travel history to Malaysia, Canada, and France, including hotels, which could form the continuous ledger stored on a blockchain.

Digital IDs are expected to proliferate in the coming years. In 2020, the International Civil Aviation Organization, the UN body responsible for establishing standards such as passports, unveiled the Digital Travel Credential (DTC) as a new standard toward next-generation solutions for individual identification. DTC could be a vital building block of future preclearance, as it would unite currently disparate forms of digital and physical preclearance, and enable governments and different actors to better communicate with each other about individuals who are travelling. Much work remains, however, due to the degree of public and private interests that need to be managed, along with the protection of personal information.

Privacy by Design—A Key Enabler for the Future of Preclearance

The privacy of information is an increasingly important aspect of border-movement dealings, regardless of whether handling personal information related to identity or commercially sensitive information. The issues related to privacy in the United States and Canada are both complex and often misunderstood. Both governments have robust frameworks for managing new processes, namely the requirement to conduct privacy impact assessments. In general, these assessments are public documents that ensure governmental adherence to privacy requirements in the use of information, data retention, and such.

However, a challenge that governments and stakeholders involved in border management face is the need to adopt a universal standard for best practices in privacy management. Without doing this, there may be potential vulnerabilities across the entire travel continuum. Breaches and theft of data, including facial biometric information and personal data, are major threats for both the security/ integrity of borders and for travellers exposed to identity theft and data misuse.

According to the 2010 edition of the International Conference of Data Protection and Privacy Commissioners, an annual forum now known as the Global Privacy Assembly, privacy by design represents the future of improved privacy management across private and public sectors. Since 2010, many jurisdictions, including Japan, Europe, and California, have adopted privacy by design into privacy laws. "Privacy by design" is based on proactive privacy management from the outset: it offers users control of how information is collected, transmitted, and retained. Instead of reacting to breaches, privacy is built into the system as the default setting and therefore embedded into the design of any process/solution. Visibility and transparency are also part of the basis of privacy by design. Some jurisdictions, such as the EU's General Data Protection Regulation, have included privacy by design in new regulations.

Cyberattacks and breaches of privacy are potential risks faced with a border environment that depends on the collection and transmission of personal data. The challenge is addressing the concept of improved privacy and border security as mutually reinforcing rather than exclusive concepts. Some, including Global Privacy and Security by Design, a group of privacy and technology experts, have promoted the idea that there is no need to forsake personal privacy for public safety, and that there are solutions to help ensure large data analytics can be privacy-protected.[4] As digital-security expert and privacy advocate Bruce Schneier (2008) wrote, "Security and privacy are not opposite ends of a seesaw; you don't have to accept less of one to get more of the other." As the volume of data grows with the implementation of new technologies and capabilities, such as block-chain and digital traveller credentials, there needs to be more evaluation. Travel history, to date, is not information that is broadly available to countries. Some countries, like Canada, the United States, and Mexico have offered their citizens participation in programs such as NEXUS; however, the sharing of biometric and travel history is limited. Another issue is that policies used are not static in time. For example, due to policies instituted by the United States, many Europeans who vacationed in Iran in 2011 suddenly could no

---

4   For more information, see https://gpsbydesign.org/.

longer travel to the United States without a visa (U.S. Department of State and U.S. Department of Homeland Security 2016). Travel history can be used against individuals in other ways as well—in 2017 Malaysia used the travel history of individuals to issue "not-to-land" orders targeted at homosexual foreigners (Pulau 2017).

At the same time, a number of U.S. cities, including Chicago, San Francisco, and Boston, moved to ban the use of facial biometrics by police and other agencies, primarily due to privacy and human-rights concerns. While any kind of biometric or biographical data needs to be protected, privacy is much broader in the protections needed, including data-retention period, access rights, data minimization, and other aspects of enclosing privacy rights into the design of the proposed border solutions.

The holistic approach in privacy by design means that every component—airline, government, technology vendor, or cloud-based data provider—is subject to a proactive view toward protecting privacy, rather than reacting to breaches of information. For the end user it means a simple-to-use mechanism to enable passengers to protect their personal information, rather than a long-scrolling privacy statement that few individuals read before clicking "accept" to install an app or submit information to a foreign government. If privacy by design were successfully infused into digital ID management, then the ownership of the information, and the record of where data has been submitted, would be fully transparent to the passenger. In practical terms, a self-sovereign identity model could be achieved through a smartphone, with a record available to the user to see their own travel history and the points in time when data has been transmitted to a government, airline, or other entity. The challenge remains that, for many countries, the ability to provide transparent information, especially when related to criminal warrants, is generally opaque. A case in point is the December 1, 2018, arrest of Meng Wanzhou at the Vancouver International Airport on a U.S. extradition request to the Government of Canada. Most notably, Meng was travelling from Hong Kong to Mexico via Vancouver when her arrest was requested.

In the future, as passengers move from the world of physical-passport swipe to digital-identity methodologies via a smartphone, some of the areas of privacy-by-design implementation will need to insist on both sovereign state powers and the rights of individuals to their own identity records.

Key Directions and Conclusions

The implementation of the 2015 Agreement on Land, Rail, Marine, and Air Transport Preclearance between Canada and the United States is an important milestone but one that prompts a theoretical and operational conversation about the future of borders. As technologies enable greater processing efficiencies, are there other aspects of aterritorial and temporal borders that need to be anticipated? Several important areas need to be further reviewed as new technologies, policies, and processes are advanced to further mature a 68-year history of preclearance between Canada and the United States.

The prevailing wisdom for border and security processing is that the responsibility is purely a government function. However, the reality is airports and land and sea ports are responsible by law to provide free-of-charge space to government agencies, including those that process border and security controls. All told, facilities across all modes of transportation total billions of dollars in assets. Starting in 2006, the dynamic fundamentally changed: airports started to invest in government kiosks and other technology to expedite travel, address growth, and improve customer service. As an example, if an airport only has space for processing a maximum of a thousand inbound passengers per hour, doubling the speed of processing has the potential to have corresponding benefits (e.g., approximately half the space needed). While the relationship is not always linear in nature, the key to success is creating the opportunity to reduce the manual work needed to conduct border security clearances, accelerate the automation of processing data, and reduce duplication. Other modes of transportation have followed suit with comparable investments that range from cruise to rail- to land-border crossings (to a lesser extent).

Accordingly, the public-private partnership model for border clearances is being reinvented. Instead of simply having a relationship with space provision in an airport, port, or other border crossing, smarter facilities could be built. Technology resulting in space savings can dramatically improve the operational experience, and improve resource allocation to better address border risks. As a result, a public-private partnership model could see greater efficiencies and effectiveness.

The traditional relationship between passenger identity, states, and non-state actors involved in border crossings is changing. The most traditional method of identity, the passport, was standardized in the 1980s and is now evolving. From its earlier origins to "'pass' a port," the contemporary passport has digital features that enable greater security. What about individuals who are stateless, such as refugees? As well, there needs to be planning to ensure that passengers with reduced mobility can still be accommodated by technologies. Kiosks that require the ability to have two arms to hold a device/document, for example, can be difficult for some passengers to use. The original plan for the e-passport called for embedded visa information. However, it remains a singular and physical object, vulnerable to loss or destruction. In the meantime, technologies have changed. Digital travel credentials (DTCs) are the future of preclearance. By having an encrypted identity owned by the individual rather than the state, there is the greater possibility to manage identity, privacy, and submission of data to a variety of actors (e.g., airlines, cruise lines, government agencies). An added benefit of DTCs is the ability to address travellers with no country or individual sensitivities. With the standards for DTCs released in October 2020, there is the potential for this method to help those whose countries may have disappeared due to war or issues related to asylum camps around the world. Individuals fleeing countries may have no documents, and/or country documentation may be irrelevant if the country no longer exists. A DTC tied to a biometric, stored on a decentralized blockchain, offers a path toward secure documentation. Although the DTC is a global standard advanced by the International Civil Aviation Organization, it is expected to take decades for global adoption. During this time there will be opportunities to ensure that the platform can address country-specific requirements and the greater individual control of identity offered in digital identities. The UNHCR is evaluating the use of blockchains, similar to KTDI, to establish a mechanism for digital identification. Currently, the UNHCR holds identity records of more than eight million refugees globally. The UNHCR has outlined a vision that each refugee should have a unique digital ID. To modernize this approach, in 2019 the UNHCR outlined a method to acquire new technologies:

UNHCR is now looking to offer a similar service to refugees and asylum seekers.

> Blockchain distributed ledgers (or other appropriate technologies) would host the eRegistry consisting of certified documents

relating to all data of UNHCR data subjects, such as individual asylum seekers, refugees stateless and other forcibly displaced persons. (UNHCR 2018)

Solutions for digital identification, smartphone applications, or other technologies need to consider mechanisms that protect rights with submitting identities to different actors in the travel and supply chain. Technology offers novel and transparent solutions to personal decision-making that can sometimes be laden with bias. User control, and the ability to have an immutable log, can help ensure that a rules-based approach can assist in limiting the perception of targeting individuals due to race, colour, creed, or sexual orientation. These abilities are also important in an age when health information or vaccination status become increasingly important requirements to board a flight. However, care and attention are needed as societal changes are advanced. For example, non-binary gender identities may be implemented in one country, but there needs to be a view toward global solutions where many countries will continue to carry legacy conventions of male/female gender conventions. For Canada, this means the need to continue to play a leadership role in the world, pushing for policy solutions that prioritize the privacy and security of individuals while establishing the infrastructure of the next-generation of border management and traveller screening.

References

Balibar, Étienne. 2002. *Politics and the Other Scene*. Translated by Christine Jones, James Swenson, and Chris Turner. London: Verso.

Bersin, Alan. 2012. "Lines and Flows: The Beginning and End of Borders." *Brooklyn Journal of International Law* 37(2): 389–406.

Brunet-Jailly, Emmanuel. 2011. "Special Section: Borders, Borderlands and Theory: An Introduction." *Geopolitics* 16(1): 1–6. http://doi.org/fnd8vt.

Canada-United States Accord on Our Shared Border. 1995. Citizenship and Immigration Canada. https://www.publicsafety.gc.ca/lbrr/archives/cn 63684181-eng.pdf.

Carpenter, Michael J. 2019. "Understanding Aterritorial Borders through a BIG Reading of Agnew's Globalization and Sovereignty." *Borders in Globalization Review* 1(1): 123–126. https://doi.org/10.18357/bigr11201919267.

CBC News. 2006. "False RCMP Info 'Very Likely' Led to Arar Deportation: Report." September 18, 2006.

Demarino, G. 1973. "Marchand Ends Preclearance." *Ottawa Citizen*, April 24, 1973.

Hiller, Harry H. 2010. "Airports as Borderlands: American Preclearance and Transitional Spaces in Canada." *Journal of Borderlands Studies* 25(3–4): 19–30. https://doi.org/10.1080/08865655.2010.9695769.

Johnson, Corey, Reece Jones, Anssi Paasi, Louise Amoore, Alison Mountz, Mark Salter, and Chris Rumford. 2011. "Interventions on Rethinking 'the Border' in Border Studies." *Political Geography* 30(2): 61–69. https://doi.org/10.1016/j.polgeo.2011.01.002.

Kaul, R. 2018. "Known Traveller Digital Identity." Speech presented at 2018 Global Distribution Conference, Austin, Texas, January 31. https://youtu.be/cBO9atrjWjg.

Konrad, Victor, and Emmanuel Brunet-Jailly. 2019. "Approaching Borders, Creating Borderland Spaces, and Exploring the Evolving Borders between Canada and the United States." *The Canadian Geographer / Le Géographe canadien* 63(1): 4–10. https://doi.org/10.1111/cag.12515.

MacDonald, L. 2018. "Getting to the Border of the Future: Policy, Pilots, and Pragmatism." Speech presented at Canada-U.S. Border Transportation Innovation, Washington. March 26. https://www.wilsoncenter.org/event/canada-us-border-transportation-innovation-the-age-america-first-moving-beyond-pre-clearance.

New York Times. 1952. "Cutting Red Tape: Airline and Customs Officials Test Plan to 'Pre-Clear' Travellers' Baggage." January 20.

Norfolk, Alexander. 2019. "Shifting, Securitizing, and Streamlining: An Exploration of Preclearance Policy in the Pacific Northwest." *Journal of Borderlands Studies* 35(4): 117. https://doi.org/10.1080/08865655.2019.1619473.

Pulau, B. 2017. "No Entry for Foreigners Going to Malaysia for Beer Fest and Gay Party." *The Straits Times* [Singapore], September 24, 2017.

Schneier, Bruce. 2008. "What our Top Spy Doesn't Get: Security and Privacy Aren't Opposites." *Wired*, January 24. https://www.wired.com/2008/01/securitymatters-0124/0124/.

Smith, Marian L. 2000. "By Way of Canada: U.S. Records of Immigration Across the U.S.-Canadian Border, 1895-1954." *Prologue Magazine* 32(3). https://www.archives.gov/publications/prologue/2000/fall/us-canada-immigration-records-1.html.

Sontowski, Simon. 2018. "Speed, Timing and Duration: Contested Temporalities, Techno-political Controversies and the Emergence of the EU's Smart Border." *Journal of Ethnic and Migration Studies* 44(16): 2730–2746.

Sulmona, Luigi G., David W. Edgington, and Ken Denike. 2014. "The Role of Advanced Border Controls at Canadian Airports." *Journal of Transport Geography* 39:11–20. http://dx.doi.org/10.1016/j.jtrangeo.2014.06.006.

Tazzioli, Martina. 2018. "The Temporal Borders of Asylum. Temporality of Control in the EU Border Regime." *Political Geography* 64:13–22. http://dx.doi.org/10.1016/j.polgeo.2018.02.002.

Transport Canada. 2018. "The Government of Canada to Test Cutting-Edge Technologies to Support Secure and Seamless Global Travel for Air Passengers." January 25. https://www.canada.ca/en/transport-canada/news/2018/01/the_government_ofcanadatotestcutting-edge technologiestosupportse.html.

United Nations High Commission for Refugees (UNHCR). 2018. "UNHCR Now Accepting Proposals on Digital Identity." November 13. https://www.unhcr.org/blogs/unhcr-accepting-proposals-digital-identity/.

U.S. Department of State and U.S. Department of Homeland Security. 2016. "United States Begins Implementation of Changes to the Visa Waiver Program." Press release, January 21. https://www.dhs.gov/news/2016/01/21/united-states-begins-implementation-changes-visa-waiver-program.

CHAPTER 9

On "Bulking Up": Humanitarian Borders and State Making in Mexico

Victoria Simmons

Economic liberalization requires a certain degree of harmonization with regards to the rules and tools that countries use to govern mobilities; in much of the Western world, this harmony did not exist in the 1980s since states largely addressed this task unilaterally, underscoring their sovereign right to define the rules about who could enter and stay within their territories, and who could enforce such rules and how. With economic liberalization in the 1990s, however, rule making and enforcement in relation to mobility became an increasingly collaborative effort among and within states, sparking more regionalized and internalized approaches to bordering and the regulation of movement. In some parts of the world, such as Europe, this triggered a process by which the borders demarcating state territories and citizenries became increasingly subordinated to emerging regional borders, spaces, and identities. The governmental effect this process produced has been described as "scaling up" (see Riemsdijk 2012).

Yet, as this chapter illustrates, scaling up is but one possible governmental effect of re/bordering resulting from globalization. In North America, I argue, re/bordering did not produce a scaling up but instead something more akin to what I call a "bulking up"; that is, an expansion or a strengthening of states' capacity to govern peoples and spaces. This was particularly (though not solely) the case in Mexico, where economic liberalization triggered a humanitarian re/bordering process involving discourses and practices concerned with migrant protection. Actors of all stripes have participated in this bulking-up process. I examine the participation of just one, however: Mexico's *Grupos Beta de Protección al Migrante*, hereafter referred to as the Beta Groups.

Touted as the "humanitarian arm" of the National Migration Institute (INM), Mexico's Beta Groups have grown numerically, geographically, and strategically since their inception in 1990.[1] Beginning as a small, undercover police unit located on the U.S.-Mexico border in Tijuana, today there are 22 Beta Groups of highly visible, orange-clad agents who patrol transit routes in nine different states of the Mexican republic in search of migrants who are lost, in danger, or in need of rescue (INM 2018). Since their inception, the migrant-protection practices and discourses of Mexico's Beta Groups, I contend, have participated in the humanitarian re-bordering of Mexico; that is, a continuous identification, classification, and engagement with spaces and populations in the name of protection and the alleviation of human suffering. By mobilizing juridical knowledges, humanitarian discourses, and policing technologies, I argue, humanitarian bordering has served to make visible, problematize, and (re)embrace those populations and spaces that operate within Mexico's territory but outside the purview of state institutions. Furthermore, as this chapter suggests, Mexico's national railway system has served as a material and symbolic scaffolding for this humanitarian bordering in Mexico.

To illustrate these ideas, I offer an analysis of the Beta Groups' field journals and internal reports from the 1990s and early 2000s. In doing so, the chapter offers valuable empirical data about a relatively understudied actor in migration politics. I also offer evidence as to how international legal instruments, such as human-rights treaties, can be mobilized to introduce and strengthen—rather than challenge—state institutions in places and populations where these are weak or absent. Finally, this chapter contributes to understandings of the dynamic nature of securitized and humanitarian bordering; it illustrates the ways in which these two seemingly distinct forms of bordering can overlap, complement, and contradict one another to produce particular border effects; it demonstrates how humanitarian bordering can comprise policing technologies, and later trade these for socio-medical techniques, without losing its humanitarian rationales

---

1   The other arm of the federal government's INM roams Mexico for the purposes of migration control; to locate, detain, and deport irregular migrants back to their countries of origin.

and aims; and it shows how securitized and humanitarian bordering rely heavily on infrastructure and routes, such as roads, walls, and railways.

Borders and State-Making in Globalization

Borders are important tools for demarcating state territories and memberships and for regulating movement there among. Borders define, distinguish, and organize places and peoples. They help determine who is here vs. there, us vs. them, who is legal vs. illegal, included vs. excluded, and so on (Casas-Cortes et al. 2015, 66–68.). Thus, any changes to the parameters of state territory and membership—or to the possibility of movement among these—always involves parallel transformations in the borders which help define them. With the end of the Cold War, the uptick in global processes of regional economic liberalization and political integration around the world generated new demands and opportunities for bordering and state making. And it is within this context that at least two novel types of borders emerged, the securitized border and the humanitarian border.

The *securitized border* emerged in response to anxieties caused by the increased volume and pace with which people, goods, and information travel the world in the wake of the disappearance of many economic and political barriers to movement and the magnificent advances in transport and communications technologies (Ticktin 2007). Typically located at the perimeters of state territories—though they are increasingly found both inside and beyond these boundaries—the securitized border is a space where there is a marked increase in use of patrols and military technologies. These are mobilized to deter or stop flows of goods or people deemed threatening while simultaneously allowing for the seamless, unimpeded circulation of people and things considered desirable (Heyman 2008; Ticktin 2007).

The exclusionary or filtering function of the securitized border produced a second border type, the *humanitarian border* (Walters 2011). This border emerges in spaces of violent transit(ion) in which human suffering is so great that its alleviation becomes the dominant rationale by which state officials and civil society exercise power. This rationale is what Fassin (2007, 2012) has called humanitarian reason (see also Walters 2011). Humanitarian borders are constituted and transformed through the exercise of power and the fabrication of certain forms of knowledge, which draw on medical expertise (i.e., recording deaths and physical and psychological traumas among border crossers) and socio-legal expertise (i.e., documenting state officials' knowledge of and training in human rights, and violations of migrants' rights while being detained or awaiting deportation). The production of truths involved in the constitution of humanitarian borders often takes place in moving and highly situated manners, such as ad hoc missions, delegations, and fact-finding missions. The primary aim of these missions is to make visible the invisible because opacity, among other factors, is thought to breed suffering (Walters 2011).

A growing body of literature recognizes the complex and intimate ways securitized and humanitarian borders can work together to (re)produce particular effects (Ticktin 2005; Aradau 2004; Walters 2011; Vaughan-Williams 2015; Pallister-Wilkins 2015; Williams 2015). This chapter builds on that literature and traces transformations in bordering and state making in Mexico at the turn of the twenty-first century.

The Birth of the Humanitarian Border in Mexico

As negotiations began on the North American Free Trade Agreement (NAFTA) in the late 1980s, Mexico came under pressure to demonstrate that it was capable of providing free-trade corridors that were secure and corruption-free (Specht 2009; McDonald and Paromchik 1996). Thus, in late 1990, Mexico's federal government disbanded its existing border-inspection group on account of corruption and created a special unit, the Beta Group Tijuana, to collaborate with San Diego Border Patrol in their fight against border crimes that targeted migrants at this U.S.-Mexico crossing (Nevins 2002; McDonald and Paromchik 1996).

Informally known as Operativo Bandido (OIM 2011), the Beta Group Tijuana was a pilot program founded by the Mexican Secretariat for Home Affairs (SEGOB).[2] During its first months and years of existence, it was described by newspapers as "an elite Mexican police unit" (Rotella 1993), "a relatively new, multi-agency border force made up of

---

2   Although INM claims to have founded the Beta Group in 1990, the INM only came into existence in 1993. It was the SEGOB that initiated the pilot project, later passing on its administration to the INM.

federal, state and city officers who are charged specifically with protecting migrants from crime" (Rotella 1992a). The Beta Group Tijuana
was considered an elite police force in that its officials were "specially
selected from other Mexican police agencies...better paid and better
trained than many of their counterparts. They report[ed] directly to
Mexico's interior minister, who report[ed] to President Carlos Salinas
de Gortari" (Rotella 1993). They also had a zero-tolerance policy on
breaches of discipline.

In order to protect migrants from crime, Beta Group Tijuana officials dressed in plain clothes so as to blend in with migrants, infiltrate
groups, and arrest people caught in the act of committing any one of
a broad range of crimes, from public drunkenness to car theft, to people and drug smuggling, extortion, and even rape and murder (Specht
2009; Rotella 1992a). Officials were armed and given sole jurisdiction
over the Tijuana border zone to prevent clashes with other Mexican
police officials working in the area (Specht 2009), and they worked in
close collaboration with San Diego's Border Crime Intervention Unit
(Rotella 1993). This crime-fighting activity was described by Javier
Valenzuela Malagón,[3] founder and initial head of Beta Group Tijuana,
as central to the group's fundamental mission, the "protection of the
migrant" (Rotella 1992a).

The initial positive results rendered by Beta Group Tijuana led
politicians and migrant-rights advocates in Mexico and United States
to call for an expansion of the program to "other border hot spots"
(Rotella 1992b), a call which was heeded. During the decade following
the inauguration of this pilot project, a series of similar protection
groups emerged at other strategic points along Mexico's border with
the United States under different names (OIM 2011) (figure 9.1). In 1994
the Beta Group Nogales was created, and in 1995 the Beta Groups were
formalized through agreements, and two more groups were created,
the Alfa Group in Tecate and the Ébano Group in Matamoros (INM
2001a, 2012; OIM 2011).[4]

In 1996, groups were also created in Agua Prieta and in Tapachula,
the latter of which responded to recommendations made by Mexico's

---

3 Trained as a psychologist and a former university professor, Javier Valenzuela
   Malagón was the brains behind the creation of the Beta Groups, as well as the first
   director of the founding Tijuana group.
4 Nogales, Tecate, and Matamoros are the names of towns and cities found along the
   U.S.-Mexico border.

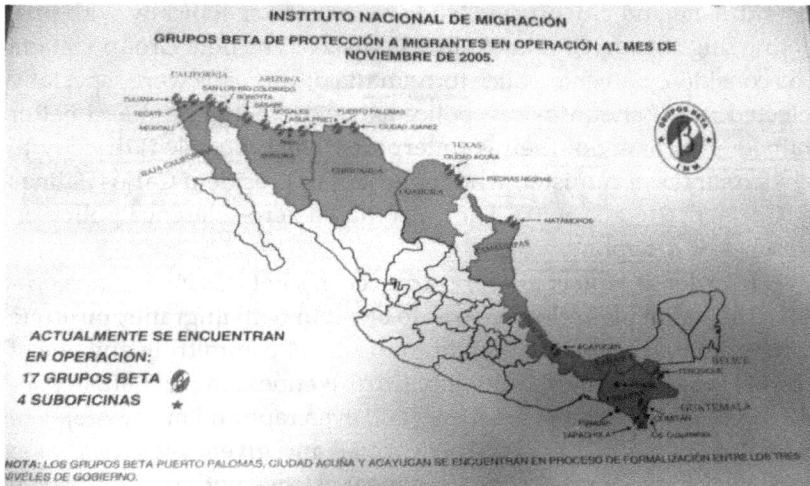

FIGURE 9.1. Map of Beta Group Operations in 2005.
Source: INM-SEGOB 2005.

National Commission for Human Rights (CNDH) that widespread
human-rights violations in southern Mexico be addressed (INM 1998c,
2001a). The analysis that follows stems from a close reading of the
1996–1998 field journals of the Beta Group Sur, which operated
between Tapachula and Pijijiapán in the southern state of Chiapas.

Rooting Out, Sorting, and (Re)Integrating Migrant Populations

When Beta Group Sur arrived in southern Mexico in May 1996, their
stated aim was "to protect the human rights, and the physical and
patrimonial integrity of migrants, regardless of their nationality or
migratory status, through actions which inhibit and prevent the
aggressions and abuses which are committed against them by criminals and dishonest authorities" (INM 1997).[5] In order to do this, they
needed to identify migrant populations and their spaces and to differentiate between the different types of migrant spaces and
populations.

Beta Group Sur identified migrant populations and spaces primarily through the practice of regular foot and vehicle patrols,

---

5   All translations from Spanish are mine.

designed to gather knowledge about the movement of migrants and the crimes committed against them. According to one report, "The preventative foot patrol allows us to continuously come into contact with migrants since these are mandatory passage points [*pasos obliga-dos*] on their way to the Central and Northern parts of the country" (INM 1998c). Patrols also offered the Beta agents a mobile means to "register complaints, descriptions of their aggressors [and] the place time and circumstances of crimes" (INM 1998c). Thus, much like the patrols of other police forces, Beta patrols involved the practice of gathering information and generating criminal profiles to develop crime-fighting and prevention programing.

Nevertheless, unlike the patrols of other police forces in Mexico, the Beta's patrols were able to supersede the jurisdictional boundaries that ordinarily place spatial limitations on the authority of other police forces in Mexico. Because it was the international human-rights framework that mandated part of the Beta's protection work, and because they were tasked to a certain extent with "policing the other Mexican police" (a point I will return to), Beta Groups were able to design patrols that were flexible and responsive to the regular changes that characterize the movement of migrants and those who target them. As one report described:

> Depending on the general characteristics of the migratory flows in each locality; the incidence and patterns of crime detected, and; the human and material resources available, each month the group coordinator will determine the general parameters of the patrols, their operating hours, the configuration of groups of agents, the zones to be closely monitored, and the general operating strategies of the group. This can be modified at any moment, according to circumstance, to attend to changes in the circumstances. (INM 1997)

This ability to transgress the spatial boundaries of ordinary police jurisdictions is what allowed for the Beta Group Sur to reorient their patrols away from the policing of the state boundary dividing Mexico and Guatemala and toward a more fluid and flexible policing of the railways. As the report noted, many months of unfruitful preventative patrols along Mexico's southern border led the Beta Group Sur to conclude that they needed to concentrate their activities along the railway tracks between the stations of Ciudad Hidalgo, Tapachula, and

Huixtla, since this was where the majority of crimes were committed against migrants (INM 1997). To adjust to the circumstances, the Beta Group Sur scheduled all its available agents to work a single shift, structured around train movements. Agents were divided into groups. One group conducted preventative patrols in a train station prior to and immediately after a train's departure. They asked anyone found around the railway to identify themselves, explain their presence, and submit to frisking to prove they were not carrying weapons.

All Beta Group Sur officials operating within this context at the end of the 1990s were required to log all the incidences of contact they had with migrants and their assailants while on preventative patrol (INM 1997). Such incidences were to be recorded in a chronological and sequential manner, noting the day of the incidence, the participating Beta agents, and the Beta lead on the shift. Beta agents were required to write a daily report, summarizing (i) all detentions (*consignaciones ante una autoridad*) and the type of legal authority to which they were channeled; (ii) all cases of direct assistance to migrants, indicating the problem and the type of assistance that was provided; and (iii) any other significant event that occurred in the day. Any incident not reported carried consequences for the person omitting it from the daily report. The Beta Groups' patrol logs and the daily and weekly activity reports that were developed from these were delivered to diverse audiences, including the Beta Group Sur's head office and the regional delegate of Mexico's INM, an inter-institutional technical committee involved in the regular monitoring and evaluation of the Beta Groups, (a transparency initiative I will address in greater detail below) and the Beta Group Sur coordinator.[6]

For the coordinator, the daily and weekly reports were a means of systematizing and analyzing the data registered in patrol logs and tailoring the group's protection activities accordingly. As the excerpt below illustrates, two key migrant profiles—the "victim" and the "victimizer"—resulted from early analyses of the patrol-log data

---

6   That the migrant-protection practices of the Beta Group Sur were so closely monitored suggests that this information likely also supported migration-control efforts in southern Mexico during this period. The regional delegate for the INM was responsible for overseeing both the migrant-protection and migrant-control programs in that region of Mexico. By requiring the Beta Groups to document and communicate their interactions while patrolling migrants' transit routes, the regional delegate would have been able to utilize the migrant-protection program as a means of police reconnaissance, which could have served to support migration-control programs in locating migrants for detention and deportation.

concerning the spaces and the behavioural patterns of diverse actors in transit routes in southern Mexico:

> [P]atrols have allowed us to identify the social composition and the contexts [*entorno*] of the major crime scenes; to study the modus operandi of the criminal actors, and; learn about the migratory practices of the undocumented [migrants]. This has also allowed us to carry out operatives [*planes operativos*] which are specific to the circumstances and causes which surround the victim-victimizer relationship. (INM 1998c)

These two figures—the victim and the victimizer—each carried their own characteristics, specific lexicon, migrant-protection practices, and indicators for measuring the protection outcomes. For example, the profile of the migrant "victim" (actual and prospective) comprised those actors who Beta agents encountered on their preventative patrols, but whose only criminal activity was their unregistered entry, stay, or passage through Mexican territory.[7] Here, the lack of registration or documentation is a defining characteristic of the migrant victim; they are also attributed with a sense of innocence that appears to stem, primarily, from an assumption of ignorance and marginalization rather than maliciousness. As the following description illustrates, these assumptions are clearly embedded in the "social assistance" class of protection practices Beta Groups engage in when encountering migrants who match this profile while on patrol. These practices are designed for:

> undocumented migrants [*los indocumentados*] with whom we have direct contact, those we meet in their places of transit or provisional stay, to those whom we offer guidance-education [*orientación*] about the human-rights protection they have in Mexico; we give them the human-rights pamphlet [*cartilla guía*];

---

7   Until 2008, unauthorized entry and unregistered transit through Mexican territory was considered a crime that was punishable with up to two years in prison and a fine of between 300 and 5,000 pesos (approximately \$30–\$500) (Grupo Coppan 2008). Thus, by definition, both local and international migrants whom the Beta Groups were tasked with protecting were engaged in criminal activities in Mexico. Though rarely enforced in this manner, article 123 of the Ley General de Población was regularly used by state authorities to extort money from unauthorized migrants as they passed through the country (González-Murphy and Koslowski 2011; Grupo Coppan 2008).

we receive their complaints, and we give them medical and food services when they require them, or social and juridical assistance when they accept or ask for it; we also alert them to the dangers and risks of particular areas; and we help prevent them from becoming involved in acts which could be considered criminal, or acts which alter our norms of social peace [*convivencia*], or which could affect the public peace. As a precautionary measure, we conduct body searches to ensure that assailants [*asalta-migrantes*] have not infiltrated among the migrants, or that no one is carrying any sort of arm which could be used in criminal acts. We take nationals and foreigners who we encounter altering the public order, under the influence of alcohol or some other stimulant, and present them to the administrative authority. (INM 1998b)

Noteworthy in this passage are the on-the-ground practices—particularly the body searches—used to distinguish the migrant victim from the migrant victimizers. Furthermore, this attempt to sort what one report called the "true" from the "harmful" migrants is also apparent in the language used in the Beta reports written at this time (INM 1998b). The terms *Migrante* and *Indocumentado* (capitalized) were used to refer to migrant "victims," whereas the "victimizers" who were not recognized public authorities were referred to as "persons," "gangs," and "foreigners," but never as *Migrantes*, despite that, by virtue of their countries of origin, many of the victimizers were also migrants (INM 1997, 1998b, 1998c). Examples of Beta Group literature are reproduced here (figure 9.2).

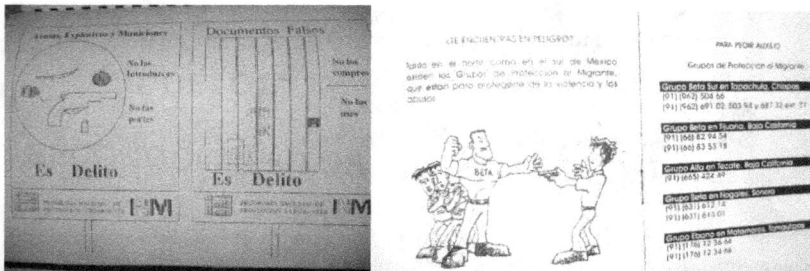

FIGURE 9.2. Posters and Pamphlets Used for Orientation of *Migrantes* in the 1990s. The poster (left) informs migrants that carrying false documents, arms, or explosives is a criminal offence. The pamphlet (right) says "Are you in danger? Migrant Protection Groups are present in both the North and South of Mexico to protect you from violence and abuses." *Source:* INM 1998b; La Biblioteca de la Unidad de Política Migratoria, SEGOB, México, D.F (personal visit).

Victimizers of migrants were profiled according to their country of origin and the frequency and the degree of organization with which they targeted the first group of *Migrantes* for crimes. A report written in 1997, for example, described this profiling process: "[W]e have started to identify these people who target migrants as members of different Mara gangs [transnational criminal organizations], and as all sorts of criminals of occasional and systematic, national and foreign character" (INM 1997). Another report presented a statistical overview of Beta Group Sur's activities during their first 18 months of operations. Their description of the crime-fighting aspect of their work is revealing. They noted that, among those persons Beta Group Sur had detained and turned over to administrative authorities while on patrols during this period,

> 52 in 1996 and 411 in 1997 were foreigners found to be violating "Police and Good Government" bylaws [*disposiciones*], disturbing the peace or public order, generally while intoxicated or under the influence of some other stimulant, such as thinner, cement or marijuana. Overall, the majority of these were persons with irregular status, without an honest livelihood. They were identified as members of one of two gangs of foreigners (Mara 13 and 18), who assault the undocumented [*indocumentados*] and who constitute, without any prejudice (sic.), a risk for migrants [*migrantes*], and a latent danger for the border community [*sociedad fronteriza*]. In terms of crime prevention, they constitute our greatest preoccupation given the antecedents and accusations [*imputaciones*] which are frequently attributed to them. (INM 1998c)[8]

Finally, it is also important to note that the reports I analyzed for this study clearly indicated the advanced development of profiles of the *civilian* victimizers Beta agents interacted with while on preventative patrols. Meanwhile, there was a total underdevelopment, if not

---

8   The Mara Salvatrucha (or MS-13) and Barrio 18 are violent street gangs that originated in Los Angeles in the 1980s. During the 1990s, the United States began to prioritize the deportation of migrants with criminal records, thereby injecting these gangs into Central America and southern Mexico. The gangs subsequently transnationalized their membership and their illicit activities through the recruitment and systematic extortion of migrants who used the railway to transit through Mexico to the United States.

absence, of profiles for those victimizers who committed crimes against migrants while acting in their roles as public authorities, such as police and customs officers. This omission is significant considering that crimes committed against migrants by public authorities were well-documented by Beta Group Sur, explicitly highlighted in their initial mission statements (INM 1997, 1998c). This contradiction is likely explained by the highly sensitive and dangerous task of policing the police.

Policing the Police and Other Governmental Dilemmas

In the first six months of operations, Beta Group Sur registered an average of 40 cases of extortion or robbery of migrants, with 41 percent of these attributed to public authorities and 59 percent to local criminal activity (INM 1998c).[9] Beta Group patrols along migrant transit routes and in migrant detention facilities were thus intended to deter public authorities in these spaces from committing crimes against migrants; their presence was also meant to ensure that justice—rather than impunity—was served when crimes were committed against migrants, as Beta Groups were to accompany and protect migrant victims through the process of filing a judicial complaint. As previously mentioned, the Beta Groups were originally meant to be a corruption-proof police force that, during the negotiation of NAFTA, would substantiate Mexico's ability to "secure" or protect the diverse mobilities that circulate within its borders, and to ensure that these were governed according to a rule of law; that is, according to rules harmonized and enforced equally throughout the free-trade region. In order to achieve this, however, the Beta Groups faced two challenges: How to ensure that *this* police force would be different from the rest? And, further, how to convince others that this *was* in fact the case?

To address these challenges, the Beta Group patrols and logs were not only used to identify, differentiate, and engage the migrant

---

9   This proportion of migrant complaints against Mexican authorities in the south was relatively larger than that registered by the Beta Group Tijuana. During the month of November in 1994, for instance, the group found that 23.1 percent of crimes committed among migrants in the Tijuana area were attributed to Mexican officials, 7.7 percent to U.S. officials, 53.8 percent to common criminals, and 15.4 percent to unknown persons. Some 61.5 percent of migrants' complaints were for assault, 23.1 percent for extortion, 7.7 percent for kidnapping, and 7.7 percent for other crimes (INM 1994).

populations but also to distinguish the diverse dispositions of state authorities. In particular, they were mobilized to deter, arrest, and support the prosecution of police and state officials who victimized migrants; and to monitor the integrity and transparency of the Beta Group itself, ensuring its strict adherence to rule of law and preventing it from becoming "ungovernable." Let's look at the use of this knowledge in greater detail, including its implication for the exercise of sovereign power in Mexico.

Safeguarding the Good Cops

In order to ensure that the Beta Groups both started and remained in their role as the "good cops," a series of checks and balances were built into the selection/recruitment, training, compensation, and monitoring methods used to compose and regulate the force. These included recruitment of Beta agents from different jurisdictional levels of policing—municipal, state, and federal—and higher pay and more comprehensive training, particularly in the area of human rights. Beta agents were required to participate in continuous training, which offered regular capacity building in three thematic areas: (1) human rights and state-level offices, (2) local juridical frameworks for combating crime, and (3) police tactics and physical fitness (INM 1997). In March and April 1997, for instance, Beta Sur agents received a total of 16 days of eight-hour training sessions, which included seven days of "Jiu Jitsu, Security and Submission techniques [*medidas de seguridad y sometimiento*], and arms training," a two-day workshop entitled "Human rights, the rape and sexual abuse of migrant women and children," and a seven-day workshop in which the UNHCR, along with Mexico's INM, the Mexican Commission for Refugee Assistance, and the National Human Rights Commission trained agents in the national and international legal frameworks for migrants and refugees in Mexico (INM 1997). With this training, Beta agents were tasked with mobilizing these knowledges and techniques to protect migrants from crime.

Internally, there were procedural guidelines that were designed to police the Beta agents "from within." Such guidelines strictly prohibited agents from engaging "in activities which differ from those which are legally ascribed to them" (INM 1997). They also prohibited anyone who was not a Beta agent from participating in the patrols without consent from the regional delegate. This included journalists and other types of police units. Beta agents were prohibited from using anything that had been confiscated in an arrest (vehicles, drugs, arms), and they were required to turn over such items, along with the person who had been porting it. Beta agents were also prohibited from using any personal belongings illegally acquired. They were required to "always wear uniforms when carrying out their work, given the preventative and dissuasive nature of crime-fighting" (INM 1997). Beta agents were only permitted to work undercover (without uniform) for approved special operations, largely to detain criminals who were identified and tracked. Finally, beginning in June 1998, Beta Group Sur began rotating agents working in supervisory roles; they also engaged in self-evaluation to assess their successes and failures, and to discuss the possible solutions to the challenges faced on the job (INM 1998b).

There were external mechanisms in place as well. These were designed to keep the Beta Groups honest. As discussed in the previous section, Beta agents were required to log all their activities and interactions when on preventative patrols. The coordinator of the Beta Group Sur was required to submit regular bi-monthly and bi-annual reports to an inter-institutional committee for review and commentary by actors from academia, civil society, international organizations, and public offices (INM 1998b). This mechanism was a product of an inter-institutional agreement signed on May 4, 1996 (INM 1998a).

Cultivating Legitimacy and Authority

The second problem that Beta Groups encountered was the dual-faced challenge of legitimacy/authority and public image; that is, how to convince others that they were different from other police forces. This meant a lot of public relations to gain the trust of migrants and other actors mistrustful of the authorities. It also meant establishing an authority that would be respected by other police forces in Mexico. The Beta reports I studied alluded to these tensions and the challenges this aspect of their work posed in terms of group morale and logistics as the Betas were relatively weaker in institutional size, influence, and material resources. For instance, one report included a (rather pessimistic) cheer Beta agents had developed in a team- and morale-building workshop: "Beta Sur. At the Service of Society. Beta Sur. With honour and dignity. I am Police. Beta Sur. I am Police. Beta Sur. Who stops us? Nobody stops us. Who criticizes us? Everybody criticizes us. And if Death happens to surprise us while on duty? Welcome it will be" (INM 1998b).

From Policing to Search and Rescue

Efforts to ensure that Beta and other police forces acted exclusively according to rule of law ultimately failed. At the end of the 1990s, reports of migrants being harassed, extorted, and trafficked by Beta Groups and other INM agents came to light in different parts of Mexico, including in Tapachula (INM 1998c, 2001a). Then, to make matters worse, in 2000, a Mexican television crew recorded two officials from Beta Group Matamoros watching passively as two migrants drowned in the Rio Grande. The agents, who were quickly dismissed, said they did not know how to swim (Puente 2001; Crosswalk 2001). This public scandal further damaged the already deteriorated image of the Beta Groups. Now, they were not only being accused of corruption but also incompetence. Critics clamoured: How could Mexico demand respect for its migrants' rights in the United States when it was incapable of guaranteeing protections for migrants in its own territory?

In an effort to rid the INM and Beta Groups of their increasingly tarnished reputations, in 2001 Mexico's federal government announced a number of measures, including over 500 personnel changes within the INM, and that more than 70 officials faced criminal charges or investigation and some 1,800 others immigration-smuggling charges.[10] The INM commissioner, Felipe de Jesús Preciado, described the measures to journalists as a "war that will be thorough" (Puente 2001). Further, as an INM report indicates, changes to migration policy introduced by the newly elected President Vicente Fox motivated a complete overhaul of Mexico's Beta Groups in 2001.

> Given the cases documented along the Northern border of migrants that have fallen victim to drowning, accidents, and

---

10 It might seem common sense and intuitive to attribute this shift in the humanitarian government of migrants in Mexico to the change in world politics that followed 9/11. And yet, in the case of Mexico, this would be a mistake. The changes to Beta Groups were proposed and implemented in May 2001 (INM 2001a).

climatic conditions—particularly in winter and summer—and those registered in the mountainous and desert regions, in the canyons and fast-moving rivers, we have decided to transform the protection functions of the Mexican state. The aim is to strengthen and adjust these functions according to the new legal frameworks [*disposiciones legales*], circumstances, and challenges in our country. The migration-related challenges which President Fox has committed to addressing, particularly those concerned with the protection and defense of the human rights of migrants, lead us to new direct actions with regards to the migrant, particularly with regards to social and institutional actions. (INM 2001a)

The change was dramatic. Fox disarmed all Beta Groups in the country, essentially transforming them from a police unit into a search-and-rescue squad. Beta Groups were reduced in size and number; they received new uniforms, with bright orange T-shirts; and their vehicles were painted orange in order to make them more readily identifiable to the public. Furthermore, new agents no longer came from other police forces, and they were trained in legal and social assistance, and in first-aid and search-and-rescue techniques (INM 2001a; Puente 2001). The orientation and social-assistance materials that Beta Groups used to engage the migrant victims (potential and actual) also shifted accordingly. As figure 9.3 illustrates, information given to

FIGURE 9.3. Posters and Pamphlets Used for Orientation of *Migrantes* following the 2001 Reform.
The poster (left) reads: "Migrant friend, your life is most important. Don't risk yourself or your family." The pamphlet (right) informs migrants of the dangers found in jungles and deserts and offers a list of essential survival items, along with the following piece of advice: "The best way to protect your life is to return home."
Source: Reynoso Nuño 2010.

migrants during their patrols (newly renamed "search-and-rescue brigades" to divorce them from their policing origins) no longer focused on the risks or threats posed to migrants by criminal groups, but rather on those risks related to the heat of the desert during the summertime or the dangers of riding atop freight trains (INM 2001b).

Thus, in little more than a decade, the Beta Groups had gone from being described as an "elite police unit" to being presented as "a civilian agency whose charge includes thousands of migrants from Central America who travel through Mexico on their way to the United States" (Puente 2001). Strangely enough, despite changes in the practices of the Beta Groups, there was great continuity in the rationales for its existence. Leaders of the Beta Groups continued to present their mandate in the exact same manner: "The function of the Beta agents is to protect the migrants" (Jaime Paz, director of the Beta Group Matamoros, cited in Puente 2001).

Likewise, Beta Groups continued to offer enormous political capital to the Mexican government in terms of Mexico-U.S. relations and state-civil-society relations, as Beta Group activities related to undocumented-migration deterrence (originally by detaining human smugglers, later by informing migrants of the dangers of border crossing and dissuading them) continued to demonstrate the Mexican government's willingness to cooperate with the United States in addressing this issue (Nevins 2002). Secondly, framing these activities as "migrant protection" gave the Mexican government a way to respond to civil society's accusations of widespread human-rights violations (i.e., corrupt officials harassing migrants); to demonstrate to the international community that it was upholding its commitments to the migrant-rights conventions it had ratified in the 1990s; and to contest critics who pointed out the hypocrisy of advocating for Mexican migrants' rights in the United States while allowing Central American migrants to face myriad forms of violence as they transited Mexican territory (INM 2001a).

Finally, the changes eliminated the contradictions and dilemmas (and perhaps also some opportunities) stemming from the condition of the Beta Groups as a police force whose job was to enforce both national and international law. As noted earlier, human rights were the raison d'être of Beta Group efforts to stop and prevent crimes against migrants. Because their mandate stemmed in part from international human-rights frameworks, it was possible to frame at least some of their humanitarian bordering practices in this way, despite that other practices—such as arrests—relied on domestic juridical tools. This presented enormous contradictions within this policing unit. One report, submitted during the period of consultation and reflections for the 2001 redesign of the Beta Groups, clearly outlines the contradictions and dilemmas that were involved in policing as the humanitarian section of Mexico's INM:

> Experience demonstrated that the deviations [*desviaciones*] which penetrated and weakened the Beta institution occurred when we allowed their public security functions to absorb their duties, particularly with respect to combatting the trafficking of the undocumented [*indocumentados*]. This natural turn to privilege policing ended up distancing the Betas from their original aims and ideals, generating suspicions and doubts about their conduct.... The preservation of rule of law [*Estado de Derecho*], without violating, and above all protecting, human rights, is an ideal which should be developed and practiced in all areas of the Institute. Nevertheless, it is a goal which is nearly impossible to reach if we pursue it through a hybrid agency, which, on one hand, searches for migrants to protect them, receive their complaints and orders, and on the other hand, detains them for violating the law. (INM 2001b)

In short, while the humanitarian rationale and juridical frameworks remained important for the Beta Groups' humanitarian bordering of Mexico in the twenty-first century, policing technologies and institutions were traded for socio-medical technologies and institutions. "Migrants rescued" replaced "criminal arrests" as an indicator of migrant-protection efficacy (Reynoso Nuño 2010; INM 1998c). Detention centres gave way to hospitals and morgues as channels for drawing populations into state institutions. And migrants were increasingly framed as victims of their own poor decisions and a (depoliticized) set of environmental risks, rather than of predatory, criminal groups.

By patrolling the railways and generating juridical knowledge that connected transgressions of state law, human suffering, and death among railway passengers and spaces, the Beta Group Sur came to constitute the railways of Mexico as a space of humanitarian governance. This is spatially significant because Mexico's railway system passes through the country's most remote corners.

By humanitarianizing the governance of the railways, the Beta Group in southern Mexico effectively made it possible to re-border all Mexico's territory so as to constitute it as one "thick" humanitarian border and one "strong" state.

Policy Considerations

Recent developments might suggest that NAFTA-era re/bordering has ultimately failed to "bulk up" the Mexican state. Over the past decade, the perpetrators of crime and violence against migrants have diversified and multiplied in Mexico. It is no longer state officials and petty criminals who assault migrants at borders. Now there is a complex, networked hierarchy of state and non-state actors who seek profit in the extraction and exploitation of migrants along transit routes throughout Mexico. This network includes non-state, armed actors, such as transnational drug cartels and street gangs, who compete and conspire to capture migrants for the purposes of trafficking, kidnapping for ransom, and smuggling.

This phenomenon has brought greater human suffering to migrants who journey through Mexico to the United States. It has also led to the emergence of new migration strategies. Since October 2018, migrants have chosen to navigate the risks along Mexico's transit routes by travelling in large groups, called caravans. Organizing their journeys around the premise that there is "safety in numbers," the caravans bring groups of migrants together (500 to 1,500 migrants per caravan) to journey toward the U.S.-Mexico border. The first caravan arrived in Tijuana in November 2018. More than six months later, an estimated 20,000 Central Americans had gathered at the U.S.-Mexico border awaiting their chance to cross clandestinely or to claim asylum.

Despite these changes in the Mexican migration-scape, Beta Group practices have not changed much. Statistics published for the first trimester of 2019 reveal an approach to migrant protection that continues to orient migrant victims and channel them into state institutions, such as hospitals, morgues, and detention centres. The Beta Groups continue to hand out informative guides that teach migrants about the dangers of the journey and their human rights (SEGOB 2019; INM 2019). They collect information about migrant spaces, identities, and movements, and they still struggle to maintain public trust

(Fernández 2019). Meanwhile, successive U.S. administrations have threatened Mexico and Central America's northern-triangle countries with sanctions—such as the reintroduction of tariffs on Mexican imports—if they fail to curb transit through their territories and stop the migrant caravans from reaching the U.S. border (Gottesdiener, Daniel, and Hesson 2021; Gambino and Agrin 2019; Torpey 1998).

Notwithstanding these developments, I would suggest that the rise of violence along migrant transit routes over the past two decades is more an indication of active state making than it is a failure to bulk up the state. These conflicts indicate a disruption of the status quo where mobility is concerned. They suggest that previous systems of regulating movement have been disturbed and, as a result, there are power struggles on transit routes today. Mexico's Beta Groups have played a central role in this disruption and the state's quest to monopolize the legitimate means of movement in spaces where it was not previously dominant.

The monopolization of legitimate means of movement is a key component of modern state making, which requires states to know their populations and territories (Torpey 1998). To do this, states must develop systems of identification and a bureaucracy capable of collecting, organizing, and administering knowledge about their populations and territories. Because of the work of the Beta Groups, the Mexican state has more contact with and knowledge of those who reside and move through the most remote corners of its territory (INM 2019). From this viewpoint, the humanitarian bordering of Mexico's Beta Groups must be seen as a contribution to state efforts to monopolize the legitimate means of movement. It is a work in progress, but not a failure to bulk up the state.

References

Aradau, C. 2004. "The Perverse Politics of Four-letter Words: Risk and Pity in the Securitisation of Human Trafficking." *Millennium: Journal of International Studies* 33(2): 251–277.

Crosswalk. 2001. "Elite Mexico Force Faces Accusations." Crosswalk Online, August 16, 2001.

Fassin, D. 2012. *Humanitarian Reason: A Moral History of the Present.* University of California Press.

———. 2007. "Humanitarianism: A Nongovernmental Government." In *Nongovernmental Politics*, edited by Michel Feher, 149–160. New York: Zone Books.

Fernández, H. 2019. "Denuncian presuntas extorsiones del INM para agilizar visa humanitaria." *El Universal* [Mexico City], April 3. https://www.eluniversal.com.mx/estados/denuncian-presuntas-extorsiones-del-inm-para-agilizar-visa-humanitaria.

Gambino, L., and David Agrin. 2019. "Trump Announces Tariffs on Mexico until 'Immigration Remedied.'" *The Guardian*, May 31. https://www.theguardian.com/us-news/2019/may/30/trump-mexico-tariffs-migration.

González-Murphy, L., and Rey Koslowski. 2011. *Entendiendo el cambio a las leyes de inmigración de México.* Washington, D.C.: Mexico Institute of the Woodrow Wilson International Center for Scholars.

Gottesdiener, L., Frank Jack Daniel, and Ted Hesson. 2021. "Tough Migration Enforcement South of Border Key to Biden Plans." *Reuters*, February 12. https://www.reuters.com/article/us-usa-immigration-military-insight-idUSKBN2AC16U.

Grupo Coppan, SC. 2008. "Despenalización de la migración indocumentada en México." *Analítica Internacional*, May 12. http://biblioteca.cide.edu/Datos/COPPAN/2008/mayo/5.12.2008%20COYUNTURA%20VC%20%20Despenalizaci%F3n%20de%20la%20migraci%F3n%20in documentada%20en%20M%E9xico%20%20%20Mayo%202008.pdf.

Heyman, J. M. 2008. "Constructing a Virtual Wall: Race and Citizenship in U.S.-Mexico Border Policing." *Journal of the Southwest* 50(3): 305–333.

Instituto Nacional de Migración (INM). 1994. *Operativo Beta: Migración Indocumentada, Vigilancia y Seguridad en la Frontera. Informe Mensual de Trabajo. Noviembre 1994.* Tijuana, Baja California.

——. 1997. "Informe bimestral de las actividades realizadas por el grupo de protección a migrantes Beta Sur con sede en la Ciudad de Tapachula, Chiapas, correspondiente a los meses de marzo y abril de 1997" [Bi-monthly activities report for the migrant protection group Beta Sur, with headquarters in Tapachula, Chiapas. March and April 1997]. Tapachula de Córdoba y Ordoñez, Chiapas: Coordinación del Programa Beta Sur.

——. 1998a. "Informe correspondiente a los meses de enero y febrero de 1998 que presenta al Comité Técnico para el Seguimiento de la Operación del Grupo de Protección a Migrantes Beta Sur" [January and February 1998 report for the technical committee for monitoring the operations of the migrant protection group Beta Sur]. Tapachula de Cordova y Ordoñez, Chis: INM Delegación Regional Chiapas.

——. 1998b. "Informe correspondiente a los meses de marzo, abril y mayo de 1998 que presenta al Comité Técnico para el Seguimiento de la Operación del Grupo de Protección a Migrantes Beta Sur" [March, April and May 1998 Report for the Technical Committee for Monitoring the Operations of the Migrant Protection Group Beta Sur]. Tapachula de Cordova y Ordoñez, Chis: INM Delegación Regional Chiapas.

———. 1998c. "Actividades, resultados, retos y líneas de acción para 1998 del grupo interinstitucional de protección a migrantes Beta Sur Tapachula-Pijijiapán" [Activities, results, challenges, and lines of action for the 1998 inter-institutional migrant protection group Beta Sur Tapachula-Pijijiapán]. Tapachula de Cordova y Ordoñez, Chis: Coordinación de supervisón y control operativo, dirección de protección a migrantes Grupo Beta Sur Tapachula-Pijijiapán of INM Delegación Regional Chiapas.

———. 2001a. "Proyecto de Reestructuración de los Grupos Beta de Protección a Migrantes." *SEGOB and INM*, May 22, 2001.

———. 2001b. "Documento de análisis y sugerencias para el funcionamiento e instalación de los Grupos Beta." Instituto Nacional de Migración.

Instituto Nacional de Migración (INM-SEGOB). 2005. "Grupos Beta de Protección a Migrante 2005." México, D.F.: INM- SEGOB. Biblioteca de la Unidad de Política Migratoria.

———. 2012. *Grupos Beta del INM. Protección al Migrante*. Instituto Nacional de Migración.

———. 2014. *Guía para los migrantes*. Instituto Nacional de Migración. http://www.inm.gob.mx/static/grupos_beta/GUIA_MIGRANTES.pdf.

———. 2018. *Grupos Beta, 28 años en la protección de migrantes*. https://www.gob.mx/inm/articulos/grupos-beta-28-anos-en-la-proteccion-de-migrantes?idiom=es.

———. 2019. *Aviso de Privacidad Integral Base de datos de los grupos BETA*. January 3. https://www.inm.gob.mx/gobmx/word/index.php/aviso-deprivacidad-integral-base-de-datos-de-los-grupos-beta/.

Casas-Cortes, M., S. Cobarrubias, N. De Genova, G. Garelli, G. Grappi, C. Heller, S. Hess, B. Kasparek, S. Mezzadra, B. Neilson, I. Peano, L. Pezzani, J. Pickles, F. Rahola, L. Riedner, S. Scheel, and M. Tazzioli. 2015. "New Keywords: Migration and Borders." *Cultural Studies* 29(1): 55–87.

McDonald, W. F., and S. Paromchik. 1996. "Transparency and the Police: External Research, Policing and Democracy." In *Policing in Central and Eastern Europe: Comparing Firsthand Knowledge with Experiences from the West*, edited by Milan Pagon. Ljubljana: College of Police and Security Studies. https://www.ncjrs.gov/policing/trans17.htm.

Mexican Secretariat for Home Affairs (SEGOB). 2019. *Acciones de protección a migrantes efectuadas por Grupo Beta, según entidad federativa, abril 2019*. Grupos de Protecci'on a Migrantes. Secretaría de Gobernación http://www.politicamigratoria.gob.mx/es_mx/SEGOB/Grupos_de_Proteccion_a_Migrantes.

Nevins, J. 2002. *Operation Gatekeeper: The Rise of the "Illegal Alien" and the Making of the U.S.-Mexico Boundary*. New York: Routledge.

Organización Internacional para las Migraciones (OIM). 2011. *Grupos Beta: El Brazo Humanitario del INM*. México, D.F. Organización Internacional para las Migraciones.

Pallister-Wilkins, P. 2015. "The Humanitarian Politics of European Border Policing: Frontex and Border Police in Evros." *International Political Sociology* 9(1): 53–69.

Puente, T. 2001. "Mexico Reforming Border Patrols." *Chicago Tribune,* September 10. http://articles.chicagotribune.com/2001-09-10/news/0109 100211_1_grupo-beta-border-patrol-migrants.

Reynoso Nuño, F. J. 2010. "Actividad Migratoria." *Delegación Regional del INM en Baja California.* Powerpoint presentation. http://slideplayer.es/slide /39202/.

Riemsdijk, M. 2012. "(Re)scaling Governance of Skilled Migration in Europe: Divergence, Harmonisation, and Contestation." *Population, Space and Place* 18(3): 344–358.

Rotella, Sebastian. 1992a. "Reducing the Misery at the Border." *Los Angeles Times,* March 10. http://articles.latimes.com/1992-03-10/news/mn-3541 _1_grupo-beta.

———. 1992b. "Border Meeting Closes in Amity." *Los Angeles Times,* April 4. http://articles.latimes.com/1992-04-04/local/me-94_1_free-trade -agreement.

———. 1993. "Border Watch: Just too Good?" *Los Angeles Times,* September 6. http://articles.latimes.com/1993-09-16/local/me-35588_1_grupo-beta.

Specht, J. 2009. "Between Immigration Control and Human Rights Protection: The Ambiguities of Mexico's Migration Policy–The Case of the Beta Groups for Protection of Migrants." Paper prepared for the International Studies Association Annual Conference 2009, New York.

Ticktin, M. 2005. "Policing and Humanitarianism in France: Immigration and the Turn to Law as State of Exception." *Interventions* 7(3): 346–368.

———. 2007. "The Offshore Camps of the European Union: At the Border of Humanity." Paper presented at the American Anthropological Association Annual Meetings.

Torpey, John. 1998. "Coming and Going: On the State Monopolization of the Legitimate 'Means of Movement.'" *Sociological Theory* 16(3): 239–259.

Vaughan-Williams, N. 2015. "'We Are not Animals!' Humanitarian Border Security and Zoopolitical Spaces in Europe." *Political Geography* 45:1–10.

Walters, W. 2011. "Foucault and Frontiers: Notes on the Birth of the Humanitarian Border." In *Governmentality: Current Issues and Future Challenges,* edited by Ulrich Bröckling, Susanne Krasmann, and Thomas Lemke, 138–164. New York: Routledge.

Williams, J. M. 2015. "From Humanitarian Exceptionalism to Contingent Care: Care and Enforcement at the Humanitarian Border." *Political Geography* 47:11–20.

PART IV

DENATURALIZING AND DECONSTRUCTING NATIONAL INTEREST AND BORDER POLICY

CHAPTER 10

Border Control and the Migration-Policy Puzzle in Japan

Edward Boyle and Naomi Chi

In the early hours of December 8, 2018, an unseemly ruckus broke out at a judicial affairs select-committee session in the upper house of Japan's National Diet (parliament). The protest occurred as opposition members of the house sought to prevent the committee's chairman from calling for a vote on revisions to the immigration-control law. The revisions were being promoted by then Prime Minister Shinzo Abe and the ruling Liberal Democratic Party, and had already been "bulldozed" through the lower house a few days earlier, on November 27 (Osaki 2018). Scheduled to come into force in April 2019, these revisions explicitly provided for an additional 345,150 foreign workers to enter the country over the subsequent five years. Opposition to the government centred on the absence of a debate on the revisions, a lack of detail in the proposals, and the heavy-handed way the bill was brought before the Diet (Gakuto and Fujita 2018). Ultimately, however, the opposition was unsuccessful in its efforts to prevent the bill's passage, and the so-called foreign-worker bill came onto the books that Saturday morning (Endo and Matsukura 2018).

Japan is currently in the midst of what has been termed its "third debate" on migration policy. This debate is occurring at the same time as questions of migration and border security have been pushed to the top of the domestic agenda in many parts of the world, and most notably among Japan's Organisation for Economic Co-operation and Development (OECD) peers. As in other parts of the world, this debate has made mention of complex issues regarding asylum, refugees, and state responsibility for the provision of support to enable migrants of all stripes to integrate into the country. That scrummages are occurring in the Japanese Diet, rather than on the streets, may be considered as representative of how this debate is conducted. Discussion is focused on how the state and its institutions should administer the border, and the ways in which this administration should respond to national challenges, rather than spilling out into society more broadly.

Broad consensus over the state's political remit shapes the conduct of this debate in Japan. While at the time many of the OECD member states are riven with "populist" opposition to both liberal migration and neoliberal economic policies, in Japan the policy program is shaped by the state's concern with maintaining its working population and tax base while mitigating opposition to immigration. The result has been an ongoing expansion in the number of temporary workers allowed into the country, in an effort to provide the flexible pool of employees necessary to keep the factories and service industries of Japan, Inc., running. This influx of migrant labour promises to dramatically affect the future demographic composition of Japan. However, the emphasis consistently placed on the presence of these foreign labourers as temporary indicates the determination on the part of the state that any movement of people into Japan does not affect the composition of the Japanese nation. It is this narrow distinction between the two notions—national demography, composed of those resident in Japan, and the nation's population, or those recognized by the Japanese government as its citizens—which constitutes the eye of the policy needle that Prime Minister Abe and the ruling Liberal Democratic Party sought to thread with the foreign-workers bill.

This chapter explains the broader context shaping this contemporary transformation in Japan's migration policy. First, it sets out the historical context within which today's border-control policy was established by focusing on the system's emergence in the aftermath of the Pacific War. That system subsequently developed into what Japanese scholars have termed the "1990s regime" of migration control. In the second section, it shows how this narrowly bureaucratic system was gradually opened up to influences from a broader cross-section of social actors over the course of two earlier migration debates. The third section provides the immediate background to the controversial bill by outlining the political context within which Abe's administration operated following his becoming prime minister for a second time in 2012. The fourth section outlines the controversial revisions to the immigration-control law and some of the criticisms it has engendered. The conclusion reflects on the changing character of Japan's borders that are likely to result from these contemporary shifts in its migration policy.

Re-Bordering an Island Nation

Central to the story of migration policy in Japan are the politics behind the process of "establishing rules of entry and exit" (Hollifield 2000, 137). Japan has traditionally been contrasted with other OECD countries for its restrictive migration laws and high degree of ethnic and cultural homogeneity (Kondo 2015, 156). This divergence between Japan and other states is frequently presented as the natural outcome of the former's "closed-country" mentality and natural predisposition to homogeneity (Akashi 2010, 39–50). However, given the recent political prominence of broadly comparable views regarding an earlier golden age of mono-cultural community in other OECD nations, what had previously been understood as reflecting Japanese ethnic chauvinism looks today to be operating in parallel with, rather than at right angles to, a discourse on migration taking place within Japan's OECD peers and, indeed, elsewhere in the world.

We argue in this chapter that, rather than an inherent hostility to foreign others, the explanation for the situation today lies in the historically contingent process through which Japan's current migration policy and foreign-resident population has come into being. It is the presence of an existing system of migration control that defines Japan's current efforts to revise these policies. The emergence and transformation of this system occurred in response to Japan's international position and relations with the wider world, rather than a unique national sense of chauvinism or shared political agreement over the importance of a "closed" country. History is therefore crucial to understand how Japan's contemporary migration and border-control system has come into being.

Japan's defeat in the Second World War resulted in the movement of vast numbers of people. Over seven million Japanese nationals were repatriated from former colonies, and indeed from further afield; around 4,000 of the 22,000 Japanese who had been resident in Canada at the outbreak of the war were stripped of their citizenship and expelled to Japan, for example (Haraguchi 2018; Roy 2015).[1] Meanwhile, perhaps 2.5 million former colonial subjects present within the borders of a shrunken Japan at the end of the war were stripped of their rights of abode and expected to return "home." The state's concern with seeking to define the "boundaries of the Japanese" (Oguma 1998) is visible in the content of the final two imperial ordinances issued by the Showa emperor before the transition to democracy under American tutelage. Issued on May 2, 1947, these defined eligibility for Japanese citizenship in advance of the proclamation of the new constitution, and deliberately excluded Japan's former Korean and Taiwanese colonial subjects from its provisions (Takemae 2002).

Later interpretations of the exclusionary nature of Japan's immigration system have largely invoked social or cultural factors, and paid little attention to either the bureaucratic imperative of defining exactly where the borders of the new Japanese nation ran in relation to its former imperial subjects, or the role of the occupation authorities in setting the parameters of this system. In the nineteenth century, Japan's desire for recognition as "civilized" in a world dominated by imperial polities of European origin had motivated its adoption of its legal and material trappings, nationality, and passports. The self-consciously modernizing state that emerged in Japan following the Meiji Restoration of 1868 rapidly learned to use such elements of international governance as a means of asserting and extending its sovereign reach. In the aftermath of the Pacific War, these same institutions were once again deployed in order to reassert the authority of the state over Japanese and foreign bodies.

Until 1952, the enforcement of border control in Japan was overseen by the supreme commander for the Allied powers (SCAP), and the period is generally characterized by efforts to strictly control migration (Kondo 2015, 157). This was conducted through the Immigration Control Order of 1951, renamed the Immigration Control Act in 1952, that had been initially drawn up by an American adviser at SCAP's general headquarters who had had 30 years of experience with the U.S. Immigration and Naturalization Service (Morris-Suzuki 2006, 137). This provided the legal framework that defined Japan's border-control and migration policy down to the 1980s, and was "exclusionary, discriminatory, and assimilatory" in requiring the

---

1   One of our anonymous reviewers noted the relevance of this to the volume. We greatly appreciate Dr. Yukari Takai introducing us to this literature.

repatriation or naturalization of Koreans and Chinese still in the country (Kondo 2002, 418). The occupation authorities and Japanese government both argued for the necessity of demarcating the postwar territorial settlement, not only at the edges of state space but also cutting through the body of the former imperial-subject population resident within the shriveled boundaries of the Japanese state at the end of the war.

This "bordering" imperative saw the adoption of a series of globalized institutional forms that sought to channel and control the movement of peoples, creating the basis for the exclusionary migration system that has famously persisted into the present. As Deokhyo Choi has noted, drawing on Seyla Benhabib, for Japan in the immediate postwar period, "the Korean imperial subject was exactly the 'frontier' that needed to become the 'boundary' of democracy when postwar Japan transformed from being a multiethnic empire to a homogeneous nation" (Choi 2021, 558). The state's concern with the disruptive potential of this population and desire for its removal was most visible in the support offered to the almost 100,000 Koreans who "re-patriated" to North Korea between 1959 and 1984.[2] At the same time, the new homogeneous democratic nation of Japan was able to countenance, and was indeed complicit in, the presence of these same former colonial subjects, most notably through the creation of the "special permanent resident" visa category that facilitated their continued presence in Japan.

Additionally, while the efforts of the occupational authorities and Japanese state administration colluded in literally reshaping Japan from an expansive imperial state into an archipelagic national one, such territorial integration did not automatically fix the border's location at the outer limits of Japanese administrative control. SCAP oversaw the repatriation of Japanese and other Asians into and out of Japan, but despite their efforts to enforce a strict border-control system there remained considerable numbers of individuals for whom Japan's border effectively failed to exist. These included not only members of the occupying forces located on bases throughout Japan, but also the considerable numbers of those who crossed between Japan and neighbouring countries without official permission (Morris-Suzuki 2010, 14–17).

---

2   "Re-patriated" is complex as the vast majority of Koreans in Japan hailed from the (vastly more populous) south of the Peninsula, but for ideological reasons many associated with and chose to move to the North.

While the former issue, of military bases, lingers on as a political issue today, and particularly for the southern prefecture of Okinawa, in which American troops are overwhelmingly concentrated, this is now seen as being a question of sovereignty rather than migration control per se. By contrast, members of the latter group, irregular migrants from neighbouring countries, have been ever-present, and played a significant role in Japan's early period of postwar economic development. While it is generally understood that Japan is distinct because its golden age of high economic growth did not rely on the import of labour from overseas, in contrast to most of what would come to be considered the "developed" world, this contrast is over-stated. As Akashi Junichi points out, there were certain areas and industries that even in the 1950s and 1960s depended upon the labour of a precarious population of workers who were not simply Japanese citizens (see Akashi, forthcoming). These included many Ryukyuans, inhabitants of the southern islands of Japan, which remained officially under U.S. administration until 1972 before reverting back to Japan as Okinawa prefecture. The labour of these individuals, whether present in Japan as the state "down-sized" from empire to nation, or migrating across its emaciated national borders at a later date, contributed importantly to the triumphant story of Japan's postwar recovery and economic development. The oft-noted "homogeneity" of Japan's population later in the twentieth century fails to account for this *ongoing* process of maintaining administrative borders between residents of the archipelago who were and were not accorded Japanese citizenship. Homogeneity was thus the outcome of policy decisions taken in response to specific historical circumstances, rather than postwar national demography blindly reflecting some inherent cultural particularism.

Given the Cold War fault lines in East Asia and the absence of multilateral economic institutions resembling those emerging in Europe, there was little incentive to alter this system for a quarter of a century. The first significant changes to Japan's postwar migration regime came about through international pressure to accept Indo-Chinese "boat people" as refugees after 1975, in the first mass movement of refugees the country experienced after the fallout from Japan's defeat in the Pacific War. The government subsequently became party to the UN Refugee Convention in 1981, implemented the Immigration Control and Refugee Recognition Act (ICRRA) the following year, and improved the rights of foreign residents thereafter.

It was only in the frothy economic bubble that emerged after 1985, though, that the country began to attract foreign workers and migrants in significant numbers. From a low base of around 850,000 registered foreigners in 1985 (of whom over 80 percent were Koreans with special dispensation to remain in the country), these numbers increased to over 1.3 million in 1995 and over 2 million in 2005, although out of a total population of more than 120 million. The Ministry of Labour continued to proclaim that while Japan would actively admit specialized and technical labour while restricting the migration of "unskilled" labour, in practice, Japan also began to see the beginnings of mass labour migration during this period.

Although it is frequently presented as an outlier in terms of its insularity, the emergence of Japan's border- and migration-control systems reveals the same factors visible in other parts of the world. As with many European states, Japan too had to grapple with the problem of imperial collapse, and responded through tightening its definition of who the Japanese were. There are two things that particularly distinguish Japan from its Western peers, however. The first is that this "tightening" occurred within a very short timeframe, especially when compared with the drawn-out decolonization processes that characterized the slow imperial retreats of Britain, France, or Portugal, for example. The government, supported initially by the occupation authorities, sought to draw a clear distinction between citizens and others on the basis of the nation's new territorial realities at the end of the Pacific War by officially ignoring the movements of people that had occurred over the previous half-century, and which would continue to occur in the war's immediate aftermath. This was done through the *koseki* system of household registration, by which the population of the Japanese "mainland," and thus future Japanese citizens, were distinguished from other colonial subjects by the record of their place of birth (on the operations of this system, see Chapman and Krogness 2014). The putative administrative clarity this offered with regards to who "counted" as a citizen of the newly democratic Japanese state provided the foundations atop which it was possible to erect a restrictive immigration regime, irrespective of the presence of those who did not fit neatly within the resultant bureaucratic boxes.

The second is Japan's geopolitical situation. The nation's archipelagic location, exacerbated by the Cold War and continuing absence of regional economic integration, led to Japan's economy and society remaining demographically insular to a much greater degree than the United Kingdom's, for instance. The absence of any multilateral regional cooperation in East Asia dramatically restricted the possibilities for labour mobility in the region, by comparison with Europe or, more recently, the Association of Southeast Asian Nations. At the same time, the Japanese economy's reliance on domestic labour during its golden age of extended economic growth was supplemented through the deployment of "hidden" minorities, resident Koreans and Ryukyuans, in specific industries to aid in this process of domestic industrial development. In this it differed from countries like Germany that accepted foreign "guest" workers from a much earlier period (Surak 2013). Yet political demands seeking the acceptance of large numbers of foreign workers to Japan have, as in other cases, tracked domestic demand for labour. It is this that has led to the emergence of migration as a political, as opposed to a merely bureaucratic or administrative, issue. It is vital to trace these shifts in the rules on entry and exit as reflecting a policy *process*, rather than merely reflecting a cultural characteristic.

The Politics of Debating Migration

The previous section has demonstrated that the historical origins of Japan's current migration regime cannot be ignored in any effort to analyze current debates over Japanese policy, for the contours of a system established in response to the collapse of the Japanese empire continues to define the terrain upon which the current debate plays out. In responding to the economic bubble of the late-1980s and accompanying increase in the number of migrants in the country, a number of changes were made to the regulations governing the migration of populations into the country. The resultant system came to be described as the "1990s regime" (Akashi 2010). This was a system in which strict migration policies were supplemented with the disguised importation of labour through ethnic repatriation and training schemes, and via irregular migration. The discussions that occurred around the establishment and operation of the regime constitute the origins of the debate on migration in Japan, as the media, politicians, and civil society began to make demands of the bureaucracy. While there is a great deal of continuity in the actors involved in these discussions today, the current debate should not be seen as merely the latest iteration of a static argument regarding the pros and cons of migration to Japan. Rather, the terms of the debate have shifted, in response to both changes in policy and the wider circumstances within which such a debate takes place.

The existing literature identifies two periods of debate down to the economic slowdown of 2008, which implies that we are now in a third period of debate regarding migration in Japan. The initial debate around foreign workers and immigration policy in Japan emerged suddenly in the late 1980s, and was in response to changes in both labour demand and supply. On the one hand, by the latter half of 1988, demand for labour was outstripping supply, with small- and medium-sized firms in particular feeling the pinch. This led to demands for the labour market to be opened. At the same time, the labour shortage encouraged a flow of irregular migration into the country in order to meet the increasing demand for labour. It was this significant increase in the numbers of undocumented workers in the country which initially led the debate around migration (Chiavacci 2014, figure 6.2). The government responded to the issue by revising the ICRRA in 1989, with the new legislation coming into force in 1990. This superficially maintained barriers to the migration of unskilled labour, but also opened what are generally referred to as two "side doors" to immigration, with new visa categories for those labelled as foreign trainees and people of Japanese descent.

Although the justification for the introduction of these two new visa categories was totally different, their effect was the same; to provide a regular source of unskilled labour for Japanese companies, even while the government continued to argue that only skilled migration was encouraged. The former group, the trainees, was labourers from East and Southeast Asian countries who were being brought to Japan for "training" before returning to theoretically use the skills and techniques they had acquired in Japan for the development of their own countries. This system was formalized with the establishment of a Technical Intern Training Program (TITP) for foreigners in 1993, and while the types of jobs in which these so-called trainees could be employed has expanded, the system continues to operate down to the present. With the recruitment of these trainees occurring in third countries via both foreign governments and Japanese firms operating overseas, the system epitomizes the manner in which certain aspects of border control expand beyond the state's administrative boundaries. The latter group, the people of Japanese descent, referred to foreign nationals of Japanese heritage. In practice, it designated the descendants of Japanese who had emigrated in the first half of the twentieth century to Brazil and Peru as eligible for a special category of visa, actively encouraging their "return" to work in their "homeland."

The result of these changes to Japan's policies of entry was to channel specific labouring bodies into the country while disclaiming the presence of a migration policy. Both of these new visa categories were able to be presented as examples of Japan's international contribution, made in order to aid the development of its Asian neighbours or to provide the descendants of Japanese with an opportunity to rediscover their roots. The priority, however, was clearly to meet the demands of the labour market while retaining a check on the uncontrolled migration of the "unskilled." The upshot of the debate is visible in the steady reduction of irregular migration recorded since. From a high of 298,646 people on May 1, 1993, the number of "estimated overstayers" steadily decreased, and reached a low of 59,061 people on January 1, 2014 (Immigration Bureau 2016, 40), after which it increased for the subsequent five years (Immigration Services Agency 2019, 60). While this reflects a number of "crackdowns" being undertaken by the Immigration Bureau, almost certainly of greater significance is the opening of these immigration "side doors" to Japan, which allowed unskilled workers access to the labour market without clandestinely overstaying their visas.

As already noted, the result was a significant increase in the number of foreigners resident in Japan, which provides the wider context within which emerged the "second debate" on Japanese migration that occurred from the end of the 1990s onwards. While the first debate was a reactive one, seeking to deal with a growing number of visa overstayers, this second debate read the question of migration and foreign labour against the nation's demographic realities, and identified foreign workers as vital in order that Japan be able to maintain its economic strength and support its rapidly aging population (Sakanaka 2007). The majority of the proposals produced during the course of this debate continued to stress skills, with a more proactive and open immigration policy solely for highly qualified foreign workers. The debate was effectively terminated after 2008, when the global recession also led to a decline in the foreign population of Japan, and particularly in many of the highly skilled occupations being targeted through these policies.

What was clear over the course of this debate is that much of the narrative remained centred on two particular aspects of security, resulting in diametrically opposed conclusions. The entry of foreign workers was presented as essential for securing the survival and prosperity of the Japanese economy while, conversely, their undocumented overstay provided a potential threat to the Japanese population. As a number of researchers documented, the discursive emphasis on the potential of "foreign criminality" was overblown, and frequently supported through the deployment of forms of "pseudo-evidence" (Shipper 2005, 306–307; Yamamoto 2004, 41–47), yet it remained prominent in arguments for restricting immigration (Vogt 2014, 58–59). The demographic imperative for increasing the number of foreign workers has therefore often been countered by arguments that argue that such an increase would, rather than supporting a putative Japanese way of life, serve to damage it. The tension between these two conflicting perspectives on Japan's "security" has continued to run through the course of policy-making in recent years.

Necessity: The Mother of Migration Policy?

Following his return to the premiership in the December 2012 general election, the government of Shinzo Abe rapidly launched a three-pronged approach to resolve Japan's most pressing problem, its moribund economic growth. Dubbed "Abenomics," the "three arrows" of this policy were fiscal stimulus, monetary policy, and structural reform. The possibility of using foreign workers within the Japanese labour market would appear to fall into the last of these categories, but it is clear that the move toward the December 2018 legislation has been a long and torturous one.

Initially, at least, the use of foreign workers, and particularly in lower-skilled occupations, does not appear to have played a significant role in the new government's thinking. In the administration's 2013 strategy paper *Japan is Back*, the only mention made of foreign contributions to the Japanese economy are those of "tourists (20), *kōdo gaikoku jinzai* (high-level foreign talents) (38), and *yūshūna* (superior, excellent) foreign students, to promote internationalization and respond to globalization (37)" (Roberts 2018, 90–91). The explicit focus on skilled migrants is consistent with government rhetoric since the late 1980s, and follows on from a series of measures introduced since the mid-2000s (Akashi 2014, 181; Milly 2014). The formal stance of the Japanese government, reflected in the policy positions put forward by both the Liberal Democratic Party, which has dominated postwar politics, and its ever-changing cast of political opponents is that Japan would not accept blue-collar migrants out of concern it would be detrimental to the social order in Japan. What has altered over the course of Abe's tenure is that the increasing urgency of securing workers is reflected in policies that, in practice, establish channels for the importation of foreign labour. Recent years have thus seen the carefully constructed ramparts of selective immigration controls being overwhelmed by an assault of extreme economic urgency.

The care sector offers a good example of this, as this is an industry in which the role of Japan's demographic transformation as a key driver of policy development is particularly obvious (Ogawa, forthcoming). Japan has long experienced low birthrates, falling to 1.26 per woman in 2005 (Cabinet Office of Japan 2017) before recovering slightly, to 1.42 in 2018 (Nikkei Shimbun 2019). These are well below replacement levels, and the population has been declining since around 2008. Additionally, this population is aging rapidly; the aging rate was 17 percent in 2000 and 23 percent in 2010, while it is expected to increase to 28 percent in 2020 and 31.6 percent in 2030 (Cabinet Office of Japan 2018a). Consequently, the growing concern surrounding the ability to care for this population has resulted in significant changes in migration policy in the care sector over the past decade, including the acceptance of care workers and nurses from Indonesia, the Philippines, and Vietnam as part of economic partnership agreements (EPAs) in 2008, 2009, and 2014, respectively, and amendments to the TITP in 2017,[3] which allowed for the recruitment of trainees directly into the care sector.[4] Yet this policy is responding to a shortfall of workers already apparent, and an increasing volume of foreign

3   Through the Technical Intern Training Act and related ordinances, under which sections of the Immigration Control Act were adopted as provisions for the TITP. The amendment also sought to halt various human-rights violations that plagued the program, including suspended pay, long hours, and unsatisfactory working environments. The new legal terms allowed for the licensing of supervising organizations, a system of accreditation for technical interns, extended training periods, and implementing quotas for technical intern trainees. See Japan International Training Cooperation Organization, https://www.jitco.or.jp/en/regu lation/index.html.

4   See "The addition of the occupation 'care worker' to the job categories covered by the Program of Technical Intern Training for Foreign Nationals" on the website of

labour is sought in order to plug already existing gaps within the care sector (Enomoto, forthcoming). As things stand, the measures taken to date will prove insufficient in and of themselves, for in May 2018 it was announced that there is a need to secure an additional approximately 60,000 care workers each year (Ministry of Health, Labour, and Welfare 2018; Japan Times 2018). With the ongoing decline in the number of Japanese entering the employment market, it is clear that foreigners will have to make up this shortfall.

This is reflected more widely across the economy as a whole. In 2017, the Cabinet Office announced that Japan has a shortage of 1.2 million in labour-intensive industries such as food and hospitality services, manufacturing, construction, agriculture and fishing (Cabinet Office of Japan 2018b), while the Ministry of Health, Labor, and Welfare reported that labour-market conditions were as tight as they were in 1992, at the tail end of the bubble economy (Milly 2018). In the 1990s, though, much of the labour shortage was due to the segmented labour market, in which many highly educated young Japanese people refused to work in low- and less-skilled jobs. Now Japan's demographic shift means that the domestic labour force is no longer there, despite considerable efforts by the government to encourage women and the elderly to enter into the employment market. A Chuo University/Persol study predicted that, left unchecked, this shortfall would rise to over six million by 2030 (Kamata 2018). The foreign-worker bill has been explicitly designed to reduce this shortfall by adding workers from overseas to the labour market.

As in the late 1980s, it is the lobbying by certain businesses and sectors for foreign workers that has been significant for the subsequent shift in Japanese policy (Deguchi 2018). It is also, though, one that is being led by the state, and specifically by a government that is reluctant to sanction anything that may be viewed as an immigration "policy" (Akashi, forthcoming; Roberts 2018). Consequently, as indicated by changes in the care sector, the policy should be viewed as a reactive one, through which the state attempts to respond to a labour shortfall that is already present within the economy. The option of foreign labour seems to have only become acceptable due to the exhaustion of other policy mechanisms. The "Basic Policy on Economic and Fiscal Management and Reform 2018—Realizing Sustainable

the Ministry of Health, Labour, and Welfare, https://www.mhlw.go.jp/stf/seisa kunitsuite/bunya/0000147660.html.

Economic Growth by Overcoming the Decreasing Birth Rate and Aging Population," approved by the cabinet on June 15, 2018, states on page 26 that "the acceptance of foreign nationals through the establishment of new statuses of residence should be limited to industries in which the acceptance of foreign workers is still necessary to the maintenance and development of the industries after measures are taken to improve productivity and to recruit domestic workers (the promotion of employment among women and the elderly, the improvement of working conditions in consideration of labour shortages, etc.)." Foreign workers are, in other words, the last resort.

The policy shift toward accepting largely unskilled foreign workers can be considered as a last piece of fletching glued to Abenomics' third arrow of structural reform. Successfully becoming Japan's longest-serving Japanese prime minister prior to his resignation in September 2020, Abe presided over improved, but hardly stellar, economic performance, which had seemed to have exhausted the benefits available through the other two arrows. Rather than economic reform, however, the increasing acceptance of the need to rely upon foreign labour should instead be seen as reflecting the ongoing structural transformation of the Japanese labour market, one driven by underlying demographic realities that remain, as yet, unresolved.

"The Year Immigration Began"

This description of 2019, by Toshiro Menju, director of the Japan Center for International Exchange, is indicative of the importance that some are ascribing to the change in policy represented by the foreign-worker bill. Before these recent revisions to the immigration-control law, the following categories of foreigners could work in Japan: highly skilled workers or those with specified knowledge and professional skills (university professors, scientists, lawyers); people with certain legal positions, such as foreign spouses married to Japanese nationals, people with Japanese heritage (the *nikkei*—primarily Brazilians of Japanese descent), and foreign permanent residents (*Zainichi* Koreans and others who had obtained residency); people who engage in certain types of paid work based on bilateral agreements signed between Japan and related countries (care workers and nurses under an EPA); trainees on the TITP; and those who have obtained permission to engage in activities outside their immigration status (largely international students who work part time).

It is often noted by people on both sides of the migration debate that the Japanese government's official focus on skilled migration is belied by the number of categories of people (spouses, *nikkei*, permanent residents, trainees, students) to whom this is largely irrelevant. Collectively, it is these categories that have made up the bulk of the foreign labour force to date (Akashi, forthcoming). The insufficiency in the labour supply has now necessitated more drastic measures. The Japanese government implemented two new visa categories as part of the recent revision (Ministry of Foreign Affairs 2019):

1. Specified Skills type 1: This status of residence is applicable to foreigners who work in jobs that require "considerable knowledge of or experience" in specified industry fields.
2. Specified Skills type 2: Status of residence for foreigners engaged in jobs that require "proficient skills" in specified industry fields.

The type 2 visa is essentially an extension or upgrade on type 1. While foreigners on the type 1 visa can work up to five years but may not bring their family, the type 2 allows foreigners to bring their family and stay for longer. People on type 2 visas are also eligible for permanent residency if and when they fulfill the other necessary requirements. Foreign workers eligible for type 1 visas must have either completed the three-year TITP or passed the technical and Japanese-language exams, and are allowed to work in 14 industrial sectors, including care, construction, shipbuilding, agriculture, and fisheries. Once a candidate possesses all the requirements, they must seek a position through job-placement agencies and obtain a contract with a company before acquiring the visa. Type 2 visas were initially only available for work in construction and shipbuilding, although this is likely to expand in the future.

Unlike the technical intern program, these new visa categories provide a status of residence that will enable foreign workers to freely live and work in Japan for a certain period of time, and thus theoretically bringing them under the provisions of the Japanese Labour Standard Law. As such, it is hoped that this will minimize some of the serious problems with TITP, such as long working hours, extremely low wages, harassment, and abuse (Uchiyama 2018). However, even though TITP has faced serious criticisms, the Japanese government has announced it will continue that program alongside the new visa statuses. It appears that, in practice, the latter will operate as an extension of the former, as it is estimated that about 60 percent of "specified skill" type 1 workers will be foreign workers who have shifted status from technical intern status, and that even after five years, former trainees will account for 45 percent of the workers on the new scheme. It remains unclear how the distinction between the two will be policed in practice, given that the same jobs will be performed by the same individuals as, initially, trainees, and then specified skills workers. This pattern of having workers shift between different visa categories has been characteristic of Japan's experience with foreign labour to date (Kimizuka, forthcoming).

Nevertheless, the Japanese government continues to emphasize that the revision and the implementation of new visa statuses do not constitute an immigration policy, nor are they equivalent to accepting the import of non-skilled workers. Instead, this latest policy tweak should be seen as a means of using talented and skilled human resources from abroad. Prime Minister Abe stated in reference to the new scheme that "the entire country is short of workers, and the new system is needed for talented foreigners to further contribute to Japan," while it is the government's intention to "set clear caps on the numbers (of additional foreign workers) and limit the period (they can stay in Japan)"—and so the new measures cannot constitute a policy of accepting foreign immigration (Oita and Aoki 2018). This "non-existence" of active immigration policies means that Japan still lacks not only the administrative and support structures but also measures for integrating foreign migrants into Japanese society, responsibility for which has largely been devolved to local administrations (Kim and Streich 2020).

The government's determination to avoid anything officially designated a migration policy is in line with public opinion, which is at best lukewarm at the prospect of increasing numbers of foreign workers coming into the country (Stokes and Devlin 2018). This is recognized by commentators like Toshiro Menju, who in describing 2019 as the year immigration began, went on to note that "The reason why the government does not refer to this as an immigration policy is due to concern for the negative image people have towards the word 'immigration.' The biggest success of this new policy was creating an opportunity for a national discussion of immigration policy, which had been taboo until now" (Menju 2019). As both the state and its advisors have already recognized the insufficiency of this latest measure, with the 350,000 foreign workers newly eligible to partici-pate formally in the economy over the next five years making up a mere 20 percent of the anticipated worker shortfall of 1.45 million, this is a discussion that will be revisited repeatedly in the near future (Takeo and Urabe 2019).

Conclusion: Missing Pieces?

It is widely accepted that the challenge for Japan and its government is to facilitate the flow of labour into Japan while avoiding public opposition to their policies. This will be achieved through an increas-ingly invasive management of migrants' movements in order to guarantee that the "guests" will conform to Japan's expectations of them, expectations which include, most notably, that they will return to their countries of origin after their term is complete (Takamura, forthcoming). It is this expectation that provides the grounds for Abe and his government continuing to insist that these new policies do not constitute an immigration policy. Given that the measures do incor-porate a "pathway to permanent residency," although not to full citizenship, this claim relies on a semantically exacting definition of immigration (Roberts 2018) that bears little relation to how Japan's foreign residents currently come to be granted bureaucratic recogni-tion by the state. The new category of recognition afforded by the policy has to date attracted little interest; the first year of the program down to March 2020 saw a mere 3,987 holders of specified-skills visas in the country (Kyodo News 2020), or far less than a tenth of the places available. Unsurprisingly, COVID-19, and the accompanying closure of Japan's borders, has not proved conducive to the policy (Ito 2021).

Concern regarding public opposition to migration continues to shape how the question is dealt with politically in Japan. It is neverthe-less misleading to assert that the inherent cultural particularity of the Japanese population is able to be evidenced through its homogeneity. As this chapter has suggested, claims to demographic homogeneity should be seen as a political response to imperial collapse, and remained discursively dominant in the absence of postwar political and economic integration comparable with that occurring in other parts of the world. The Cold War isolation of Japan from Asia led to the now-circumscribed, archipelagic borders of the Japanese nation being performed as barriers to the outside world, a performance granted meaning through the practices of import substitution and export promotion that characterized Japan's economy during most of the postwar period. Nevertheless, this border performance ultimately created the conditions for the demise of Japan's export economy, as the costs of maintaining such a restrictive labour pool came to be borne by domestic producers, and led to the adjustments detailed in this chapter. While recent years have seen major changes in the legislative framework controlling the entry of people into the country, this limited and gradual acceptance of selected skilled immigrants to the country remains paired with the commitment to securing and protecting Japanese society, a commitment whose contours have been shaped by earlier cycles of the policies and politics of migration.

The borders of Japan are currently transforming in response to this domestic demand for labour, through the increase and expansion of migration channels into the country. The hard shell of the "1990s regime" is coming to resemble the porous and permeable membrane that was characteristic of borders under globalization. Yet while Japan is seeking to fine-tune the management of its borders under similar socio-economic and demographic pressure as Canada, it continues to espouse a migration policy and border governance that is essentially opposed to the Canadian multicultural model. The objective behind the restricted opening of Japan's comparatively closed labour market remains to support domestic industry and the tax base in the face of an ongoing decline in Japan's own working-age population. Achieving this objective while protecting the traditionally homogenous understanding of who it is that comprises Japan offers a distinctive set of policy challenges for the government. Japan's case reminds us "that variation in labour migration results not from ineluctable economic and demographic forces but from political processes that mediate economic and demographic pressures" (Bartram 2005, 11). A full account of such processes remains essential for understanding changes in borders, and how they shape what crosses them.[5]

5   This chapter grew out of the "Hokkaido Workshop on Immigration Policy and Border Security", held at Hokkaido University on April 21, 2018, organized by the Jean Monnet Network "Comparing and Contrasting EU Border and Migration Policy – Are They Exemplary?", and supported by Erasmus+ and the Borders in Globalization project. Particular thanks are due to Akashi Jun'ichi, Enomoto Yoshihito, Kimizuka Hiroshi, Ogawa Reiko, and Takamura Kazue, as well as to

References

Akashi, Junichi. 2010. *Nyukoku Kanri Seisaku – "1990-nen taisei" no seiritsu to tenkai* [Japan's Immigration Control Policy: Foundations and Transition]. Tokyo: Mekanishiya Shuppan.

——. 2014. "New Aspects of Japan's Immigration Policies: Is Population Decline Opening the Doors?" *Contemporary Japan* 26(2): 175–196.

——. Forthcoming. "From Export Powerhouse to Importing Manpower: The Policy towards Foreign Workers under the Abe Administration." Unpublished manuscript, consulted June 26, 2019.

Bartram, David. 2005. *International Labor Migration: Foreign Workers and Public Policy*. New York: Palgrave Macmillan.

Cabinet Office of Japan. 2017. "White Papers on Japan's Birthrate." https://www8.cao.go.jp/shoushi/shoushika/whitepaper/measures/w-2017/29webhonpen/html/b1_s1-1-1.html.

——. 2018a. "White Papers on Japan's Aging Society." https://www8.cao.go.jp/kourei/whitepaper/w-2018/html/zenbun/s1_1_1.html.

——. 2018b. "Monthly Topics: Recent Economic Indicators." https://www.cao.go.jp/keizai3/monthly_topics/2018/0302/topics_052.pdf.

Chapman, David, and Karl Jakob Krogness, eds. 2014. *Japan's Household Registration System and Citizenship: Koseki, Identification and Documentation*. London: Routledge.

Chiavacci, David. 2014. "Indispensable Future Workforce or Internal Security Threat? Securing Japan's Future and Immigration." In *Governing Insecurity in Japan: The Domestic Discourse and Policy Response*, edited by Wilhelm Vosse, Reinhard Drifte, and Verena Blechinger-Talcott, 133–158. London: Routledge.

Choi, Deokhyo. 2022. "The Empire Strikes Back from Within: Colonial Liberation and the Korean Minority Question at the Birth of Postwar Japan, 1945–47." *The American Historical Review* 126(2), 555–584. https://doi.org/10.1093/ahr/rhab199.

Deguchi, Haruki. 2018. "A New Immigration Policy for Japan." *Japan Times*, December 4, 2018. https://www.japantimes.co.jp/opinion/2018/12/04/commentary/japan-commentary/new-immigration-policy-japan/#.XRpelvZuLMR.

Endo, Shuhei, and Yusuke Matsukura. 2018. "Japan Ushers in Major Immigration Policy Change with Revision to Boost Foreign Workforce." *The Mainichi* [Tokyo], December 8. https://mainichi.jp/english/articles/20181208/p2a/00m/ona/013000c.

Endo Ken, Iwashita Akihiro, and Emmanuel Brunet-Jailly. Portions of this work were supported by the NIHU Transdisciplinary Project "Area Studies Project for Northeast Asia," and JSPS KAKENHI Grant Numbers JP 16K17071 and 20H01460.

Enomoto, Yoshihito. Forthcoming. "Unwelcome Embrace? Foreign Nurses and Care Workers in Japan." Unpublished manuscript, consulted June 26, 2019.

Gakuto, Takako, and Yuki Fujita. 2018. "Japan's Lower House Passes Foreign Worker Bill as Concerns Mount." *Nikkei Asia*, November 28, 2018. https://www.japantimes.co.jp/news/2018/12/07/national/politics-diplomacy/japan-set-enact-controversial-immigration-bill-paving-way-foreign-worker-influx/.

Haraguchi, Kunihiro. 2018. "Dainiji Sekai Taisen no chokugo ni Nihon ni 'soukan' sareta Nikkei Kanada-jin no sono ato – Kanada kikoku / Nihon teijyu wo meguru mondai" [Japanese Canadians who were "repatriated" to Japan immediately after WWII: Issues surrounding re-entry to Canada and domiciliation in Japan]. *Journal of the Japanese Overseas Migration Museum* 13: 49–70.

Hollifield, James. 2000. "The Politics of International Migration: How Can We Bring the State Back In." In *Migration Theory: Talking Across Disciplines*, edited by Caroline Brettell and James Hollifield, 137–186. New York: Routledge.

Immigration Bureau. 2016. *Immigration Control*. Ministry of Justice, Japan.

Immigration Services Agency. 2019. *Immigration Control and Residency Management*. Ministry of Justice, Japan.

Ito, Kazuya. 2021. "Japan Sees Six-Fold Rise in Number of Foreign Workers on New Skills Visa." *The Asahi Shimbun*, May 26, 2021. https://www.asahi.com/ajw/articles/14358579.

Japan Times. 2018. "Fill the Gap in Nursing Care Workers." Editorial, June 26. https://www.japantimes.co.jp/opinion/2018/06/26/editorials/fill-gap-nursing-care-workers/#.XRw5augzaUk.

Kamata Tomoko. 2018. "What's at Stake: Inside Shinzo Abe's Efforts to Bring More Foreign Workers into Japan." *NHK World*, November 20. https://www3.nhk.or.jp/nhkworld/en/news/backstories/302/.

Kim, Viktoriya, and Philip Streich. 2020. "*Tabunka Kyōsei* Without Immigration Policy: The Role of Centers for International Exchange and Their Challenges." *Contemporary Japan* 32(2): 174–196.

Kimizuka, Hiroshi. Forthcoming. "Filtering Migrant Flows and Abuse in the System." Unpublished manuscript, consulted June 26, 2019.

Kondo, Atsushi. 2002. "The Development of Immigration Policy in Japan." *Asian and Pacific Migration Journal* 11(4): 415–436.

———. 2015. "Migration and Law in Japan." *Asia & the Pacific Policy Studies* 2(1): 155–168.

Kyodo News. 2020. "Japan's New Working Visa Falls Far Short of Expectations in 1st Year." *Kyodo News*, May 29. https://english.kyodonews.net/news/2020/05/29193315631c-japans-new-working-visa-falls-far-short-of-expectations-in-1st-year.html.

Menju, Toshihiro. 2019. "Imin 'Gannen' Kadai to Tenbo" [Immigration year one: prospects and challenges]. *Sekai*, no. 918 (March): 27–30.

Milly, Deborah. 2014. *New Policies for New Residents: Immigrants, Advocacy, and Governance in Japan and Beyond*. Ithaca, N.Y.: Cornell University Press.

———. 2018. "Abe's Choice for Japan: Thriving Migration without Immigration." *Georgetown Journal of Asian Affairs* 4(1): 20–28.

Ministry of Foreign Affairs. 2019. "Specified Skills Worker." Ministry of Foreign Affairs. https://www.mofa.go.jp/files/000459527.pdf.

Ministry of Health, Labour, and Welfare. 2018. "Dai-7-ki kaigo hoken jigyo keikaku ni mototsugu kaigojinzai no hitsuyosu ni tsuite" [Number of care workers required according to the 7th comprehensive care insurance plan]. Ministry of Health, Labour, and Welfare press release, May 21, 2018. https://www.mhlw.go.jp/stf/houdou/0000207323.html.

Morris-Suzuki, Tessa. 2006. "Invisible Immigrants: Undocumented Migration and Border Controls in Early Postwar Japan." *Journal of Japanese Studies* 32(1): 119–153.

———. 2010. *Borderline Japan: Frontier Controls, Foreigners and the Nation in the Postwar Era*. Cambridge: Cambridge University Press.

Nikkei Shimbun. 2019. "18nen no Shuseisu 918 man, Saitei o Koushin, Shusei Ritsu 1.42" [Total number of births in 2018 was 918,000, record low, birthrate at 1.42]. *The Nikkei Shimbun*, June 7, 2019. https://www.nikkei.com/article/DGXMZO45809520X00C19A6MM8000/.

Ogawa, Reiko. Forthcoming. "Migration and 2030 Agenda for Sustainable Development in Japan." Unpublished manuscript, consulted June 26, 2019.

Oguma, Eiji. 1998. *'Nihonjin' no kyōkai: Okinawa, Ainu, Taiwan, Chōsen shokuminchi shihai kawa fukki undō made* [The boundaries of the Japanese]. Tokyo: Shinyōsha.

Oita, Naoki, and Jun Aoki. 2018. "Abe Reiterates Need to Accept More Foreign Workers in April Next Year." *The Mainichi* [Tokyo], December 11, 2018. https://mainichi.jp/english/articles/20181211/p2a/00m/0na/004000c.

Osaki, Tomohiro. 2018. "Immigration Bill Clears Lower House despite Opposition Filibuster and No-Confidence Motion." *Japan Times*, November 27. https://www.japantimes.co.jp/news/2018/11/27/national/politics-diplomacy/immigration-bill-set-clear-lower-house-despite-opposition-filibuster-no-confidence-motion/.

Roberts, Glenda. 2018. "An Immigration Policy by *Any* Other Name: Semantics of Immigration to Japan." *Social Science Japan Journal* 21(1): 89–102.

Roy, Patricia E. 2015. "Canadian and American Treatment of the Nikkei, 1890–1949: A Comparison." *American Review of Canadian Studies* 45(1): 44–70. https://doi.org/10.1080/02722011.2015.1022309.

Sakanaka, Hidenori. 2007. "The Future of Japan's Immigration Policy: A Battle Diary." *The Asia-Pacific Journal: Japan Focus* 5(4): 1–9.

Shipper, A. W. 2005. "Criminals or Victims? The Politics of Illegal Foreigners in Japan." *Journal of Japanese Studies* 31(2): 299–327.

Stokes, Bruce, and Kat Devlin. 2018. *Despite Rising Economic Confidence, Japanese See Best Days Behind Them and Say Children Face a Bleak Future.* Pew Research Center Report, November 12. https://www.pewresearch. org/global/2018/11/12/despite-rising-economic-confidence-japanese -see-best-days-behind-them-and-say-children-face-a-bleak-future/.

Surak, Kristin. 2013. "Guestworker Regimes: A Taxonomy." *New Left Review* 84:84–102.

Takamura, Kazue. Forthcoming. "The Migrant Surveillance Regime and the Plight of Migrant Detainees in Japan." Unpublished manuscript, consulted June 26, 2019.

Takemae, Eiji. 2002. *Allied Occupation of Japan.* Translated by Robert Rickets and Sebastian Swann. London: Continuum.

Takeo, Yuka, and Emi Urabe. 2019. "Japan Needs More Foreign Workers, New Government Adviser Says." Bloomberg News, March 5, 2019. https:// www.bloomberg.com/news/articles/2019-03-04/new-voice-on-abe -s-economic-panel-calls-for-more-foreign-workers.

Uchiyama, Osamu. 2018. "Foreign Trainees Describe Harsh Realities before Diet Members." *The Asahi Shimbun*, November 9, 2018. http://www. asahi.com/ajw/articles/AJ201811090049.html.

Vogt, Gabriele. 2014. "Friend and Foe: Juxtaposing Japan's Migration Discourses." In *Governing Insecurity in Japan: The Domestic Discourse and Policy Response,* edited by Wilhelm Vosse, Reinhard Drifte, and Verena Blechinger-Talcott, 50–70. London: Routledge.

Yamamoto, Ryoko. 2004. "Alien Attack? The Construction of Foreign Criminality in Contemporary Japan." *Japanstudien: Jahrbuch des Deutschen Instituts für Japanstudien* 16: 27–57.

CHAPTER 11

The Failure of the European Union's Promise for Transnational Solidarity: The Challenge of the Refugee Crisis

Franziska Fischer

German President Frank-Walter Steinmeier called for more solidarity within the European Union concerning the refugee influx during a visit to Rome in May 2017. More specifically, he asked for a solidary distribution of the "tasks and the burdens" that come with such an influx between the European partners (Handelsblatt 2017). Already in August 2015 German Chancellor Angela Merkel had appealed to solidarity, not only within Germany but also by pointing to the other member states, when welcoming all refugees to Germany. The concept of solidarity is one of the building blocks of the EU's set of values that forms its normative power, an ideological framework to pursue its agenda through a persuasive or attractive character. Alongside peace, liberty, the rule of law, and anti-discrimination, the EU supports bonds among its member states through a value system and not through military or economic enforcement. Through the attractiveness of the value system, it operates as a normative power, or in other words through the power of persuasion, which ought to move beyond the borders of the member states. The question arises: How capable is the EU in taking on this supranational role by providing normative guidelines that exceed national borders, especially when facing a crisis?

What we have seen in the European Union since 2015 with the influx in refugees and the resulting discourse is, rather than solidarity, the upheaving of the concepts of sovereignty, nationalism, and border enforcement. Populist movements have received more recognition; demands for the securitization of space and culture have grown increasingly loud. The refugee discourse within the European Union presents just one example of how the European value system is challenged, and with it, a European identity that has struggled from the beginning, if it even existed to begin with. Other examples include Brexit, responses to the financial crisis in 2008, and the revoking of the Schengen Agreement. The European Union's normative ideology seems to be clashing against a social force within the member states that resist the union's pursuit for a common agenda to protect its own national space. As a result, borders are becoming increasingly important, as well as the preservation of the national identities of the member states. There are counter examples that show that this argument is indeed more complex. The EU project is a multi-layered, multifaceted ideational, economic, social, and political cogwheel, and some situations, like the influx of refugees, unearth faults in the construction of this cogwheel.

This chapter aims to examine the limits to cross-border EU solidarity, and the EU's failure to facilitate and organize a European-wide solution to a crisis of the influx of refugees since 2015. In order to understand how the idea of a pan-European solidarity project is failing, this chapter will examine the construction of the value system of the European Union and juxtapose it with the frameworks of the modern nation-state and its constructed community and identity reflected in a cultural sphere of belonging, contained by borders of the nation-state. These spheres of belonging have established much more than physical borders, they have entrenched psychological boundaries in the mind, which have damaged efforts at solidarity and fractured the European Union into its component nation states. This phenomenon is explored through observing political and media narratives in member states such as the United Kingdom and Germany, by presenting examples of established, widely read, and recognized news outlets such as *The Guardian*, the BBC, *The Times, die Tagesschau, das Handelsblatt, Die Zeit,* and *die Sueddeutsche,* among others. This chapter also investigates political and public reactions to refugee influx, such as breaching the Schengen Agreement and the Dublin regulation.

Investigating how pan-European solidarity has fared under contentious circumstances may offer insights into policy-making in other jurisdictions. In an increasingly interconnected world, transnational solidarity ought to be an important building block of global responses to the needs of millions of people on the move. Understanding why solidarity might break down in certain situations when the principle needs to be extended to real-life challenges should be of interest to researchers and policy-makers concerned with borders and migration. The example of the EU and its asylum policy in the context of the 2015 refugee influx presents an important moment in history and a reference point for the study and governance of these issues.

The Absence of Coercive Measures

Hedley Bull (1982) claimed that it seems likely that Europe will ever become a strong actor in international affairs, pointing at the absence of a military power. Despite increasing securitization issues due to terrorism and increased mobility of people through globalization, the European Union has refrained from building its military power but rather put its efforts toward building its normative power within and outside of the union (Manners 2002, 235). Ian Manners agrees with Bull's argumentation in the context of the time in which it was written, however he opposes Bull's proposition in a contemporary timeframe and suggests that the developments of the 1990s "in international relations lead us to rethink both notions of military power and civilian power in order to consider the EU's normative power in world politics" (236).

Manners argues that the EU has the potential to play a more significant role in establishing norms on an international level than the individual member states (236). His argument suggests that a European value system may eventually be perceived more influential than value systems on a smaller scale, such as the nation-state, and may outweigh the hard power of military and economic enforcement. This ultimately leads to the suggestion that there can be a stronger identification with a set of European norms and values than with national ones. However, that would require a homogenous shift in the minds of the people within a very heterogeneous population of the European Union, to identify as a European citizen first, or at least identify with a European set of values, before identifying as a German, Dutch, or French citizen.

Also contradicting Bull in his opinion, Teresa La Porte (2011) argues that even though the EU does not have hard-power capabilities, such as economic and military enforcement, it "maintains all of the conditions necessary to practice an effective power of persuasion (soft power) [...] and the capacity to establish international norms of behavior (normative power)." She suggests that the normative strategy of the European Union "represent a real alternative to more unilateral or aggressive political visions" (7). According to Manners and La Porte, the European Union does not need military and civilian enforcement in order to be recognized as an international actor, and even more so, to be recognized as a guiding authority by its member states. One of the building blocks of this guiding authority is the concept of solidarity that binds together the member states beyond their national borders in situations of need and crisis—theoretically.

What we witness in practice is a different story, one that can be illustrated by reference to the current influx in refugees in the European Union. The influx has provoked a resentful reaction within parts of the population that now seek solutions within the national parameters rather than a European-wide approach. Chantal Mouffe (2018, 11) argues that we currently are witnessing a populist moment in Europe and beyond, when right-wing social movements are harnessing and rearticulating nationalism, racism, and xenophobia, proposing alternative narratives to the one of the established elites.

The normative value system of the European Union does not hold when faced with an actual crisis, such as the influx of refugees since 2015 that forces the theoretical concept of solidarity to move from abstraction to a concrete plan. What can be witnessed is the deterioration of the normative claim and the ineffectiveness of European soft power that leaves room for political action motivated primarily, but not exclusively, by national interest. While the European Union aims to overcome physical and ideological boundaries with the moral force of its normative claim, its legal language fails to uphold this provision in times of crisis. Instead, the people tend to return to their traditional sphere of belonging, which is intimately tied to the nation-state and national identity, and search for national solutions that promise to protect national interest. This normative deterioration is not total, though it becomes especially evident in extreme cases such as the migrant influx.

The EU and Its Member States—Caught Between Realism and Idealism

The Westphalian system of territorial states became deeply entrenched and institutionalized by the mid-1800s and was relatively stable until the 1970s (Middell 2016). European national movements for self-determination peaked after the First World War, during the "Wilsonian Moment" in the context of Wilson's famous Fourteen Points, which championed the self-determination of all (European) nations (Gould and Pasquino 2001, 1). Self-determination facilitated two phenomena: first, the organization of space in spheres of belonging and, second, it provided the toolbox to create a social identity, heavily linked to the sphere of belonging. Gould and Pasquino observe that the "democratic principle of self-determination has come to be accepted as an integral part of international law" (2001, 2). They define the notion of national self-determination "as the idea that nationalities may rightfully determine the boundaries, membership, and political status of their own communities, including asserting a right to statehood" (4). Gould and Pasquino argue that the ethical justification for self-determination "begins from the idea that individuals, as moral agents, have rights to their own well-being." Among the conditions for well-being is the ability to engage in the expression of one's cultural norms, values, and customs. Yet to do this, "one must have a right to engage in cultural expression and to the conditions that allow this" (4). In short, the concept of self-determination provides the tools to form a social identity, which is heavily linked to the cultural and ideological sphere of belonging, framed by the nation-state and its borders.

In that sense, the notion of self-determination links to the sentiment of belonging, as it creates a sphere of ownership over physical and abstract resources, such as territory and culture. This sphere of belonging is legally protected by the concept of sovereignty, which the European Union, through international agreements, has challenged in order to preserve supranational harmony. More specifically, the implementation of the Lisbon Treaty has significantly increased the powers of the European Parliament and changed the voting and institutional policies of the union (Reznick 2012). This results in a supranational policy system, or an overarching approach to certain economic, political, and social issues such as migration, in which individual member states must sometimes adhere to EU guidelines put forth by supranational institutions, such as the Parliament, the European Commission, and the Court of Justice of the European Union, to pass certain policies or to commit to certain political actions (Wallace 1999). One of these systems is the Common European Asylum System, outlining EU-wide guidelines on how to organize the influx and distribution of asylum seekers that theoretically contains, channels, and, in extreme cases, overrides a purely nationalist approach.

In its legal framework, the EU urges that member states together carry out the tasks that come with such an influx. Recital 22 of the Dublin III Regulations calls for "mutual trust" and "solidarity" in the face of crisis. Further, the European Union justifies its role as a creator of an overarching rule system in recital 40. This legal provision suggests that member states might lack the capacity to implement appropriate measures to manage an influx of asylum seekers to the satisfaction of other EU member states. Thus, recital 40 states that establishing and implementing measures to deal with a crisis can "by reason of the scale and effects of this Regulation, be better achieved at Union level" (Dublin Regulations III 2013).

Two main issues can be observed through these examples. First, the language of the norms is extremely vague, which leaves room for interpretation by the member states. Second, in order to prevent a great divergence in interpretation, the provision reserves the right to make this interpretation for the member states if need be. Thus, legal provisions reserve the possibility on a supranational level to facilitate the ideal scenario in case the reality of the member states prevents it. Therefore, these provisions challenge the respective opinion and national interests of member states. As a result, there is a discrepancy in established norm by the union and actual behaviour or action taken by the member states. One example is the breach of the Schengen Agreement by several member states, such as France, Austria, Poland, and Germany. Since 2015, the respective governments have issued temporary re-installment of border controls to their national spheres from potential security threats via the arrival of large numbers of refugees in the southern and eastern Schengen zone.[1] In order to understand this discrepancy and how the European Union's values fail to overcome national borders, the concepts of the spheres of belonging and social identity need to be explored in more detail.

Wimmer and Glick-Schiller (2003) address the issue of identity by suggesting that "Most scholars of nationalism [including Calhoun, McCrone, and Smith], discussed the nation as a domain of

---

1   Investigating the discussions that ultimately led to the Schengen Agreement, as well as the Dublin regulation, could aid in understanding the tension between the realism and idealism of EU policy. Further, looking into discussions after Schengen and Dublin had been revoked could offer insight into an evolution of the realism/ idealism tension.

identity—far removed from the power politics of modern state formation" (582). They argue that the nation is defined through common origins and history that has been built through a shared culture, language, and identity. On the other hand, the "state" is a political and economic system with a leading authority executing sovereignty within a particular territory. In that sense, the state provides and protects a legal space for the nation to exist. However, cultural, ethnic, historic, and many other social spheres that make up and create a nation are always in fluctuation and are not congruent to an established sovereign territory of a state or a supranational entity such as the union. Rather, these spheres overlap, barely touch, or heavily exceed one another, forming a messy picture of what one society looks like, hinting at why it may be so difficult to agree on a singular approach to a crisis on a national level, let alone on a supranational level, such as the European Union.

Refugees "are perceived as foreigners to the community of shared loyalty towards the state and shared rights guaranteed by that state" (583). As foreigners, they have been "absorbed into the national body through the politics of forced assimilation and benevolent integration" (583–584). Thus, they are "not meant to be part of the system of social security that the national community has developed [...] because they come 'from outside' into the national space of solidarity" (584). Therefore, Wimmer and Glick-Schiller argue that "Due to this tension, immigrants' integration into the welfare systems had a touch of illegitimacy and abuse" (584). Appadurai (1996) similarly argues that the "isomorphism of people, territory, and legitimate sovereignty that constitutes the normative character of the modern nation-state is itself under threat from the forms of circulation of people characteristic of the contemporary world" (191). By requesting solidarity and promoting an action plan for the distribution of refugees, the European Union acts as a driving force behind the threat of losing sovereignty, territory, and a perceived homogenous culture, and therefore drives this tension.

In that sense "Sovereignty and the nation-state appear to be threatened, both literally and metaphorically, as Europe's permeable southern borders are constantly breached by refugees and migrants" (Zetter 2007, 186). Kamens (2012, 13) observes that "This process too undermines the sense of nations as 'exceptional' and culturally distinctive." Thus, the nation-state, intending homogeneity through a cultural entity, is challenged through the flow of migration enabled by the European Union. Therefore, the European Union appears to be paralyzed by trying to balance realism, experienced through the actions taken by its member states, and idealism, by its effort to uphold its value system and soft power structure (Haine 2004, 73).

Narratives in the UK and Germany

This section highlights some examples of the media representing a specific political narrative voicing concerns about refugees. Examples from established news outlets demonstrate one aspect of how public opinion is shaped, though the analysis is not meant to be comprehensive on the topic. In 2015, then UK Prime Minister David Cameron stated to ITV news, while on a trip to Vietnam, that he was aiming for better protection of Great Britain's borders, referring to migrants in France waiting to cross the channel as a "swarm of people coming across the Mediterranean" (Taylor, Wintour, and Elgot 2015). He also hinted at enhancing immigration rules, thus protecting the economy and jobs, especially for citizens and taxpayers, by increasing deportations and reducing the number of work permits issued to asylum seekers (Elgot 2016). Furthermore, he synchronized the inability to speak English to radicalization by arguing that "If you are not able to speak English, not able to integrate, you may find therefore you have challenges understanding what your identity is and therefore you could be more susceptible to the extremist message" (Elgot 2016). The political representation of the situation paints a strong "us" and "them" picture and attaches a simplified picture of the situation, undermining the humanitarian need of a large share of the refugees and the disgraceful situation of people in refugee camps aspiring to move to Great Britain.

This narrative concerning refugees entering national territory is not unique but is widespread over the European Union. This may not always be portrayed and represented by the majority of governments, but some political parties use such messaging. For example, the former leader of the right-wing populist party Alternative for Germany (AFD), Frauke Petry suggested in 2015 to make use of firearms in protecting the national border in order to prevent illegal immigration. While this caused an uproar on the political and social landscape, the percentage of the population supporting and voting AFD has risen considerably and crossed in many German *länder* beyond the 5 percent threshold, which allowed the party to enter into regional parliaments. This suggests that there may be a significant portion of the public that received the populist messages as acceptable solutions. The populist message is well represented in the media. This specific narrative dehumanizes the refugees as a grey mass, a threat, and as an illegal homogenous entity, unable to perceive the narrative in view of the devastating reality of the Syrian civil war but, rather, the reality of a nation-state in distress due to economic and security concerns.

This narrative portrays refugees beyond the control mechanism of the nation-state, and therefore leads some in society to react in protective ways for their space, which can erupt in resentment or in violence. Appadurai observes that "violence is [thereby a] peculiar mobilization of social uncertainty and ideological certainty" (2006, 90). In order to gain certainty, Zetter (2007) identifies "The securitization of migration, and fear of the increasingly diverse 'other,'" contrasts with an earlier period when there were more effective entry controls and fewer but more clearly defined migrant ethnicities—at least in the public mind" (180). Violent behaviour can specifically be observed in Germany, where there are thousands of incidents of public attacks on refugee accommodations and on individuals.

The Case of Violence in Germany

According to official statistics of the Germany federal police, the Bundeskriminalamt (BKA), broadcast by Tagesschau, the main evening news on German television, in the first quarter of 2016 there were 347 criminal offenses in Germany against refugees and their accommodations. Most of the perpetrators were nationalist and right-wing extremists. This number compares to 1,031 violent incidents over the whole of 2015, a dramatic increase over previous years (BKA-Statistik 2016). In 2016, there were more than 3,500 total violent incidents against refugees and their accommodations, including men, women, and children, alongside attacks on volunteers helping refugees (Fremdenhass 2017). Both the motivation for attacks on accommodations and on individuals stems from nationalist and right-wing belief systems. However, there is a lack of political narrative addressing this problem. Ulla Jelpke, a spokesperson for the Die Linke (The Left) party in Germany argued that the absence of recognition and acknowledgement of such attacks as a national security threat is worrisome, as was the failure of the government to react (Fremdenhass 2017). Strikingly, on the contrary, violent incidents committed by refugees, though outnumbered by attacks against refugees by the thousands, are reported on a completely different scale. Further, violent incidents supposedly carried out by refugees are in many cases not confirmed. Rather, all people with a migratory background, whether first, second, or third generation, are perceived as one single homogenous mass under the term "refugee." Representation of attacks against refugees and their accommodation receives less attention by media, by the political landscape, and the public perception. However, media tends to connect violent incidents carried out by people with migratory background to refugees.

This misrepresentation can be observed through the presentation of an attack in a Munich shopping mall, the attack in the Berlin Christmas market, and the sexual harassment attacks in Cologne on New Year's Eve 2015. In all cases, the first reaction of the media was to imply a refugee connection, often with ambiguous framing or questions marks. The Huffington Post suggested the men responsible in Cologne came just prior to New Year's Eve with a new wave of refugees, however later in the article they quote the BKA, which states that many of the suspects had previously attracted attention by the BKA through suspicious behaviour (Kosch 2016). According to this timeline, the potential suspects had already been European residents for several years and, in fact, did not enter the European Union along with the recent refugee influx. Further, the nationalities of the suspects were later identified as mainly from countries in North Africa. People migrating from countries in North Africa to Europe would not have qualified as refugees in most cases, and thus should not have been identified as such. Der Spiegel stated that refugees were among the suspects; however, it admitted that there was no evidence that any refugees were offenders (Diehl et al. 2016).

Such representation of refugees often fuels anger that can result in violence. The immediate association with refugees to a violent incident is facilitated by a public perception conditioned to react emotionally, rather than to rationally assess the evidence. This is not to say that there are no incidents including refugees and violence against other refugees or non-refugees. Furthermore, the representation supports an image that connects every person that appears to have a migratory background to the term "refugee." This connection leads any future incidents to the immediate public conclusion to blame refugees. Vice versa incidents are often just dismissed by arguing that it was a separate incident carried out by extremists, which are not perceived as a recurring and growing trend (Middelhoff 2015). The public's undifferentiated perception of the grey mass that is constructed through the media and elite narrative translates into an oversimplified picture of the situation that allows polarizing and totalizing narratives to take hold.

Establishing Mental Borders—Us and Them

Tensions between Western societies and immigrants are reproduced and enhanced by oversimplification. After the sexual assaults in Cologne during New Year's Eve, the BKA pointed out similarities to sexual harassment incidents in Cairo during the Tahir Square protests during the Arab Spring (Connolly 2016). This established a precedent for public opinion to perceive these sorts of crimes as an Islamic phenomenon (Meaney 2016). An array of separate and unconnected violent incidents involving people with a migratory background and a Muslim heritage followed the Cologne incidents. A teenager from Afghanistan attacked people with an axe in a train in the area of Würzburg, while claiming a connection to the Islamic State. A German with Iranian roots shot nine people at a shopping mall in Munich, wounding several others. The police took hours to identify and contain the situation, initially portrayed as a terrorist attack. In Reutlingen, a small town in the southwest of Germany, a Syrian man killed a pregnant woman with a machete at a kebab shop, and another Syrian man injured several people outside a nightclub in Bavaria, then committing suicide with a bomb.

While the Merkel administration addressed the unique character of each event, as the Munich attack was related to right-wing extremism, the attack in Reutlingen was a family-based crime, and the suicide attack a psychiatric incident, other voices in Germany connected all incidents to a common cultural heritage that justifies such a behaviour. The AFD's Petry spoke in an interview with the *New Yorker* of a "liberal tendency to suppress politically inconvenient truths" (Meaney 2016). In Petry's opinion, her political opponents "absolutely avoid acknowledging the factors of illegal migration and open borders in these attacks." According to Petry, all the attacks were connected to social and cultural heritage. She argued that "These people coming into Germany are used to being in completely different social circumstances." This narrative is reproduced in public opinion as a recent study of the Friedrich-Ebert-Stiftung confirmed. According to their survey, one in five Germans has xenophobic and Islamophobic attitudes (Zick, Küpper, and Berghan 2019). The label "refugee" is thus constructed on the premise of a homogenous collective identity of a group, which does not fit in the cultural sphere of the European nation-states. The identity that is connected to the label triggers an emotional response in public opinion, mainly mistrust, fear, and anger, or at the least skepticism.

At this point, however, it is important to acknowledge the strong counter narrative that exists in Germany and many other member states of the European Union, that refrains from an oversimplification of the identity of the refugee, and a welcoming culture has pushed back against xenophobic activities. For a period of time, Germany took in unprecedented numbers of asylum seekers. Nevertheless, while a minority opinion, xenophobic narratives against refugees provokes significant outcomes, not only within society as violent incidents but also in the political sphere and the rise of right-wing nationalist and populist movements.

Appadurai (1996) identifies this uncertainty as a "crisis of legitimation" of the nation-state through migration, arguing that "states lose their monopoly over the idea of nation" (157). One way of protecting the nation is the imposition of creating a narrative for immigrants by representing them in a certain way. So, even though there was a transgressive accession of that space, through creating a narrative for the transgressive unit, the notion of control, or at least the illusion of control is handed back to the sovereignty regime. Further, by revoking supranational agreements, such as the freedom of mobility through Schengen and the distribution of burdens through the Dublin III regulation, nation-states aim to reclaim control over their physical and ideological landscape.

Social Tension Leading to the Halt of Solidarity

The representation of refugees has shaped public opinion considerably by provoking an emotional response. It has created a discourse that has resulted in a defensive and rejectionist behaviour, not only toward refugees, but also toward the European Union as an institution that seems to attack the need for the securitization of national space with its overarching policies. Thus, parts of the refugee discourse provoke a rejection of the core values that the European Union is built on. The attraction of concepts such as solidarity, liberty, and the rule of law exceeding the limits and border of the nation-state, in this case, seems to work as an abstract concept, however not in an actual context. Therefore, identifying the European Union normative power per se does not mirror its actual role. When faced with turmoil the seemingly homogenous ideological landscape of the EU splits into national spheres and provokes the member states to actions motivated by self-interest rather than solidarity.

The first example for these kinds of actions is the breaching of the Schengen Agreement, a key achievement based on the concept of liberty and freedom within the European Union, which was first encoded in the Treaty of Rome and enhanced with the Treaty on European Union within the Treaty of Maastricht, and later amended by the Treaty of Lisbon. The second example is the breaching of the Dublin regulation, which rests on the concept of solidarity between the member states, in order to identify the member state responsible for examining an application. The concept of solidarity is directly or indirectly incorporated in almost all the main treaties of the European Union and implicitly addressed within several regulations, and in speeches from officials within the member states and the European Union.

The Schengen Agreement represents one of the most successful translations of the core values of the European Union, liberty and freedom, into actual policy adapted by the member states, with very few opt-outs. It ensures free movement of people within the territory of the European Union by abolishing internal border controls and relying on a single external border. However, the Schengen Agreement has also caused tension between the member states, as it requires one standardized regulation on external border control, police coordination, and legislation concerning securitization of national space in the face of terrorism and other criminal networks. Yet, it was not until the refugee influx that tensions and concerns rose to the level for some member states of partially revoking the Schengen Agreement. With the perception of a mass of reported or unreported migrants coming from Syria by land and sea to Greece and Italy, or through Turkey, the Schengen Agreement was perceived as a liability for securitization, in context to terrorism but also economic dependency and cultural imposition. Therefore, countries like Hungary or Bulgaria have built fences in order to regain control over their territorial space and contain the refugee influx. Additionally, there has been a resurgence of borders within the Schengen area, sometimes temporarily due to attacks or in other cases more permanently. Thus, nation-states have deliberately rejected provisions set in place by the EU to secure national interest and territory. The momentum to commit to these moves has been set in motion by the perception of the refugee influx as an uncontrollable situation by the EU and its normative regulations.

The provisions of the Dublin III regulations experienced a similar rejection due to the perception of the refugee influx. Dublin III determines the responsibility of asylum application to member states based on a set of criteria. The distribution of responsibility to member states remains, despite the reform of criteria, uneven, due to the fact that most asylum seekers arrive by land or foot and thus enter the EU through the external borders in the east or south. Most of them then fall under the responsibility of periphery countries, such as Greece and Italy, which lack the institutional and financial capacity to take on such a task and risk to fail the fundamental human-rights provision. This shows the system was flawed from the beginning; however, its flaws became crucial with the refugee influx since 2015.

Due to the lack of sufficient institutional and financial capacities, the process of welcoming and registering in Italy and especially Greece has led to extremely long wait periods. This lack of capability not only put further strain on the national economies and infrastructures to provide housing, health care, and food, but also allowed for illegal movement to other member states due to the lack of an overview and supervision within the country of first arrival. Within new Dublin regulations, asylum seekers gained the right to refuse registration processes and refuse relocation requests back to their country of arrival. While this enhanced the rights of asylum seeker themselves, for the member states it added another layer of bureaucracy and led to disputes between member states, as Dublin III also determined a bilateral coordination between member states. Instead of evoking solidarity between the member states, it resulted in the member states acting for their own national interest rejecting refugees, such as Hungary, Poland, and Slovakia, which stated they would not accept asylum seekers at all, or only accept non-Muslim asylum seekers (BBC News 2017; O'Grady 2015).

The other side of this coin can be seen by the example of Germany, when Merkel took an optimistic stand in a press conference in 2015, suggesting that Germany has the capacity to accommodate all refugees who wished to settle there. Thereby she suspended the Dublin III regulations by processing asylum applications out of their sphere of responsibility. Other member states, such as Hungary, the United Kingdom, and France, instead of perceiving Germany's example as an act of solidarity or as a good example to follow, rejected Germany's course of action in public declarations. Thus, the public perception of the refugee influx has created a strong voice in public opinion that rejects the consequences of adopting solidarity in the context to the refugee influx and thus the provisions of the EU that are based upon it. Instead, nationalist political and social programs emerge, which are celebrated by a large number when taking a stand against welcoming refugees within their territorial space.

Ian Manners suggested that the "EU is not what it does or what it says, but what it is" (Manners 2002, 252). What it is, is a union of member states with increasingly domestic national developments within the political and social landscape. The most predominant example may be Brexit and the United Kingdom's decision to leave the EU. This is of course not entirely based upon the refugee policies of the EU; however, it has been a strong narrative for the UK Independence Party, for example. *The Guardian* suggests that Britain left the European Union years ago when it came to asylum and refugees (Travis 2017). The paper quotes Theresa May saying that she "declared in her 2015 conference speech that 'not in a thousand years' would she take part in a new common EU immigration and asylum policy" (Travis 2017). In France's recent general election, we witnessed the continued rise of far-right and Eurosceptic party National Rally (previously the National Front), with second-place presidential candidate Marine Le Pen faring better against liberal incumbent Emmanuel Macron than she had in the previous election of 2017 (Clarke and Holder 2017). With her message of a strong national identity, she rejects the welcoming of refugees on European Union provisions, and a large minority of public opinion agrees with her. Other politicians have started to align with her narrative regarding refugees (Marlière 2016).

In many more member states, such as the Netherlands, Denmark, Poland, Hungary, Austria, and so on, such narratives can be observed as a constitutive element of the political and social landscape. This is not to say that there is not also a strong counter narrative; however, by observing the contemporary political discussion and the support and recognition the nationalist, Eurosceptic, and anti-immigration narratives received by the public, the EU as a normative concept is arguably in distress. In his state of the union address in 2015, Jean-Claude

Juncker, who served as president of the European Commission from 2014 to 2019, critiqued the European Union as not being in a good state (Juncker 2015).

But how can we explain this lack of emotional bond to the Union? The EU has been foremost an economic project that evolved into a political institution but fell short in the creation of an identity through nation-building efforts and the creation of an emotional attachment of its citizens. The historicity of the European continent forged the "self" of the nation-states since their emergence after the peace of Westphalia and provided a foundation for the collective identities within the nations. The EU is a project that rose out of the aspiration for peace and economic advantage, which was intended to be harnessed for national interests. It does not hold the merit to build a collective identity that outweighs the attachment to the nation-state for the normative power to become effective internally, at least not yet.

Solidarity Failing to Overcome Borders

The problem with the adaptation of cross-border solidarity falls on similar grounds. "Solidarity, which mean to do what is good for all of us, depends on a collective or shared identity" (Eriksen 2015, 252). But according to Eriksen, "this is poorly established in the EU" (252). He explains the lack of a shared identity or bonds between the member states and to the European Union that would enable solidarity and form "a collective identity enabling redistribution and socioeconomic justice." To his understanding "solidarity is in short supply: it tends to stop at national borders" (253). This, however, would not be accomplished by also implementing hard-power structures, such as a police force within the European Union, as Therborn (1997) had suggested. Solidarity is a value that cannot be administratively or legally enforced. It depends on an emotional bond, especially since it is so vaguely phrased. Therefore, the interpretation of the respective member states needs to be influenced by the notion of a collective identity, or at least comradeship (Eriksen 2015, 253). According to Eriksen's understanding, the concept of solidarity asks for actions that exceed the demand of duty, however, are not merely a case of altruism (253–254). According to his understanding, "actors are called upon to help others in need through the establishment of a more just economic system, a better political regime or policy in the common interest." The issue, not only in the context of solidarity, is to identify and agree on a common interest on the scale of the EU.

However, the lack of unified action in context to refugees leads to the assumption that the European Union's weakness does not result so much from the absence of hard power, but rather "the absence of a unified voice and the inability to effectively represent the EU as a singular entity" (La Porte 2011, 7). This claim also suggests a failure, or the non-existence of a collective European identity established through the union's endeavours within its set of values. It seems what is lacking is time to forge, enhance, and strengthen its values; to give them opportunities to prove themselves beyond national spheres.

The European Union's Potential—Celebrating Diversity

Teresa La Porte (2011) raises an interesting argument by asking if, in order to be a normative power, the European Union needs homogenous appearance within and to the outside world, or if the diversity within the union can be used as an asset and to the advantage of the normative power. According to La Porte, "diversity is an asset, not an inconvenience" (7). And she makes an important point in the context of contemporary Western society. Through increasing globalization, the mobility of people has become one of the main phenomena within this process. In most places of the developed world, heterogeneity in culture and political and economic orientation is the predominant societal structure. Instead of fighting it, acknowledging and embracing heterogeneity, and using it as an extended set of resources, may be key for the European Union as a normative power. La Porte acknowledges that "Europe will never constitute perfect unity: it is neither its intention, nor does it correspond to the EU's political nature" (7). She suggests the EU as a role model to manage this pluriverse on a global scale. However, she also reminds us that it is "necessary, to know how to present this diversity in an articulate and coherent way, and not neglect to emphasize the evident unity that the member states demonstrate in multiple aspects" (7). Here, the EU is struggling to find the right voice with its member states, and on an international level, to present itself as strong in diversity. The lack of a unified voice, however, may also be partially because of a strong voice within the respective member states, still rejecting the idea of a heterogenous collective identity, but rather focus on the securitization of its artificially constructed homogenous perception.

La Porte is nevertheless optimistic about the potential of the European Union to act on behalf of its normative structure based on its own diversity. Her optimism about the potential of the European Union as a normative power is refreshing yet it is ahead of its time, as the EU at this moment in time seems to be struggling to identify its potential as an atypical actor itself. With the increasing notion of nationalism resulting in action of the member states to contradict the union's influence as a normative power, such as Brexit and the rise of right-wing social movements and political parties in France, Poland, Hungary, and Germany, and many other member states. Hocking and Bátora (2009) have a more moderate suggestion in defining the EU as a "large scale experiment in governance beyond the state" (14). Rather than translating the potential of the EU into reality, Hocking and Bátora suggest that it "can be seen as a fascinating laboratory to study the evolution and adaptation of diplomacy" (quoted in La Porte 2011, 8–9). This moderate determination of the European Union's potential as a normative power may hit closer to home than a rather over-optimistic assumption by La Porte, by simply observing the political landscape within the European Union at this moment. Solidarity may have yet to overcome national spheres, but we can witness humans coming together on supranational and global scales on other social issues. The "Fridays For Future" climate strikes, for example, have reached a global scope and show the capacity of the driving social force of collective human action. The solution to finding a unified voice in helping refugees thus may not be found within a supranational normative state structure such as the EU, but rather by addressing the urgency for collective action by representing the conflict that caused the influx as a global issue.

References

Appadurai, Arjun. 1996. *Modernity at Large*. Minneapolis: University of Minnesota Press.

——. 2006. *Fear of Small Numbers: An Essay on the Geography of Anger*. Durham, NC: Duke University Press.

BBC News. 2017. "EU to Sue Poland, Hungary and Czechs for Refusing Refugee Quotas." Europe. December 7. https://www.bbc.com/news/world-europe-42270239.

BKA-Statistik. 2016. *Mehr als 900 Angriffe auf Flüchtlingsheime*. Tagesschau, Inland, December 28.

Bull, Hedley. 1982. "Civilian Power Europe: A Contradiction in Terms?" *Journal of Common Market Studies* 21(2): 149–170. https://doi.org /10.1111/j.1468-5965.1982.tb00866.x.

Clarke, Seán, and Josh Holder. 2017. "French Presidential Election May 2017 – Full Second Round Results and Analysis." *The Guardian* [UK], May 26. https://www.theguardian.com/world/ng-interactive/2017/may/07 /french-presidential-election-results-latest.

Connolly, Kate. 2016. "Tensions Rise in Germany over Handling of Mass Sexual Assaults in Cologne – Police and Media Accused of Cover-up to Avoid Stoking Anti-immigrant Feeling after Witnesses Say Men Who Carried out Attacks Were of Arab Appearance." *The Guardian* [UK], January 7. https://www.theguardian.com/world/2016/jan/06/tensions -rise-in-germany-over-handling-of-mass-sexual-assaults-in-cologne.

Diehl, Jörg, Sven Röbel, Fidelius Schmid, Barbara Schmid-Schalenbach, and Benjamin Schulz. 2016. "Was bis jetzt zu den Übergriffen in Köln bekannt ist – Wer sind die Verdächtigen von Köln?" *Spiegel Online*, Panorama, January 8. https://www.spiegel.de/panorama/justiz/koeln -was-ueber-die-uebergriffe-bekannt-ist-a-1071191.html.

Dublin Regulations III. 2013. *Regulation (EU) No. 604/2013 of the European Parliament and of the Council*. June 26. https://www.asylumlawdatabase. eu/en/content/en-dublin-iii-regulation-regulation-ec-no-6042013 -26-june-2013-recast-dublin-ii-regulation#toc_32.

Elgot, Jessica. 2016. "How David Cameron's Language on Refugees Has Provoked Anger; Immigration and Asylum." *The Guardian* [UK], January 27. https://www.theguardian.com/uk-news/2016/jan/27/david -camerons-bunch-of-migrants-quip-is-latest-of-several-such-comments.

Eriksen, Erik O. 2015. "The Eurozone Crisis in the Light of the EU's Normativity." In *The Future of Europe: Democracy, Legitimacy and Justice after the Euro Crisis*, edited by Serge Champeau, Carlos Close, Daniel Innerarity, and Miguel Poaires Maduro, 247–262. Lanham, Md.: Rowman & Littlefield International.

Handelsblatt. 2017. "Steinmeier fordert mehr Solidarität." May 5. https:// www.handelsblatt.com/politik/deutschland/fluechtlingspolitik-stein meier-fordert-mehr-solidaritaet/19752066.html?ticket=ST-3664601-6vlT b6qAci9WL3212PAb-ap6.

Gould, Carol C., and Pasquale Pasquino, eds. 2001. *Cultural Identity and the Nation-State*. New York: Rowman & Littlefield Publishers.

Haine, Jean-Yves. 2004. "The EU's Soft Power: Not Hard Enough?", *Georgetown Journal of International Affairs* 5(1): 69–77.

Hocking, Brian, and Jozef Bátora. 2009. "Diplomacy and the European Union." *The Hague Journal of Diplomacy* 4:113–120.

Juncker, Jean-Claude. 2015. "Time for Honesty, Unity and Solidarity." State of the Union Speech. Strasbourg, September 9, 2015.

Kamens, David H. 2012. *Beyond the Nation-State: The Reconstruction of Nationhood and Citizenship.* Bingley, UK: Emerald.

Kosch, Lea. 2016. "Köln-Attacken: Silvester-Täter kamen mit Flüchtlingswelle nach Deutschland." Huffpost, June 9.

La Porte, Teresa. 2011. "The Power of the European Union in Global Governance: A Proposal for a New Public Diplomacy; USC Center on Public Diplomacy at the Annenberg School." CPD Perspectives on Public Diplomacy, Paper 1. https://uscpublicdiplomacy.org/sites /uscpublicdiplomacy.org/files/useruploads/u35361/2011%20Paper%201 .pdf.

Meaney, Thomas. 2016. "The New Star of Germany's Far Right, Frauke Petry Is a Mother, a Scientist, and the Leader of the Country's Most Successful Nationalist Phenomenon since the Second World War." *New Yorker,* October 3, 2016. http://www.newyorker.com/magazine/2016/10/03/the -new-star-of-germanys-far-right?mbid=social_facebook.

Manners, Ian. 2002. "Normative Power Europe: A Contradiction in Terms?" *Journal of Common Market Studies* 40(2): 235–258.

Mouffe, Chantal. 2018. *For A Left Populism.* London: Verso.

———. 2014. "The Information Revolution and Soft Power." *Current History* 113(759): 19–22.

Marlière, Philippe. 2016. "French Politicians Are Now Marching to Marine Le Pen's Immigration Tune – As the Mood Darkens in Europe, French Opposition to Migration Now Extends to a Category of EU Worker." *The Guardian* [UK], Opinion, November 20. https://www.theguardian.com /commentisfree/2016/nov/20/french-politicians-dancing-marine -le-pen-tune-immigration.

Fremdenhass. 2017. "Mehr als 3500 Angriffe auf Flüchtlinge." *Süddeutsche Zeitung,* February 26. https://www.sueddeutsche.de/politik/fremdenhass -mehr-als-3500-angriffe-auf-fluechtlinge-im-jahr-2016-1.3395560.

Middell, Matthias. 2016. "Kein Grund in Panik zu verfallen, Matthias Middell über Flüchlingsbewegungen und Verlustängste." *Das Leipziger Universitätsmagazin,* January 19.

Middelhoff, Paul. 2015. "Karte der Gewalt - Über 500 Angriffe gegen Flüchtlinge und ihre Unterkünfte zählte die Polizei allein in diesem Jahr. Wo leben sie besonders gefährlich?; Politik, Flüchtlinge." *Zeit Online,* August 26. https://www.zeit.de/politik/deutschland/2015-08 /gewalt-gegen-fluechtlinge-rassismus-deutschland-anschlaege -koerperverletzung?utm_referrer=https%3A%2F%2Fwww.google .com%2F.

O'Grady, Siobhán. 2015. "Slovakia to EU: We'll Take Migrants – If they're Christians." *Foreign Policy,* August 19, 2015. https://foreignpolicy .com/2015/08/19/slovakia-to-eu-well-take-migrants-if-theyre-chris tians/.

Reznick, Gabriel. 2012. "Shared Sovereignty and the European Union: The Transition to Post-Westphalian Sovereignty." Research paper, Academia. https://www.academia.edu/2763366/Shared_Sovereignty_and_the_European_Union_The_Transition_to_Post_Westphalian_Sovereignty.

Taylor, Matthew, Patrick Wintour, and Jessica Elgot. 2015. "Calais Crisis: Cameron Pledges to Deport More People to End 'Swarm' of Migrants." *The Guardian* [UK], July 30. https://www.theguardian.com/uk-news/2015/jul/30/calais-migrants-make-further-attempts-to-cross-channel-into-britain.

Therborn, G. 1997. "Europe in the Twenty-First Century." In *The Question of Europe*, edited by P. Gowan and P. Anderson, 357–385. London: Verso.

Travis, Alan. 2017. "On Asylum and Refugees, Britain Left Europe Years Ago." *The Guardian* [UK], March 1. https://www.theguardian.com/uk-news/2017/mar/01/how-britain-hard-stance-refugees-reshaping-european-policy.

Wallace, William. 1999. "The Sharing of Sovereignty: The European Parliament." In *Sovereignty at the Millennium*, edited by Robert Jackson, 81–99. Malden, U.K.: Blackwell.

Wimmer, A., and N. Glick-Schiller. 2003. "Methodological Nationalism, the Social Sciences, and the Study of Migration." *International Migration Review* 37(3): 576–610.

Zetter, Roger. 2007. "More Labels, Fewer Refugees: Remaking the Refugee Label in an Era of Globalization." *Journal of Refugee Studies* 20(2): 172–192.

Zick, Andreas, Beate Küpper, and Wilhelm Berghan. 2019. "Verlorene Mitte - Feindselige Zustände. Rechtsextreme Einstellungen in Deutschland 2018/19." Mitte Studie. Hg. für die Friedrich-Ebert-Stiftung v. Franziska Schröter. April 2019. https://www.fes.de/referat-demokratie-gesellschaft-und-innovation/gegen-rechtsextremismus/mitte-studie.

CHAPTER 12

Canadian News Media Coverage and Discourse of the Refugee and Migrant Crisis in Europe, 2015–2016

Claude Beaupré

The refugee and migrant crisis (RMC) in Europe, also known as the refugee crisis or the migration crisis, refers to a period of time in 2015 and 2016 when human migration from the Middle East and Africa toward Europe was the object of alarm, scrutiny, and debate. The international community became captivated in April 2015 after the sinking of five boats in the Mediterranean Sea carrying nearly 2,000 individuals who had hoped to reach Europe. This period—which arguably ended with the EU-Turkey refugee-return agreement of March 2016, when Europe agreed to pay Turkey 6 billion euros in exchange for restricting the number of migrants crossing into Europe (see chapter 3 of this volume; also Papademetriou 2017)—saw attention toward human migration raised in the media internationally. Ultimately, the RMC led to a mixture of regional and national debates about immigration, identity, and security in many parts of the world, most of which are ongoing today.

In 2015 and 2016, there were a staggering 2.3 million individuals found to be in Europe irregularly, the highest number in decades (European Parliament 2017). For some of Europe's portal countries, such as Greece, Italy, and Hungary, gaining thousands of incomers daily, while administering to those already present, pushed capacities to the breaking point. In addition to this, there were an estimated 4,000 deaths in the Mediterranean linked with the surge in migration

(UNHCR Data Portal, n.d.), an unusually high number that does not include the many who succumbed along the way. For the vast majority of Europeans, however, having no concrete, first-hand experience of the events other than media reports and the political captivation, meant that the RMC remained a faraway, abstract notion that had little to do with the actual events and everything to do with how it was supposed to affect them (Krzyżanowski, Triandafyllidou, and Wodak 2018; Wallace 2018). For the majority of Europeans, therefore, the RMC was first and foremost a perception of events rather than an experience of events, quite removed from the actual experience of the migrants or asylum seekers. As such, analysts must be careful not to add to the sensational discourse of crisis that surrounds the RMC from the European perspective, while also not understating the urgency of the plight of those undertaking the forced migration. In many ways, these were unusual and trying times for Europe, yet labelling the European experience a "crisis" hyperbolizes the reality. Doing so not only stigmatizes the individuals involved by rendering them as mere statistics to be handled or withstood, but also sets an alarmist and politicizing tone to the events (Krzyżanowski, Triandafyllidou, and Wodak 2018).

The role of the media during the RMC was "more crucial than usual" (Georgiou and Zaborowski 2017, 13). This was not only because of the scale and speed of the events that transpired, but mostly because of the power various mass media hold in influencing national public and political attitudes, framing debates and setting agendas toward asylum and migration. Some scholars, such as Krzyżanowski, Triandafyllidou, and Wodak (2018) and Triandafyllidou (2018), advance that, jointly and interactively, the media and political spheres fanned the flames of hysteria surrounding the discourses of migration and security throughout, and arguably since, the RMC. A handful of "turning points"—important events that are reported in the national media and influence or mark significant shifts of public discourse and policy (Triandafyllidou 2018)—were associated with heightening urgency and fuelling mobilization in several European countries. By comparing the media coverage of key EU member states throughout the RMC, Triandafyllidou found that there is an interactive relationship between media depiction and the migration discourse in each case, one conditioned by historical precedent and political climate.

This raises the question of the role of discourse in public policy and the social perception of immigration in countries such as Canada, which would have been chiefly dependent on the national media coverage to understand the situation in Europe. To ascertain this, I have looked into Canada's existing national discourses on immigration prior to the RMC to contextualize the research. This was followed by an analysis of two identified "turning points" of the RMC in Canada: the publication of the Alan Kurdi photograph and the Paris attacks of November 2015, both of which were linked with significant discursive and political shifts in the country. Each will be further explicated with the help of a previous analysis of the Canadian media coverage of RMC-related events (Beaupré 2018).

This research suggests that Canada's approach to migration is sensitive to the influence of media coverage. If the post-9/11 world heightened the emphasis on security in the country's rhetoric vis-à-vis refugees and migrants, the photograph of a dead child and all that it came to signify appears to have sharpened humanitarian sentiments among the electorate and boosted calls for a more proactive refugee-resettlement program, one which dovetailed into the Liberal Party's return to government with the October 2015 federal election. However, following the November 2015 Paris attacks, what might be understood as a discursive pendulum swung back. What have remained since are competing discourses on human mobility ranging from a fear-based, xenophobic, securitized conception of migration to a call to uphold humanitarian values of helping those in need.

Media in Migration Discourse

In being perceived as a credible provider of information, the media allows civil society and policy-makers alike to access knowledge on issues that could be relevant to them; an apprising role of greater importance still when the audience stands physically distant from the events taking place. Media coverage can have complex, multi-layered, and indeed long-term impacts on perception and discourse creation, not least with regard to politically charged issues such as human mobility. A 2018 study, for example, found that the media's informative role, especially in times of election, create "attitudinal uncertainty," especially surrounding issues in which the audience may not have first-hand experience (Gavin 2018). This uncertainty may in turn influence political attitudes, debates, and, ultimately—albeit at times indirectly—policy outcomes. The same study found, moreover, that the power of influence held by the media is particularly important when there are persistent patterns of coverage across a range of media (Gavin 2018).

Concerning the RMC specifically, while some may have witnessed an unusual number of newcomers in their surroundings, there is a likelihood that they were not directly affected in terms of their work, their space, and/or their daily habits. This is where the media exercised its influence, presenting their oftentimes incomplete and rushed (Feinstein and Storm 2017) version of the narrative which was, in turn, filtered and interpreted once more to fuel conversation and debates (Wallace 2018). These derivative retellings are what Strömbäck (2008) referred to when he stated that "mediated reality matters more than any kind of actual or objective reality" (239). This notion was also supported by Wallace (2018) and Krzyżanowski, Triandafyllidou, and Wodak (2018), who added that the representation of an individual or a group of people within a physical space through the mediatization of politics is one of the main carriers of migration discourse, and that exploring the news coverage of refugees and migrants is vital to understanding how citizens formulate and justify their opinions toward them.

Building on this, Wallace and Krzyżanowski, Triandafyllidou, and Wodak have suggested that, around the world, the politicized "mediatized visions" of human mobility are often depicted negatively. Media, it seems, has become a platform for the spread of "anxious politics" toward immigration (Albertson and Gadarian 2015), which are chiefly constructed on fears and misinformation propagated by sensationalistic media and xenophobic and/or Islamophobic rhetoric, infusing discourses with marked elements of security. While such negative views were traditionally attached to far-right politics, they have now been found to varying degrees across the political spectrum (Krzyżanowski, Triandafyllidou, and Wodak 2018, 15). This discursive shift is perceived as the result of the increasing tendency to link migration and security and/or terror in the aftermath of the 9/11 attacks of 2001 (Huot et al. 2015; Nail 2016; Bose 2020).

As Hier and Greenberg (2002) pointed out, trends would suggest that migration-related news coverage is most often episodic and considered "hard news" (i.e., salient stories with some degree of urgency attached to their reporting) following the reporting of any substantial influx. These periods are often labelled as "crises" and usually lead to a discursive focus on immigration, security, and resource management. Correspondingly, media and political rhetoric are seen to focus on the administrative and economic demands of caring for and integrating refugees within their societies, and suspicions about refugees' genuineness in their claims (Wallace 2018). This stems from the rising number of refugees globally and their perception as burdens, threats, bogus "asylum seekers," "illegal" migrants, criminals or, worse, potential terrorists (Aiken 2001). Moreover, the term "migrant" or "economic migrant" implies that an individual aims to join the workforce of the receiving country. These terms, moreover, are often conflated with "immigrants," who become fixed members of the local society. Such perceived and / or potential permanence, however, musters various fear-based discourses, not least of which is that they are a drain on social-welfare services; they present a security threat; they "steal" available jobs, compromising locals' chances of employment; and they "blemish" the local status quo with their own diverse cultures. As such, by using the terms "refugee" and "migrant" interchangeably, the wariness that stems from migrant and immigrant arrivals is transferred unto refugees, creating confusion while withdrawing attention from the individuals who require—and are entitled to—legal protection (Beaupré and Fischer 2020).

Triandafyllidou (2018) set out to investigate how the RMC had been covered and debated in European countries more or less directly involved in managing the influx (i.e., Greece, Italy, Hungary, Serbia, Croatia, Austria, Germany, and Sweden) and a few others which were less involved but remained important geopolitical players (i.e., the United Kingdom and Poland). The research was based on the premise that for each individual country there was an interactive relationship between specific events that took place, their coverage, and their de-/re-construction through national discourses. Her research aimed at identifying what she called "turning points" (206) for each country, meaning the memorable events of the RMC reported locally, which have in turn influenced the discursive shifts within each country. The comparative overview found that while there is a storyline of events common to all, the selection of turning points for each state had more to do with the geographical and political proximity and/or relevance of the events in question, and "the ways in which the events resonate with underlying national themes and historical legacies" (214). In simpler terms, how a state responded to the RMC was anchored in its notions of identity, its values, and its geopolitical context and the ideology of its administration.

The research concluded that the resulting adopted policies of each country in response to the RMC reflected the respective national recontextualization of historical patterns vis-à-vis the perception of the "other" (i.e., asylum and migration) and the existing national discursive traditions. Triandafyllidou found that the existing migration discourse, based on historical precedence and the current political climate of each country, is reflected in and influenced by the media coverage of the RMC, and vice versa, that there is an interactive and mutually reinforcing relationship between media coverage, migration discourse, and political action.[1] The frameworks Triandafyllidou and Krzyżanowski, Triandafyllidou, and Wodak developed for analysis in the European context can be applied to the Canadian experience of the RMC, even though, or especially because, Canada was geographically removed and dependent on media reporting to understand the situation in Europe. To demonstrate this, I have looked into Canada's existing national discursive traditions on immigration prior to the RMC and identified "turning points" of the RMC that appear relevant to the country.

The media-coverage section of this research was conducted first through a historical analysis of the RMC as a means of identifying its main themes and events (Beaupré 2018). Each of these, in turn, were subjected to an empirical media analysis based on four of the highest-circulation daily Canadian newspapers: in English, the *Globe and Mail*, the *National Post*, and the *Toronto Star*, and, in French, *La Presse* (Boumans et al. 2017, 2). The media analysis of this research relies heavily on the Factiva global news database, which allows users to compile and compare the outputs of various news outlets. Through Factiva, it was possible to generate a list of all articles published in both French and English by these four media outlets, both in print and online from January 1, 2015, until December 31, 2016, which pertained in a general manner to the European continent. It is worth noting, however, that the data was organized in a way that it would exclude republished articles, pricing and market data, obituaries, sports, and calendar articles. Examining the way these four news sources covered the RMC from a quantitative standpoint enabled the

---

1   It should be noted that with the advent of social media and other online communications tools, the role and influence of traditional media sources (i.e., print media, radio broadcasting, television, and so forth) is more limited than in the past. Further research into the influence of social media, therefore, within the same framework as this study would be complementary.

identification of potential turning points. The quantitative analysis in this text serves to highlight which key RMC events were met with heightened coverage by the Canadian media, which in turn can be associated with moments of discourse elaboration and shift in Canada.

Other studies have looked at the potential links between the Canadian media and the migratory wave that occurred in 2015–2016. A few notable examples, with illustrative titles, are Petra Molnar's (2016) "The Boy on the Beach: The Fragility of Canada's Discourses on the Syrian Refugee 'Crisis,'" Tyyskä et al.'s (2017) "The Syrian Refugee Crisis in Canadian Media," Rebecca Wallace's (2018) "Contextualizing the Crisis: The Framing of Syrian Refugees in Canadian Print Media," and Winter, Patzelte, and Beauregard's (2018) "L'imaginaire national, l'asile et les réfugiés syriens en Allemagne et au Canada." Each of these, however, focused on the Syrian refugee crisis and Canada's role in it, and either briefly allude to Europe's RMC or simply ignore it altogether. This latter omission could be understood mainly because, if the RMC seemed abstract and far away to the majority of Europeans, Canadians were at an even greater distance. However, this does not mean that Canadian media paid no attention to the events in Europe.

Altogether, the four newspapers generated nearly 17,000 articles on issues related to Europe in a general manner between January 2015 and December 2016 (Beaupré 2018). Of these, 2,300 articles made direct mention of the terms "refugees" and / or "migrants." These articles are considered henceforth as articles containing the refugee and/or migrant (RM) criteria. These are the articles concerning the events that surrounded the RMC in Europe. When looking at figure 12.1, on the overall Canadian coverage of European matters between 2000 and 2017, one can see that 2015 and 2016 were not extraordinary years in terms of general media coverage. However, when looking at the bottom line, which exhibits the number of articles with the aforementioned RM criteria, there is an appreciable rise over these two years in media attention. This increase averages to 300 percent from the overall median average, meaning that throughout 2015 and 2016 there were three articles per day in the four selected newspapers written about refugees and/or migrants in Europe instead of the median one article per day between 2000 and 2017.

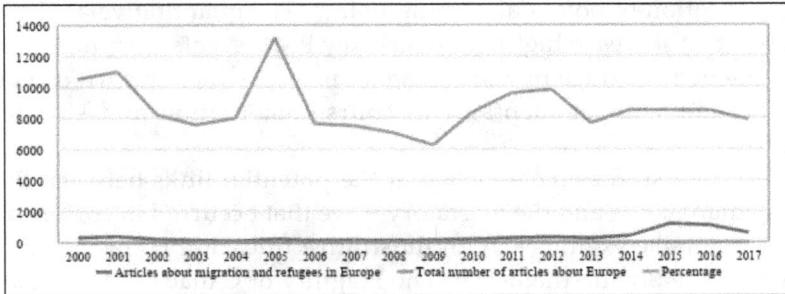

FIGURE 12.1. Overall Numbers of Articles Written by Selected Newspapers Concerning Events in Europe and total Number of Articles Linked with Migration and Refugees between 2000 and 2017.

Source: Claude Beaupré.

Pre-RMC Migration Discourse

In Canada, immigration is a key element of the national history and identity. This is not only because the country has a long history as a leader among Western nations in refugee protection and resettlement (Molnar 2016) but also because the country prides itself on its immigration background and its multiculturalism. As a per capita percentage, Canadian immigration and refugee resettlement have been sizeable since the nineteenth century, due mostly to an expansionist policy pursued in relative continuation since the end of the Second World War (Reitz 2012). For most of the past two decades, the country has consistently taken in around 0.8 percent of its population annually, resulting in a per capita gain nearly twice the size of the US's, even including irregular immigrants from Latin America (Reitz 2012). Even so, the aforementioned migration discursive trends are also present in Canada, as refugees are vilified as "queue-jumpers," resource-drains, and security threats (Huot et al. 2015). Although personal stories have been known to soften refugees' reception, the reality remains that refugees are often negatively portrayed as inevitable burdens to the state in Canada (Wallace 2018).

In the aftermath of the 9/11 attacks, Canada was not immune to the increased global focus on national security and the prevention of terrorism. This influenced discursive shifts in Canadian immigration that had an increased security component focused on potential terrorists in a process that implicated refugees and migrants of Muslim and

Middle Eastern backgrounds. Consequently, the Liberal-led administration of the time, followed by Prime Minister Stephen Harper's Conservative governments, diverted resources from resettlement and integration programs to strengthening border controls in an effort to "root out" potential terrorists (Antonius, Labelle, and Rocher 2021). It meant that from 2006 to 2015, the reception of refugee claims was significantly reduced overall, allowing for a steady decrease since 2008 more specifically (Statistics Canada 2019). This decrease followed restrictive policies in an attempt at discarding "bogus" applications meant to save the government $1.6 billion over five years (Goodspeed 2018). The securitization of migration post 9/11 created the perception that the Canadian immigration system was vulnerable to exploitation, a sentiment bolstered by domestic media (Winter, Patzelte, and Beauregard 2018; Krzyżanowski, Triandafyllidou, and Wodak 2018). As Goodspeed (2018) put it, the reforms were also accompanied "by a marked shift in rhetoric" under Conservative governments (287). Refugees were depicted as "economic freeloaders." After 9/11, the fear of a similar terrorist attack happening on Canadian soil led many to perceive foreigners with uncertainty and fear, and Middle Eastern individuals in particular experienced racial profiling; "This translated into a new focus on security issues, with demands to patrol borders, intercept migrants, and seek safeguards from foreign threats. Combined with 'law and order politics,' the result has been a demonization of immigrants and refugees, and a focus on 'fraud' and 'abuse'" (287). By 2015, this meant that it was harder for refugees and asylum seekers to come to Canada than at any other point since the twentieth century.

Even within this context, it should be noted that support for refugee resettlement in Canada continued. Indeed, as reported by the Transatlantic Council on Migration, public-opinion polling showed that Canadians were far more open to human migration than their European or American counterparts (Bloemraad 2012; Hiebert 2016). The way Canadians perceived migration in 2015 allowed for a wide range of discourses, ranging from highly securitized to welcoming and humanitarian.

Turning Point One: The Photograph, September 2015

With the 2015 federal elections in full swing, the photograph of the deceased Alan (Aylan) Kurdi, a two-year-old Syrian boy who drowned while crossing with his family from Turkey to Greece, became a focal point of a series of discursive changes in the country. This photograph, taken by Turkish photojournalist Nilüfer Demir, proved significant for Canadians, not only because it horrified the world, reproduced *en masse* in the international media, but also because the country was directly implicated with it. Within a week of its publication, it became known that members of the extended Kurdi family in Canada had attempted to sponsor them as refugees for resettlement but had been refused for administrative reasons (Kurdi 2019). The rejection led Alan Kurdi's immediate family to attempt the journey to Europe irregularly.

A quantitative media analysis indicates a link between the viral dissemination of the photograph and the uptick in popular attention to the events in Europe. Out of 17,000 articles prior to September 2015 and the photograph, there was an average of two articles per day about Europe with the RM criteria in all four newspapers. Afterwards, it tripled to six articles per day, a decidedly high number considering that this is from only four newspapers. Moreover, when looking at the overall 17,000 articles, even those without direct relevance to the RMC, 97 percent that mentioned Syria (e.g., the war but not the refugee and migrant flows into Europe) were published after the Kurdi tragedy. This suggests that the photograph did bring Syria—and indirectly the RMC—more to the fore of Canadian attention even when the child was not directly mentioned in the articles. As such the image, published initially on September 2, 2015, in the Netherlands, can be considered a turning point of the coverage of the RMC.

The image's media resonance has to be understood in the context of the 2015 federal election. Elections are a time of heightened political scrutiny and debate, rendering media coverage constant and more consequential (Gavin 2018). Had the story of the Kurdi family and its linkages to Canadian refugee-resettlement policies, particularly toward Syrian refugees, occurred at a time when Parliament was sitting, one may expect that its coverage would have been less, as it might have been, moreover, had the incumbent Conservative administration not been resisting a more expansive refugee response for the previous two years, in the face of the RMC scrutiny and heightened public demand for increased resettlement. Indeed, prior to the publication of the Kurdi photograph, there had been limited public outcry about the lack of a federal response to the Syrian war that had been raging since 2011, and about the lack of Canadian solidarity toward Europe's challenges with the RMC (Molnar 2016, 68). Until then, "the political debate remained largely impersonal and focused on numbers and targets" (Goodspeed 2018, 300). In July 2013, Canada, under Prime Minister Harper, had promised to resettle 200 government-sponsored and 1,100 privately sponsored Syrian refugees by the end of 2014. It remained, however, that a year later, as Syria's war entered its fourth year, Canada had resettled fewer than 150 Syrians. At that same time, Sweden, which has only about a quarter of Canada's population, had opened its doors to more than 30,000 Syrians, and Germany was expecting to receive 800,000 refugees (Goodspeed 2018, 285). As such, in September 2015, in the last few weeks leading up to Canada's 42nd federal election, the Kurdi tragedy, the RMC, and the Syrian refugee crisis became politicized, prompting Canada's major parties to distinguish themselves by promising refugee-resettlement policies, with special attention to Syrian refugees. Indeed, some have attributed the Liberal Party's welcoming position on refugee resettlement among the factors that contributed to its victory over the Conservatives on election day, October 19 (Molnar 2016, 70; Bose 2020, 14).

The source of the migration influx toward Europe was regionalized. According to the European Parliament, the vast majority of the first-time asylum seekers to the EU in 2015–2016 originated from Syria (28 percent), Afghanistan (15 percent), and Iraq (11 percent) (Eurostat 2016). Together, these three countries were the origin of more than 50 percent of all newcomers, with the remaining percentage being made up of smaller pockets of Nigerians, Pakistanis, Eritreans, and multiple others. Even so, the Canadian media focused almost exclusively on Syrian refugees, seldom mentioning Afghans and Iraqis, and doing so only passively and never as individual groups (Beaupré 2018, 50–52). Media coverage focused on Syrian refugees rather than the other nationalities involved in the RMC because of three factors: Syrians made up the largest pocket of refugee claimants in Europe; attention toward the Syrian civil war was already heightened because of the ongoing debate, since 2013, on Syrian refugee resettlement; and because the Alan Kurdi story hit a chord with the Canadian people because his death, and that of his mother and five-year-old brother (Kurdi 2019), were tied to reports of their failed attempt to receive asylum in Canada.

The latter point, more specifically, was because, as Goodspeed (2018) stated, the photograph reminded civil society of their power to act as they did in 1978 with the overcrowded Indo-Chinese *Hai Hong* ship. Denied permission in surrounding countries, the world's media in 1978 brought the plight of "boat people" into Western living rooms. Following a chain of reports and photographs of the conditions on the *Hai Hong*'s cramped quarters, Canadians "fretted" over the world's unwillingness to help the refugees, according to Goodspeed (288), comparing this developing situation with that of the Second World War Jewish population. Consequently, stirred by the media coverage of the events, civil society mobilized and the Canadian government agreed to resettle 604 of the *Hai Hong*'s passengers in the final months of 1978. The story of this ship coincided with the beginning of Canada's unique tradition of private sponsorship of asylum seekers in the 1970s. Forty years later, civil society seemed ready to revamp this tradition as the top Google search term in the country after publication of the Kurdi photograph was "How to Sponsor a Syrian?" (Goodspeed 2018). This call for action was mirrored in varying degrees in the articulation of all party positions throughout the 2015 election, seen in statements regarding RMC responses and refugee-resettlement plans beyond the already agreed-upon annual numbers (Molnar 2017).

It has been argued that following the Kurdi photograph, the prevailing negative perceptions of Middle Eastern refugee claimants in Canadian migration discourse, which had prevailed for over a decade were mitigated by a strong desire to help, and Canadians were called upon to welcome those in need (Tyyskä et al. 2017; Winter, Patzelte, and Beauregard 2018). It is even said that, at times, the widespread call to action from coast to coast seemed so grand that, if anything, refugee advocates felt that the resulting self-congratulating news coverage "amounted to a massive Internet 'selfie' in which Canada's admiration for its own response to the Syrian crisis threatened to overshadow the narratives of the Syrians themselves" (Goodspeed 2018, 301). In an interview with an official from a provincial partner agency, Bose (2020, 17) found that "this mayor or that councillor or this family [called] asking when were they getting the Syrians [...] like they all wanted their own Syrian doll family." Such statements were also supported by Tyyskä et al. (2017), who found in their own media-coverage analysis that the stories usually ignored the program recipients altogether by instead fixating on the deeds and generosity of the Canadians involved.

To put the influential capacity of the Alan Kurdi photograph into context, it is worthwhile to compare the scale of its media coverage with that of other similarly unfortunate RMC events. The first is the lorry incident of August 2015, when 71 individuals were found dead and abandoned in the back of a truck along an Austrian highway (International Organization for Migration 2015, 1). There were three reasons which rendered this incident one of the most marked tragedies of the RMC. The first was the sheer gruesomeness of the story as the bodies were found in an advanced stage of decomposition. The second was the fact that it broke away from the more commonplace stories of migrants and refugees drowning at sea (Strohecker 2015). Last, it was also that it occurred merely a week before the pictures of Kurdi were first published. Upon looking into this incident's media coverage, however, only four articles were found from the four considered newspapers, some of which ignored the story altogether.

The second incident to be contrasted with the Kurdi photograph is the image of five-year-old Syrian Omran Daqneesh, dazed and bloodied, sitting in the back of an ambulance after being rescued from a collapsed building in Aleppo, Syria (Sajir and Aouragh 2019). The photo made international headlines a year after the Kurdi photograph in August 2016. Like the lorry incident, it also generated little attention in Canada, with only three articles being published, each by a different newspaper. The reception of both photographs in Canada was largely due to the contexts in which they were received. As Goodspeed (2018, 297–298) puts it:

> The repetitive tragedies that dominated the end of the last century and the beginning of the twenty-first have left a legacy of callous disregard. In an era of twenty-four-hour, all-news television, the public has had a surfeit of tragedy to deal with. [...] The photo of Alan Kurdi, dead on the beach, was an exception. One stark, shattering image seemed to suddenly change everything.

The Kurdi photograph is attributed with placing a face to the RMC; a humanizing element said to break away from abstract and impersonal statistics such as 71 refugees/migrants, or 3,000-plus deaths in the Mediterranean Sea (Goodspeed 2018). In September 2015, the photo of the child is thought to have galvanized a mobilizing force for Canadians to take a greater role in alleviating the Syrian refugee crisis (Tyyskä et al. 2017; Winter, Patzelte, and Beauregard 2018).

That some events could suddenly capture public attention while others did not highlights the susceptibility of both attention and rhetoric in Canada, and the potential rapidity with which it may be overturned to the detriment of those men and women on the receiving end of these policies. While Molnar (2016) might attribute this fickleness in attention toward the Daqneesh photograph to the eventual "numbing" of the Canadian public to the Kurdi photograph, Goodspeed (2018) would associate it with the natural outcome of the fast-paced media coverage of our modern world. Either scenario, to which I would add the time-specific context of the Canadian election, would help explain why, merely a week earlier with the former example or a year later with the latter, Canadian newspapers felt less inclined to cover the incident.

Turning Point Two: Paris Attack, November 2015

It did not take long after the Kurdi photograph for the national migration discourse to be swayed once more in reaction to RMC-related events. Two months after the initial surge in Canadian willingness to take in Syrian refugees, and one month after the Liberals had been put into power, the conversation seemed to have circled back once more toward fear and insecurity in the wake of terrorist attacks in Europe (Showler 2015; Molnar 2016). This brings us to our second discursive turning point, the November 2015 Paris terrorist attacks.

By the time the RMC began, in April 2015, the continent was already attending to the complexities of the increased frequency of Islamist militant attacks since 2006 (Europol 2018). In 2015 and 2016 alone, multiple attacks occurred (Foster 2017), notably *Charlie Hebdo* (January 2015), the Paris attacks (November 2015), the Brussels bombings (March 2016), and the Berlin Christmas-market attack (December 2016). While each of these were devastating events, none sparked the same level of coverage in Canadian newspapers as the November Paris (Bataclan) attacks. It was mostly due to that it was not only deadlier, resulting in the loss of 130 lives, but also because of what I have labelled Canadian "post-colonial nostalgia" toward France and the UK.

In Beaupré (2018), I show that nearly 50 percent of the total 17,000 articles between 2015 and 2016 on Europe focused on events that occurred in these two countries, a statistic mirrored in the number of articles containing the RM criteria. In total 3,409 articles written about France in a general manner, 34 percent related to terrorism linked with the November 2015 attacks and, to a much smaller degree, the July 2016 Nice truck attack. Of course, it would be inaccurate to state that neither

France nor the United Kingdom played a role in the events of the RMC, or that they were not affected by its developments. Yet, despite the importance of the Calais "jungle," the Eurotunnel crossings, and the Paris attacks, just to name a few, these two countries were not the ones the initial historical research singled out as having played a key and active role in the RMC, unlike Greece, Italy, Germany, or Sweden (Beaupré 2018). Even so, Canadian media appear to spotlight the colonial powers that founded Canada. The Paris attacks generated a significant amount of attention in the Canadian RMC media coverage, resulting in the publication of an average of six articles per day (between November 2015 and January 2016), meeting the RM criteria. This continued the post-Kurdi-photograph media hype of the RMC, which was, however, diminished come January 2016, with a still significant, but greatly reduced, three articles per-day average.

To bluntly link migration and terrorism is perpetuating unwarranted labels on the men and women who simply wish to secure a safer and better future for themselves. Unfortunately, this association is often made, resulting in statements such as this one by Nail (2016, 158–159):

> The refugee crisis in Europe can no longer be understood as separate from the crisis of terrorism after the Paris attacks on 13 November 2015. In fact, the two crises were never really separate in the nationalist imaginary to begin with. […] It should hardly go without saying that migration and terrorism are not the same thing, but the fact that they have become each other's doppelgänger in contemporary politics, at least since 9/11, cannot simply be dismissed or ignored.

Sensibility toward Muslims in Europe became increasingly apparent in the aftermath of the November 2015 attacks (Oztig, Gurkan, and Aydin et al. 2021). A reality made worse when a Syrian passport was found near the body of one of the aggressors (Funk and Parkes 2016; Ball 2015; Vinocur 2015). The document, however, had supposedly belonged to a completely unrelated party, an asylum seeker who had arrived in Greece a few weeks earlier and had his documents stolen (Kingsley 2017), a detail that was at times left out in the reporting of the event. Unsurprisingly, many linked the threat of Islamic-extremist terrorism to the ongoing RMC despite all the attackers holding either French or Belgian nationalities (Farmer 2016). This reinforced the prevailing post-9/11 association of refugees and migrants from the Middle East with extremist violence and ultimately depicted them as potential threats to national security.

In 2015, Canada experienced a 61 percent rise in the number of police-reported crimes motivated by hate against the Muslim population (Statistics Canada 2017). In Toronto, for example, a Muslim mother picking up her children from school was accosted and told to "go back to [her] country" (Rieti 2015); a mosque was torched in Peterborough, Ontario (CBC News 2015b), and another mosque was defaced twice in Alberta (CBC News 2015a). To blame this discursive shift solely on the Paris attack perpetrators and the influx of refugees and migrants of Middle Eastern backgrounds into Canada would be unjustified. Islamophobia in Canada was already on the rise, and the Paris attacks only served to fuel it. In 2016, there was a 13 percent decrease in the number of police-reported crimes motivated by hate against the Muslim population; in 2017, however, there was a 150 percent increase (Gaudet 2018; Armstrong 2019).

Coinciding with the Paris attacks, the Liberal government published a number of statements that suggested that its refugee-resettlement program would prioritize women and complete families rather than individual men, promoting its pre-selection vetting processes for the incoming Syrian refugees (Canadian Council for Refugees, n.d.). It should be noted, however, that single men could still be eligible for resettlement if they identified as LGBTQ; they along with families and single women were the preferred candidates. Doing so corroborated "the assumption and implication that single [and presumably religious] Middle Eastern men are a greater security risk and should be feared because they fit the stereotype of most terrorists" (Molnar 2016, 71).

This statement exemplifies the dominant Canadian migration discourse. It states that while the federal government remained engaged in the protection of Syrian refugees, demonstrating that it still regarded them as individuals worthy of protection, it simultaneously insinuated that they carried a potential for danger. As the RMC in Europe was coming to an end, these two messages highlight the complex reality of migration discourse in Canada: a contention between the pervasive security rhetoric of migration post 9/11 and the humanitarian "values" that influence the country and its citizens to mobilize to help those in need.

Conclusion

Four years after the initial surge in migration toward Europe, one of the main perceived outcomes of the RMC was the discursive entanglement of regional and national debates vis-à-vis immigration, identity, and security in most of the Western world. This did not stem solely from the RMC. These linkages first became salient post 9/11, which resulted in an "us versus them" attitude reflected in increased border controls, selective migration reform, and a rise in Islamophobia in many societies. The RMC, in turn, is merely the continuation, entrenching these correlations into the discursive mainstream. As stated earlier, the RMC was not a migration crisis per se, despite what its name suggests, but first and foremost a discursive one. While the events that occurred throughout the RMC were indeed lamentable, the exigencies that resulted from them had more to do with the public and political perception of the events that transpired in Europe rather than the actual surge in migration itself or the precarious realities of the non-European men and women implicated in it.

In the midst of the RMC, the media played a pivotal role. It allowed civil society and policy-makers alike to access knowledge on matters of relevance on which they could inform their opinions and actions, an especially important function in faraway places where citizens had no first-hand experience. This was the premise of Triandafyllidou's (2018) research, which proposed that the existing migration discourse of any given country, being based on historical precedence and the reigning political climate, is reflected and influenced by its media coverage, and vice versa. It suggests that there is an interactive and mutually reinforcing relationship between media coverage, migration discourse, and political action. In each European country studied, a handful of detected "turning points" accompanied discursive shifts that amplified the urgency of the situation and fuelled mobilization.

It is no stretch to say that the RMC has impacted Canada, and is likely to continue doing so in both the near and distant future, socially and politically. This is not only because the RMC has raised important questions surrounding migration within the country but also because the "crisis" will undoubtedly leave its mark in contemporary history in ways still to be uncovered. The RMC was significant in Canada, not only because it occurred simultaneously with the 2015 federal election but also because it mobilized the country to reconsider the Canadian government's focus on the securitization of migration. While the country enjoyed an ocean-wide level of separation from the 2015–2016 events in Europe, it was not immune to their discursive ripples. Building on Triandafyllidou's model and my own research (Beaupré 2018), it was found that Canada's turning points in the RMC were the publication of the Alan Kurdi photograph in September 2015 and the November 2015 terrorism attacks in Paris. Prior to September 2015, the Canadian media paid relatively little attention to the events in Europe on matters linked to human migration. After the publication of Kurdi's photo and story, however, the growing negative perception of refugees that had been dominating Canadian migration discourse for over a decade was challenged by a public desire to help and rekindle the perceived Canadian tradition of welcoming those in need. It is plausible that political and civil-society mobilization around this issue helped the federal Liberals secure a majority government in October 2015. The eagerness to help, however, was soon mitigated. A mere two months later, the conversation seemed to have returned to one infused with fear and insecurity after the Paris terrorist attacks. While this event was not directly related to the migratory wave in Europe, the fact that the men who initiated or participated in the attack were of Middle Eastern origins, like many of those involved in the RMC, left many to call for heightened security measures toward migration. This sentiment was echoed by the Government of Canada, which began prioritizing the resettlement of women and complete families rather than individual men; at once reinforcing the conflation of refugees and security threats.

These two contrasting messages highlight the Canadian discursive spectrum as the RMC in Europe was coming to an end: a contention between the previously upheld security rhetoric of migration post 9/11 and the welcoming "values" that binds the country to those in need following the appearance of the Kurdi photograph. When tracking the Canadian media coverage of the RMC in Europe throughout 2015 and 2016, the two turning points are easily identifiable. Out of 17,000 articles that appeared prior to September 2015 and the publication of the photograph, there was an average of two articles per day about Europe with the RM criteria in the four reviewed newspapers. Afterwards, the average tripled to six articles per day and remained as such from November 2015 until December 2016, after which it halved for the remainder of 2016. The numbers show a distinguishable Canadian interest in the RMC linked to the turning points.

When inputting Canada into Triandafyllidou's framework, it can be seen that the turning points had nothing to do with the geographical proximity of the events and everything to do with their relevance and resonance within the existing national migration discourses and the underlying historical and ideological precedence of the country. This chapter suggests that Canada's migration discourse is indeed sensitive to the influence of highly reported events. The rapid nature of each discursive transition highlights the fragility of migration policies and rhetoric in Canada, which concurs with their notion that there exists an interactive relationship between specific events that took place, their coverage, and their de-/re-construction through national discourses.

References

Aiken, Sharryn J. 2001. "Of Gods and Monsters: National Security and Canadian Refugee Policy." *Revue québécoise de droit international* 14(1): 117–139. https://ssrn.com/abstract=2494101.

Albertson, Bethany, and Shana Kushner Gadarian. 2015. *Anxious Politics: Democratic Citizenship in a Threatening World.* Cambridge: Cambridge University Press.

Antonius, Rachad, Micheline Labelle, and François Rocher. 2007. "Canadian Immigration Policies: Securing a Security Paradigm?" *International Journal of Canadian Studies / Revue internationale d'études canadiennes*, no. 36: 191–212. https://doi.org/10.7202/040782ar.

Armstrong, Amelia. 2019. "Police-Reported Hate Crime in Canada, 2017." Statistics Canada. April 30, 2019. https://www150.statcan.gc.ca/n1/pub/85-002-x/2019001/article/00008-eng.htm.

Ball, Sam. 2015. "Syrian Passport Puts Spotlight on Refugees after Paris Attacks, but Real Threat Closer to Home." *France 2.* November 16, 2015. https://www.france24.com/en/20151116-syrian-passport-puts-spotlight-refugees-after-paris-attacks-but-real-threat-closer-home.

Beaupré, Claude. 2018. "Analysis of the Canadian Media Coverage of the Migrant and Refugee Crisis in Europe, 2015-2016." Master's thesis, University of Strasbourg.

Beaupré, Claude, and Franziska Fischer. 2020. "The Label 'Refugee' and Its Impacts on Border Policies." *Borders in Globalization Review* 1(2): 71–83.

Bloemraad, Irene. 2012. "Understanding 'Canadian Exceptionalism' in Immigration and Pluralism Policy." Migration Policy Institute, Washington, D.C. https://www.migrationpolicy.org/pubs/Canadian Exceptionalism.pdf.

Bose, Pablo S. 2020. "The Shifting Landscape of International Resettlement: Canada, the US and Syrian Refugees." *Geopolitics* 27 (2): 1–27.

Boumans, Jelle, Damian Trilling, Rens Vliegenthart, and Hajo Boomgaarden. 2017. "The Agency Makes the (Online) News World Go Round: The Impact of News Agency Content on Print and Online News." *International Journal of Communication* 12:1768–1789.

Canadian Council for Refugees. n.d. "Did You Know…? Facts about Refugees and Refugee Claimants in Canada." https://ccrweb.ca/en/myths-facts.

CBC News. 2015a. "Cold Lake Mosque Hit by Vandals, Again." November 28, 2015. https://www.cbc.ca/news/canada/calgary/cold-lake-mosque-vanda lized-again-1.3342228.

———. 2015b. "Peterborough Mosque Arson Is Suspected Hate Crime." November 15, 2015. https://www.cbc.ca/news/canada/toronto/mosque -peterborough-fire-1.3320013.

European Parliament. 2017. "Asylum and Migration in the EU: Facts and Figures." News, June 30, 2017. http://www.europarl.europa.eu/news/en /headlines/society/20170629STO78630/eu-migrant-crisis-facts-and -figures.

Europol. 2018. *European Union Terrorism Situation and Trend Report 2018.* Europol. https://data.europa.eu/doi/10.2813/00041.

Eurostat. 2016. "Record Number of over 1.2 Million First Time Asylum Seekers Registered in 2015." Eurostat Press Office, March 4, 2016. http://ec.europa.eu/eurostat/documents/2995521/7203832/3-04032016 -AP-EN.pdf/790eba01-381c-4163-bcd2-a54959b99ed6.

Farmer, Ben. 2016. "Who Is Salah Abdeslam and Who Were the Paris Terrorists? Everything We Know about the Isil Attackers." *The Telegraph* [UK], March 18. https://www.telegraph.co.uk/news /worldnews/europe/france/11996120/Paris-attack-what-we-know -about-the-suspects.html.

Feinstein, Anthony, and Hannah Storm. 2017. "The Emotional Toll on Journalists Covering the Refugee Crisis." Reuters Institute for the Study of Journalism, University of Oxford. https://reutersinstitute. politics.ox.ac.uk/our-research/emotional-toll-journalists-covering -refugee-crisis.

Foster, Alice. 2017. "Terror Attacks Timeline: From Paris and Brussels Terror to most Recent Attacks in Europe." *Express.* https://www.express.co.uk /news/world/693421/Terror-attacks-timeline-France-Brussels -Europe-ISIS-killings-Germany-dates-terrorism.

Funk, Marco, and Roderick Parkes. 2016. "Refugees versus Terrorists." EU Institute for Security Studies. https://doi.org/10.2815/469903.

Gaudet, Maxime. 2018. "Police-Reported Hate Crime in Canada, 2016." Statistics Canada. April 25, 2018. https://www150.statcan.gc.ca/n1/pub/85-002-x /2018001/article/54915-eng.htm.

Gavin, Neil T. 2018. "Media Definitely Do Matter: Brexit, Immigration, Climate Change and Beyond." *The British Journal of Politics and International Relations* 20(4): 827–845. https://doi.org/10.1177/136914 8118799260.

Georgiou, Myria, and Rafal Zaborowski. 2017. *Media Coverage of the "Refugee Crisis": A Cross-European Perspective.* Council of Europe, report DG1(2017)03. https://rm.coe.int/1680706b00.

Goodspeed, Peter. 2018. "Back to the Future: Shifts in Canadian Refugee Policy over Four Decades." In *The Criminalization of Migration: Context and Consequences,* edited by I. Atak and J. Simeon, 283–312. Montréal and Kingston: McGill-Queen's University Press.

Hiebert, Daniel. 2016. "What's So Special about Canada? Understanding the Resilience of Immigration and Multiculturalism." Migration Policy Institute, Washington, D.C. https://www.migrationpolicy.org/research /whats-so-special-about-canada-understanding-resilience -immigration-and-multiculturalism.

Hier, Sean P., and Joshua L. Greenberg. 2002. "Constructing a Discursive Crisis: Risk, Problematization and Illegal Chinese in Canada." *Ethnic and Racial Studies* 25(3): 490–513. https://www.migrationpolicy.org/sites /default/files/publications/TCM-Trust-Canada-FINAL.pdf.

Huot, Suzanne, Andrea Bobadilla, Antoine Bailliard, and Debbie Laliberte Rudman. 2016. "Constructing Undesirables: A Critical Discourse Analysis of 'Othering' within the Protecting Canada's Immigration System Act." *International Migration* 54:131–143. https://doi:10.1111/imig .12210.

International Organization for Migration. 2015. "European Migration Crisis IOM Emergency Response Plan for Serbia and the Former Yugoslav Republic of Macedonia." https://www.iom.int/sites/default/files /country_appeal/file/IOM-European-Migration-Crisis-WB-Response -Plan-Appeal.pdf.

Kingsley, Patrick. 2015. "Why Syrian Refugee Passport Found at Paris Attack Scene Must Be Treated with Caution." *The Guardian* [UK], November 15. https://www.theguardian.com/world/2015/nov/15/why -syrian-refugee-passport-found-at-paris-attack-scene-must-be-treated -with-caution.

Krzyżanowski, Michal, Anna Triandafyllidou, and Ruth Wodak. 2018. "The Mediatization and the Politicization of the 'Refugee Crisis' in Europe." *Journal of Immigrant & Refugee Studies* 16(1–2): 1–14. https://doi:10.1080/15 562948.2017.1353189.

Kurdi, Tima. 2019. *The Boy on the Beach: My Family's Escape from Syria and Our Hope for a New Home.* Toronto: Simon & Schuster Canada.

Molnar, Petra. 2016. "The Boy on the Beach: The Fragility of Canada's Discourses on the Syrian Refugee 'Crisis.'" *Contention* 4(1–2): 67–76.

https://www.berghahnjournals.com/view/journals/contention/4/1-2
/conto40106.xml.

———. 2017. "Canadian Response to the Syrian Refugee Crisis." *The Canadian Encyclopedia*, March 13. https://www.thecanadianencyclopedia.ca/en /article/canadian-response-to-the-syrian-refugee-crisis/.

Nail, T. 2016. "A Tale of Two Crises: Migration and Terrorism after the Paris Attacks." *Studies in Ethnicity and Nationalism* 16(1): 158–167. https://www. doi.org/10.1111/sena.12168.

Oztig, Lacin Idil, Turkan Ayda Gurkan, and Kenan Aydin. 2021. "The Strategic Logic of Islamophobic Populism." *Government and Opposition* 56(3): 446–464.

Papademetriou, Demetrios G. 2017. "The Migration Crisis Is Over: Long Live the Migration Crisis." Migration Policy Institute, Washington, D.C. https://www.migrationpolicy.org/news/migration-crisis-over-long -live-migration-crisis.

Reitz, Jeffrey G. 2012. "The Distinctiveness of Canadian Immigration Experience." *Patterns of Prejudice* 46(5): 518–538. https://doi.org/10.1080/0 031322X.2012.718168.

Rieti, John. 2015. "Muslim Woman Sworn at, Told to Go Back to Her Country on TTC Bus." *CBC News*, December 3. https://www.cbc.ca/news/canada /toronto/sundus-a-ttc-bus-abuse-1.3349601.

Sajir, Zakaria, and Miriyam Aouragh. 2019. "Solidarity, Social Media, and the 'Refugee Crisis': Engagement Beyond Affect." *International Journal of Communication* 13(28): 550–577. https://ijoc.org/index.php/ijoc/article /view/9999.

Showler, Peter. 2015. "Syrian Refugee Debate a Tale of Two Stories." *Toronto Star*, November 22. https://www.thestar.com/opinion/commentary/2015/11 /22/two-competing-stories-about-syrian-refugees.html.

Statistics Canada. 2017. "Police-Reported Hate Crimes, 2015." The Daily, June 13. https://www150.statcan.gc.ca/n1/daily-quotidien/170613/dq170 613b-eng.htm?HPA=1.

———. 2019. "Just the Facts: Asylum Claimants." https://www150.statcan. gc.ca/n1/pub/89-28-0001/2018001/article/00013-eng.htm.

Strohecker, Karin. 2015. "Truck of Corpses, New Shipwreck Intensify Europe's Migrant Crisis." *Reuters*, August 27. https://www.reuters.com/article /us-europe-grants-eu-austria-idUSKCN0QW19H20150827.

Strömbäck, Jesper. 2008. "Four Phases of Mediatisation: An Analysis of the Mediatisation of Politics." *Journal of Press/Politics* 13(3): 228–246. https:// doi.org/10.1177/1940161208319097.

Triandafyllidou, Anna. 2018. "A 'Refugee Crisis' Unfolding: 'Real' Events and Their Interpretation in Media and Political Debates." *Journal of Immigrant & Refugee Studies* 16(1-2): 198–216. https://doi.org/10.1080/1556 2948.2017.1309089.

Tyyskä, Vappu, Jenna Blower, Samantha DeBoar, Shunya Kawai, and Ashley Walcott. 2017. "The Syrian Refugee Crisis in Canadian Media." Ryerson Center for Immigration and Settlement, Working Paper No. 2017/3.

UNHCR Data Portal. n.d. "Operation Portal: Refugee Situation." https://data2.unhcr.org/en/situations/mediterranean.

Vinocur, Nicholas. 2015. "Passport Points to Syria, but Officials Urge Caution." *Politico.* November 14. https://www.politico.eu/article/paris-attacker-slipped-into-europe-with-refugees-isil-molins-france-syria-greece-migrants/.

Wallace, Rebecca. 2018. "Contextualizing the Crisis: The Framing of Syrian Refugees in Canadian Print Media." *Canadian Journal of Political Science* 51(2): 207–231. https://doi.org/10.1017/S0008423917001482.

Winter, Elke, Anke Patzelte, and Mélanie Beauregard. 2018. "L'imaginaire national, l'asile et les réfugiés syriens en Allemagne et au Canada : une analyse discursive." *Canadian Ethnic Studies* 50:15–33. https://doi.org/10.1353/ces.2018.0013.

Mobility, Borders, and Comparative Research

Emmanuel Brunet-Jailly

As illustrated in the chapters above, there should be no doubt that for the last ten years states have been struggling with controlling human mobility (Guterres and Swing 2010). With over one percent of humanity displaced, there should be little surprise that the numbers of "irregular" migrants, asylum seekers, and displaced individuals are on the rise because of war, conflict, poverty, and climate and environmental changes (UNHCR 2020). Such a small proportion hides a much graver problem: the total number of forcefully displaced individuals worldwide. In 2020, the UNHCR documented 48 million internally displaced people, also known as IDPs (UNHCR 2020). Indeed, what remains the core problem is that because humanity is growing by the billions, mobility has also increased, almost *exponentially*, because the numbers are in the hundreds of millions of human beings. As clearly stated by Filippo Grandi, UN commissioner for Refugees, "we are witnessing a changed reality in that forced displacement nowadays is not only vastly more widespread but is also no longer a short term and temporary phenomenon" (6).

As underscored in the introduction and in the chapters of the first section, the question of short- versus long-term is at the core of this volume, and brings forth one of the major lessons of this edited collection: that human mobility is a defining feature of the beginning of the twenty-first century. This is the case simply because the sheer *number* of individuals on the move has increased beyond what pre-existed: 100 million forcibly displaced (UNHCR 2020, 4), and current policies, as surveyed above, were *never conceived* to deal with a long-term situation of ongoing mobilities across the world. Furthermore, the number of people who are suffering and who are on the move, in an attempt to improve their lives, continues to be dealt with by governments according to international standards set in the aftermath of the Second World War. In addition, there is increasing consensus among scholars and policy-makers that both climate change and the deepening economic disparities of the twenty-first century (McLeman and Hunter 2010), now further exacerbated by the coronavirus pandemic of 2020, also contribute to increasing this mobility (Chakraborty and Maity 2020). Yet, we also know that migrants contribute positively to their place, country, or city of destination, and in particular that their arrival does not affect, for instance, the wages of existing residents (Card 1990).

This volume aims to highlight that international and national legal regimes, and subsequent regulatory and policy systems, have been struggling, resulting in a tug of war between ideas, in particular liberal ideas, concerned with what to do about millions of humans on the move. It must be clear to readers of this volume that in the second decade of the twenty-first century, humans on the move generally hope to exchange a difficult economic or political situation (Samers and Collyer 2017) for what is often a legal regime conceived for *temporary* situations, or a deregulated legal regime implementing precarious rights systems. And, when labour regimes organize the status of these humans, they fall into cheaper and much less protected labour categories.

The original goal of our research program, which was structured partly around four workshops held between 2017 and 2018, was to review how Canada, the European Union, and Japan compared when faced with increased migration and mobility (Jean Monnet Network 2020). More broadly, this volume focuses on Canada in an international context, and also asks how borders and migration policies had progressed in their dealings with such situations comparatively. Indeed, we started this research program assuming that the EU response to the 2015 migration crisis offered exemplary policy responses, and should be studied in comparative perspective and context. We elected to compare Canadian policy responses to the European Union, Japan, and Mexico, assuming there would be many differences and similarities. Our findings were that although Canada and Mexico have long traditions of immigration, currently, Canada and Mexico, and the European Union and Japan, realize that migration matters because their economies have been expanding but the natural demographic growth of their populations remain stagnant. What we document in this volume is that those situations, in turn, lead to major unresolved policy struggles.

First, these governments, alongside their bureaucracies, have been overwhelmed with mobility issues and seem continually behind the last crisis. Indeed, the governments of those countries are, more than ever, unable to control such mobilities. Hence, for instance, the usage of the word "crisis" to describe the arrival of nearly two million individuals in 2015 at the borders of the European Union (Juncker 2015), or the notion of 2019 as "the year immigration began" in Japan by Boyle and Chi in chapter 10.

Second, as detailed frequently in the chapters of this volume, many policy solutions have assumed such mobility would be *temporary* (chapters 1, 2, 10). Empirical evidence consistently shows this is not the case. Continuing to assume that mobile individuals and irregular migrants are *not* a permanent feature of our twenty-first-century human history is an error; one lesson could be that much needs to be done to adapt legal regimes to that new permanence. Indeed, the UNHCR notes in "Global Trends" for 2019 that only about 35 million refugees had found a durable solution (UNHCR 2020).

Third, human mobility is indisputably a structural feature of human history (Mackova and Kysucan 2016; Swing 2011). And, although there are no doubts that mobile individuals, irregular migrants, and most refugees are hosted in countries of the Global South, as discussed repeatedly in this collection, mobile individuals and irregular migrants are a *permanent feature* of the contemporary history of our world, and also affect politics and policies of the Global North; that is, of Canada, the EU, Japan, Mexico, or the United States in particular. And because they are a structural characteristic of our world, governments ought to consider adapting and developing policies of management, welcome, and integration of those irregular migrants and their human ambitions and hopes, because these are the policies that ought to address the rights statuses of those human beings.

This is a point eloquently made by William L. Swing (2011), director general of the International Organization for Migration: "We live in an era of the greatest human mobility in recorded history." And yet, most of the contributors to this volume describe procrastination, difficulties, and tensions between neo-liberal views and humanistic ideals when it comes to human migration. For instance, the international community, the Western world, and countries such as Canada, Japan, or the 27 member states of the European Union, have until recently been satisfied with short-term policy approaches that *commodify* mobile individuals and deregulate labour standards, thus leading to a pauperization of labour and human-rights standards (chapters 1, 2, and 3).

Furthermore, the chapters here suggest (1) that contemporary borders and migration policies are more *intertwined* today than ever before; (2) that border scholars can contribute a great deal to *the role of borders* as mechanisms used by states to control mobility; and (3) that the bordering of states was not only about enforcing the respect of their own individual sovereignty at the international boundary lines but also resulted from (4) complex governance and policy mechanisms that required multitudes of tools enforcing limits across the traditional territories of states—their territoriality—beyond their territory, and across the territories of neighbouring states, and sometimes extraterritorially; that is, beyond their proximate neighbour.

In this conclusion, those assumptions are reviewed. Our findings clearly underscore and clarify the surprisingly complex mobility and bordering regimes of the past 10 years. Legal and regulatory systems are at the centre of a profound transformation of what borders are and how mobile individuals are legally labelled, filtered, parked in camps, and therefore identified as human beings, or indeed not. In the United States, for instance, a person is a legal subject of which rights and duties are attributes—and thus a person is recognized by law as human only because of those rights and duties—not because they are humans (Taylor 1985, 97); indeed, such a legal system does not grant inherent rights to human beings but recognizes a person as a legal being only. If a human being has no rights, they are just a body. Although Agamben (1995, 2005) never discusses the United States in his work, he discusses other such cases as "bare life," what ancient Greeks called *zoē* (the biological fact of life). The next four sections discussed how border and mobility legislation and regulatory/policy frameworks have continually adapted to increase control over mobility in *piecemeal* policies in Canada, the EU, Japan, and Mexico.

In the end, contrary to what a number of scholars have argued, that borders were "vacillating" (Balibar 2002) and "mobile" (Amilhat Szary and Giraut 2015; Sassen 2015), we find that these discussions do not go beyond a territorialist logic. Also, we suggest that by stressing the concepts of "border-zone" (La Pradelle 1928), "bending border" (Chen 2005), "border regions" (Paasi et al. 2018), "states' border realism" (Iwashita 2016), "borderities" (Amilhat Szary and Giraut 2015), or "borderscapes" (Rajaram and Grundy-Warr 2007; Brambilla 2015) to understand the nature of borders, these literatures posit states and the territorial delineation of state sovereignties as central to border questions. For instance, innovative concepts such as "borderscaping" (Brambilla 2015) underscore the importance of hegemonic and counter-hegemonic imaginaries in their "territorialist imperatives" but are still only partial glimpses into the changing logic of borders because they remain conceptually grounded in a statist / territorialist view of borders (Agnew 1994, 2017; Brenner 1999; Stark 2016). What we find is markedly different. Borders and mobility policies of the EU, Canada, and Japan are dependent on the legal regimes that mesh them together, beyond their territoriality, with the non-profit and private sectors across territorial spaces grander than any one state. For instance, as detailed below, the EU, Canada, and Japan border and migration policies depend on agreements spanning their regions of the world, but also networks of policy actors sometime reaching around the world, as is the case for the airline industries.

Big Picture: Canada and the European Union Struggle to Adapt to Mobility

In both Canada and in the European Union, our findings are that over the past decade border and mobility legislations have continually struggled to adapt to increased mobility. A cross section of this volume points to Canada's specific changes over the last few years. Comparing border—and migration-policy changes in Canada and the EU is striking: the Canadian context has evolved, but marginally— indeed, undocumented migrants arriving from the United States across the land border have increased, but the EU's demographic context is much graver; while millions are at the gates of the Union, in a number of countries and many in camps, the number entering Canada over the last few years reached 25,000 in 2017 and 28,000 in 2018. Unlike the EU, Canada has not had to completely revisit its border and migration policies because of mass migrations across its boundary lines. Consequently, there has not been any profound rethinking or massive pressure to review policy and responses to a spectrum of issues dealing with the management of borders or human mobility. Also, contrary to the EU, xenophobia and hostility have not driven Canada to implement extreme *de-bordering* and *re-bordering* of its policies, except with respect to refugee claimants and asylum seekers (see chapters 5 and 6; the EU-specific phenomenon is well documented in chapter 3). However, there are similar policies in areas concerned with controlling mobility prior to migrants reaching the boundary line. For instance, to manage asylum seekers that are already in North America, Canada has relied on the United States and the Safe Third Country Agreement (STCA) (IRCC 2020). The agreement applies to refugee claimants who seek right of entry into Canada from the United States at a port of entry by land or air. According to Canada's Immigration and Refugee Protection Act, Canadian officials should be able to assume that the third country is safe and party to the 1951 Refugee Convention and the 1984 Convention Against Torture. Also, the third country's policies and practices have to be in-line with both conventions, as do its human-rights record. Further, it has to have a "shared responsibility agreement" with Canada regarding refugee claims. The Canada-U.S. STCA, however, is unique for Canada. Interestingly, contrary to the European Union and the United States, Canada does not have any other policies to hold migrants away from its own boundary lines. Canada does not have camps, or the use of extraterritoriality procedures (e.g., carrier sanction, interception of migrants at sea, posting immigration officers in foreign countries for the external processing of asylum seekers).

However, two phenomena are affecting Canada with regards to mobility and borders: first, as a world leader and exemplar in migration and refugee protection and management, and a model for refugee integration, Canada has seen its reputation weakened given revisionist policies under Conservative-led governments from 2006 to 2015 (Carlaw 2017); indeed, Canada under Prime Minister Harper revisited its legislation to make it harder for refugees to gain status. Today, according to Watson (chapter 2), Canada qualifies as a status-quo state that is benevolent with revisionist tendencies. Its leading position in global governance is perceived as self-serving and driven by a determination to preserve the status quo. Such a strategy may have served Canada well in the past but, in the face of new worldwide mobility developments, it diminished Canada's credibility in the 2017 Global Compact negotiations. In sum, as discussed in chapter 2, Canada lost its leading voice in the migration debates. Second, those policy choices are reflective of two further transformations, summarized by Schmidtke, in chapter 1, as a commodification of migrants and an erosion of labour standards. Indeed, when looking specifically at foreign-worker programs it becomes clear that the number of "temporary" foreign workers has increased so much that, since 2017, they have represented 70 percent of all long-term residents with no citizenship rights (the number increased from about 250,000 in 2011 to over 470,000 in 2019). Clearly, such programs raise a number of questions that fail to address the foundational reasons for Canada's migration policies; that is, increasing its workforce and population. Schmidtke shows that such policies lead to an erosion of labour standards, and to lowering the cost of labour, while also increasing abuses (a problem well identified by Immigration, Refugees and Citizenship Canada), and, overall, result in the growth of an "under" class of non-citizens that experience continuous forms of social and political exclusion.

In other words, it is clear that over the last few years, contextual changes have affected Canada deeply as well as the EU. Since 2015, the EU faced serious difficulties adapting to migration. In both Canada and the EU many tensions have been pulling and pushing policy responses across a wide political spectrum of ideas. It is led by a sentiment of hostility and xenophobia in parts of the Union, and along concurrent efforts to manage and welcome migrants both in Canada and the EU. The authors, here, analyzed this tension as continuous pressures to limit or enable mobility with difficulty, a phenomenon described in border studies as *de-bordering* and *re-bordering*. As further discussed in the following section, the Union expanded its policies outside the Union's borders to southern and eastern neighbourhood countries, increasing various forms of extra-territorialisation including procedures being implemented and staffed, and camps being built around the Mediterranean region, to increase control over mobility. Furthermore, simultaneously a number of EU member states closed their national borders *within* the Union, which contravened with the Schengen Agreement. Unfortunately, such controversies over policy making inside the Union have also raised international concerns regarding the status of migrants in and around the Union, with human rights and charitable organizations raising alarms. Human rights and international law records have been tarnished in a number of Union member states. Also, because of states of exception/emergency, the lawful implementation of both the Dublin regulation and the Schengen Agreement ended up being disregarded. In Canada, as detailed in chapters 5 and 6, during the Harper years making border crossing difficult took administrative and procedural forms, that resulted in a narrower ambit of interpretation of what a safe third country is. The resulting picture is that anxieties and insecurities regarding the status of temporary foreign workers or Syrians attempting to enter the Union or Canada, has led to a further deterioration of the status of those individuals with regards to human rights, labour laws, and a large portfolio of border management policies across all countries across much more complex governance mechanisms. These expand spatially the border and bordering procedures beyond the international boundary line into other countries where mobility statutes and border policies are blurred; it is explored in further detail below.

Borders and Mobility Policies: Legislative Tug of War

A second theme of this volume has to do with how states in their attempts to *re*-gain control over mobility struggle to retain respect for human rights and migratory principles established during the post–Second World War period. In Canada, a set of policies implemented between 2014 and 2019 illustrates partially unsuccessful attempts to regain control over incoming refugee claims outside the spirit of such principles. The most notable in terms of legislative change is Bill C-97, i.e., the Budget Implementation Act of 2019 (see Galloway, chapter 6). This legislative change prevents claimants from coming to Canada if they have already submitted a claim elsewhere. Galloway suggests that the legal justification for such is thin, born out of a distinction between citizen and non-citizen that is expanded on xenophobic grounds. For Galloway, xenophobic ideas are "unfounded or irrational fear" that are arbitrarily implemented. While Canadian governments struggle to harden legal interpretations and administrative processes, Galloway points to procedures designed to make it particularly difficult for claims to be successful: mandatory detention, denial of reviews of detention, short timeline for claims, and, toward making claimants' stays uncomfortable, denial of health-care protection.

Furthermore, the one piece of legislation that brings Canada and the United States together to administer refugees came under tremendous judicial pressure. Kiyani (chapter 5) reviewed the STCA to argue that (1) the agreement's core provision of safety is in question and (2) the United States is not a safe third country. Here again, we have an interesting case whereby the Canadian government struggles in its attempts to rely on a partner government to deal with its own migration concerns. Kiyani suggests that Canada has become dependent on the United States' own refugee regime, and it is a regime that cannot be called "safe" anymore—a further example of blurred complex border/mobility-policy governance spanning the boundary line and expanding bordering policies inside the U.S. administration. The U.S. regime has evolved procedurally to make asylum claims excruciatingly difficult, because (1) it weighs asylum requirements against illegal entry into the United States but also (2) includes a long list of reasons for denials, including asylum seeking because of violence originating from private spheres or non-state actors, gender-based persecutions, and ethnic, religious, and persecution of national origin. In sum, both Canada and the United States have been using procedures to make claims nearly impossible, which contravene the intent of the 1951 Refugee Convention. Concurrently, a joint border-and-mobility regime emerges from such partially dysfunctional cooperation.

In the European Union, it is not process or procedures that are changing but claims of state of exception; that is, states' ability to transcend the rule of law (Agamben 2005; Mbembe 2019). Member states have been claiming that they are facing situations of a *state of exception* and implementing new border policies within the Union, on its borders, and across neighbouring countries, but they are also taking exceptional measures, such as taking away people's rights, as suggested by Agamben (2005). Documenting both the *de-bordering* and *re-bordering* processes as core challenges to the EU ideals of free mobility and of European integration, Wassenberg points to the solidarity principle and suggests it is being undermined, noting in particular that border policies and fences have a "disastrous humanitarian dimension" (chapter 4). For Wassenberg, because of the migration crisis, European integration and the ideal of a "Europe without borders" are both in question. Indeed, the application of the Dublin regulation illustrates the failure of the EU's multinational approach because it puts the onus on each peripheral member state to prevent irregular mobility of asylum seekers, undocumented migrants, and refugees in the Schengen area. Such implementation clearly illustrates failures both of solidarity and integration across the Union. Those failures also point to tensions across tier levels of governments inside the EU, and failures to implement policies of effective mobility control across the territory of the Union and beyond. Nationalistic and sovereign reflexes appear strong—yet also fragmented, hence their real but partial success—but also underscore the increasing intertwining of border and mobility regimes and policies. The following section illustrates how border policies continually adapt to those pressures to control mobility; how states attempt to control mobility at points of entry into global transportation systems, or within the procedures of their own recruitment policies designed to attract migrants, and, ultimately, inside their own territory.

Borders Continually Adapt to Mobility—below and beyond the Scale of the State

Our third lesson is that mobility is affecting borders and bordering policies in multiple ways. In partnership, states lead the expansion of the reach of their regulatory systems outside the perimeter of their international boundary lines and develop policies that focus on transportation corridors inside and across their own territories to further control mobile individuals across the jurisdictions of subnational-level governments. These initiatives require a multitude of policy and administrative innovations that enforce boundary limits at the periphery of states and beyond the periphery, across the territories of neighbouring states and across the world.

An outstanding example of such important policy changes concerns the transformation of border security at airports and seaports. Today, border checks and security are provided by multiple agencies that do not exclusively rely on government functions and operations but, more than ever, require the involvement of private-sector actors. Airport operators are continually looking for ways to increase the speed at which passengers can be processed. They struggle with limited space and increased international standards and procedures to deal with increasing numbers of passengers. Recently, preclearance has become a way of facilitating increases both in security levels and processing speeds in Canada, the EU, and Japan. Obviously, such changes affect procedures in other transportation industries, such as rail and cruise / ferry ships, and to a lesser extent trucking. Operators rely on information and communication technologies to automate processing visas and travel authorization and identity checks. Experts assume that such authentication will also include biological checks against the spread of contagious diseases, including such epidemics as SARS or a pandemic like COVID-19. Interestingly, our findings, as suggested by Wong in chapter 8 are that the international security of states results from partnering with the private sector, hence enhancing further usage of information and communication technologies and further entanglement of public-private actors. Being pre-cleared prior to departure becomes the point of entry into international travel networks.

In the same vein, the protection regimes of states can extend beyond their own bureaucracies to the non-profit sector, for instance. This is the case of Canada's regime of refugee sponsorship and protection, which, as documented by Lehr, in chapter 7, increases the Canadian state's reliance on the non-profit sector and on private citizens' ability to organize to sponsor individuals and families. Refugee sponsorship has existed in Canada since 1976 and has seen a number of adaptations over time. The most recent version of the refugee-sponsorship regime (2016), however, includes some important pitfalls. For instance, states such as Canada are able to plan and regulate the reach of their sponsorship programs. But they cannot predict the changing and sometimes variable support of their own population vis-à-vis international migrants, and migrants coming from very different regions of the world. These developments illustrate the increased dependency of the Canadian government on the non-profit sector, and the overall evolution of those partnerships.

To increase its reach in monitoring and controlling mobility, Mexico has been adapting to increase the protection of migrancy across its own territory. Indeed, as shown by Simmons in chapter 9, Mexico created the Beta Groups (Grupos Beta de Protección al Migrante) to monitor and prevent violence against mobile individuals. These are twenty-two state groups whose primary task is the protection of migrants travelling across Mexico on their way to the northern border and the United States. They are found along the major transit routes. Their presence signals Mexico's authority in controlling and managing mobility but also re-bordering mobility across Mexico. Remarkably, it is a humanitarian approach to controlling mobility. The national jurisdiction of the Beta Groups goes beyond the traditional jurisdiction of Mexican police forces, which stop at the state or *municipio* boundary line. Beta Groups jurisdiction encompasses different geographies, such as train lines and train stations, but also railway networks across the country. Their mandate includes policing the police, specifically in regard to crimes of extortion committed against migrants by police forces. They are an interesting illustration of a government's attempt to regain and recentralize control over increased mobility with a primordial humanitarian approach. Their targets include non-state armed groups, such as cartels and other gangs, and the trafficking, ransoming, and / or smuggling of migrants.

In sum, it is striking that these border policies are not about holding, protecting, or fixing a boundary line, but are more about expanding the scale and reach of state policies beyond the confines of their limited territoriality along important means of transportation and targeting specific mobile individuals; although this is a confirmation of pre-existing literatures in border studies, in this volume, chapters 7–10 detail how such policies both bound territory and also expand the governing/bordering spaces concerned beyond the territoriality of states. It is specifically a governance of mobility rather than a governance of space. The scale of those border policies is not specifically territorialized, not bounded by any one particular international state territory, but delimited by the ultimate goal of those particular states' partnerships with the private and security or caritative and humanitarian sectors to enhance—or limit—the mobility of individuals and also to protect transportation routes used by migrants. Indeed, the examples above are specific to contexts. For instance, airport security is transnational, and reaches very high standards and homogeneity across the world, thanks to the transnational role of the International Air Transport Association. Yet both the examples from Canada and Mexico confirm counter intuitive mechanisms that extend their policy reach across their territory and beyond, and protect mobile individuals. And, indeed, the rights of a travelling elite are protected in Canada, whereas in Mexico a policy initiated to protect mobility rights is now used to restrict mobility.

Borders and Mobility—Polarized Politics

Our fourth major finding is that current international mobility is polarizing the politics of all the countries studied in this volume. Our work adds to the literature that points to politics as being an important determinant of government policy response in every country but, what it also contributes is an extensive review of how politics has influenced national and regional border policies, and concurrent states' ability to partner across contiguous boundary lines. In Canada, refugee and immigration policy took centre stage in the 2015 general election, and the Liberal Party, vowing to work with the public to welcome more Syrian migrants and asylum seekers than the incumbent Conservatives, won a majority in Parliament. As detailed by Beaupré (chapter 12), the photo of Alan Kurdi's lifeless body on a beach in Greece shocked Canadians and led to an overwhelming desire to help Syrians. Most likely this event provided a new perspective through which media reportage of European difficulties with incoming migrants swayed Canadians. It took a public outcry for the federal government to develop a more humanitarian approach to the crisis and to increase the number of asylum seekers from Syria.

In Japan, Boyle and Chi discuss how, because of labour shortages, political discussions address the need to transform borders and migration policies. Indeed, despite a long history of being a closed labour market and being a culturally homogeneous country, Japan has recently been reckoning with the idea that foreigners can contribute to its economic success. Indeed, because the country is faced with an aging population, it is opening its doors to skilled and unskilled foreign workers. A 2017 government report pointed to a labour-market gap of 1.2 million workers, and a joint 2018 study by Chuo University and Persol Research and Consulting forecasted that the gap would further increase to 6.4 million. As a response, legislation in 2018 proposed to create 350,000 visas for mid-term foreign workers. Explanations for this acute need for foreign workers include attempts to change the course of Japan's long and well-documented economic stagnation and its aging population. Indeed, 2019 is deemed "the year immigration began" in Japan; it has been well over 20 years in the making, and piecemeal policies address labour need without an overall immigration strategy. In the European Union, political parties and other groups clearly struggled to agree on a pan-European policy dealing with increased mobility. Fischer, in chapter 11, suggests that while there may have been efforts of solidarity among the member states, many populist, nationalistic, and xenophobic movements have prevented the EU from emerging as a truly effective *normative power*. On the contrary, national border policies re-emerged as a major determinant of national identity for many EU countries, not just Hungary and Poland. The *de-bordering* and *re-bordering* tug of war between states' sovereign powers was only limited by cost and the choice to federalize those costs. In sum, and unsurprisingly, politics is important to particular policy responses, but it also seems clear that both Canada and Japan are adapting to their own challenges, yet at scales that are much less dramatic than in the European Union, where 27 member states toil to find an agreement on both border and immigration policies and a common discourse on how mobile individuals serve the economies of the Union. But the overwhelming empirical lesson is that governing mobility is the core challenge, and that border and immigration policies have to be considered together to reach agreement on security and humanitarian standards to satisfy policy partners across the wide political spectrum of the Union.

All in all, over the last 10 years, when faced with significantly more mobile individuals, the EU, Canada, and Japan have struggled and partially failed to establish border and mobility policies that would match the deep-seated humanitarian and security challenges greater numbers of mobile individuals have raised. Contemporary answers continue to fail to settle those questions. Crises persist. Instead, short-term policy responses, bringing mobility and border policies together, exposed the limitation of understanding borders as single boundary lines and the need for ambitious, long-term, and multilateral mobility and border-governance agreements across regions of the world. These are explored further in the last section of this conclusion.

Is there Hope in the EU, or Canada and Japan, for Entrenched and Long-Lasting Border and Mobility Regimes?

Interestingly, in Canada there is a controversy underway regarding the application of the STCA; a July 2020 decision by the Federal Court has found that the federal government's process in implementing the STCA is unconstitutional (Federal Court Decision 2020). Justice McDonald's reflection on the designation of the United States as a "safe third country" argues that the provisions enacting the STCA infringe the guarantees in Section 7 of the Charter, which protects "Life, liberty and security of the person," and further explains, "I have also concluded that the infringement is not justified under Section 1 of the Charter." In particular, Justice McDonald's statement 139 reads: "The penalization of the simple act of making a refugee claim is not in keeping with the spirit or the intention of the STCA or the foundational Conventions upon which it was built." Justice McDonald concludes with statement 140: "Applicants have established a breach of Section 7 of the Chapter."

The court gave Parliament six months to remedy the law. However, the government is appealing the decision. If the appeal is successful, the government will be handing back to the U.S. refugee claimants currently in Canada. Importantly, the Federal Court decision is the second that finds the STCA unconstitutional (Imrie 2020) because it expands the ambit of application of Section 7 to refugees.

In Japan, in the early summer of 2020, despite a reputation of isolationism and xenophobia, commentators suggested that Japan had radically increased immigration without a major political backlash because of a clear government argument that, for economic reasons, a yearly decrease of 400,000 per year in the general population justified a new visa policy to welcome temporary unskilled foreign workers while highly skilled workers would be allowed to apply for permanent residency (Gelin 2020). The number of foreign-born workers expanded threefold to reach three million in 2020, thanks primarily to a "a la carte globalization, where Japan custom-orders labor force in the 14 sections where [workers] are most urgently needed." Contrary to Canada's politics, support came from the most conservative parties, while Red Tories and Liberals raised concerns about labour rights and exploitation.

In the European Union, until September 2020, the common view was that EU member states were deeply divided on what was acceptable common policy on migration and borders. Southern countries such as Cyprus, Greece, Italy, Malta, and Spain aligned in their demand for "a mandatory relocation mechanism among all member states." For those countries, the relocation of undocumented migrants had to include all search-and-rescue sea operations. Basically, their call was a plea for a rewriting of the Dublin regulation that makes EU-peripheral countries responsible for the welcome, checking, and processing of asylum claims of anyone undocumented entering the EU via their territory. Their claim was that the burden was too high, and too few countries were responsible.

Central European and Baltic countries disagreed and suggested that each country should have the choice to decide how solidarity could be enacted. Countries such as the Czech Republic, Estonia, Hungary, Latvia, Poland, Slovakia, and Slovenia argued that, in the face of the problem, they had not been denying solidarity efforts; that they would be willing to demonstrate their solidarity efforts further at the borders of the Union by contributing to stronger border policies. Their view is that stronger borders and procedures are necessary, and can take various financial, technical, and expert forms, but that relocation is not possible.

To sum up, since 2015, borders and mobility have become intertwined in more ways than ever. On the one hand, border policies have become more a-territorial. Our Jean Monnet Network research findings are expanding beyond Sassen's (2015, 45) "notion of borderings and bordering capabilities." Our research findings suggest that it is not boundary markers that delineate boundary lines, or boundary maps that are at the core of the current transformation in delineating sovereign exercises, but *the regulatory processes that give rights to individuals and goods*. These legal processes have further individualized and, thanks to information and communication technologies, the bordering of goods and people are markedly not taking place at the peripheries of states along their internationally recognized boundary lines but *inside* states' territories and also *outside* their exercise of territoriality. Such unexpected paradigm change links both the border and mobility-migration literature, justifying some of the ongoing, conceptual, tug of war at play in this volume.

The core findings of this volume, however, are that rights' regimes are the contemporary borders that do or do not permit mobility: thanks to international agreements, many governments, certainly in the European Union, Canada and Japan or Mexico, have the ability to preclear and follow the movements of mobile individuals. First addressing the preclearance of goods, those agreements have expanded to include individuals. Undeniably, while most customs documents are processed electronically, at source, inside the accounting offices of global corporations, whereby electronic accounting transactions include customs duties and destinations, there are still goods in transit in customs warehouses at the very peripheries of states in the proximity of border-gates where agents work at clearing customs and excises and process customs slips. Today, government agencies and the private and not-for-profit sector agencies have the ability to also check individual documents at source and prevent human mobility from the place of origin of specific departures; a clear break from traditional checks upon arrival at the boundary line.

Our volume paints a picture of the situation in Canada, Japan, Mexico, and the European Union in a comparative perspective that suggests many nuances. Mobile individuals fall in a wide range of taxonomies that illustrate mobilities with rights, mobilities without rights, and mobilities during which rights are lost, as foreseen in the philosophical works of Giorgio Agamben. Fortunately, our volume fully illustrates those groupings; individuals on the move have been a serious challenge to states' capacities to welcome them and for those states' legislation regarding the rights of newcomers, including asylum seekers. What is most striking is the realization that, across all our case studies, there has been a generalization of a situation of the hardening of regimes of rights and regulatory processes dealing with mobile individuals. Indeed, it is a mostly stable percentage of the overall world population, about two percent, but it is growing, growing in proportion to the overall world population, whereby 270 million are mobile; they are potentially Agamben's *bodies* without rights, bodies who, during the mobile process, lose all humanity: bare life, the Greek *zoē* (Agamben 1995).

References

Agamben, Giorgio. 2005. *State of Exception*. Chicago: University of Chicago Press.

——. 1995. *Homo Sacer: Sovereign Power and Bare Life*. Stanford: Stanford University Press.

Agnew, John. 1994. "The Territorial Trap: The Geographical Assumptions of International Relations Theory." *Review of International Political Economy* 1(1): 53–80. https://doi.org/10.1080/09692299408434268.

——. 2017. *Globalization and Sovereignty: Beyond the Territorial Trap*. 2nd ed. Lanham, U.K.: Rowman & Littlefield.

Amilhat Szary, A.-L., and F. Giraut, eds. 2015. *Borderities and the Politics of Contemporary Mobile Borders*. New York: Palgrave.

Balibar, Étienne. 2002. *Politics of the Other Scene*. London: Verso.

Borsch-Supan, Axel, Duarte Nuno Leite, and Johannes Rausch. 2019. "Demographic Changes, Migration and Economic Growth in the Euro Area." European Central Bank Forum, Sintra, Portugal. https://www .ecb.europa.eu/pub/conferences/shared/pdf/20190617_ECB_forum _Sintra/paper_Boersch-Supan.en.pdf.

Brambilla, Chiara. 2015. "Exploring the Critical Potential of the Borderscapes Concept." *Geopolitics* 20(1): 14–34. https://doi.org/10.1080/14650045.2014 .884561.

Brenner, Neil. 1999. "Globalisation as Reterritoralisation: The Re-scaling of Urban Governance in the European Union." *Urban Studies* 36(3): 431–451. https://doi.org/10.1080/0042098993466.

Card, David. 1990. "The Impact of the Mariel Boatlift on the Miami Labor Market." *Industrial and Labor Relations Review* 43(2): 245–257. https://doi.org/10.2307/2523702.

Carlaw, John. 2017. "Authoritarian Populism and Canada's Conservative Decade (2006–2015) in Citizenship and Immigration: The Politics and Practices of Kenneyism and Neo-conservative Multiculturalism." *Journal of Canadian Studies* 51(3): 782-816.

Chakraborty, Indranil, and Prasenjit Maity. 2020. "COVID-19 Outbreak: Migration, Effects on Society, Global Environment and Prevention." *Science Total Environment* 728:138882. https://doi.org/10.1016/j.scitotenv.2020.138882.

Chen, X. 2005. *As Borders Bend: Transnational Spaces on the Pacific Rim.* Lanham, U.K.: Rowman & Littlefield.

Court of Justice of the European Union (CJEU). 2017. "Judgment in Joined Cases C-643/15 and C-647/15 Slovakia and Hungary v Council." Press release, no. 91/17, September 6, 2017. https://curia.europa.eu/jcms/upload/docs/application/pdf/2017-09/cp170091en.pdf.

Federal Court Decisions. 2020. *Canadian Council of Refugees v. Canada (Immigration, Refugees and Citizenship).* Federal Court Decisions, 2020 07 22 file number IMM-2229-17, IMM02977-17, IMM-775-17. https://decisions.fct-cf.gc.ca/fc-cf/decisions/en/item/482757/index.do.

Gelin, Martin. 2020. "Japan Radically Increased Immigration—and No One Protested." *Foreign Policy,* June 23, 2020. https://foreignpolicy.com/2020/06/23/japan-immigration-policy-xenophobia-migration/.

Guterres, Antonio, and William Lacy Swing. 2010. "Making the Most of Human Mobility." UNHCR – The UN Refugee Agency, April 2010. https://www.unhcr.org/news/editorial/2010/4/4c18cf459/making-human-mobility-antonio-guterres-united-nations-high-commissioner.html.

Immigration, Refugees, and Citizenship Canada (IRCC). 2020. "Canada-U.S. Safe Third Country Agreement." Agreements. https://www.canada.ca/en/immigration-refugees-citizenship/corporate/mandate/policies-operational-instructions-agreements/agreements/safe-third-country-agreement.html.

Imrie, Alison. 2020. "Federal Court Declares the STCA Unconstitutional." Court.ca, October 2, 2020. http://www.thecourt.ca/federal-court-declares-the-stca-unconstitutional/.

Iwashita, A. 2016. *Japan's Border Issues Pitfalls and Prospects.* New York: Routledge.

Jean Monnet Network. 2020. "Comparing and Contrasting EU Migration and Border Policies." EU Borders and Migration. https://www.uvic.ca/humanities/intd/europe/eu-grants/network/eubamp-16-19/index.php.

Juncker, Jean Claude. 2015. "State of the Union Address 2015 by Jean Claude Juncker, President of the EC: Highlights." Filmed September 2015 at the European Parliament, Strasbourg, France. https://ec.europa.eu /commission/priorities/state-union-speeches/state-union-2015_en.

La Pradelle, Paul de. 1928. *La frontière : étude de droit international*. Paris: Les Éditions internationales.

Mackova, Lucie, and Lubor Kysucan. 2016. "The History and Politics of Human Mobility." *Development, Environment and Foresight* 2(1): 23–34.

Mbembe, Achille. 2019. *Necropolitics*, Durham: Duke University Press.

McLeman, Robert, and Lori Hunter. 2010. "Migration in the Context of Vulnerability and Adaptation to Climate Change: Insights from Analogues." *WIREs Climate Change* 1(3): 450–461. https://doi.org/10.1002 /wcc.51.

Paasi, A., E.-K. Prokkola, J. Saarinen, and K. Zimmerbauer, eds. 2018. *Borderless Worlds for Whom? Ethics, Moralities and Mobilities*. London, U.K.: Routledge.

Rajaram, P. K., and C. Grundy-Warr, eds. 2007. *Borderscapes Hidden Geographies and Politics at Territory's Edge*. Minneapolis: University of Minnesota Press.

Sassen, S. 2015. "Bordering Capabilities versus Borders: Implications for National Borders." In *Borderities and the Politics of Contemporary Mobile Borders*, edited by A.L. Amilhat Szary and F. Giraut, 23–52. New York: Palgrave Macmillan.

Samers, Michael, and Michael Collyer. 2017. "Explaining Migration across International Borders: Determinist Theories." In *Migration*, 2nd ed., 54–89. London: Routledge.

Stark, Heidi Kiiwetinepinesiik. 2016. "Criminal Empire: The Making of the Savage in a Lawless Land." *Theory & Event* 19(4). Project MUSE.

Swing, William Lacy. 2011. "Human Mobility in the 21st Century: Perception and Realities." Public address, International Organization for Migration. https://www.iom.int/speeches-and-talks/human-mobility -21st-century-perceptions-and-realities.

Taylor, Charles. 1985. "The Concept of a Person." In *Philosophical Papers*, 97–114. Cambridge: Cambridge University Press.

United Nations High Commissioner for Refugees (UNHCR). 2020. "Global Trends: Forced Displacement in 2019." Copenhagen: UNHCR Data Service. https://www.unhcr.org/5ee200e37.pdf.

Politics and Public Policy

Series Editor: Geneviève Tellier

There has been a resurgence of the study of politics, inspired by debates on globalization, renewed citizen engagement and demands, and transformations of the welfare state. In this context, the study of political regimes, ideas, and processes as well as that of public policy contribute to refreshing our understanding of the evolution of contemporary societies. Public policy is at the heart of political and state actions. It defines the course and the objectives adopted by governments and steering citizen initiatives and collective actions. Political analysis is increasingly complex and dynamic, embracing more diverse political, social, economic, cultural, and identity-related phenomena. The *Politics and Public Policy* series is an ideal forum in which to present titles that promote an exploration of these questions in Canada and around the world.

Recent titles in the *Politics and Public Policy Series*

For a complete list of the University of Ottawa Press titles, please visit:
www.press.uOttawa.ca

www.ingramcontent.com/pod-product-compliance
Lightning Source LLC
Chambersburg PA
CBHW050625280326
41932CB00015B/2531